1,000,000 Books

are available to read at

www.ForgottenBooks.com

Read online
Download PDF
Purchase in print

ISBN 978-0-282-98561-5
PIBN 10875726

This book is a reproduction of an important historical work. Forgotten Books uses state-of-the-art technology to digitally reconstruct the work, preserving the original format whilst repairing imperfections present in the aged copy. In rare cases, an imperfection in the original, such as a blemish or missing page, may be replicated in our edition. We do, however, repair the vast majority of imperfections successfully; any imperfections that remain are intentionally left to preserve the state of such historical works.

Forgotten Books is a registered trademark of FB &c Ltd.
Copyright © 2018 FB &c Ltd.
FB &c Ltd, Dalton House, 60 Windsor Avenue, London, SW19 2RR.
Company number 08720141. Registered in England and Wales.

For support please visit www.forgottenbooks.com

1 MONTH OF FREE READING

at

www.ForgottenBooks.com

By purchasing this book you are eligible for one month membership to ForgottenBooks.com, giving you unlimited access to our entire collection of over 1,000,000 titles via our web site and mobile apps.

To claim your free month visit: www.forgottenbooks.com/free875726

* Offer is valid for 45 days from date of purchase. Terms and conditions apply.

English
Français
Deutsche
Italiano
Español
Português

www.forgottenbooks.com

Mythology Photography **Fiction**
Fishing Christianity **Art** Cooking
Essays **Buddhism** Freemasonry
Medicine **Biology** Music **Ancient Egypt** Evolution Carpentry Physics
Dance Geology **Mathematics** Fitness
Shakespeare **Folklore** Yoga Marketing
Confidence Immortality Biographies
Poetry **Psychology** Witchcraft
Electronics Chemistry History **Law**
Accounting **Philosophy** Anthropology
Alchemy Drama Quantum Mechanics
Atheism Sexual Health **Ancient History**
Entrepreneurship Languages Sport
Paleontology Needlework Islam
Metaphysics Investment Archaeology
Parenting Statistics Criminology
Motivational

TRANSACTIONS
OF THE
CONGREGATIONAL
HISTORICAL SOCIETY

VOL. III
1907 — 1908

Edited by
T. G. CRIPPEN

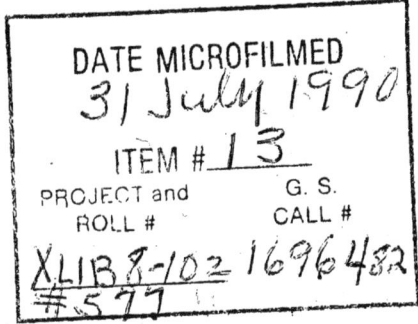

Printed for the Society by
Fred. S. Thacker : 3 Dyers' Buildings : Holborn : London.

CONTENTS

	PAGE
Academies, Early Nonconformist	272, 387
Academic Discipline in 18th Century	67
Achurch, Parish Register of	126
Ancient Sacramental Plate	25, 116, 153
Asty, John, and the Fleetwoods	187
Baptists, History of Early, in London	88
Broadway Meeting, Somerset	357
Browne, Robert, and the Achurch Parish Register	126
„ „ Later Years of	303
Burton-on-Trent, History of Congregationalism in	81
Button's Academy	285
Bury Street Chapel, Contemporary Account of its building, etc. ...	117
Channel Islands, Puritans and Presbyterians in	110
Chapel Building under the Stuarts	67
Church Building in the West Riding, Seventy Years of	293
Church, "Profes of Aparent"	257
Congregational Historical Society—Annual Meeting, 1907 ...	75
„ „ „ Annual Meeting, 1908 ...	269
„ „ „ Meeting at Wolverhampton ...	1
„ „ „ Meeting at Blackpool ...	209
„ „ „ Balance Sheet, 1907 ...	144
„ „ „ Lists of Officers and Members 73, 266, etc.	
Conventicles, London, 1683	364
Cumberland and Westmoreland—Nonconformity in	212
„ „ Notes on Map of	229
„ „ Early Conventicles in	300
Doddridge, Dr. Philip—Memorials of	145
„ „ Unpublished Correspondence of ...	319
Doolittle's Academy	286, 395
Editorial 1, 77, 139, 209, 269, 337	
Episcopal Returns, 1665-6	339
Flavel Cup, The	153
Fleetwood Family, The	187
Frankland, Richard	21
Gale's Academy	274
Hanover Chapel, Peckham	155
Islington, Academies at	285
Jessey Church, The, 1655-1678	233
Leek, Nonconformity in	4
London, Religious Condition of, 1672	192
„ Conventicles in, 1683	364
„ Academies in and near	274, 395
Longdon and Lichfield, Story of Congregationalism in	33
Maesyronen Chapel	354
Maidwell, Rev. Thomas, Pastoral Letters of	367
Martock, Pound Lane Chapel	244
Mill Hill School, Centenary of	171
Morton's Academy	277, 396
Newington Green, Academies at	274, 396

Nightingale Lane, Contract for Building Chapel, 1682	67
Peckham, Hanover Chapel	155
Penry, John—Some Dates	114
,, Last Years of	182
,, Last Journey to London	291
,, in Scotland	379
Pilgrim Fathers' Church Communion Plate	154
Pound Lane Chapel, Martock	244
"Profes of Aparent Church"	257
Puritans and Presbyterians in the Channel Islands	110
Ravenstonedale, Ancient Meeting-House	91
Religious Condition of London in 1672	192
Scott, Jonathan, Apostolic Labours of	48
Sheriff Hales Academy	387
Surrey Congregational History (Cleal) Review	331
Taunton Communion Plate	116
Veal's Academy	289, 395
Wales, The Oldest Chapel in	354
Walpole, The Ancient Meeting-House at	317
Wapping, Academy at	289
Wattisfield, Ancient Meeting-House at	251
Watts, Dr. Isaac, Tomb of	240
,, ,, Unpublished Letter of	241
West Bromwich, Ebenezer Chapel	104
Wiggenton, Giles, His "Visitation"	27
Yorkshire, Seventy Years' Chapel Building in the West Riding	293

NOTES AND QUERIES

Books, Brief notices of :	
Boseley, Rev. Ira., The Independent Church in Westminster Abbey	3, 79, 142
Brown, John, D.D., The Colonial Missions of Congregationalism	271
Browne, Robert, His Retraction	80
Clowes, Chronicles of the Congregational Church, Great Yarmouth	1
Dale, R. W., D.D. (posthumous), History of English Congregationalism	78
Merchant, H., M.A., Wem, History and Guide	141
Nightingale, B., History of the Lancashire Congregational Union	3
Penney, Norman, The First Publishers of Truth	79
Pierce, W., Historical Introduction to the Marprelate Tracts	337
Powicke, F. J., Ph.D., History of the Cheshire Union of Congregational Churches	79
Wyatt, F., Brief History of the Congregational Church at Axminster	141
Canting Names	78, 141, 210
Corrections	2, 140, 271
Deaths, Recent :	
Dale, Rev. Bryan, M.A.	139
Le Brun, Rev. E.	77
Lord, Rev. Thos.	338
Ryland, Mrs., Litt.D.	270
Tuck, W., Esq.	77
Doddridge Relics	337
Globe Alley, Wooden Meeting-house	1
Mallock, Rawling and Rogers	140
Milton Relic—A Probable	3
Pilgrim Fathers' Church	209

Queries:—
  Cote, Oxfordshire, Baptist Chapel at 211
  Extinct Theological Academies 1
  McNeely, Rev. Charles, and his congregation 77, 211
  Scottish Families near Horningsham 211
  Watts and Doddridge Relics 3, 77
Ravenstonedale, Quakers at 140
Watts, Dr. Isaac—Expenses at his Funeral 2
  ,,   ,,   Memorial of 211

CONTRIBUTORS

Atkinson, Dr. S. B., M.A., J.P. 187
Barker, Rev. John 327
Cater, Rev. F. I. 126, 303
Clapham, J. A., Esq. ... 293
Colligan, Rev. J. H., M.A. 212
Crippen, Rev. T. G. 91, 155, 229, 272
Dale, Rev. Bryan, M.A. .. 21, 91
Doddridge, Ph., D.D. ... 323
Gasquoine, Rev. Thos., B.A. 182, 291
Gould MS. 88
Huntingdon, Selina, Countess of 329
Iliff, John S., Esq. 81
James, N. G. B., Esq., M.A. 171
Kelly, Rev. W. (revised) ... 104
Le Brun, Rev. E 110

Lovatt, J., Esq. 4
Lloyd, Rev. D. C. 351
Macfadyen, Rev. D., M.A. 48
Maidwell, Rev. H. 367
Mitchell, Rev. A. T., M.A., F.S.A. 387
Miles, Dr. Henry 319
Pierce, Rev. W. 379
Scamell, John, Esq ... 244
Standerwick, W., Esq. ... 357
Stevens, Rev. A. J. ... 33
Turner, Rev. G. Lyon, M.A. 142, 192, 300, 339, 395
Watts, Dr. Isaac 241
Whitley, Rev. T., LL.D. ... 233
Williams, Joseph 327
Wiggenton, Giles 27
Wood, Rev. S. 324

ILLUSTRATIONS

Achurch Parish Registers, Leaves from 126, 130
Burial Place at Rushton, Staffordshire 6
Chapels:—
  Bury Street, London (Plans of) 123, 124
  Langdon Green, near Lichfield 34
  Maesyronen, Wales (2) 354
  Martock, Somerset (2) 248
  Peckham, built 1717 163
  Ravenstonedale, before renovation 90
    ,,   ,,   after renovation 98
  Walpole, Suffolk 316, 31
  Wattisfield, Suffolk 250, 253
Communion Plate:—
  The Flavel Cup 152
  Pilgrim Fathers' Church 154
  South Petherton 26
  Taunton, Paul Street (3) 116, 117
Kettering, The Conventicle House 368, 376
Mill Hill School—The School House 170
  ,,   ,,   Ridgway House 179
Scott, Rev. Jonathan 51
Sheriff Hales Manor House 392
Thorp Waterville, "The Old Chapel House" 308
  ,,   ,,   door of supposed meeting-room 312
Trowbridge Baptismal Bowl 26
Woodhouse Green Farm, near Rushton 6
Map to illustrate Early Nonconformity in Cumberland and Westmoreland 216
Map of Surrey (from Cleal's *History*) 334

EDITORIAL

The usual AUTUMNAL MEETING of our Society was held on Wednesday, 17th October, in the lecture room of the Wesleyan church, Darlington Street, Wolverhampton, kindly lent for the occasion. In the absence of our President the chair was occupied by E. B. Dawson, Esq, of Lancaster.

The Rev. D. Macfadyen, M.A., of Highgate, read a paper on *The Apostolic Labours of Captain Jonathan Scott*, for which a hearty vote of thanks was tendered, and Mr. Macfadyen was requested to place the paper in the Secretary's hands for publication.

The Secretary read a paper contributed by J. Lovatt, Esq., of Leek, on the early history of Nonconformity in that town and neighbourhood.

The Rev. A. J. Stevens, of Lichfield, read extracts from a memoir on *Early Congregationalism at Longdon*, with which Lichfield was from the first intimately connected.

Papers on the *Origin of Congregationalism at Burton-on-Trent* and *West Bromwich* were taken as read, and will appear in a future issue of our *Transactions*.

*

We wish to call attention to Mr. Dale's paper in our present issue, which usefully supplements the account of Frankland's academy given in our last.

*

We are particularly desirous of obtaining information respecting extinct theological academies, including names of students. Especially we would welcome particulars of Newport Pagnell, Fakenham, Gosport, Cotton End, and Bedford.

*

Adverting to the tradition mentioned of a wooden meeting-house in Globe Alley, Maid Lane, erected for Wadsworth (see II. 377), we have ascertained from Bp. Sheldon's Return of Conventicles, 1669, that the edifice was *then* in actual use. This is an important link in the evidence for the continuity of the Pilgrim Fathers' church with the church of Jacob and Jessey.

*

Two remarkable memorials of Dr. Isaac Watts have lately come to light. One, in the custody of C. W. Toms, Esq., of Meaburn

Editorial

House, Putney, is a contemporary record of the original assignment of seats in Bury Street chapel, 1708, with a plan thereof. This has been copied for the Society, and Mr. Toms has given permission for its publication.

The other, in the possession of G. Brocklehurst, Esq., of Lyminge, Kent, is the deacons' account book of Bury Street from 1728 to 1756. From this it appears that the stipend received by the two pastors, Messrs. Watts and Price, in 1728, was £70 each, *i.e.*, £17 10s. quarterly. From 1729 to 1735 this was augmented by "gratuities" of various amounts; from 1735 onward the quarterly payments were usually £22 15s.; and lately, to the end of Dr. Watts's pastorate, varied from £25 to £30, *i.e.*, £100 to £120 per annum.

Mr. Brocklehurst has kindly furnished the following transcript of the entries relating to Dr. Watts's funeral :—

Cash.   Cr.

1748
December 6   Pd Mr. Day, Clarke for mourning for the Doct^r - - - 3 3 0
—   Pd Mr. Niblett £3 : 3. Mrs. Niblett £2 : 2 ditto - - - 5 5 0
—   Pd Mrs. Davis £2 : 2. Mary Daniel £2 : 2 ditto - - - 4 4 0
13   Pd Mr. Jennings, Funeral Sermon, with request to Print - - 2 2 0
—   Pd Mr. Chandler, Oration at ye Grave do. - - - - 2 2 0
—   Pd the two Constables, attending when ye Serm^n was Preach^d - 10 0

*

The object of the Society being the ascertainment of facts rather than the promulgation of opinions, we always welcome corrections vouched by adequate authority. We therefore thank the Editor of *The Christian Life*, of 7th October, for the following :

BIBLIOGRAPHY, vol. ii. p. 432.—The treatise *Pzzicopcovii Samueli Dissertatio*, &c., is wrongly ascribed to Hales by Anthony à Wood : Hales had nothing whatever to do with it.

ON MR. PIERCE'S QUERY, vol. ii. p. 377.—The correct title is *Ecclesiasticae Disciplinae, et Anglicanae Ecclesiae ab illa aberrationis, plena a verbo Dei, & dilucida explicatio*. The English edition of 1574 is *not* " dated Geneva "; it names no place, but was probably printed at Middelburg. There is a Geneva reprint, 8vo., 1580.

*

We have to thank several correspondents for photographs and prints of ancient meeting-houses, communion plate, and other relics

Editorial

of olden Nonconformity. We hope in due time to reproduce all, or nearly all, of these much esteemed contributions.

*

The Rev. Ira Boseley has completed his *History of the Independent Church of Westminster Abbey*, which is ready for publication. The price will be 3/6 to subscribers. We hope many of our members will, by subscribing, shew their appreciation of a piece of painstaking and commendable research.

*

Among recent publications we are glad to notice a *History of the Lancashire Congregational Union, 1806-1906*, by the Rev. B. Nightingale. Another useful contribution to Free Church history is the *Chronicles of the Congregational Church at Great Yarmouth*, by J. E. Clowes, Esq., of which, however, only a limited edition has been printed for private circulation.

*

A PROBABLE MILTON RELIC.—Personal memorials of Milton are so rare that it is with some gratification we call attention to a small agate handled knife and fork, which were *certainly* in the possession of the poet's widow at the time of her death, and may very probably have been used by her illustrious husband. There is distinct evidence as to the persons by whom they were successively owned until about forty years ago, when they were bought by Mr. Partridge, bookseller, of Wellington, Salop. By the recent death of Mr. Partridge's widow they have become the property of her niece, Mrs. Hammond, The Villas, Woodlesford, Yorks., who would be glad to receive an acceptable offer. They ought to be in some public collection.

*

The Council of New College, Hampstead, have granted permission to our Secretary to examine and make extracts from the valuable records and other MSS. in the college library. A beginning has been made, and, although not much has yet been effected, it has been ascertained that there are important stores of information, especially regarding some of the early Nonconformist academies. This, it is hoped, will at some future time be placed before our readers.

*

The Secretary would be glad to hear of any autographs or other personal relics or memorials either of Dr. Isaac Watts or Dr. Philip Doddridge, whether in public or private custody.

Nonconformity in Leek

THE task I have undertaken does not allow of many preliminary words; only that I should acknowledge the *Historical Notice* by the Rev. J. Hankinson, who commenced his ministry at the Leek church fifty years ago, and is now living at Cheltenham.

When, in 1862, the new church was built, and a document prepared to put under the foundation stone, the trustees stated that nothing was known by them of the history of the old church prior to 1782. Fortunately, however, Mr. Hankinson was led to a study of its origin; and in 1878, and again in 1888, privately printed records which shew a much older history. I have been able, I am glad to say, by much tedious hunting and reading, to add materially to Mr. Hankinson's *Historical Notice*, but in the following pages I have freely used this valuable record, although in most cases I have, in my researches, found the source whence Mr. Hankinson's facts were derived.

My chief sources of information are:—*Leek Parish Church Registers, 1633*, the *Congregational Magazines* (1820, &c.), Calamy's *Memorial, etc.*, Clark's *Lives*, Urwick's *Nonconformity in Cheshire*, *Dictionary of National Biography*, Sleigh's *History of the Parish of Leek*, Miller's *Olde Leeke*, Henry Newcome's *Diary*, &c. I am also very much indebted to the Rev. G. Lyon Turner, Mr. J. Watkinson, the Rev. T. G. Crippen and other gentlemen who have rendered me valuable help.

The history of Nonconformity in Leek and the

neighbourhood can, in my opinion, best be treated by giving short sketches of the men who, by their holy lives and faithful ministry, brought the Gospel to the moorlands of Staffordshire where there was the greatest need for it.

In the early part of the 17th century the inhabitants are described as living in worse than heathen darkness, and it would be easier to ask the question than to answer it, as to what the Church of England had been doing. Glimpses of light were occasionally seen, however; and as men's consciences became even a little more free at the Reformation, private judgement, with all its advantages, was exercised. Although one and another were silenced and even martyred, the free Gospel was being gradually established.

Beginning at the Commonwealth period there are three names which stand out most prominently as having influenced this neighbourhood and established Congregationalism at or near Leek. These are:—

  John Machin (1624-1664),
  George Moxon (1603-1687),
  Henry Newcome (1627-1695).

As, however, there are well written biographies of these worthies, it is not needful for me to give even a summary of their lives. They all three held pastorates not far from Leek, but with praiseworthy zeal they went about the district weekdays and Sundays, "as much in the saddle as an Arab," one says, and being learned and devout men they left an indelible mark on the district.

John Machin seems to have organized a band of ministers, likeminded with himself, who used "some of their Sundays and many of their weekdays in holding services in the towns and villages of Staffordshire. He for six years paid £100 per year out of his private income to maintain 'a double lecture' (*viz.*, two sermons once a month), the ministers to be the most orthodox, able and powerful that can be procured for love of Jesus Christ." The first of these was held at Newcastle-under-Lyne, August 4th, 1653; and the other places included in the plan were: Leek, Uttoxeter, Lichfield, Tamworth, Walsall, Wolverhampton, Stafford, Pencridge, Eccleshall, Stone and Mucklestone, all in the county of Stafford. Besides George Moxon and Henry Newcome the following, amongst others, would probably give their services:—John Gartside, Joseph Cope, Randal Sillito, of Newcastle; Thomas Edge, of Gawsworth; Job Wilson, John Cartwright, of Bosley; William Bagshaw, "the apostle of the Peak"; Thomas Brook, of Congleton; John Hieron, of Bradsall; and many more, most of whom were honoured by ejectment from their pastorates in 1662.

George Moxon was at Astbury in 1653 in conjunction with John Machin; and they also took charge of Rushton, near Leek, preaching there alternately. After his ejectment Mr. Moxon remained at Rushton, and went about the moorlands preaching in private houses and where he could.

There is a farmhouse, Woodhouse Green, near Rushton, where he held services regularly, and there exists still a burial ground close by. This house was situated about five miles from any town, and so Mr. Moxon was able to avoid the Five Mile Act for a time. Worshippers from Leek would probably resort thither. Henry Newcome was friend and biographer of John Machin, and one of his chief assistants in the itinerant work. He published a *Diary* which makes frequent reference to Mr. Machin and his work, and has been of the greatest use in compiling this paper.

WOODHOUSE GREEN FARM, NEAR RUSHTON.
(Old Baptist Preaching-place.)

OLD BURIAL-PLACE, RUSHTON, NEAR LEEK.

Nonconformity in Leek

Coming directly to Leek there is much uncertainty as to the exact state of things.

The Rev. Francis Bowyer, son of Sir John Bowyer, M.P., of Knypersley, Staffs., was vicar of Leek from 1633 to Nov. 4th, 1648, where he was buried. I have no evidence as to his signing the "Engagement," but as his family connections were favourable to Cromwell, it is possible that he did, and so there would be no ejectment; and the fact of Mr. Bowyer keeping his appointment so long is evidence that he was a worthy man and conducted the services in the parish church in a devout and creditable manner. His nephew, Sir John Bowyer, M.P., was Governor of Leek for Cromwell, and did good service. In 1645 Francis Bowyer signs the certificate of people taking the covenant at Leek, and he signs the Leek parish church register until 1647. I notice in the Bowyer pedigree several intermarriages with the family of Sir George Gresley, who fought with Cromwell in the Civil Wars. Mr. Bowyer was succeeded, in 1649, by the Rev. Robert Fowler, who is described by Mr. Sleigh as "pastor," and, according to the same authority, he remained at Leek until 1654. This would be the first distinctly Nonconformist appointment, and, as Mr. Fowler remained in the office six years, we can hope that his services were appreciated and that he would render Mr. Machin every assistance; and that his spirit was not embittered by having one relative cruelly butchered in cold blood by the Royalists, and another, the Rev. Richard Fowler, plundered at Barthomley in Cheshire. There seems to be some family connection with T. Edge, a Parliamentary commissioner, who lived at Horton Hall, and was a friend of Mr. H. Newcome, the Fowlers acquiring the property some time later. Mr. Fowler commences to sign the Leek registers in March,

1648, and adds the word "pastor"—Mr. Bowyer having signed "vicar."

The Rev. Ralph Worsley, B.A., is another minister who was at Leek parish church during the Commonwealth. His family was of considerable importance, and, being thoroughgoing Puritans, gave Cromwell assistance during this period in various ways. Ralph Worsley was a distinguished scholar, and was trained at Cambridge. He is often mentioned in H. Newcome's *Diary*, and not always favourably, owing to Newcome being a strict Presbyterian. He was connected with the Worsleys of Platt, who were Nonconformists and famous in the annals of Lancashire Nonconformity. He was ordained at Chelford, in Cheshire, in 1653. The Leek parish church register has the following entry :—

> "A Register of all Christian marriages and burials in the parish church of Leeke, by me, Ralph Worsley, A.D. 1654, in the first year of Oliver Cromwell, Lord Protector of the Commonwealth, beginning at Feb. 12th, 1654."

He does not sign the registers, and does not appear to have remained long at Leek. The writing is by a different hand soon after the above entry. There are some marriages during Mr. Worsley's stay which are stated as having been published at the Leek market cross.

In 1654 the name of "Henry Newcombe" appears on the Leek church register as being present at two separate marriages, and at one it seems to be his own signature as "minister in the parish," but as he then held the appointment of minister at Gawsworth, it could only be a visit. There were, he says in his *Diary*, "motions made for my brother Richard Newcombe to come to Leek, and after to Bosley, but the Lord appointed him employment elsewhere." The vacancy, which evidently existed at Leek, was filled by Thomas Wynnell.

The Rev. John Hieron is mentioned in Henry Newcome's *Diary* as being of Leek (1653), but I think this would be a visit only. That gentleman was at Breadsall, and was ejected from the church there in 1662. He did a good deal of itinerant work such as we have seen that Mr. Machin did, and during his long ministry of fifty-two years he "preached in 96 churches and little sanctuaries innumerable." He was born at Stapenhill in 1608, and died at Losco, Derbyshire, in 1682, aged 74. He suffered great persecution, but maintained a fine Christian character through all. There is a grand eulogy of him in the *History of Ashbourne*, in Derbyshire, to which county his life and work mainly belong. We hope Leek appreciated the visit of so learned and good a pastor. He had, like many of the others I have named, been trained at Cambridge and received episcopal ordination.

Thomas Wynnell,* M.A., is a name which has caused me much trouble. I have succeeded in finding very little about him. He is stated by Wood and local historians to have been vicar of Leek in 1662, and in that year to have "resigned or abandoned it."

Was he ejected? By the courtesy of the Rev. J. Menzies, of Bridport, I learn that he was born at Askerswell, in Dorsetshire, about 1590, entered Brazenose College, Oxford (1622), took degree in Arts, and became rector of Craneham, near Gloucester, in 1642. He was also prebendary of Wolverhampton, and was buried at Carworth in 1662, aged 72. He was author of several theological books.† How long he was at Leek, and whether the Act of Nonconformity was the cause of his

---

*Also spelled Whynell and Winnell.

†According to A. Wood, Mr. Wynnell's principal publications were *The Covenants Plea for Infants, or the Covenant of Free Grace, pleading the Divine Right of Christian Infants unto the Seal of Holy Baptism* (Oxford, 1642); and *Suspension Discussed, or Church Members' Divine Right to Christ's Table-Throne of Grace Discussed and Cleared* (L. 1657).

leaving, I cannot say, nor can I say how far it may have led to his death that same year. The Leek parish church registers, which date from 1633, contain nothing about him except the following:

> "Memorandum that Thomas Wynnell, clerk, was chosen by the consent of the Parish of Leeke to be register of the Parish abovesaid and was sworn and approved to execute the office of a register according to an Act of Parliament made in that behalf, bearing date of Wed. 24th Aug. 1653, on August 12, 1655.
> Signed B. Rudyerd, Justice of the Peace for the County of Stafford and resident in Leek aforesaid."

The registers are very clearly written in English and well preserved. Mr. Wynnell did not sign the pages, but the entries are in apparently the same writing until 1661, when they commence in Latin, and in 1662 are signed by Geo. Roades, vicar.

So far then as we have any proof, a Leek minister cannot definitely claim the honour of being among those in the county who were ejected in 1662; but, if not, Mr. Wynnell very narrowly escapes this honour. His father, also named Thomas Wynnell, was rector of Askerswell 44 years, and died in 1638, aged 78. His mother bore the honoured name of Lyte, and there were family connections with the equally honoured name of Locke. These facts and names suggest a probably interesting biography if it could be written.

The Sir Benj. Rudyerd, M.P., above mentioned, was called the "silver trumpet" of the Long Parliament; and, although not following Cromwell in all respects, he threw in his lot with the Parliament, and was a tower of strength to the people's cause and to Nonconformity.

The Quakers seem to have been firmly established in Leek and the surrounding villages in the 17th century, some of their registers dating from 1648. Their present chapel was built in 1694, and so is almost a contemporary with the Congregational cause in Leek. They had, however, a "Gospel-house in Leek" in 1654 and 1655, as is seen by their own documents, and appear to have suffered some persecution.

Up to the time the Wesleyans formed separate churches, the Quakers shared with the parish church and the Presbyterians (as our own church was then called) the honour of being the only three places of worship in Leek.

It would make this paper too long to attempt to touch upon many more names of ministers who, in the itinerant method of the time, went about the towns and villages of North Staffs. at this period, and doubtless sowed that good seed which soon afterwards led to the formation of churches.

This reminds me that I must say something as to the origin and foundation of the church at Leek.

After the Restoration, and when Mr. Winnell had left Leek, the episcopal form of worship was recommenced in the parish church, the Rev. Geo. Rhodes being vicar in 1662.

What persecutions and hardships our Free Church ancestors suffered we can only conjecture from what we know went on all over the country. There is much evidence, however, that dissent was not dead, nor nearly so; and particularly in the villages around Leek can we trace numerous meeting-places in spite of the despicable Acts of Parliament to forbid them. I cannot now stay even to mention them, but if the full history of Nonconformity in Staffordshire is written, some day, I trust these places and people will not be overlooked.

"For few remember them. They lived unknown
Till persecution dragged them into fame,
And chased them up to heaven. With their names
No bard embalms and sanctifies his song;
And History, so warm on meaner things,
Is cold on this."

By the courtesy of the Rev. G. Lyon Turner I have been furnished with a list of the "Presentations in Ecclesiastical Courts for Nonconformity" for this part of Staffordshire, and this clearly shews that the authorities had no easy task even to check the spread of dissent, much more to root it up. The same courteous gentleman furnishes me with a copy of the licences taken out in this district in 1672, when some measure of freedom was granted to Nonconformists.

From this list we are pleased to notice that Jane Machin, the widow of our pioneer John Machin, not only takes out a licence for her house as a preaching-place at Seabridge, but also for one at Stoke-on-Trent, so keeping alive the memory of her husband and the cause of Christ.

At Leek, Thomas Nabbs got a licence for his house, and doubtless this was the foundation of a church which has had a continuous history ever since that period. The family of Nabbs was well known in this district, and the name frequently occurs in the parish church register, but unfortunately I have been unable to locate the place of Thomas Nabbs' house. Mr. Lyon Turner again comes to my rescue by giving me copies of the *Hearth Rolls*, and we find that Thomas Nabbs paid this strange tax for a house at Heaton, near Leek and Rushton, where Mr. Moxon lived, and probably would be owner of property in Leek, for which he got the licence; or did our ancestors walk from Leek to Heaton, about five miles, to the services?

The first documentary evidence we have of a church in Leek is an indenture dated 1683, or two years before the death of Charles II., shewing that certain property, which stood on the exact site of the present Leek Congregational church, was sold to men with distinctly Nonconformist names, and a fair inference is that the cottages were bought for the purpose of a meeting-house. A few years later the property was rented and licensed for that purpose by the first known minister, the Rev. Josiah Hargreaves, who was resident in 1695. He purchased the property in 1716, as an indenture of that date shews, and in 1732 it was made over to trustees by Mr. Hargreaves.

The exact date of the coming of the Rev. J. Hargreaves to Leek is unknown, as is the date of the formation of the church; but it is a very probable conjecture that a remnant of the flock who attended Mr. Wynnell's services in the parish church would keep together and meet as occasion offered. Mr. Machin had died two years after the Act of Conformity was passed, but Mr. Moxon remained in the neighbourhood; and other itinerant ministers are mentioned as doing their best to defy or evade the Acts, and give comfort, support and encouragement to the scattered Nonconformists. After the passing of the Act of Toleration in 1688 doubtless the Leek friends would form themselves into a regular congregation or church.

Mr. Hargreaves took part in the ordination of Mr. John Ashe in 1696; and, as one would suppose that very young ministers would not be likely to officiate at such a ceremony, the inference is that Mr. Hargreaves was at Leek much before that time. He left Leek for St. Ives in 1725, when he is said to have been at Leek "many years." I regret to learn from a member of the church at St. Ives that their records from 1650 to 1742 are lost, so I have not been able to learn anything further about him.

In 1730 the Rev. Hugh Worthington, jun., came as a young man to Leek, and entered upon his pastoral duties. His father was minister at Dean Row, Cheshire. Young Worthington had been educated in his father's academy, from which sprang many noted preachers. He was ordained at Knutsford, his father taking a leading part in the ceremony.

In 1732 the property was put in trust, it being described as:—

> "commonly called the meeting-house and as being used by Protestant Dissenters commonly called Presbyterians."

On the death of his father in 1735 Mr. Worthington took his place at Dean Row, and remained there about thirteen years, afterwards holding the pastorate of Hale chapel for about twenty years.

He is spoken of, as was his father, with the highest praise, and there must have been, one would think, a very strong church at Leek to command the services of such a talented man, who after "conflicting with many difficulties in the world, peaceably left it Oct. 1st, 1773, aged 62 years."

The celebrated Dr. Harwood is the next minister of whom we have any record. He was born in 1729, and died in 1794, but I have no date of his appointment. He preached at Leek and Wheelock on alternate Sundays, and superintended the grammar school at Congleton on week-days. The probable date of his coming to Leek is 1754, and so we have a gap in our history of nineteen years. He removed in 1765 to Bristol, taking Presbyterian ordination, and became distinguished as a clever scholar, critic and divine, publishing many books. He was a very close friend with Dr. Priestley, then at Nantwich, and became, first an Arian, and ultimately a Unitarian.

The dual pastorate was continued by the minister who followed Dr. Harwood, at both places. This was Rev. Benjn. Ratcliffe, who commenced about the year 1765 and remained until 1772, when the Wheelock chapel was closed. It after-

Nonconformity in Leek 15

wards became a Baptist church. What became of Mr. Ratcliffe we do not know, but he was the same year succeeded at Leek by the Rev. Evan Lewes, and in 1775 the property was transferred to this gentleman. He remained at Leek about five years, but forty-three years later he is mentioned on another deed as living at Coton Cottage, Milwich, near Stone.

In 1780 the Rev. James Evans was minister, and in this year Mr. Hankinson says the first old chapel was taken down and rebuilt, a minister's house erected in the adjoining garden, and an endowment fund was raised. Mr. Evans remained at Leek until 1782.

There is a minute on the church books dated July 22nd, 1782, which says that "this day the Rev. George Chadwick received an invitation from a very respectable majority of the subscribers and the same day accepted the same." This gentleman, however, did not actually assume the pastorate ; and another minute dated Nov. 12th, records that the Rev. Robert Smith was that day elected minister. This minute is signed by thirty-six subscribers.

Mr. Smith's election was disputed by a number of the congregation, and a law suit followed: "At the Assizes held at Stafford, 1783, before the Hon. Mr. Justice Nares and a special jury, was tried the cause of the Protestant Dissenters of Leek, which was sent down from the Court of King's Bench." The matter in dispute was whether certain persons coming into their place of worship during a pastoral vacancy, attracted there by special services held by Captain Scott, and becoming subscribers during the vacancy, were qualified to vote, or whether the right of election was vested only in those who were subscribers to the last stated ministry. After a hearing of more than four hours the jury gave a verdict for the old congregation, and Mr. Smith's election was confirmed.

This Captain Scott played a very important part in the history of the Free Churches about that time, and many of the Congregational churches in Cheshire and Staffordshire owe their origin and development to him. I am pleased to know that the Rev. D. Macfadyen is undertaking to write his biography.

Mr. Smith remained at Leek until 1807, when he removed to Nantwich and was pastor there for eleven years, when he resigned. He died at Nantwich, 1822, aged 73, having been a minister of the Gospel forty years. During his ministry at Leek the Non-parochial Registers were commenced. These cover the period from 1787 to 1837, and are now at the General Registry Office, London. They are for for births and deaths only. It was also during Mr. Smith's pastorate that the Leek Sunday school was formed. This was in 1797, the Anglicans, Independents and Wesleyans all joining in the work and meeting in the old theatre in the "Swan" yard. Sunday schools afterwards became denominational, each church having a flourishing school.

The Wesleyans also became established in Leek about this period, their first chapel, "Mount Pleasant," being built in 1787. John Wesley visited Leek several times from 1772 to 1788, holding meetings in a room in the "Black's Head" yard.

Mr. Smith was succeeded in Leek by the Rev. Stephen Johnson, who was pastor until 1813, when he removed to Wickham, and after a pastorate of twenty-five years there, during which time the cause had been greatly enlarged, he died in 1838.

He was followed by the Rev. Joseph Morrow, who came to Leek in 1813 and died in harness in 1836.

During his pastorate, *viz.*, in 1830, a number of his hearers, by the advice of the county ministers, left the Derby Street chapel and formed another church which met for a time in the "Black's Head" yard. This new church elected the Rev. Wm. Parker Bourne, then a student at Highbury College, as their pastor, and the congregation increasing a new chapel was built in Union Street, and opened May 6th, 1834. Day schools were also built about the same time and put in trust, and a useful and flourishing school for girls and infants has continued there until the present day. Our oldest known Sunday school register dates from 1830. Mr. Bourne married, during his stay in Leek, Margaret Crusoe, the daughter of Mr. Crusoe, solicitor, and has two daughters still living who are frequent visitors to Leek. Mr. Bourne, owing to failing health, was soon obliged to resign his charge, and removed to Teignmouth in 1836, but was spared to labour there only a few years, and died in February, 1840, aged 37, "having a full hope of immortality."

Mr. Morrow, as we have seen, died about the same time as Mr. Bourne resigned, and when the Rev. Robert Goshawk was elected in 1837 the two churches soon afterwards came together again, and thus the six years' division was healed. Mr. Goshawk continued his charge until 1856, having been minister for about nineteen years. After several pastorates in various parts of England he settled in Norwich, and died there in 1883, aged 73.

There are a few persons yet living in Leek who remember Mr. Morrow, Mr. Bourne, and Mr. Goshawk, and of them all I hear the kindest comments.

The next pastor was the Rev. Josiah Hankinson, who in August, 1856, undertook pastoral duties at

Leek, and remained until February, 1892, having faithfully served the church and town of Leek for nearly thirty-six years. During Mr. Hankinson's pastorate the present church was built in Derby Street and the mission church in Alsop Street commenced.

As we write (1906) we are glad to know that Mr. Hankinson is still hale and hearty, and that arrangements are made for him to occupy his old pulpit on the 50th anniversary of his settlement in Leek.

The Rev. Wm. Aylmer Stark, M.A., a student of Mansfield College, Oxford, was elected to succeed Mr. Hankinson in 1893, and was followed in 1897 by the Rev. Andrew Hamilton, also of Mansfield College, and in 1900 the Rev. John Hoatson, the present minister, received a unanimous call.

This concludes the list of the "band of men whose hearts God had touched," who have held aloft the banner of truth so long and so well.

> "God wrote His name upon a little child,
> And as it grew, the fret of worldly care
> Effaced that name, the manuscript defiled,
> Writing care, interest, sorrow there.
>   An angel visited the child and smiled,
> For through all else
> The old sweet name was there."

* * * *

> "We bless Thee, Lord . . . . . .
> For Pisgah's gleams of newer, fairer truth,
> Which ever ripening still renew our youth ;
> For fellowship with noble souls and wise,
> Whose hearts beat time to music of the skies ;
> For each achievement human toil can reach ;
> For all that patriots win and poets teach ;
> For the old light that gleams on history's page,
> For the new hope that shines on each new age."

J. M. WHITE

(*British Congregationalist*, Aug. 9th, 1906).

Leek Congregational Church Ministers

AT LEEK

Rev. John Machin, B.A.	1649-1662	(occasional)
„ George Moxon	1653-1664	„
„ Henry Newcome, M.A.	1647-1660	„
„ John Hieron, M.A.	1649-1662	„
„ Francis Bowyer	1633-1648	(at Leek parish church)
„ Robert Fowler	1649-1654	„ „ „
„ Ralph Worsley, B.A.	1654-1655	
„ Thos. Wynnell, M.A.	1655-1662	

Mr. Thomas Nabbs' house licensed, 1672
Derby Street property bought, 1683
Rev. Josiah Hargreaves   (?) 1695-1725
„ Hugh Worthington, jnr. 1730-1735

. . . .

„ Dr. Edward Harwood	(?) 1754-1765	
„ Benjn. Ratcliffe	1765-1772	
„ Evan Lewis	1775-1780	
„ James Evans	1780-1782	
Capt. Jon. Scott	1771-1807	(occasional)
Rev. Geo. Chadwick	1782	(elected only)
„ Robert Smith	1782-1807	
„ Stephen Johnson	——1813	
„ Joseph Morrow	1813-1836 }	
„ Wm. Parker Bourne	1830-1836 }	
„ Robt. Goshawk	1837-1856	
„ Josiah Hankinson	1856-1892	
„ Wm. Aylmer Stark, M.A.	1893-1897	
„ Andrew Hamilton, M.A.	1897-1900	
„ John Hoatson	1900	

The above dates are in some cases only approximate.

J. LOVATT.

Richard Frankland

IN addition to the excellent summary of the life of Frankland given in the last number of the *Transactions*, a few further particulars concerning that early and eminent tutor may be of interest.

There is an account of the writ of Privy Seal issued by Oliver Cromwell, Lord Protector, May 15th, 1657, in *A Collection of Historical Pieces*, by Francis Peck, M.A., London, 1740. The names of the first provost, fellows, tutors and visitors are mentioned, but the name of Frankland is not among them. Some post may have been designed for him in the college of Durham (*Dict. of National Biography*); but there is no evidence, so far as I am aware, that he was ever appointed to it.

The story of his admonition to Charles II. is contained in *Extracts from the Day-book of Dr. Henry Sampson* (formerly in the possession of Thoresby), in Birch MSS., Brit. Mus. 4460. But it is, I think, somewhat doubtful. His interviews with Thomas Sharp, Archbishop of York (son of a Parliamentarian of Bradford), are described by himself in a letter to Thoresby, November 6th, 1694 (*Correspondence of Ralph Thoresby, 1832*, I. 171).

A marble tablet to Frankland's memory, placed over the door of the south side of Giggleswick church, bears the following inscription, which I copied some years ago:—

H. M.
Richard Frankland, A.M.,
Ex celebri Franklandorum de Thirtilbe [Thirkleby] in
agro Eboracensi gente connubio vero stabili juncto uni

ex filiabus D. Sanderson de Hedley Hope in agro Dunel: viro optimo et ab optimo dilecto, theologo venerando, pio philosopho excogitandum, acuto ad explicandum; Felici Patri bene merenti posuere filiæ fratribus, eheu, ante parentes defunctis, vixit An. 67. Mens: 11 ob: An. Aeræ Xtian. 1698.

In the register of burials I found the following entry:

"1698. Richardus Frankland de Rathmell cler. quinto die Octobri."

He married Elizabeth Sanderson, of Hedley Hope, in the parish of Brancepeth, Durham, who died at York, 1706, and had two sons: John, entered the academy May 3rd, 1678, died January 1679; and Richard, entered the academy April 13th, 1680, died of the smallpox at Attercliffe, May 4th, 1689; and three daughters: Barbery (named after Mrs. Lambert, of Calton Hall), Elizabeth, and Margaret, who survived him. There are tablets in the church porch at Giggleswick to later members of the Frankland family, *i.e.*, Richard Frankland, of Close House, who died April 23rd, 1803, aged 70 years; John Frankland, his brother, who died April 26th, 1804, aged 68 years; also Isabella, their sister, who died December 3rd, 1811, aged 71 years.

On the passing of the Toleration Act "the house of Mr. Richard Frankland at Rathmell" was recorded at the quarter sessions as a public meeting-place for Protestant dissenters, Oct. 8th, 1689, on the certificate of John Hey, of Horton in Craven, a near neighbour of Richard Mitchell, of Marton Scar (many miles distant from Calton Hall and Winterburn). After the death of Frankland, October 1st, 1698, the academy was carried on for a short time under Mr. John Owen, his student (admitted Nov. 23rd, 1689) and assistant, of whom William Tong wrote:—

"He was a student of Mr. Frankland, and after some years

spent with him as a pupil was chosen to be his assistant, and while he was so his example and endeavours were of very good use to several young men in the family. He had made great improvements in religion and learning before he left that place, and entered upon the ministry with great seriousness and great acceptance, and chose to spend his time and strength in the same place where his father lived and died. He was, I think, the only dissenting minister in Merionethshire. Some occasions leading him to Salop he fell sick there at Mr. Orton's house, and in 9 days died [Jan. 1700] (being about 30 years of age), to the great grief of all his acquaintance and to the unspeakable loss of the Church of God." (*Life of Matthew Henry*, 1716, p. 277).

Oliver Heywood wrote to Thoresby, Nov. 7th, 1698 :—

"They have not yet got a tutor for the scholars at Mr. Frankland's; they desire Mr. Tong of Coventry, but are in suspense. Mr. Owen stays till Christmas." (*Thoresby's Correspondence*, I. 335).

He also wrote at the end of his list of Frankland's students :—

"After Mr. Richard Frankland's death the academy was broken up, the scholars dispersed. Not long after Mr. John Charlton set up a teaching university learning in a great house in Manchester, Lanc.—the names of his scholars are these [19 names, of which 14 were those of Frankland's students]. I received this catalogue. Sept. 4, 1699." (*Diary*, 11.16).

Religious services continued to be held at Rathmell for some years subsequently by James Towers, one of Frankland's students (admitted April 14th, 1694, who was in some way related to his tutor, and who had forty hearers in 1715 : Evans' list). Towers removed to Tockholes, Lancashire, in 1722, and from the time of his removal his congregation appears to have been scattered. It was not until a century later that a Congregational chapel was built at Settle, three miles distant, as the result of the visit paid in connection with "the West Riding Itinerant Society" (formed in 1811) by that distinguished evangelist Joseph Cockin, of Halifax, his worthy son, John Cockin, of Holmfirth, and other ministers.

In answer to an enquiry made by the late Mr. Joshua Wilson concerning the history of Independent churches in Yorkshire, John Cockin wrote April 21st, 1821, (among other things) the following account of a visit he paid to the chief scene of Richard Frankland's labours :—

"Some years ago when I was itinerating in Craven I passed through a village and saw Rathmil painted on a board. The name struck me, and after pausing a little I recollected it was the residence of Mr. Frankland, the tutor of the first dissenting academy in England. I asked the first man I met if there were any remains of an old chapel in the place. 'No,' said he, 'but there was once a college here.' (From this you learn what name these institutions had in days of yore). I then enquired what person in the village was most likely to give me information about it. According to the direction I received I waited on one person and another, and at last I went to one family whose ancestors had resided within a stone-cast of Mr. Frankland's house for several centuries. They received me courteously, entertained me to dinner, shewed me the premises, answered my enquiries and told me all the traditions of the place respecting the 'old college.' It was an extensive establishment, bounded by a high wall, which enclosed an acre of ground. Over the gate of the yard there was a large bell, which rung at stated times to call the students up, and to summon them to family prayer, meals, &c. Some of the buildings have been taken down, and those which are yet standing are converted into cottage houses. There was a long row of small windows to the different studies, most of which are now walled up. Over the principal door there yet remain the initials $R^E F$ (Richard and Elizabeth Frankland) cut in stone. The kitchen was described to me as having been very large, and my guide told me that when she was a girl she had often hid herself in the oven at the game of 'hide and seek.' The garden and orchard were also extensive, but they are now converted into grass land. I could learn no anecdotes of the personal character of Mr. Frankland, or any of the students ; and all the traditions I heard related to the mischievous tricks which the young men played to the country people. From the number (303) I am inclined to think that the children of dissenters were educated there for commercial life [some were doubtless educated by him for the learned professions, but most of them became ministers]; and experience has proved that plan to be attended with many evils. When I had seen all that could be shewn and heard all that could be told, I went forward to Giggleswick church in which Mr. Frankland lies interred. There is a black tablet to his memory fixed in the wall, with a Latin inscription which speaks highly of his attainments as a scholar, a philosopher and a divine. Having thus paid all the respect I could to his memory, I pursued my journey, and preached that evening at a house at Settle. How singular are the revolutions of the world, that the country which once produced so many burning and shining lights, and from which our forefathers received the benefits of knowledge and the blessings of religion, should now be visited by our itinerants as a district benighted in ignorance!"

BRYAN DALE.

NOTE.—On p. 425 vol. II. it is said that "The only colleague [of Frankland] of whom we have certain knowledge is his old pupil Mr. Issot." The author of a kindly notice in *The Christian Life* mentions two others: Richard Frankland the younger, entered at Natland 13th April, 1682; and John Owen, entered at Rathmell 23rd November, 1689. The same writer informs us that "Hartleborough or Hallburrow" is really Hart Barrow, near Cartmell Fell, and just within the Lancashire border; also that Frankland was buried in Giggleswick *church*, not churchyard.

T. G. C.

Ancient Sacramental Plate

BY the courtesy of J. Scamell, Esq., of Westbury, we are enabled to present a couple of prints of considerable historic interest :

I. Two silver beakers formerly used in celebrating holy communion in the "old meeting" at South Petherton, Somerset. The church was founded in 1688, just after King James's "Declaration of Indulgence." It was originally Presbyterian, at least in name, though practically Independent, and in 1747 formally adopted Congregationalism. The successive ministers were the Revs. Samuel Bulstrode, 1688-1725 ; Henry Rutter, 1725-46 ; James Kirkup, 1746-84 ; David Richards, 1786-1842. On Mr. Richard's retirement, or soon after, worship was discontinued, and the building has since been demolished.

During Mr. Kirkup's ministry the church became for the most part Arian. In consequence of this a secession took place, and the present Congregational church was organised in 1775, the first minister being the Rev. R. Herdsman, one of Lady Huntingdon's students from Trevecca.

The cups here figured were exhibited before the Society of Antiquaries on the 21st June, 1888, being then in the possession of J. P. Daniel, Esq., the senior surviving trustee ; and are now (1907) in the custody of his niece.

The following description is from the *Proceedings* of the Society of Antiquaries :—"The older of the two cups is $3\frac{3}{8}$ inches high, and is enriched a little below the lip by a broad band of flower work in *repoussé*. Hall marks, London 1691-2 ; maker's mark, a goose or duck. The other cup is also $3\frac{3}{8}$ inches high, but has nearly vertical sides with a belt of upright acanthus leaves in

26 Ancient Sacramental Plate

repoussé round the bottom. A little above is a narrow belt of laurel leaves, also in relief. Hall mark, London, 1697-8 ; maker, A. N."

H. Norris, Esq., a local antiquarian, furnished the following additional particulars to another periodical :—" They are of beaten silver . . . . each containing precisely eight ounces."

II. The silver baptismal bowl presented to Silver Street Chapel, Trowbridge, in 1767, by T. Jeffries, goldsmith, of Cockspur Street, London. (See *Transactions* vol. II., p. 209.) It is of beaten silver, and weighs 21.2 oz. troy, equivalent to $23\frac{1}{2}$ avoirdupois. It is $8\frac{3}{4}$ inches wide at the top, $4\frac{1}{2}$ inches wide at the base, and $4\frac{1}{2}$ inches high. It has the London hall mark, Old English capital 𝔐, maker's initials E. A. It is inscribed : "The gift of Thomas Jeffries, of London, 1767."

The South Petherton Communion Cups

The Trowbridge Baptismal Bowl.

Wiggenton's *Visitation*

THE following is from a MS. in the Congregational Library, of which a description appeared in *Transactions*, ii., 147, *et seqq*.

It is in the handwriting of Giles Wiggenton, the Puritan vicar of Sedbergh; and may be fairly called A Series of Articles ministered in a Mock Visitation.

and theife articles doe conteine in effect the some of al such matters as the sincere brethrē and true lovers of reformatiõ would have practised in the church both by y^m selves and also by others to the high glorie of god almightie.

Certeine articles ministred by the Arch: at noe time leaste he should hurte or shame his owne prophane hirelings for neglecting of most Excellent and waightie matters and duties: as well is knowne they doe neglect and despise them.

1. In primis: whether have you any moe Pastorall cha[r]g then one? and having but one whether came

one charge.   you lawfullye & honestlye into the same, yea or noe? and whether are you resident thereuppon? Tell where? when? by whose meanes & in what manner?

2. Itm̄ whether doe you labor by p̄yer and by all good meanes possible that the people of yor church, namelye such

honest entrance.   as are knowne to be v[ir]tewous maye willinglye, Joyfullye & lovinglye enterteyne & reteyne & mainteyne you as y^e^u^r Pastor; not contenting y^r selfe w^t the lame entrannce of putacōn Institution & Induction (as they are termed) nor w^t any kinde of Intrusion or enforcement w^tout the goodwill of the good christians but rather purposing in yor hearte to become a nursing father unto them in yor Pastorall charge by naturall kindnes, naturall love, tender pittye &c, sithence yor

Edge of page frayed and a few words illegible.   ministerye & rulling is thus established; not onelye according to the recvd l[awes] of this realme, but also according to the [? holye] word of god? Tell in what manner? &c.

3. It͞m whether doe yoᵘ in a godlye wise manner wᵗout holding the faith of Christ in respect of p̄sons joyne & con-
Elders. sult wᵗ the most forward of the congregcōn for the more godlye & quiet ordering of the residewe according to the holy word of god & the good lawes of this realme : and whethʳ doe you direct and pswade the faithfull in yoʳ flocke to make choicē of, allowe & confirme this consultacōn & governaunce? Tell in what manner? &c.

4. It͞m whether doe you wᵗ consent of all the forward christians chosen to joyne wᵗ you for over syght of the residewe;
Marginal notes on this page are lost through the fraying of the outer edge of the paper. set downe good ord̄ers from tyme to tyme, to meet wᵗ pticular inconveniensens as they growe : according to the holye worde of god & the good lawes of this
The Elders their realme ; for example against contentious psons : that
practice of yⁱʳ none may flee at the lawe till the sainctes & godlye
godlye govnment brethren be first delt wᵗ all to arbytrate the matter. & agaynst inflamable vayne talkers, lyers, swearᵉˢ, Sabaoth breakers, unlawful resorters to yoʳ towne to hinder yoʳ good orders &c some convenient admonition, complainte, penaltye & such lyke, before you seeke for excommunication & extremitye against them? Tell in what man͟ⁿ? [*manner*]

5. It͞m Whether doe you direct and perswade the faithfull in your flocke likwise to make choice of allowe & con-
Deacons. firme A certeyne nomber of godlye wise psons in their office weeklye or from tyme to tyme to gathʳ reserve & bestowe uppon the poore, especiallye of the household of faith, their maintenance necessarye & competente, soe as there maye be noe begger amongst you, according to the holye word of God & the good lawes of this realme? Tell in what manner &c.

6. It͞m whether doe you not wᵗ advice & discretion sue for
assistance of faith- the usefull favour & assistance of all her maᵗⁱᵉˢ most
ful injoined
or craved lawfull & worthy officers to theise yoʳ good orders making them privye [?] of them in sincere & orderlike manner?

7. It͞m whether doe you not praye daylye and by name both
privatlye and publicklye for her maᵗⁱᵉˢ most honorable
pticular prayer for counsaile . . . . . in authoritye under them ; yᵗ god will
the queen's maᵗⁱᵉ
and all maᵗrats give them more & . . . . . to . . . love & cherishe . . . . . .
lawful. and all the sound fil . . . . [*an entire line is apparently missing, through the bottom of the page being worn*]
. . . . followers thereof and to espye, hate. correct and punishe the contrarye. Thus building up the church of christ daylye; to their great honnor & comfort? Tell what manner &c.

8. It͞m whether doe yoᵘ soe earnestlye hate all Idollatrye and antechristianitye wᵗ all the enormityes and deformityes
al christians their thereof, yᵗ you labor by all meanes to rid out of the
zealous further
ance of godlye churche or congregacōn every garment and remnāt
discipline against
false worshippe defiled wᵗ sinn, all outward shewe and offensive ap-

pearance of evell: remembring the pure & precise doctrigne of oͬ saviour christe, & the parables thereto according, in the scripture, as of the leane the halting and lukewarme Brethren & the curse of god uppon all those yͭ doe his worke negligentlye & serve him not with their whole hertes, soules & strenght &c and remembring yͭ by suche degrees of yielding to small corruptions Sathā seeketh & useth to overthrow Gods grace in the pͬessors & to bring them to destruction as you may see daylye: Tell in what manner, &c.

9. Itᵐ whether doe you carefullye refrayne the companye of all heretiques, & of all obstinate & pphane worldlings, except uppon good occasion offered to win their soules: whoe after sundrye admonitions doe not refraine frō their wicked waye, remembring howe it is written wͭ

<small>al christians their like furtherance against al false brethren doges, and Swine.</small>

such an one eate not ne bid him god speed, ne knowe him not by having any familliar acquaintance wͭ him. depͭ from him & have noe fellowship wͭ his unfruitfull workes of darknes: but reprove them rather. An angrye countenance putteth awaye sin & sclaunder. And whether doe you willinglye & in good zeale zeale [*sic*] seake in due order for yͬ pte and according to yoͬ calling to bring them to publicke reprof & excommunication that they may be ashamed and converted (?) that othͬs maye feare & be edified, and that yoͬ dutyes herein maye be discharged and god maye be glorified by this his healthfull ordinance in the great congregacōn: & whether doe you after they be excommunicated, pittyfullye and Brotherlye endevour as you maye, to reclayme them to the fayth of christ yt God maye be highlye glorified, and good spirites reioyced in his happye conͮsion.

10. Itᵐ whether doe you travayle by all godlye wise meanes possible, as well privatelye as publiquelye to prevente & preserve the sheepe of yͭ flocke from this heavy vengeance of Just excommunication for grievous

<small>The pastors & elders — special furtherance & tender care thereof.</small>

offences as being the verye entrance and assurance to everlasting damnation accoumpting it greater wisdome & a richer crowne beyond all comparison, for you to win soules than to obteyne any worldlye lucre, ambitious Roome [*i.e. place or position*] or vayne pleasure, yea the whole world, & all therein conteyned?

11. Itᵐ whether doe you instruct & mainteyne your owne houshold in good & godlye order using morning & evening pͬyer amongst them & catechizing unto the wͭ ofte reading of the Scripture & wͭ suche other holye

<small>houshold instruction & discipline</small>

exercises: soe as yͬ people pceiving yoͬ house to be as it were a litle church doe now & the͂ repayre unto you for their sp[irit]uall comfort & edyefieng by yoͬ godlye household exercises; & yͭ wͭout all suspicōn or liklyhood of private convinticles, or such like absurd sclanders wᶜʰ yoͬ adversaryes used to obiecte agaynst yͬ well doinges. Tell in what manner &c.

12. It^m whether doe you some tyme (uppon Just occasion offered) use the same or like godlye exercises in other folkes houses alsoe, beside y^r owne to th' ende to traine & direct their housholdes thereof, being kinges & pphetes there, to teache & rule their houshold ye better and godlier? Tell in what manner? &c.

Trayninge of other folkes housholdes In like manner.

13. Itm whether doe you keepe good hospitallyty yor selfe & exhorte other of abillity soe to doe not frequēting the alehouses nor such unmeete places; nor being nigardlye misers at home: but going before yor flocke to their good example, in all vertuous & godlye conversation: soe as even those w^t out & the strangers maye reporte well of yor good doctrigne, life, & order to the greater praise of god & of his ghospell wch you professe: Tell in what manner? &c.

hospitalitie and good example.

14. Itm whether doe you give yo^rselfe muche to privat p^ryer, fasting. sober behaviour, studye & meditacōn on gods holye worde all the weeke longe, soe as yo^u maye be the better able, publiquelye & pryvatlye to understand & deliver the true meaning of the Text of holye scripture & to applye the same fitlye for reformacōn of manners of the people: and whether doe you hold yor selfe to the pure Analogie or pporcōn & platforme of gods worde in yor preachīgs not mixing any forraigne doctrigne unto it; as of other mens devises & of yor owne brayne; Tell in what manner? &c.

godlye private exercises & right devidig of the worde of god.

15. Itm whether doe you preache every Sabath daye in the forenoone? & preach or catechize every Sabath daye in the afternoone? and at all oth^r tymes when the people of yor charge maye convenientlye assemble together, dealyng faithfullye & painfullye w^t them in the worke of yor ministerye, in season & out of season? Tell in what manner &c.

Sabot^u daye exercises for preaching.

16. Itm whether doe you minister the holye comunion unto them often, & in most reverent manner after due examinacōn of every one of them, & in earnestwise inviting them to become newe creatures in christe more & more? & likewise the holye Baptisme & layeng upp treasure for the poore: & whether doe you use solempne fastings, & love feasts & suche like holy meetings, as occasion & necessity doth require? Tell in what manner &c. &c.

Sabath dayes exercises for the Sacramet namelye the lordes supper

17. Itm whether doe you not account it dangerous for yo^u uppon yor allegeance to god & uppon payne of yor owne & of yor congregacōns greate hinderance in spūall thinges to be absent from them but one Saboth daye, or tyme appoynted for holye exercises, remembring howe the Israelytes made a calfe, & fell to sundry greivous sins in moses his shorte absence from them (though uppō necessarye occasions in their singuler behoofes) & howe o^r savio^r christ bad peter feede,

continewal necessitie of observing the saboths.

feede, feede, both Sheepe & Lambes, y^t is, never cease feeding of them as peter him selfe expoundeth it : feede as much as in you lyeth the flock of christe. and likewise paul as aforesayde. Preach in season and out of season, and agayne Wo be to me if I preache not the ghospel : and finally the ministerye is often compared to the most painfull & faithfull office y^t can be ; as Sheepherdes, Builders, trompetteres, warriours, watchmen, &c. All wch places w^t sundrye the like places & reasons dulye considered whether dare you or ever durst you w^t out urgent & enforcing cause of necessitye be absent from yor flocke any one saboth daye & being soe enforced to be absent wheth^r doe you use to leave a deputye in yor roome yea or noe ? and yf you leave a deputye whoe & what manner of deputye is he ? whome you doe trust in soe wayghtye a matter of trust ? & if he have the like office elsewhere ? w^t what conscience dare yo^u pull or hold him from thence ? by what equitye & uppon what occasiō ? Tell what &c. ?

18. Itm̄ whether doe you use & applye all yor possible meanes for the winning & comforting of christe his sheepe & *private conferece in dealing wth ye flocke* lambes in yor congregacōn, as by making of peace, visiting & comforting the poore & sicke, & anyway troubled eaven house by house as need requireth, & for the punishing & rooting out (as aforesaid) of obstinate sinnes from the lords flocke, as comōn drunkardes, usurers, quarellous, whorem^rs, sclanderers, Idollaters, & such like : and wheth^r doe yo^u pticularly visit every howse for the better direction of them in grace & peace? Tell in what manner, &c. &c. ?

19. Itm̄ whether doe you nowe & then take a surveye & reckoning in yor minde namelye at the tymes of yor *private examinacōn & sensuringe* Catechizing for preparation for the Lordes Supper, howe god blesseth or curseth yor labors in the pceedinges or backslidings of yor selfe or of yor flocke or any pte of it. heartily praysing god for the successe of the one, & humbly prayeng his grace for redresse of the oth^r duly considering the right cawses of both, & soe laboring thence forward, to encrease in grace & truth, wisdome & courage, humilitye & good hope, & in all vertue all the dayes of yor life ? Tell in what manner &c. ?

20. Itm̄ whether doe you everye weeke, or soe often as you can convenientlye make yor repayre to some places nere *Sinods and general councelles* to you to th' end y^t then & there you maye be edified, comforted, & confirmed, by yor godlye brethren of the ministerye & maye edyfie Comforte & confirme them in the aforesaid godlye doctrigne honest life & good order; namelye by conferences, disputacōns, reasonings, prayers, Singing of psalmes, preachings, readings, pphesings, fastings, & feastings and such like holye exercises & wherby you & they may become the better able both to teach & rule yor severall charges at home & alsoe to

fournishe & adorne the Sinodes and generall councells abroade for government & direction of the whole churche, according to the holye word of god & good lawes of this realme. Tell in what manner? &c.

21. Itm̄ whether is not the drift of all yor sermons & dealings according to the drift & dealings of the holye ghost & word of god, w^t all g^rce and truth : & w^t out fleshlye worldlye & devillishe affeccōn, as of wantonnes & vanitye, covetousnes & subtiltye, pride, pompe, boasting & ambition, feare or favo^r, envye or disdayne or anye such lyke evell affecōn to trayne & leade the people by fayth & love to frame their lives daylye more & more religouslye and zealouslye before god ; charitablye and peaceablye toward their neighbours faithfullye & obedientlye toward their supiours ? Tell in what manner ? &c.

<small>precise & pure affection to be sought for.</small>

As for the other 3 articles being the last in nōber of his petitionarye articles ppounded to her gratious ma^{tie} at her first enterance w^t all the rest of those articles they are pticularlye confuted & th' absurditye of them is disclosed : first by 2 or 3 schrols of doubts latlye moved by certeyne ministers to the B. of Norwiche. secondlye by one schroll of counter articles entituled from the highest pastor &c 3^{lye} by 2 severall aunswers made of purpose unto them th' one longer th' other shorter ; beside all other treatises before & since concerning the cause of reformcōn.

I heare morover of 1 other article to be ministered w^t the former to make them up 22 namelye to this effect

Whither [*sic*] have you at any tyme or by any meanes spoken against my L. A. or his dealings ; or shewed y^r selfe to mislike thereof. & whether doe yo^u thinke he dealeth not well & like a good p^rlate, & according to his place & authoritye. yea or noe ? Tell wherein, when & where ? &c.

The Story of Congregationalism in Longdon and Lichfield

ABOUT midway between the market towns of Lichfield and Rugeley, with the main road connecting them as its near boundary, lies a triangular plot of common land known as Longdon Green. An ancient inn and a few cottages are scattered irregularly about; and, crossing the green, we are led along a by-road on the opposite side to a tiny graveyard, and a small plain building called Longdon Green Chapel. The situation is sequestered even to loneliness. The building is devoid of ornament; only four walls, stuccoed and whitewashed, and a tiled roof, moss-grown in patches; there is nothing but the Gothic shaped windows to distinguish it from some outbuilding of a farm. Entering through one of the side doors of the tiny vestibule, we see across the rear one old-fashioned high-backed pew, divided in the middle to admit of a cupboard, on the top of which the baptismal vessel formerly stood. Between this and the communion table beneath the pulpit are straight-backed benches, cushionless and narrow. A harmonium, a stove, and a few oil lamps complete the furniture. There is no vestry, nor any other usual accommodation. Bare and uninviting as we of the well appointed town churches may think, it is the spiritual home wherein a little flock regularly and devoutly gathers, whose story we have now to tell.

The Staffordshire ministers ejected at the Restoration, or by the Act of Uniformity, were fifty-six in number, of whom only six afterwards conformed. In the neighbourhood with which we are particularly concerned were Rev. John Butler, M.A., vicar of St. Mary's in the market square, Lichfield; Rev. Thomas Miles, rector of St. Chad's, or Chadstowe as it was called; John Mott, of King's Bromley: Nathaniel Mansfield, of Armitage; Richard Dowley, B.D., of Elford; Richard Chantrye, of Weeford, and several others. But though they lost their houses and their incomes, these true-hearted men did not lack friends or faithful adherents.

The vicar of St. Mary's, John Butler, for example, though deprived of his church, did not leave the city. His activity, though necessarily curtailed, was not entirely suppressed. In Harwood's *History of Lichfield* we read: " Butler was of Edmund's Hall, Oxford, and was silenced after the Restoration; after which he sometimes preached in his own house. Mr. Minors, of Lichfield, was kind to him and his family; set up one of his sons in trade, and sent another to the University, where he was at the expense of his education; and when he died left him £12 a year. Butler died about 1670, aged about 50." This Mr. Minors is evidently he of whom Harwood had written on an earlier page: "Thomas Minors also left a house and lands to trustees for a schoolmaster and thirty poor boys, inhabitants of the city, to read the Bible," &c. The house still stands at the end of Bore Street, and bears the name of "Minors' House," though the endowments were long ago transferred, we understand, to the grammar school.

When, in 1672, King Charles—in order to favour the Roman Catholics and afford them facilities without openly avowing himself—issued the Declaration of Indulgence, the following applications for licence (amongst above 4,000 others) were made, and stand on record in the State Paper Office:—

> "The House of John Barker in Litchfield, Stafford, Pr. [*i.e.* Presbyterian] Meeting-place, 15 May.
> Like for the House of Wry Jeslem in Litchfield.
> Like for the House of Thomas Minors in Litchfield."

A few months later the following occur:—

> "The House of Job Hathersick of Lichfield, Staffordshire.
> The House of Alice Nockin of Lichfield, Pr."

It is evident from this alone that Nonconformist principles were not confined to the ministers; and that in the case of Minors his adherence was not merely a matter of friendship for his late minister, who had died two years earlier, but of personal conviction. It is fair to assume that Nonconformist services were held in the house in Bore Street in 1672, as well as in other houses in and near the city.

We now revert to Thomas Miles, the ejected rector of St. Chad's. Calamy says of him:—"He suffered much by his Nonconformity. Besides his annual income, he lost £40 which should have been paid to him in the beginning of the year; and he left his living in a very low state. He continued in the town till the Oxford Act came out [*i.e.* the "Five Mile Act" of 1665], when he was forced to leave his family, tho' he had a very dangerous cold upon him. He did not see his wife and children for eleven weeks, nor durst he come to them in eighteen months. Having no certain dwelling, he travelled about from place to place, near 300 miles on foot. If at any time he stole home by night, he durst not stir out of his chamber; and when he went out it was either very late or very early, for fear of being taken. He was once sent for by a magistrate who lay sick, and continued his night visits for a fortnight. The evening before his death Mr. Miles was sent for in haste by

LONGDON GREEN CHAPEL, NEAR LICHFIELD.

daylight, and being seen to go into the house was complained of to the chief magistrate of the town by a curate, which made him hasten away the next morning. This gentleman, who had been twice applied to for a warrant to apprehend him, was so kind as to send notice to his wife (that he should be safely conveyed away). He was afterwards cited into the Ecclesiastical Court for baptizing his own child; and was often forced into the country, in snow and rain, to preach before day, and to shift from house to house, for fear of a certain magistrate who said he would have him dead or alive. He was sometimes constrained to retire into the fields and solitudes, to keep Sabbaths alone, and his life was often in danger from extreme heats and colds. He lived entirely upon Providence, which took care of him, and he was not forsaken, nor did his seed beg their bread."

This, doubtless, is the man to whom Nonconformity, especially in the form of Congregationalism, owes its being as a collective force in this neighbourhood. Among the records in the diocesan registry at Lichfield is an entry, made in 1665, of the names of some 40 or more persons who at that time were "presented" in the parish of St. Chad's, from which Thomas Miles had been ejected, for non-attendance at their parish church. Presumably some at least of these, faithful to their conscience and their pastor, had gone with him, and formed the nucleus of his congregation, which—tradition says—gathered at first in a farmhouse kitchen at Curborough, a hamlet near by. This congregation, like many others, appears to have been broken up by the Conventicle Act of 1664; under the pressure of which we can well understand how Miles was "forced into the country . . . to preach before day," &c. The Five Mile Act coming into force the following year, tradition affirms that the meeting-place was changed to a remote part of King's Bromley, just beyond the limit decreed; and though no actual records remain, the subsequent course of events appears to corroborate the tradition.

The brief respite from persecution afforded by the short-lived Declaration of Indulgence was not neglected, either by preacher or people. Among the State papers before mentioned are found these entries of licences applied for:—

"Licence to Thomas Miles, to be a Grall Pr. [*i.e.* General Presbyterian] Teacher." This application appears to have been made about the middle of June, 1672, and desires that he should be allowed to preach "in general and at large," in *any* place "licensed" or "allowed" under the Declaration. It is an open question, however, whether the licence was granted; it was made out, but there is no indication—as in many instances—of its having been signed by the king and issued.

But there were certainly issued licences for three houses in Longdon in which worship might take place, the third of which introduces us to one who, it would seem, became Mr. Miles's successor about this time :—

> "The house of Christian Hood in Longdon."
> "The house of Edward Brughton in Longdon."
> "Mr. Tho. Bakewell, minister, Presbyt^n, ye town, Longdon in ye county of Stafford, in ye house of Richard Browne, yeoman in ye s^d towne."

This last application is endorsed "Given in by Mr Richards, 2^d May." The licences were issued within about ten days; for there are these further entries among those which were granted :—

> "The House of Richard Brown in Longdon, Stafford, Pr Meeting-place, 13 May."
> "Licence to Tho. Bakewell to be a Pr Teacher in the house of Richard Brown in Longdon, Stafford, 13 May."

With the application for a "general" licence made by Thos. Miles our acquaintance with that brave and worthy gentleman ceases. Of his subsequent career, his doings, death, and burial, we have no information. That his cordial relations with his people remained unbroken is clear, from his application for a licence to preach " in generall and at large," a few weeks after his successor had been authorized to preach " in the house of Richard Browne at Longdon." We cannot conceive of his leaving the neighbourhood where he had laboured for so many trying but faithful years. It may be that physical infirmity, the result of anxiety, hard work and exposure, had made him feel no longer equal to the duty of effectively ministering to the spiritual needs of so widely scattered a following. We must remember that his sphere of labour embraced Lichfield and Longdon; and most likely included Rugeley, eight miles away, with the whole intervening district. There were the houses licensed for preaching in Lichfield, John Barker's, Wry Jeslem's, Job Hathersick's, Thomas Minors', and Alice Nockin's. All these good people, with of course many others who met with them, would almost certainly be under his pastoral oversight; and probably some at Curborough, King's Bromley, and Armitage. There was no Nonconformist minister at or near either of these places; for N. Mansfield, who left Armitage in 1662, had removed to Wolverhampton, and thence to Walsall, where he died; and John Mott, who came out at King's Bromley, after four years of farming, removed thence to Stafford. We do indeed find a licence to preach issued to Richard Swinton, and one for the house of William Palmer, both at Fisherwick, four miles east of Lichfield, but we know nothing of them. They would no doubt be known to the Lichfield Nonconformists; and Swinton *may* have cooperated with Miles. It seems, however, a reasonable suggestion that Miles, finding himself no longer equal to the strain and responsibility of so laborious a pastorate, may have advised that one more vigorous should take it up, leaving him free to preach and travel as his strength might permit. Here, then, we must leave him, and thank God for him and such as him.

Our interest is now turned to Thomas Bakewell, ejected from Burton-on-Trent, of whom Calamy, fortunately, gives a pretty full account, as follows :—

"He had episcopal ordination, and was first ejected in 1661 from the rectory of Rolleston, [between Burton and Tutbury] value 120£ per annum. The stipend for the lecture at Burton, which was 30£ per ann., was paid by the Company of Clothworkers in London. Being silenced on Bartholomew day, he rented a house in the same parish, where he afterwards preached. In about half a year he was cited before Bp. Hacket, and this was charged upon him as a thing highly criminal; for which (tho' already ejected) the bishop in open court suspended him *ab officio*, and gave orders to one of the clerks to send a letter of complaint to the justices and deputy-lieutenants. In a little time a warrant was issued out by the magistrates, and sent to the Constable of Burton Extra, by the Bp's apparitor, who came with the Constable upon the Lord's Day, while Mr. Bakewell was preaching, to see the warrant executed. The Constable not only took him, but also Mr. Thomas Ford, (an ejected minister who sometimes preached in his own house at Winsall, but was then only a hearer) and carried them before Sir Edward B—, (? *Bagot of Blithfield*) who told them they must either be bound to their good behaviour or go to prison. Mr. Bakewell desired to know whether preaching in his own house would be deemed a breach of good behaviour. The justice answered that it would; upon which Mr. Bakewell replied, He would give no bond to tie himself from preaching; and Mr. Ford concurring with him, they were both sent to jail, where they were detained ten weeks, before the Act against conventicles was passed. They were then released without having anything imposed upon them."

Calamy seems to be slightly inaccurate as to his dates. The entries relating to the case in the Lichfield Consistory Court records are these :—

"6 Oct. 1663. Thomas Bakewell of Burton-upon-Trent for Keeping Conventicles.
Also that he preacheth but to improve his guifts in his family, and setts open the door, & if people do come in he forbids them nott, nor calleth conventicles."

"22 Oct. 1663. In the name of God, Amen. We, John, Bishop of Lichfield and Coventry, in the business of the correction and reformation of Thomas Bakewell, clerk, &

Thomas Ford of Burton-upon-Trent,—by reason of his holding private conventicles & preaching in his private house within the Parish of Burton-on-Trent, against the tenor of the Act of Parliament, as well as against the tenor of Ecclesiastical law—

Suspend Thomas Bakewell from exercising his ministry & the celebration of divine things (service), whether in the parish of Burton upon Trent or elsewhere in this diocese.

And excommunicate the aforesaid *Thomas Ford* on account of his contempt of this episcopal command & for not obeying our monition."

Calamy continues:—" Mr. Bakewell, on returning home, was not discouraged, but held on preaching. When the Oxford Act came out he was forced to leave his wife and children, and to go into a desert place twenty-five miles from his habitation; where he continued several months with a poor people who were glad to have the gospel preached to them; though he was forced to live at his own expense, and at the same time maintain his family out of the little he had of his own. At length he returned home, and continued preaching at Burton till the Indulgence in 1672. He was then earnestly invited to Longdon,* and he went to preach to a people who had been great sufferers, leaving Mr. Ford to preach at Burton. There he continued as long as the Indulgence lasted; but afterward warrants were sent to the constables to search the houses where the people used to meet; upon which they assembled in the fields and woods, that they might worship God without molestation. But the informers followed them thither, and executed upon them the Act against Conventicles; so that he and his people suffered greatly. Among other instances of cruelty, the huntsmen set their dogs upon them. (Conform. 4th Plea, p. 56). He published *A Justification of Infant Baptism*." [And several other treatises, chiefly against Antinomianism, which are in the Congregational Library.]

In connection with the Indulgence we notice a fact of some importance. In May, 1672, Mr. Bakewell applied for his licence as a " Presbyterian," and the houses in which preaching is permitted are called Presbyterian. But within three months fresh applications are made and granted under the title " Congregational." This is the first time in our local history that the word is used. The applications, now, are for himself and the houses of Messrs. Broughton and Browne, that of Christian Hood not being mentioned. They are contained in a long list of over 20 names from various parts of the country, which is headed " Congregationall." This is the form of them :—

---

* Calamy says London; but this, as the licence clearly shews, is a mistake.

Longdon and Lichfield 39

Cong. Mr Thomas Bakwell. The house of Michal Mere in Magdalen Parish in Oxford. The houses of Mr Broughton, and Richard Browne, in Longdon. Staff :"

Only the applications for Mr. Bakewell and the house of Richard Browne were granted. The entry reads :—

"The house of — Brown in Longdon. Staff. Congr. 25 July."
"Licence to Tho : Backwell to be a Congr. Teacher in the house of — Brown in Longdon, Staff. 25 July."

It would seem, therefore, that the church at Longdon first became distinctly and avowedly Congregational in 1672. In many cases, about this time, the distinction between Congregational and Presbyterian is confused, and the terms are used almost interchangeably; but that our people preferred their true title is very evident from their making a new application.

The Indulgence afforded but a transient relief; it was revoked in the following year, persecution was renewed, and went on with varying degrees of rigour for nearly sixteen years longer. Magistrates, constables and informers conspired together to hunt down the hated Dissenters; fines were exacted and multiplied, prisons were crowded : yet the result was not to destroy Nonconformity, but to promote its increase both in numbers and strength of character; and at length, in 1688, the Revolution put an end to an intolerable tyranny, and was quickly followed by the substantial and permanent, though incomplete, relief of the Toleration Act.

We now lose sight of Bakewell; it may be that, after enduring so many years of hardship, he sought a well-earned retirement, preferring to leave the new and springing activities to a younger man. Or it may be that he had entered the eternal rest, whither, in all probability, Miles had preceded him. We have no knowledge of the date when his successor was called; but there is extant an old church book which contains entries of baptisms in 1695; signed by Robert Travers as minister. Several of these entries are of baptisms of infants in private houses in Longdon, Lichfield, and other places in the neighbourhood, shewing that Travers's ministrations, like those of his predecessors, were not confined to Longdon, but covered a district extending over several miles, and including both the places mentioned, and the villages, hamlets and isolated farmhouses and residences round about.

Longdon Green, being about the centre of this sphere of ministration, and accessible by roads from every quarter, was chosen as the site of a permanent house of worship—the building described at the outset of our narrative. It was the first Nonconformist church building erected within a circuit of many miles, and is still in a good state of preservation. It was built and furnished by subscriptions and free-will offerings ; and towards its erection, and the subsequent building of the house adjoining as a residence for the minister, sums up to £40 were individually given. When we consider the much greater purchasing power of money in those days than in our own, we shall better appreciate the liberality and spirit of sacrifice displayed. The records in the old church book above referred to shew that among the adherents were some who might be regarded as well-to-do, a few even who ranked as county families; but the majority were in moderate or poor circumstances.

The exact date of the erection cannot be determined ; tradition places it in 1692, and strong presumption in favour of this generally accepted date is furnished by the old church book. The entries therein, above the signature of Robert Travers, extending from 1695 to well into the next century, make frequent allusion to matters taking place within the building, but never mention its erection. The obvious conclusion is that it was already occupied when Travers settled, not later than 1695. It was not, however, till 1722, when the generation which had built it was passing away, that the property was transferred to a body of trustees.

One notes here with satisfaction how impotent had been all the efforts of the Stuarts to destroy Nonconformity. In the Evans Manuscript, [preserved in Williams's Library,] which gives statistics compiled between 1717 and 1729, the congregations of Lichfield and Longdon are coupled together as one, and called by the old title of Presbyterian. They are returned as having 280 hearers, 60 of them being county voters, under Robert Travers as their minister. So flourishing was their condition that the church was able not only to maintain itself, but to lend substantial help to others. This was the period when "Briefs" were in vogue, *i.e.*, letters setting forth the hard circumstances of various communities, with appeals for relief, which were read in various places of worship. For what remarkable purposes collections were made may be gathered from a few examples :—

"To help pay for losses at a disastrous fire at Bruges."
"To assist the sufferers by inundations in the Low Countries."
"To ameliorate the condition of the Huguenot refugees."
"To relieve the distressed silk-weavers in Brabant."

These and the like, with many nearer home, were not disregarded, but met with a response proportionate to the pressure of the case and the means at disposal. That their own poor were not neglected appears from entries such as these, of which there are many :—

"Item. To Sarah Jones, 6^d."
"Item. To Goody Smith, 9^d."
"Item. To Widow Brown, 6^d."
"Item. To Goody Hughes, a shilling."

These sums were, of course, worth more then than now. The use of "Goody" in place of the prefix "Mrs." is very quaint and genial, and quite in the spirit of the evidently affectionate relationship between pastor and flock.

Other entries shew that Travers was able to keep a man-servant, who possibly served also as clerk, seeing that in the old furniture of the church was a clerk's seat situated in front of and beneath the pulpit. The wages of this worthy were, according to an entry of his engagement in the minister's handwriting, "forty shillings a year, and an old coat of mine for to make him a new one." The minister not only kept a horse for riding, but also kept cattle, as we gather from reading in the book—which seems occasionally to have been used for private accounts as well as church affairs: "Item. To vetches for Two Stirks 1^s· 8^d." Quite the "country parson!"

The whole time of this long pastorate appears to have been one of peace and prosperity, of close unbroken Christian fellowship and love, of hearty and sustained interest and generosity in the church, and of quiet but sincere and earnest piety. Mr. Travers was assiduous in his labours, not only in his church but in surrounding homes, and frequently—it would seem regularly—in houses at Lichfield. Previous to 1747 the worshippers resident in this latter place must have detached themselves, and formed a separate community—probably because of the inconvenience of travelling 3½ miles, at all seasons, to worship—though they still retained Mr. Travers as their pastor, so cannot have been entirely disunited. This is shewn by a deed executed in 1747, by which "Robert Travers, Teacher," left forty pounds to be applied to the churches of Longdon and Lichfield, and providing that if either cause should lapse the money should be devoted to the other which survived. This constitutes the first intimation of a distinct Nonconformist "church" at Lichfield.

Again, as with his predecessors, we have no record of the death of Travers, or the place of his burial. Nor, unfortunately, have we any knowledge of his immediate successor. Indeed, we enter now on a period of obscurity, unrelieved by either record or tradition, except a glimpse which is afforded by two deeds. One, executed in 1757, is the settlement of freehold property upon the church at Longdon. The other, executed a year later, is the settlement of a copyhold, including the church building, in like trust, and its enrolment in Chancery. But these, if they tell us no more, speak clearly of interest maintained, of jealous and watchful care over their little sanctuary and its belongings on the part of those who loved it, and a determination to make its legal foundations secure.

We come now to a stage in our history for which we must depend on what is told by word of mouth by those still living, though in the evening of their days, who had it at first hand from the persons concerned. It is said that, toward the end of the eighteenth century, the church at Longdon—like many others—fell under the control of Unitarians. How it came about is not stated, but it was presumably rather through the perversion of the existing body of worshippers than through the intrusion of others.—change of belief, not of persons. So complete was the change that the property was at one time in imminent danger of being entirely diverted to the support of Unitarianism. Happily a Mr. George Birch, of Armitage, interested himself in the matter, and succeeded in getting an altogether new body of trustees appointed.

Scarcely had the church passed through this experience, with the dissension which would almost inevitably attend it, when about 1794 Congregational worship began to be held at Rugeley. These services would attract many who had formerly worshipped at Longdon, but to whom Rugeley was within a more convenient distance.

A few years later, and what may be called the Nonconformist centre of gravity in the district was changed. Hitherto it was at Longdon, which must still be accounted the mother church; but now it was transferred to Lichfield, with which, henceforth, the fortunes of Longdon were inseparably bound up. How this came about must be told, quoting from the earliest pages of the *Lichfield Church Book* :—

"The city of Lichfield has been proverbial for ages past in the opposition of its inhabitants to the introduction of the Gospel; so that while the light of Divine Truth was spreading in most other towns in the neighbourhood, the ministers and friends of Religion were discouraged in their wishes to come to this place by the cloud of thick darkness which appeared to envelope and surround the city.......But God, who had mercy in store, was pleased to hear the prayers of His people on the behalf of this place; several persons previous to 1790 were brought to a knowledge of the truth, and soon became earnestly desirous to promote the spiritual welfare of their friends and neighbours."

We have already seen that a separate " Dissenting interest " existed in Lichfield in 1747 or later, the members of which presumably met for worship in each other's houses. Whether they were affected by the Unitarian flood which almost overwhelmed Longdon we do not know; but we can well understand that a small community, seated in the very stronghold of Episcopacy, would find the maintenance of their worship and discipline no easy matter. There are persons still living who remember the obloquy and contempt which were cast on Nonconformists in Lichfield in their youth; and places are still pointed to, outside the city, where they were compelled to worship in the open air. In 1790 these good people, " with the advice and encouragement of ministers and Christian friends, engaged a building in Tunstall's Yard, Sandford Street, which was repaired and fitted up for public worship." In July of that year the place was opened by Rev. G. Burder, of Coventry, and Rev. J. Moody, of Warwick; and continued to be supplied by neighbouring ministers, or by a preacher stationary for a time in Lichfield, till 1796. After six years, however, the little company was reduced by force of circumstances to so small a number that "it was determined to desist from regular preaching; and soon after, the attempt was given up, and the place shut up for several years....... Now the enemy triumphed, and those few who had favoured the meeting were at times shamefully treated on that account." The spirit of persecution was still abroad; but it was, as ever, powerless to destroy the work of God. Reading on, we find that "About the year 1802 several persons were, by the providence of God, brought to reside in the town and neighbourhood, who were much concerned to have the preaching of the Gospel resumed; and, though not without considerable opposition, they had the above mentioned place re-opened, and occasional service again established."

In spite of contrary influences the congregation began to increase; and in 1805 it was thought warrantable to obtain a settled minister. The choice fell upon a Mr. Guard, of whose antecedents it is known only that he had intended to become a missionary, but had been prevented. He remained at Lichfield two years, and then left for Cornwall. After an interval of six months Mr. William Salt, of Hoxton Academy, accepted an invitation to take up the work. Up to this time no regular church had been organized; for we read in the minute book that "on the 13th of June, 1808, after much serious prayer for the Divine blessing, a meeting was held in an upper room in Dam Street, [why not in the regular place of meeting is not explained,] when six persons afterwards named formed the Christian Society or Church which, by the blessing of God on the ministry of the Word, has continued to this day." The names are Henry Fairbrother, William Daniel, Mary Austin, Mary While, Alice Daniel, and Elizabeth Siddons. At the same meeting Articles of Faith were drawn up, and rules for personal conduct and church order and discipline. The newly formed church at once entered on a course of activity and expansion; and on 24th November, 1808, they "opened a house for preaching at Burnt-wood Green, where the people are as ignorant as heathens, but many disposed to hear the Gospel."

The church at Longdon was still maintained, though with diminished numbers and without a minister. The want was supplied by a bequest, somewhere about this time, of two closes of arable land, the rent of which was to go to the Independent ministers of Lichfield in succession, so long as services, or in default a Sunday school, were maintained by them at Longdon. This endowment, with others formerly made at different times, and including the rent of what was originally the minister's house, produce a present income of about £20 a year, which is still forthcoming, and the conditions enjoined are fulfilled.

Some events of a painful character seem to have transpired about this time, whether persecution or dissension is not known; several leaves having been cut out of the church book, with the evident purpose of suppressing the record. The first words on the next remaining page are suggestive: "..... can truly say with the Apostle, The things which have happened to us have turned out to the furtherance of the Gospel. A spirit of enquiry was excited, and God blessed His word to many." The result was the adding of new names to the church roll in quick succession, and the building of a new chapel in Wade Street. The certificate of its entry in the diocesan register, as then required by the Toleration Act, is dated 26th September, 1811, and the opening services were held on the 18th March, 1812. Mr. Salt's ordination took place at the same time, the attendance being—as might be expected—"very numerous." A crowning day for Nonconformity in Lichfield, indeed!

As an indication of the strength and whole-heartedness of the church it is recorded that, on 18th September of the same year, 1812, after a sermon by Rev. Rowland Hill on behalf of the Missionary Society, the collection amounted to £15. Twelve months later, on 17th September, 1813, the foundation of the chapel-house, attached to the rear of the chapel, was laid. The expense was chiefly defrayed by the bounty of Miss Newnham, of Birmingham, who was to receive a small rent during her life, after which the house was to belong "to the Meeting and cause of Christ for ever." By 1815 the evening congregations were so increased that a front gallery was erected, which was opened on Christmas Day by Rev. J. A. James, of Birmingham. About this time the church was much exercised by the fact that two members —notwithstanding serious admonition—had married ungodly partners, and suffered severely in consequence. Thereupon a resolution was unanimously passed "That this church, deeply deploring the evil consequences that arise from members of churches intermarrying with the ungodly, concerned for the credit of religion and the comfort and peace of the society, do resolve as a matter of church discipline to interfere in every case where a connection is likely to be formed so contrary to the Word of God and so injurious to the peace of the soul."

During the continuance of Mr. Salt's pastorate several cases of discipline are noted, mostly for various forms of immorality. In 1823 "Robert Bayley addressed the church on his dismission to the Academy to study for the work of the ministry." Meanwhile

Longdon and Lichfield

other Congregational churches were formed in the neighbourhood: Brownhills in 1816, Cannock in 1817, Armitage in 1820, and—a little later—Gentleshaw in 1835. All these would afford convenience to some who formerly worshipped at Longdon, and as a result that ancient congregation was still further depleted. There are indications that about 1830, and for some time after, affairs there were managed by the church at Rugeley.

In the autumn of 1831 Mr. Salt removed to Erdington. During his pastorate 109 names had been enrolled in the church book. He was succeeded by Rev. John Parry, from Rotherham College, who after five uneventful years resigned, owing to a change in his doctrinal opinions. He preached an admirable and touching farewell sermon from Acts xx. 32.

The next minister was Rev. Edward Gatley, from Malton, Yorks., who took charge on 21st October, 1837. He attracted large congregations, so that side galleries were added to the chapel for their accommodation. Disaffection on the part of certain members led to the matters in question being referred to Revs. J. A. James of Birmingham and J. Hammond of Handsworth, who signed the following note:—" We see no cause to lessen our confidence in Mr. Gatley, nor that we should in any degree withdraw our sincere and cordial affection from him; but would confirm our love towards him, while we express our sympathy for him under these painful trials." The church accepted this verdict, requested Mr. Gatley to reconsider his proffered resignation, and excluded the disturbers from fellowship. In 1844 Mr. Gatley removed to Thirsk, Yorks., preaching farewell sermons at Longdon as well as Lichfield.

Rev. J. Gossley became pastor in 1846, but remained only a few months. He was followed, in May, 1847, by Rev. David Griffiths, from Tean, who for about sixteen months laboured with commendable zeal and hopeful success, gaining general esteem and affection. In September, 1848, he visited his kinsfolk in South Wales; and exposure to wet and cold on his return journey brought about an illness which in a short time proved fatal. He was buried in Green Hill graveyard, and a tablet to his memory was placed in the chapel by subscription. His funeral sermon was preached by Rev. Wm. Salt, then of Hinckley; who in April, 1849, accepted a call to resume the pastorate which he had vacated more than 17 years before. He continued to preside over the church, and to fulfil the duties of his ministry, till within a few days of his death, which took place after a short but painful illness on 1st June, 1857, in the 74th year of his age and the 50th of his ministry. A few months later the esteem and affection in which he was held were testified by a beautiful marble tablet to his memory which was placed over the pulpit.

The interest at Longdon meantime declined, perhaps in part

owing to Mr. Salt's growing age and infirmity. Whatever the cause, it reached low water mark, and services were discontinued except on infrequent occasions. This lasted only till the coming of Mr. Salt's successor, when the old meeting-house was re-opened and services resumed, which, with the aid of an efficient staff of lay preachers, are still continued. It was about this time that the meeting-house was renovated and modernized; the old-fashioned pews with high backs and doors, and the singers' pew in the corner, were removed, to be replaced with unsightly and less comfortable benches. This was done by a Mr. Chetwynd, resident in the neighbourhood; and why such vandalism should have been permitted is a marvel, unless the old fittings were found to be hopelessly decayed. This was certainly the case with the pulpit last year. It was a somewhat ponderous and ornate structure, but was found to be unsafe and crumbling with dry rot.

The successor of Mr. Salt was Rev. G. B. Scott, from Brotherton in Yorkshire; who remained till June, 1862, and then removed to Whitchurch, Salop. At that time the number of church members was 68. During his pastorate Henry Fairbrother, the first member on the church roll, died on 29th April, 1859, in the 88th year of his age. He had honourably fulfilled the office of deacon for nearly 30 years, and was the father of Rev. William Fairbrother, the well known missionary to China.

An illustration of the healthy condition and sympathetic spirit of the church in those days is found in a collection of £7 4s. 9d. which was taken up on Sunday, 16th October, 1862, on behalf of the distressed cotton operatives in Lancashire.

Later events must be very briefly narrated. Rev. William Bealby, from London, entered on the pastorate in March, 1863, and left, owing to ill-health, in 1868. Rev. R. F. Brown followed in November, 1869; his ministry was not highly successful, and he left in December, 1871. During a vacancy of a year and a half the affairs of the church were managed by a committee, and the pulpit supplied by neighbouring ministers and students from Spring Hill College. In 1873 Rev. E. H. Reynolds, from Armagh, was invited to the pastorate, and remained till near the end of 1876, when he removed to Great Ayton, in Yorkshire. During his time the communicants worshipping at Longdon were received into membership at Lichfield—an arrangement which lasted until recently.

About nine months after Mr. Reynolds' removal Rev. G. Hobbs, from Nottingham Institute, was installed as pastor. The church members now numbered 54. In 1878 the chapel was renovated and re-seated; and on 4th May, 1884, a new organ was inaugurated, the preacher being Rev. Dr. Paton, of Nottingham, and the collections amounting to £30. The 19 years of Mr. Hobbs' ministry were marked by quiet usefulness, without any very striking incident. He retired in 1895, engaging in secular business, but preaching occasionally. After a few months' interval Rev. W. F. Dawson from Madeley, Salop, undertook the pastorate in July, 1896. Three years later painful disaffection was manifested, and the congregation dwindled almost to nothing. The affairs of the church were then submitted to the direction of the Trustees and the Executive of the Staffordshire Congregational Union; and on their advice the building was temporarily closed, Mr. Dawson's association with the church being brought to an end. This was in March, 1902. After repairs and improvements the doors were again opened in June, 1903, with the co-operation of the aforesaid Union, the present writer being called to the pastorate. The actual number of church members is 47, with a Sunday school of about 90 children.

In 1903 the ancient church at Longdon was reconstituted, and a separate church book commenced. Last year the old meeting-house was put in thorough repair. The pulpit was found to be so decayed that it was impossible either to repair it or to remove it entire; a small but fitting rostrum was therefore erected in its place, as much of the old woodwork as was sound and suitable being used for the purpose; and the effect is said to be not entirely disappointing. At the same time a Sunday school was commenced, which progresses hopefully. And week by week there gathers within the ancient walls a handful of faithful and devoted worshippers, not unworthy successors of the men who reared it in old time, when the worship of Almighty God was commonly a more serious business, and when all the ease and comfort men sought or desired was of the heart and soul.

A. J. STEVENS.

The Apostolic Labours of Captain Jonathan Scott

IN Staffordshire, Cheshire, Shropshire, and Lancashire there are 22 Congregational churches which trace their origin wholly or in part to the work of Captain Jonathan Scott. A man who left so rich a legacy of living influences deserves to be well known and affectionately commemorated in the counties and among the churches which he served so well.

I picture to myself a stalwart, soldierly man, with broad shoulders, high forehead, compressed determined lips, and, in later life, long curling hair falling down over his broad shoulders. As a rule dressed as a clergyman, on occasions Captain Scott could ride into a town in the full regimentals of a captain-lieutenant of his Majesty's Dragoons, and going into the pulpit in that garb he would preach to a full chapel; or he might suddenly throw off an overcoat, display his uniform, and command the disturbers of an open-air meeting to hear his message in the name of King George III. His style of eloquence was, we are told, "fearless and forcible, somewhat rugged, altogether unadorned," and if not a style fitted for building up a reputation for oratory, it was mighty to the pulling down of the strongholds of Satan. Whitefield playfully described it to his congregation as Captain Scott's "artillery," with which he had invited him to occupy the Tabernacle "rampart" where he was sure to do much "execution."

Apostolic Labours of Captain Jonathan Scott 49

Whether preaching in a building, or on a horse-block in the open air, as in Hanley, Captain Scott was a man who could hardly fail to command the attention of his hearers—mighty in the Scriptures, stern in rebuke, feeling the truth he proclaimed, gracious in urging the offers of the Gospel. To his hearers his voice had something of the final trump in it, well suited to rouse sleepers from the death of sin that Christ might shine upon them.

Such I suppose was Captain Jonathan Scott at the time of his apostolic labours. His history, like his presence, was a challenge to the attention of men. By birth he might claim as good blood as any in the land. His father was Captain Richard Scott, of Scott's Hall, Kent, and his mother the daughter and heiress of Jonathan Scott, of Belton Grange, near Shrewsbury. Both on his father's and his mother's side he was descended from the Scotts of Kent, who were of the line of John Baliol, the Scottish king, who had the ill-luck to have for his rival Robert the Bruce. The family was known as Baliol le Scott, till for brevity and convenience they dropped the Baliol and became simply Scotts. A genealogy of this kind is not an irrelevance, for in religion as in everything else blood tells, though Jonathan Scott took his stand on grace and not on heredity. He probably owed some of the commanding qualities which made him a leader of men to heredity, though it was grace which accounted for the use he made of them.

Jonathan Scott was born at Shrewsbury, on November 15th, 1735. At the age of 17 he became a cornet in his Majesty's 7th Regiment of dragoons, following the profession of his father. He rose to be a captain-lieutenant, and in this capacity saw service in three campaigns. He was present at the battle of Minden, August 4th, 1759;

but being posted on the right wing of the allied army in a detachment under Lord George Sackville, he was prevented from taking part in the engagement.

The great change in his life must have come shortly after this. His tone and temper had been much like that of other army officers of the time; if anything he was more seriously minded than most, for he tells us that he was occasionally chaffed by his brother officers for his habit of serious reading. "Well, Scott," they would say, " have you read your psalms and lessons to-day ?" From the Pisgah height of his conversion he looks back on these days of his "religious fits" as days spent in the cities of the plain, and can say nothing too bad of them. But he tells enough of his own history to make it plain that there had been a preparation for the breaking of the light which seemed to himself so sudden. In one town through which the regiment passed books were distributed to the soldiers by the bequest of a pious benefactor. Scott received a book containing a prayer which ended with the words "for Jesus' sake." He describes the extraordinary emotion which shook his frame when he first came to use these words in prayer. A riding accident which all but dislocated his neck, and which might have been fatal but for prompt medical aid, contributed to bring him into a serious frame of mind. His conversion took place while his regiment was stationed at Brighthelmstone in Sussex. He had been out shooting and was caught in a storm. He found himself near a farm where some of the regimental horses had been at grass, and sought shelter with the farmer. His host urged him to hear the Rev. William Romaine, representing him, Scott says, as "a very remarkable person." The end of it was—also a great beginning—that Scott

Rev.d Jonathan Scott,
late of Matlock.

Pub by Williams & Smith, Stationers Court 1 Oct.r 1807

went to hear Romaine preach at Oat Hall, a house fitted up by the Countess of Huntingdon. The sermon on "I am the way," gave Scott exactly what he wanted. "This," he said, "is the thing, the very thing I want, and have wanted so long, and knew not what it was nor how to obtain it." He dated his conversion from that day.

For about four years Scott faithfully bore witness to his new allegiance in the army. Wherever his regiment went he found an opportunity of declaring the good news which had meant so much to him. In this way he first preached at Berwick, York, Leeds and Manchester. It is clear from his letters that these were years of considerable trial to him. There is no more thorough convert than a converted soldier ; for a soldier understands from the beginning the meaning of obedience as few men ever learn to do ; indeed, the military type of Christian represented by such men as General Charles Gordon, General Havelock, Captain Vicars, Sir Henry Lawrence, Colonel Gardiner, and Captain Scott, compares favourably with any other type. We can read between the lines of Scott's letters to Richard Hill, afterwards Sir Richard, the brother of Rowland Hill, that it was at no small cost that he maintained a consistent Christian profession. He writes in 1766 in a careful hand :*—

> "I have not yet been attacked by any of the officers in the Regiment, nor had one single word said to me, but have been suffered to do what I please ; but I do not expect that Satan will let them be long silent, but will stir his people up against me ; indeed, if he does not I shall begin to be alarmed and suspect that he does not hate me so much as I hope he ever will have cause to do, and undoubtedly will if I hate myself and love my adorable Jesus as much as I ought to do. God grant therefore that soon open hostilities may commence betwixt us and last as long as I remain on earth. And here let me entreat, my

---

*MS. letters in Memorial Hall Library.

dear Friend, pray to God for me that I may be enabled to go forth in the strength of the Lord and to fight the good fight of faith manfully under Christ's banner, Who is the glorious Captain of my Salvation, my Almighty Chief and Leader, that I may be His faithful soldier and follower, then I am sure to come off more than conqueror." . . . .

"I find that before I left the Regiment in order to go to Shrewsbury I began to be a suspected person. Attending such a notorious person as Dear Romaine's ministry, and associating with some Christian people was sufficient to cause such suspicions as that I was turned this and turned that, &c., as our dear friend Mr. Fletcher (of Madeley) justly observes, the people always say when anyone lays the eternal interest of his soul to heart. Upon my rejoining the Regiment now I found that it was no longer bare suspicion, for now they are convinced I am turned an arrant methodist. And this their persuasion is a very lucky one for me, for now they begin to think my company not worth being over solicitous about : and I am sure you will readily believe that a very little of theirs is enough to satisfy me, or more properly speaking to dissatisfy me, since their whole conversation consists only in idle vain nonsense larded with horrid oaths and filthy obscenity ; this is the more shocking to me as I must sometimes be present at it and have it not in my power to remedy it." . . .

"But I must not here omit to thank and praise God for His goodness in giving me one dear Christian friend, a faithful brother in Christ : the adjutant of the Regiment, Mr. Barrett ; he is a most gracious child of God indeed."

Captain Scott's military duties must have left him a good deal of leisure for correspondence, for these letters are lengthy and rambling. We get occasional glimpses in the letters of the little circle of evangelicals who kept one another's hearts warm by constant visits and correspondence; and it is equally clear that they had two soul sides, and turned a somewhat frigid aspect towards the outsider who belonged to " the world " and was not of the charmed circle. In August, 1766, he writes to Richard Hill :—

"Sunday last the Sacrament of the Lord's Supper

> having to be administered at Olney I went over there, and heard two very excellent discourses from Mr. Newton. What a monument of the mercy and free Grace of God is he, and still, my dear Friend, I think there is not so great a one on earth as myself. I never was so much charmed with the lot of God's children as I was with those at Olney. They seem all love and gratitude. They are mostly poor people, and the grace of God is seen in all its native richness and beauty."

Then Richard Hill is going to visit Mr. Venn, and wants Scott to go with him. Scott replies that he will gladly go if he can get leave. "I hope and trust the Lord is extending his mercy and grace still further in our Regiment, as there seems to be a desire amongst some of our men to wait upon the Lord, and to seek after Him. We have a meeting at my lodgings twice a day, to which all come that will. To attend to this as long as such a poor creature as I am is in the least made serviceable, is undoubtedly my first duty."

In December he writes to Hill again :—

> "I saw and spent a few hours with great delight and I trust much profit with dear Mr. Fletcher, who I think grows in grace—like a Cedar in Lebanon."

On the other hand it was with the greatest difficulty that Scott, before his conversion was known, could persuade Romaine to speak to him except on most distant terms, and he had to follow him to London "to see if there was any difference between the air of London and the air of Brighthelmstone." Eventually he went with an introduction from Romaine to call on a Mr. Powis, who was one of the children of light. Mr. Powis was entertaining Mr. Venn, and was in no mind to have his spiritual converse disturbed. When he saw Scott across the lawn he broke out, "There is Captain Scott; what can he want here? I am determined not to see him if I can avoid it." However, the man-servant had not been taught to dissemble; Captain Scott was shewn in, explanations ended in embraces, and he entered the circle as the "dear captain."

Although Captain Scott was willing enough to combine the service of King George and the service of the Captain of his salvation, we cannot wonder that his official superiors looked with some suspicion on what must have seemed to them a divided allegiance. They gave him a hint, or a series of hints, which led to his selling out of his regiment in March, 1769. He was probably the less unwilling to do this that in June of the previous year, 1768, he had married Miss Elizabeth Cley, of Wollerton, in Shropshire, a lady who had all the virtues and other assets with which eminent ladies in the eighteenth century were so singularly endowed—eminent piety, remarkable prudence, a handsome estate, economical habits and an affectionate disposition.

On his marriage Captain Scott removed to Wollerton, in Shropshire, but though married he did not "settle down." He at once began preaching at Wollerton, and soon gathered a congregation which became an Independent church. Wollerton gradually became a centre from which radiated an evangelising force over a steadily increasing area.

It is convenient to classify Scott's work according to the counties in which the churches he founded are situated; but it is obvious that such a classification supplies no chronological guidance to the order of his labours. Captain Scott was not concerned with county boundaries. He was ready to go wherever he found an opening for preaching the Gospel. Indeed, the evidence seems to shew that a door emphatically closed was more attractive to him than an open door. So, for example, it was at Market Drayton. There services in the open air had been repeatedly interrupted and broken up by those strenuous upholders of all established customs in Church and State whom we should now call hooligans. The worshippers had been offered shelter by a brave Welsh woman, a Miss Elizabeth Vernon. When they met on her premises the pious inhabitants broke all her windows. This was Captain Scott's opportunity. He came over from Wollerton and conducted the meetings for some time in person, secured a site, erected a building and organised the people into an Independent church. The church was formed in 1776, and the indenture of the deed which transferred the ground for the chapel to Scott describes it as for a meeting-house of Protestant Christians of the Independent persuasion.

Captain Scott's connection with Newport (Salop) was more chequered. In 1765, before Scott had left the army, he had received a gift of a plot of land for a chapel in Newport from Mr. Jones, one of the six students who were expelled from Oxford for holding meetings for prayer, reading of the Scriptures, and spiritual conversation. *O si sic omnes!* A chapel was erected and the work begun, but Scott was only able at times to give it intermittent attention, and it soon had to be closed. In 1792 Mr. Moses Silvester, an earnest and resolute adherent of the Gospel, settled in business in Newport. He revived the local interest in the chapel, and on his undertaking to keep the pulpit well supplied with suitable preachers Captain Scott transferred the chapel to him. It became the home of a church which still flourishes in Newport. Mr. Silvester bequeathed to the church at Newport a fragrant name, which descended to a Newport lad, and in the person of Mr. Silvester Horne seems likely to be long associated with the newest developments in Congregational history.

Besides Wollerton, Drayton and Newport, Scott's name is associated with the founding of the churches at Wistanswick and Ollerton, in Shropshire. For the benefit of the latter Mrs. Scott left an endowment of £300, which was lost through the negligence of the trustees.

In Cheshire Captain Scott is connected with the foundation of six churches — Nantwich, Congleton, Middlewich, Macclesfield, Northwich, and Chester; Urwick calls him the Cheshire Whitefield.

At Nantwich a beginning had been made by a visit from George Whitefield in 1753. He was attacked by a mob, taken out of the town over the Flood Gates to a place called Marsh Lane, where an attempt was made to drive an infuriated bull among the congregation. The bull, however, fell into a pit, and the hooligans, lacking either the courage or the kindness to extract him, left him there. The little company left by Whitefield's visit had various fortunes, but kept together till 1778, when they took a coachmaker's shop and fitted it up for worship at a cost of £40. This place was opened in 1780 by Captain Jonathan Scott and William Armitage of Chester. It was some time before the church was able to maintain a minister, but both before that time and after Captain Scott kept in close touch with the people and did much to sustain the church by his visits. The last public service in which he took part was at Nantwich. There he administered the sacrament on the 12th of April, 1807, a month before his death.

The incidents which led to the founding of the church at Congleton are an illustration of the Captain's methods. In 1780 he was preaching at Hanley in Staffordshire, about twelve miles from Congleton. Two or three persons from Congleton went over to hear him, and invited him to visit them as soon as possible in their own town. They had no room to offer him, and could not secure even a barn ; but difficulties of this kind only put the captain on his mettle. He went to Congleton and preached either in the street or in the yard of the inn where he had lodged. Rowland Hill happened to be in the neighbourhood, and followed up the beginning made by Scott in the following week. The reception given to him encouraged Scott to believe that there was work to be done in Congleton ; so he fitted up a room at his own expense, where he, or some supply obtained by him, preached every Sunday. Ten years later, in 1790, he erected a chapel in Mill Street, mainly at his own expense, which served the church until the present building was erected.

At Middlewich the Rev. William Maurice, of Stockport, afterwards of Fetter Lane, London, revived an old Independent cause which had been throttled by Socinianism and endowment. In 1792 a small chapel was fitted up and opened by the Rev. James Boden, of Hanley, and Captain Scott. The opening of the new place was made an occasion for hostilities which must have satisfied Captain Scott that he was still an object of dislike to the Enemy of religion. A mob assembled outside the chapel, and as soon as dusk hid the aggressors the worshippers were assailed with brickbats. In this case the instigator of the attack was a certain notorious Parson Adams.

Townley Street, Macclesfield, might almost be called a "forlorn hope" till Captain Scott generaled it and led it to victory. The little company of " them that feared the Lord and spake one with another" was driven from house to house. They rented and furnished a barn, but three weeks afterwards were turned into the street by the owner, a clergyman. They got some help from the church at Mosley Street, Manchester, and they had various uneasy experiences with errant evangelists. It is with a sigh of relief that the minute books of the church record

> "We were afterwards supplied with ministers from different places till the Lord sent, to our great assistance, the Rev. Mr. Scott of Drayton in Shropshire (better known as Captain Scott). In May, the same year above mentioned, Mr. Scott ordered, at his own expense, the communion pew to be made, and twelve pews next to the same; the chapel being finished with forms or benches by the Manchester friends. The Lord's kindness in raising this congregation such a kind friend in the Rev. Mr. Scott, we hope will be gratefully remembered by us and by our posterity."

In 1788 a new chapel was built, and opened with a communion service at which Captain Scott presided. His interest in the church was unremitting as long as he lived. On the death of the first settled minister, Mr. Kingston, in January, 1789, Captain Scott preached his funeral sermon; and the second minister, Mr. Wildbore, was invited on his recommendation. It is recorded how when he rode into the town and preached in full regimentals half the town was there to hear. His function was that of a true overseer watching over the flock in its own interest. In financial matters he was its chief supporter, and he came to exercise an authority more than episcopal. His military training had left a certain severity in reproof which made him a terror to evil doers. It is recorded on one occasion that when he was expected to visit a church one of the brethren prayed that it might please God to bring this brother safely to them, but that he might *leave the rod behind him.* There is a characteristic mingling of kindly feeling, strategic caution, and sound judgement in the following letter to the Macclesfield church concerning the settlement of the Rev.

Daniel Dunkerley, who was ordained in August, 1798 :—

> "I am glad Mr. Dunkerley is so well liked. I have not the pleasure of knowing (him); having never, that I recollect, seen him. I hear nothing but good of him; therefore 'twill be well to engage him to supply you for some time. Perhaps it may be better for him to go and return as he does at present, than to quite leave his business. I think preachers should take such an important step deliberately; and a people not be hasty in persuading to such a measure; for if we draw anyone out of certain bread, we are bound to maintain those who leave it for our sakes—that is if they behave well. . . .
> In haste—much haste,
> Your servant in the Lord,
> JONATHAN SCOTT.
> Matlock : very late. Saturday night, 10th Dec., 1796."

In Chester itself Captain Scott had a share in establishing the Queen Street Independent chapel. When he first visited Chester there was already a considerable nucleus of Independents and Presbyterians who had seceded from the church where Mathew Henry had once been minister, on the ground that two successive ministers had fallen into Socinianism. They commenced their separate existence in a room adjoining the old common hall and part of St. Ursula's hospital, where they met for prayer and Christian fellowship, and to read the particular copy of Mathew Henry's *Commentary* which had been left for his people's use. After 1770 they met in a larger room, and there Captain Scott frequently visited them to their great profit. Two years later a church was formed, and in October, 1772, William Armitage became minister. He and Captain Scott remained lifelong friends and allies in the work of the Kingdom.

It is not possible with the material now available to collect all the traces of Captain Scott's influences in Cheshire. Here and there one comes across a footmark, and it is always the step of a

Hercules. At Marple Bridge we hear of him preaching in full regimentals in the open space near Mill Brow chapel. At Northwich he took up a decadent cause and made it the opportunity for securing an addition to the evangelizing forces of this county. In 1795 he introduced to Northwich the Rev. Job Wilson, a man of "primitive simplicity and apostolic zeal," who for forty-one years remained the minister of that church. He found it a small despised community, meeting in an upper room, with a dubious record in the town, and left it a prosperous church well housed and high in the esteem of the whole countryside.

This is the kind of work associated with Captain Scott's name in Cheshire. Where he could not go himself, from sheer inability to be in six places at once, he would find some one else to go; and he had a soldier's eye for a man. Perhaps the right men were drawn to him by some affinity of character; perhaps he was drawn to them. In the result the men of his choice justified their selection better than is usually the case where one minister has to nominate another.

In Lancashire there are several churches where there is some tradition of Captain Scott's influence, but only three where we have definite record of the work he did. At Elswick in 1774 his work began in considerable excitement, for the Independent minister refused to unlock the doors of the chapel to let in Captain Scott. He had no sympathy with either the views or the methods of the evangelical revival, and in those days they were not content with circumambulatory resolutions as a method of expressing opinion. The trustees forced the door, and Captain Scott preached to a large audience. This was the genesis of his influence at Elswick; and it led to the exodus of the unwilling minister, and presently to the introduction by Captain Scott of an evangelist who became minister of the church.

At Preston there was no church formed till 1828, but when the time came for its organisation the members who formed it recalled that the Gospel began first to be preached in connection with dissenters in Preston by Captain Scott, and some of them owed their first impressions to him.

It was with Lancaster that Scott's connection was closest. In December, 1773, he began to visit there, and his visits continued till about 1776. He found the people of Lancaster a "sincere, hearty, catholic people with good large hearts," and formed a strong attachment to them. He would stay two or three months at each visit; Lancaster would then be his headquarters while he made gospelling expeditions to Ulverstone, Garstang, Elswick, and other places. In February, 1774, in the midst of one of these visits, he writes to a friend: "I know you love Zion; and it will rejoice you to hear of her prosperity. I hope I may in truth tell you the good news that the Lord is abundantly blessing His word in and about this place. I have had several doors opened to preach; some in the File (Fylde) country (west of Preston), which is the barrenest part of Lancashire; where at present there is the most pleasing and promising prospect of much good, through the divine blessing, being done." In 1774 the church at Lancaster tried to draw closer the tie with Captain Scott. They pressed him affectionately to become pastor of the church. This invitation he did not see his way to accept, but he decided on another step which greatly pleased his friends. On September the 18th, 1776, he was ordained at Lancaster, not as pastor of the church, but as "presbyter at large." The fact is worth commemorating as an illustration of the freedom of the time from some of the stricter constructions of the doctrine of a "stated ministry"—a doctrine which sometimes claims exclusive rights in the independency of the past. Three pillars of northern Nonconformity took part in his ordination: Mr. Allat of Forton, Mr. Edwards of Leeds, and Mr. Timothy Priestly, then of Manchester. The ordination charge was given by Mr. Edwards from Acts xi. 15: "Go thy way; for he is a chosen vessel unto me"; and surely the familiar words, were never more fitly appropriated than to Captain Scott's apostolic zeal and consecration.

From Market Drayton it is some eight miles to Newcastle-under-Lyme. There Captain Scott succeeded in gathering converts and establishing a church. At Newcastle he was on the border of a district unlike any of those he had hitherto evangelised. In appearance the district is so bleak, barren, and murky, that someone in one of George Eliot's books (I think Mrs. Poyser) says of it that even the crows flying over it fly straight over and won't stop there. Even at that time it was relatively a busy centre of population, chiefly composed of potters. Thither about 1782 Captain Scott found his way. In Stoke-on-Trent more than a thousand hearers would collect to hear him when he appeared. In Hanley he began to preach from a horse block at the lower end of High Street, facing the market square, and there, in the language of the time, he introduced the Gospel to Hanley. His preaching had immediate and striking results. In 1783 there were enough converts to form a church, and in 1784 they built a chapel "13 yards square with galleries on three sides," we are told. The building was registered as a "place of public worship for Protestant Dissenters of the Independent persuasion," on January 15th, 1784. This was the beginning of the

Tabernacle Church, Hanley. After enlarging the building more than once, the community migrated across the road and erected a building which is recognised as the Congregational cathedral of North Staffordshire.

To Captain Scott the church also owed its first minister, the Rev. James Boden, whose apostolic vigour built up the Hanley church, so that during his ministry he admitted 135 persons to fellowship. He also began open air preaching in Stafford. This was a bold proceeding in a county town, and led to much opposition; but an excise officer named Davis invited Mr. Boden to preach at his house. There a congregation was gathered, and in 1788 a stable opposite the Vine inn, Fuller Street, became its regular place of meeting. Hearing of this little community Captain Scott came to the rescue, found a suitable minister, and maintained him in Stafford at his own expense.

The church at Stone owes its origin to one of Captain Scott's converts. It must have been when Captain Scott was with his regiment, and his regiment was stationed at Manchester, that he preached in that city. His preaching was blessed by the conversion of *two respectable persons*—so says the record, with a proper eye for those operations of the Spirit which are rightly described as "great marvels." One of these was a gentleman who heard him preach in a timber yard, and who afterwards removed to Stone and became the foundation of a "Gospel interest" in that place. No doubt Captain Scott visited his convert and encouraged him frequently in his good work.

The chapel at Newcastle was built in 1795, largely by the help and under the inspiration of Captain Scott; and it is said the chapel at Cheadle, founded in 1800, owes him a similar debt. So that Newcastle, Hanley, Stoke-on-Trent, Stone, Stafford and

Cheadle, six churches in all in Staffordshire, bear witness to Captain Scott's apostolic labours.

About the year 1779 Captain Scott formed a friendship which had the effect of greatly increasing his influence. He was introduced by a mutual friend to Lady Glenorchy, a lady who in the profusion and purpose of her gifts might be coupled with the Countess of Huntingdon. At the time of her introduction to Captain Scott she was on the lookout for someone to take the direction of her giving department, and she promptly offered the work to Captain Scott. He became her recognised counseller, advising when and where and how to give, and in many cases becoming himself the channel of her gifts. He was now able to get young men educated for the ministry at her ladyship's expense, and sent several to Dr. Williams' academy at Oswestry, and later to Newcastle-under-Lyme, whither the academy was moved under the care of Mr. Whitridge. Her ladyship took the place of a pastors' sustentation fund, and frequently augmented the salaries of underpaid ministers. She also acted as a chapel building fund, of which Captain Scott was secretary, treasurer, and committee.

In 1786 Lady Glenorchy died, and among other bequests left a chapel and dwelling-house at Matlock to Captain Scott. This led to his removal in 1794 from Wollerton to Matlock; and this was his home till his death.

In 1799 he had lost his wife, and three years later, in 1802, he married a widow, a Mrs. Barrow. The portraits of him in later years are very attractive and pleasing. The face is clean shaven, shewing firm lips set in a genial smile, high smooth forehead, double chin, alert kindly eyes, and over the whole countenance the look of serene kindliness which settles on the face of those who give

Apostolic Labours of Captain Jonathan Scott

themselves to ministries of love and faith. Although he was no longer able to preach six times a week, he contrived to travel and preach till within five weeks of his death. On the 12th of April, 1807, he administered the sacrament at Nantwich; and on 10th of May was present at public worship for the last time at Matlock. Then for several weeks he lay dying. It was the custom of the time to preserve with special affection the deathbed sayings of gracious souls, and Captain Scott's deathbed testimony was both doctrinal and eloquent. This ruling passion was strong in death, and was maintained to his last breath. In an experience like his, the witness to the sufficiency of Christ, and the sense of sinfulness swallowed up in the grace of the Redeemer, are the utterance of a mind which has lived in these great sufficient truths. He died on May 28th, 1807, and was buried at Queen Street chapel, Chester, where the remains of his first wife had also been laid.

He was a man of whom men loved to talk, and they had many stories to tell of him in the district where he had done his strenuous work; how, for instance, when he thought his horse was being neglected in a friend's house, he had gone to the stable, stripped, and thoroughly cleaned him down with his own hands, and fed him before he sat down to eat; or how, at an inn at Coventry, the captain heard an ostler swear, and seeing his horse turn his head he said to the man: "Do you see how my horse stares at you? He is not used to such words at home; he never hears an oath there, and doesn't know what to make of it"; or how a lady had tried to remind him of some youthful fun they had shared together: "Yes, madam," said the captain, "I remember it well; but you and I are many years older now and so much nearer death and eternity," and so plunged into the greater matters which were ever his chief concern.

They told of his liberality; how he took only personal necessaries out of his income and gave the rest away, and how the more he gave the more he was able to give. He scattered and increased. They told how old age robbed him of none of his zeal; but to the last he continued to plead and wrestle, exhort, reprove, command, entreat, in season and out of season, for the salvation of souls. And when men were tired of telling his several virtues, they said he was a Christian gentleman. I do not wonder that they loved him. I cannot even write of him now without feeling my heart warm towards him.

DUGALD MACFADYEN.

Academical Discipline in the 18th Century

THE following curious report has lately been found amongst a heap of MSS. in the library of New College. It relates to the academy of the Congregational Fund Board, which at the date mentioned was located in Tenter Alley, Moorfields; the students living with their kinsfolk, or boarding in private families. The academy existed from 1712 to 1744; the tutors during the last few years were John Eames, Esq., F.R.S., and the Rev. Jos. Densham. The students whose course was unfinished were then transferred to Dr. Jennings.

"Mr. Northcroft. Is sober & Regular in his Conduct where he lives, but they have little Religious Conversation with him & he very seldom prays with 'em lately. They say 'tis perhaps because their Hours & Method of Living are sometimes unsettled by their Business.

Mr. Madgwick & Mr. Grigson. The Gentlem^n they live with says they seem to improve in their Manners & Behav^r to one another & the Family, go to Prayer with him in Turns. & are very quiet & Regular, excepting that Grigson sometimes lies out at some Friends. he don't at all Suspect his going into bad Company. He is upon the whole more out with one or Another than Madg^k who scarce keeps any Company at all.

Mr. Jolly. 'Tis a Family of Gentlewomen he lives with, & they all speak very handsomly of him : he is very modest, sober, Regular &c. & goes to Pray^r with them.

Mr. Thomas. also has a good word from the Person he boards with ; he goes to Prayer with him in Turn.

Mr. Davies. The Gentleman he lives with says he is a good natur'd civil young man, & is very sober & goes to Prayer with 'em sometimes ; but he spoke as if he was not thorough diligent in his

Studies, but said moreover he talked of reforming & sitting closer to it this Winter.

These Six in their 4th year

Mr. Pearson. Mr. Rawlins at Ludg^t with whom he lives speaks well enough of him. he goes to Prayer, is sober &c.

Mr. Sheldon (*a*). His Brother in Law & Sisters give him a very good Word. he's much at home, sober, regular; & goes to Pray^{rs} with them.

Mr. Savage (*b*). his mother speaks very well of him, he's very sober & studious, she's affraid he hurts himself by studying too hard. He goes to Pray^r sometimes, but is very modest & Diffident wch hinders him a little.

Mr. Sheafe. his Father says he's always above by himself, & sure (says he) he must spend his time there in Study. he seems to speak as if he was not very tender and dutifull to his Parents. he goes to Pray^r sometimes.

These four in their 3^d Year

Mr. Thompson (*c*) has where he lives now as well as before a very good Character for a sober pious young man; seems to be, they say, an Experimental Xn. & goes to Pray^r much to their Edification.

Mr. Furnace (*d*), has also a very good Word from his Relations. is almost always in his Study, & sometimes goes to Prayer with them.

2^d Year

Mr. Hoyle behaves very well.

Mr. Smithson. his Unkle & he seem not thoroughly to agree, but I don't find the young man much to blame

I exhorted both these to perform Family Prayer. I think they ha'nt begun yet.

Mr. Brewer———

First Year

I have Lectur'd this Year to one Class or another on Logic, Geography, Geometry, Algebra, Trigonometry, Physics & Conic Sections.

Joseph Densham.

L^n. Feb: 3^d 1743/4

(*a*) Probably the Rev. John Sheldon of Canterbury.
(*b*) The Rev. S Morton Savage, D.D., successor of Dr Watts.
(*c*) Perhaps the Rev. Josiah Thompson, Baptist, who became Dr Savage's assistant.
(*d*) The Rev. Philip Furneaux, D.D.: author of *An Essay on Toleration*, &c.
(*e*) The Rev. S. Brewer, B.D., of Stepney.
The rest we have been unable to identify.

Chapel Building under the Stuarts

THE following builder's contract, dated 8th May, 1682, has lately been acquired by the Congregational Library :—

THIS WRITING of agreement indented made the Eighth day of May Anno Domini 1682 And in the thirty fowerth yeare of the raigne of our Soveraigne Lord King Charles the second of England &c. BETWEEN Henry Tabor of Nightingale Lane in the parish of St. Mary Matfellon als Whitechapple in the County of Midlsx Carpenter on the one part and Philip Narraway Cittyzen & Glazier of London and William Hodges Cittyzen and Merchant-taylor of London on the other pt WITNESSETH That aswell for and in consideracōn of the Summe of Seaventy poundes of lawfull money of England to the s^d Henry Tabor at and before then-sealeing and delivery hereof well and truly paid by the said Philip Narraway and William Hodges or one of them the receipt whereof the said Henry Tabor doth hereby acknowledge accordingly As also for the consideracōns hereafter mencōned. He the said Henry Tabor for himselfe his Executors Administrators & assignes Doth covenant grant and agree to & with the sd. Philip Narraway & William Hodges and either of them their Executors Admrators & assignes and every of them by these p̄sents in manner and forme following (that is to say) Inp̄ris that he the said Henry Tabor his Execut^{rs} Adm^{rs} servants workmen or Assignes or some of them shall and will at his and theire owne proper costs and charges by or before the twentyeth day of August now next ensueing the date hereof in good artificiall and substantiall manner with good sound timber Deales and other materialls hereafter mencōned erect and build or cause to be erected built and compleately finished for the sole use and benefitt of the said Philip Narraway and William Hodges their Executors and assignes in and upon a certaine peece or parcell of ground lyeing & being in Nightingale Lane aforesaid which doth abutt East on a garden now in the occupacōn of   North on a Warehouse in the occupacon of William Smith, West on the Dwelling house of the said Henry Tabor, and South on ground in the occupacon of John fforth. One new frame Edifice or building like unto the building knowne or called by the name of Mr Ryther's meetinghouse scituate at the Lower end of Meetinghouse ally neare Old-gravell Lane in the parish of Stepney in the said county of Midlsx according to the Dimensions and other Directions and in such forme and with such materialls as is hereafter perticularly mencōned (that is to say) Imprimis the said Edifice or building to containe in length from North to South fforty and six foot of assize little more or less and in breadth from East to West fforty foot of assize little more or less to be covered with plaine tiles; from the upperside of the Raizeing to the underside of the plate to be eighteene foot Item the Raizeings to be tenn and seaven inches, the Beames nine and eight inches, the King posts nine and seaven inches the Basis seaven and five inches. Item the principle rafters tenn and eight inches, the purlings nine and seaven inches, the smale rafters three and fower inches, the maine posts nine and seaven inches, the punchions six and five inches, the Quarters two and three inches, the outside to be weather boarded with good deales; and tarred, and to be lined round within from the raizeing to the plate with good two kirt slitt deales, the ground plate with good oake five and nine inches. Item the ground floor to be laid with good yellow deales and oaken Joyces with a good brick foundation and to goe upp one stepp into the building. the Beames to be kneed and dogged with Iron. Item the principle rafters to be banded to the Beames with Ironplate, the Kingposts to be likewise banded to the Beames with Iron, and with sufficient lights and Casements according to a draught to them the said Philip Narraway and William Hodges given [*something obliterated*]—and to make three Double Doores with Locks, Keys bolts, and hinges. Item to lay the windowes and doores twice in oyle colouring. The Edifice to be plaistered over head and in every particular thing suitable and answerable to Mr Ryther's Meeting house. And the same Edifice or building to be erected as aforesaid shall be as substantially effectuall and in as good workmanlike manner done performed and finished as the said building knowne by the name of Rythers Meetinghouse is. In CONSIDERACŌN whereof the said Philip Narraway and William Hodges for themselves and either of them, their and either of their Executors Administrators and assignes and for every of them Doe covenant grant and agree to and with the said Henry Tabor his Executors Administrators and assignes by these presents That they the said Philip Narraway and William Hodges or either of them, their or either of theire Executors Administrators or assignes or some or one of them, shall and will well and truely pay or cause to be paid unto the said Henry Tabor his Executors Administrators or assignes the full sume of One hundred poundes of lawfull money of England over and besides the sume of seaventy poundes above mencōned in manner following (that is to say) ffifty poundes part thereof when and as soone as the roofe of the said Building shall be laid on and [*paper torn*] ffifty poundes residue thereof when and as soon as all the said Building shall be compleately finished and done according to the true intent and meaning of these presents And to and for performance of all and every the covenants grants and agreements by the said Henry Tabor his Executors Administrators servants workmen and assignes to be performed in all things as above he bindeth himselfe his Executors and administrators unto the said Philip Narraway and William Hodges their Executors Administrators and assignes in the penall sume of three hundred and fforty poundes of lawfull money of England truely to be paid by these presents. And Likewise to and for performance of all and every the Covenants payments and agreements by the said Philip Narraway and William Hodges their Executors Admrators and assignes to be paid and performed in all things as above, They bind themselves their Executors and Administrators unto the said Henry Tabor his Executors Administrators and assignes in the like penall sume of three hundred and fforty poundes sterling truely to be be paid by these presents. IN WITNESS whereof the said parties to these presents interchangeably have put to theire hands and seales the day and yeare above first written.——

[*The signatures and seals have been torn off.*]

The following receipts are written on the back of the contract :—

(1) June ye 23^d 1682 Reseved the sum of fifty pound of William Hodges & phillip Naraway   *ll s d*   50 : 0 : 0

          y mee Henry Tabor

(2) August the 18th 1682 Reseved then of William Hodges and phillipe Narawaye the sum of fifty pound beinge in full payment of the within mentioned contract and all acounts I saye Resed y mee   *ll s d*   50 : 0 : 0

          Henry Tabor

(3) August the 18th 1682 Reseved of William Hodges & phillip naraway twenty & seaven shillings for 4 Casements and som other Iron work I say Resed y me   *ll s d*   1 : 7 : 0

          Thomas Mumford

NOTE.

The meeting-house in Nightingale Lane seems to have been built for a congregation under the pastorate of the Rev. John Knowles, who had been ejected from a preachership in Bristol Cathedral. The very fragmentary records of the church give Mr. Knowles two predecessors: the Revs. Samuel Slater, ejected from St. Katharine's by the Tower, and Thomas Kentish, ejected from Overton, Hants. All three are commemorated as early pastors of what became the King's Weigh House Church; and Knowles was not successor to, but colleague with, Kentish. It would appear therefore that about 1682, during Kentish's ministry, a separation took place, in consequence of which the new meeting house was built. Knowles died 10th April, 1685; and was succeeded by the Rev. John James, the ejected minister of Flintham, Notts., who died in 1696 or 7. The Rev. Christopher Midall or Meidel followed for a short time; he was a native of Denmark, and in 1699 joined the Society of Friends. Thomas Loyd became pastor on 24th September, 1700. In his time a strongly Calvinistic Confession of Faith—including the dogma of "Imputed Righteousness"—was drawn up, to which all members were required to assent. Mr. Loyd becoming infirm, the Rev. John Mitchell was elected co-pastor on 9th December, 1719; and on the death of Mr. Loyd, 9th January, 1721, became sole pastor. In 1722 the meeting house was rebuilt on the same site. The succeeding pastors were the Revs. Thomas Toller, 1754-1760; Henry Mayo, D.D., 1762-1792; John Knight, 1793-1803. In that year the meeting-house was pulled down, the site being required for the construction of the new London Docks. After using temporary accommodation for nearly three years in King Henry's Yard, the congregation obtained possession of a chapel in Pell Street, near Wellclose Square. The first minister there was the Rev. Thos. Cloutt (afterwards Russell), a literary man of some note in his day. Several pastors followed, but after a somewhat troubled history the church became extinct before the middle of the 19th century.

List of Members

Hon. Members marked *H*, Life Members marked *L*.

Adeney, W. F., Rev., Prof., M.A., D.D.
Anderton, W. E., Rev., M.A.
Andover (U.S.A.) Theological Seminary
Astbury, F. T., Rev.
Atkinson, S. B., Esq., M.A., J.P.
Avery, John, Esq.
Baptist Union, The
Bartlet, J. V., Rev., Prof., M.A., D.D.
Basden, D. F., Esq.
Bate, Frank, Esq., M.A.
Bax, A. Ridley, Esq.
Beaumont, E., Esq.
Boag, G. W., Esq.
Bragg, A. W., Esq.
Brown, J., Rev., Dr., B.A.
H Brown, W. H., Esq.
Brownen, G., Esq.
Burrage, Champlin, Esq.
Campbell, R. J., Rev., M.A.
Carpenter, J. Estlin, Rev., M.A.
Carter, W. L., Rev., M.A.
Cater, F. I., Rev., A.T.S.
Chevalier, J., M.
Clapham, J. A., Esq.
Clark, J. H., Esq.
Clarkson, W. F., Rev., B.A.
Claydon, George S., Esq.
Cocks, J., Esq.
Colborne, F. N., Rev.
Congregational Library, Boston, Mass
Cribb, J. G., Esq.
Crippen, T. G., Rev.
Dale, A. W. W., Esq., M.A.
Dale, Bryan, Rev., M.A.
Davies, J. Alden, Rev.
Davis, C. H., Rev.
Davis, J. E., Esq.
Davy, A. J., Esq
Dawson, E. B., Esq.
Didcote, C. Page, Esq.
Dimelow, J. G., Esq.
Dixon, H. N., Esq., M.A., F.L.S.
Dixon, R. M., Esq.
L Dore, S. L., Esq., J.P.
H Ebbs, A. B., Esq.
Ebbs, W., Rev.
Ellis, C. W., Esq.
Evans, A. J., Esq., M.A.
Evans, G. Eyre, Rev.
Evans, Jon. L., Esq.
Evans, R. P., Esq.
Firth, C. H., Prof., M.A., LL.D.
Flower, J. E., Rev., M.A.
Forsyth, P. T., Rev., Dr.
Gasquoine, T., Rev., B.A.
Glasscock, J. L., Esq.
Gordon, A., Principal
Gosling, Howard, Esq.
Green, Joseph J., Esq.
Green, T., Esq.
Grice, T. E., Esq.
Grieve, A. J., Rev., M.A., B.D.
Groser, W. H., Esq., B.Sc.
Hall, C. W., Rev.
Hall, W. H., Esq.
Harker, F. E., Rev.
Harris, W. J., Esq.
Harrison, G. W., Esq.
Harwood, W. Hardy, Rev.
Hawkins, F. H., Esq., LL.B.
Henderson, A. D., Esq.
Hepworth, F. N., Esq.
Hepworth, J., Esq.
Hepworth, T. M., Esq.
Heslop, R. Oliver, Esq., M.A., F.S.A.
Hewgill, W., Rev., M.A.
Hills, A. M., Miss
Hitchcock, W. M., Esq.
Hodgett, C. M., Esq.
Holt, Edwyn, Esq.
L Hounsom, W. A., Esq., J.P.
Huckle, Attwood, Esq.
Iliff, John S., Esq.
Jackson, S., Esq.
James, Norman G. B., Esq.
H Johnston, W., Esq.
Keep, H. F., Esq.
Kenward, Herbert, Rev.
Key, James, Rev.
King, Jos., Esq., M.A.
Knaggs, J., Rev.
H Lancashire Independent College (Goodyear, C., Esq.)
Lawrence, Eric A., Rev.
Layton, F. J., Rev., A.T.S.
Le Brun, E., Esq.
Lester, E. R., Esq.
Lewis, D. Morgan, Prof., M.A.
Lewis, Geo. G., Esq.
Lewis, H. Elvet, Rev., M.A.
Lloyd, E. Lewys
Lloyd, J. H., Esq.
Lovatt, J., Esq.
Low, G. D., Rev., M.A.
Luke, R., Esq.
Macfadyen, D., Rev., M.A.
Mackintosh, R., Rev., Prof., D.D.
Massey, Stephen, Esq.
H McClure, J. D., Dr.
McCrae, A., Esq.
McKnight, E., Esq.
Minshull, John, Esq.
Mottram, W., Rev.

List of Members (continued)

Muir, W., Esq.
Mumford, A. A., Esq., M.P.
Musgrave, B., Esq.
H New College
    (Staines, Howard, Rev.)
Nightingale, B., Rev.
H Palmer, C. Ray, Rev., Dr.
Palmer, W. M., Esq.
Parnaby, H., Rev., M.A.
Pearson, S., Rev., M.A.
Pierce, W., Rev.
Pitt, Walter, Mrs.
Powicke, F. J., Rev., Ph.D.
Poynter, J. J., Rev.
Pugh, Mrs.
Rawcliffe, E. B., Rev.
Rees, J. Mackreth, Rev.
Richards, D. M., Esq.
Ritchie, D. L., Rev.
Robinson, W., Rev.
Rollaston, Arthur A., Esq.
Rudge, C., Rev.
Rutherford, J., Esq.
H Rylands, Mrs., D.Litt.
Scamell, W., Esq.
Serle, S., Esq.
Shaw, H., Rev.
Silcock, P. Howard, Esq., B.A.
Simon, D. W., Rev., D.D
H Smith, W. J., Esq., M.A.
Society of Friends
Souter, Alex., Prof., M.A.
H Spicer, Albert, Sir, Bart., M P.

H Spicer, George, Esq., M.A., J.P.
Standerwick, J. W., Esq.
Stanier, W. H., Esq.
Sykes, A. W., Esq.
H Thacker, Fred. S., Esq.
Thacker, Henry, Esq.
Thomas, D. Lleufer, Esq.
Thomas, John, Esq., J.P., C.C.
Thomas, Wm., Rev.
H Thompson. J., Esq.
Titchmarsh, E. H., Rev., M.A.
H Toms, C. W., Esq.
Tuck, W., Esq.
Turner, G. Lyon, Rev., M.A.
Tyson, R. G., Esq.
U.S.A. Congress Library.
Walmsby, L. S., Esq.
Watkinson, J., Esq.
H Webster, Is., Esq.
L Whitley, A. W., Esq.
Wicks, G. H., Esq.
H Wilkinson, W., Esq
Williams's Library.
Williams, Mrs.
Williamson, David, Esq.
Williamson, David, junr., Esq.
Windeatt, E., Esq.
Wing, Lewis, Esq.
Winterstoke of Blagdon, Baron
Wontner, A. J., Esq.
Wood, Leonard B., Esq., M.A
Woodall, H. J., Esq.
Young, Hugh P., Rev.

OFFICERS OF THE SOCIETY.

President   Rev. Dr. John Brown, B.A.,
                              Hampstead, London, N.W.
Hon. Treasurer   Rev. G. Lyon Turner, M.A.,
                            Crescent Lodge, St. John's, London, S.E.
Hon. Auditor   Mr. John Minshull, Memorial Hall, London, E.C.
Hon. Editor & Librarian   Rev. T. G. Crippen,   ,,   ,,   ,,
Hon. Secretaries   Rev. T. G. Crippen,   ,,   ,,   ,,
                Mr. Henry Thacker,   ,,   ,,   ,,

CONDITIONS OF MEMBERSHIP.

(a) LIFE MEMBERS, paying twenty guineas in lieu of annual subscription.
(b) HONORARY MEMBERS, paying an annual subscription of one guinea or more.
(c) ORDINARY MEMBERS, paying an annual subscription of five shillings.

Subscriptions should be made payable and remitted to the Hon. Treasurer, as above; and are payable *in advance* on January 1st in each year.

New members are entitled to all the publications issued by the Society in the year they join.

Transactions

[Vol. III., No. 2]   [MAY, 1907

Contents

Congregational Historical Society : Annual Meeting	75
Editorial	77
Burton-on-Trent	81
John S. Iliff	
Early Baptists in London	88
The Ancient Meeting-house at Ravenstonedale	91
Bryan Dale, M.A., and T. G. Crippen	
Ebenezer Church, West Bromwich	104
Puritans and Presbyterians in the Channel Islands	110
E. le Brun	
Some Penry Dates	114
Wm. Pierce	
The Taunton Communion Plate	116
Bury Street Chapel	117
Robert Browne and the Achurch Parish Register	126
F. Ives Cater, A.T.S.	
List of Members and Officers, &c.	137

Can be obtained direct from the Book Saloon, Congregational Union of England and Wales, Memorial Hall, London, E.C.

Printed for the Society by
Fred. S. Thacker, 2 Dyers' Buildings, Holborn, London.

Congregational Historical Society

Annual Meeting

Our seventh Annual Meeting was held on Wednesday, 8th May, in the council chamber of the National Temperance Federation. There was a fairly good attendance of members.

The Rev. J. BROWN, D.D., occupied the chair. Prayer was offered by the Rev. B. Nightingale. The Report consisted mainly of a summary of documents published during the year, and of such as are in hand awaiting publication; with reference to research work effected or still in progress by members of the Society. The arrangements made last year as to meetings of committee had proved quite impracticable, with the result that the officers of the Society had been compelled to act mainly on their own responsibility—a state of things which it was desirable to amend. It was also urged that efforts should be made largely to increase our membership, so as to make it possible—which it is not at present—to issue the *Transactions* quarterly.

The TREASURER presented his financial statement, which reports a fair balance in the bank, although expenditure had somewhat exceeded income during the year. [The balance sheet, not having been yet audited, is held over for publication in our next issue.]

On the motion of E. B. DAWSON, Esq., seconded by the Rev. B. NIGHTINGALE, the Report, &c., were adopted *nem. con.*

The Treasurer, Secretaries, and Chairman were unanimously re-elected.

Some discussion ensued as to the future constitution of the Committee. It was ultimately agreed that "there should be a working Committee consisting wholly of members resident in or near London, with an indefinite number of corresponding members resident in the country."

The Committee was then chosen as follows:—

S. B. ATKINSON, Esq., M.A., M.B., J.P.	J. D. McCLURE, Esq., LL.D.
J. AVERY, Esq.	Rev. H. ELVET LEWIS, M.A.
Rev. G. BARRETT.	Rev. D. MACFADYEN, M.A.
	RIDLEY BAX, Esq., F.S.A.

With authority to co-opt two others.

Officers of the Society

The following were approved as corresponding members :—

    Rev. BRYAN DALE, M.A., Bradford.
    H. N. DIXON, Esq., M.A., F.L.S., Northampton
    Rev. T. GASQUOINE, B.A., Upper Bangor.
    W. A. HOUNSOM, Esq., J.P., Brighton.
    Rev. B. NIGHTINGALE, Preston.
    Rev. W. PIERCE, Northampton.
    JOHN SCAMELL, Esq., Westbury.
    Rev. C. W. SMYRK, Barnstaple.

The Rev. T. GASQUOINE read a short paper on *The Later Years of John Penry*.

The Rev. G. LYON TURNER read a transcript from a MS. which he had discovered in the British Museum, consisting of a contemporary review of ecclesiastical affairs in London in 1672.

Hearty thanks were accorded to the readers, and they were requested to place the papers in the hands of the Secretary for publication.

A letter was read from A. A. MUMFORD, Esq., M.D., urging that steps should be taken towards publishing the Bunhill Fields Registers. This was referred to the Committee.

Conversation ensued about the Autumnal Meeting at Blackpool. It was arranged that the Rev. B. NIGHTINGALE should read a paper on the Ancient Chapel at Ellswick ; and the project of an excursion thither was favourably entertained.

Officers of the Society, 1907-8

Chairman : Rev. JOHN BROWN, D.D.
Treasurer : Rev. G. LYON TURNER, M.A.
Editorial Secretary : Rev. T. G. CRIPPEN.
Financial Secretary : HENRY THACKER, Esq.
Auditor : JOHN MINSHULL, Esq.

EDITORIAL

We regret to announce the death of two of our members, both of whom have done good service in various departments of research : Mr. Tuck, of Bath, whose *History of Argyle Chapel* we noticed a year ago ; and Mr. Le Brun, of Jersey, from whose pen we have in our present issue an interesting memoir on *Puritanism and Presbyterianism in the Channel Islands*.

An interesting event of the present year is the 250th anniversary of Hanover Chapel, Peckham, which was celebrated on 14th April and following days. This church is believed to have originated in 1657, through the labours of the Rev. John Maynard, who from 1646 to 1651 held the sequestered vicarage of Camberwell. Several men of great eminence have held the pastorate ; especially Dr. Samuel Chandler in the 18th century, and Dr. W. B. Collyer in the 19th. We hope in a future issue to give a brief sketch of the history of this historic church.

We should be glad of any information about the Rev. Chas. McNeely, who in 1806 preached on one part of the day in the ancient chapel in Monkwell Street ; but who in 1813 was no longer in the list of London ministers. We are desirous of tracing his congregation from 1806 to about 1820.

We should also be glad to receive information about the origin, application, variation, or diversion of Congregational charities of any kind, especially endowments.

Several correspondents have kindly answered the inquiry in our last issue about autographs and memorials of Doddridge, which appear to be pretty numerous. We should be glad to hear of similar relics of Dr. Watts ; which, there is reason to believe, are decidedly scarce.

Editorial

The following communication may be of some interest:—

"It is well known that the familiar story of a Kentish jury in Puritan times, every one of whom bore a canting name, is a pure fabrication. Nevertheless there is a belief still current that such names were not uncommon, a belief which finds support in respectable works like Grainger's *Biographical History* and Brook's *Lives of the Puritans*. I therefore thought it worth while to examine several lists of indisputable authenticity; and the results are worth notice.

"Of the 479 persons commemorated in Brook's *Lives of the Puritans*, *the only one* who bears a canting name is the worthy Praise-God Barbone; though there is the rather heathenish name of Hannibal Gammon. Neither in the roll of the Long Parliament, of the Westminster Assembly, nor of Cromwell's second Parliament, is a single canting name to be found. In the lists of officers in the Parliamentary army of 1642 there are several eccentric names, such as Ornall, Mount, Agmondesham, and Wendy; but the only approach to a canting name is that of Sir Faithful Fortescue. In Cromwell's Little Parliament the name of Praise-God Barbone is alone of its kind. Finally, the names of the 2,237 ejected ministers in the *Nonconformists' Memorial* have been examined: 381 of these have no Christian name specified; but of the 1,856 full names there is a larger proportion of Bible names, especially from the Old Testament, than is now usual, and there are a very few eccentric names, as Onesiphorus Rood, Philologus Sacheverel, and Dositheus Wyar. Of what might properly be called canting names, however, *seven only* are to be found, *viz.*: Ichabod Chauncy, Sabbath Clark, Gracious Franklyn, Increase Mather, Thankful Owen, Comfort Steer, and Faithful Teate; another appears in the roll of Frankland's students—Godsgift Kerby. In short, amongst above 4,000 persons of the Civil War and Commonwealth period, by far the greater number of whom were of pronounced Puritan opinions and sympathies, the canting names amount to *ten altogether*."

We should be glad to note the discovery of any other fully authenticated names of the same class in the Puritan age.

*

The most important publication of the season as regards Congregational Church history is the long awaited posthumous work of Dr. R. W. Dale, completed by his son, the learned chancellor of Liverpool University. Instead of occupying space with any lengthened commendation of the *History of English Congregationalism* we simply advise our readers to buy it, read it, and lend it to their neighbours. It is not faultless, it exhibits some lack of proportion, and there are some omissions, of which notice is taken in an appreciative review in the current *Contemporary;* but it is far away the best book of the kind accessible. We hope that in due time the publishers will be encouraged to produce an edition in a handier form, and at a lower price (though 12s. for 800 pages of large 8vo. is by no means dear), that it may find a place in many thousands of homes and in all our Sunday school libraries.

*

We have pleasure in calling attention to a remarkable publication of the Friends' Historical Society, entitled *The First Publishers of Truth*. It is a collection made about 1720, but now first printed, of early records of the rise and growth of Quakerism in every county of England. It is carefully edited by Norman Penney, Esq., librarian at Devonshire House, (who is a member of our Society), and has an introduction by Dr. T. Hodgkin, whose *Life of George Fox* is widely and deservedly esteemed. As illustrating a curious phase of earnest Christian life, which is still very imperfectly understood beyond a narrow circle, the book deserves a place in every public library. It is handsomely printed, 16 + 410 pp., with five facsimiles; price 15s. net.

*

The Rev. Ira Bosely has published his promised *History of the Independent Church in Westminster Abbey*. It gives an interesting account, in a popular style, of a church which originated under the Commonwealth, first worshipped in the Abbey, was driven into concealment at the Restoration, had many persons of distinction among its ministers and members, and after numerous vicissitudes was finally disbanded about 80 years ago. Incidentally it refers to many stirring events associated with the places where the church successively assembled; and gives divers little known facts relating to Congregational churches worshipping in buildings which, belonging to the Church of England *as a whole*, have been reserved by law since 1662 for *that part of it* which accepts Episcopacy and the prayer book. The book is well got up, except for one or two provoking misprints; the price to non-subscribers is 5s.

We are glad to call attention to the Rev. Dr. Powicke's *History of the Cheshire Union of Congregational Churches*. It is a well arranged and useful sequel to Urwick's *Historical Sketches of Nonconformity in Cheshire;* and brings the story of Congregationalism very satisfactorily up to date.

Mr. Burrage has printed, in a limited edition, the important MS. of Robert Browne which he discovered in 1905. This treatise, which occupies 65 pp., is an apologetic reply addressed by Browne to some persons, possibly Barrowe and Greenwood, who had circulated writings of an ultra-Separatist character, maintaining that it was positively sinful to hear the preaching of the State Church clergy. Being written after his partial conformity the treatise is unquestionably—as Mr. Burrage calls it—a "Retraction" of some harsh utterances in his earlier writings; but it does not seem inconsistent in principle with the leading thoughts in his *Reformation without Tarying for Anie*. Barrowe's *Four Grounds of Separation* appears to have been his answer to this *Retraction*; and it must be confessed that as regards general tone a comparison of the two is not wholly favourable to the Separatist martyr. Indeed, except in a few passages Browne exhibits a gentleness and self-restraint only too rare in the controversial writings of the period.

We have secured a few copies of the *Retraction*, which will be supplied to members, as far as they will go, in order of application; price 2/6 net.

Burton-on-Trent

THE church at High Street, Burton-on-Trent, is stated to have been founded in 1670 through the instrumentality of the Rev. Thomas Bakewell, a clergyman who held the rectory of the village of Rolleston (about three miles from Burton) for fifteen years—from 1646 to 1661. In the latter year, the year before the Act of Uniformity was passed, he was ejected from his rectorship, for what reason the chronicles are silent[1]; but as there is a blank of several years in the parish registers of the period, the late rector of Rolleston (the Rev. Canon Fielden, deceased since this paper was written) humorously suggested to the writer that possibly Mr. Bakewell was ejected because he did not keep the registers properly!

Mr. Bakewell also held a lectureship at Burton of the value of £30 per annum, paid by the Clothworkers' Company in London, and from this he was ejected on Bartholomew's Day.

He subsequently preached in his "own hired house" at Burton, and apparently was assisted in his ministrations by Mr. Thomas Ford, an ejected (or silenced) minister living at "Winsell," *i.e.* Winshill, a neighbouring Derbyshire village now incorporated in the borough of Burton.

[Of his subsequent career an account, substantially identical with what was given in this paper as originally written, is contained in the Rev. A. J. Stevens's *History of the Church at Longdon and*

---

[1] It can scarcely have been to replace a formerly sequestered rector, as no such person is mentioned in Walker's *Sufferings of the Clergy*.—T. G. C.

Lichfield, published in the last issue of *Transactions* (vol. iii., pp. 33-47); to which the reader is referred. Mr. Bakewell's writings are noticed in *Early Nonconformist Bibliography* (*Transactions*, vol. ii., p. 440).]

From its formation down to the year 1838 a living representative of Mr. Bakewell's family was connected with the church. The name of Henry Bakewell appears as a trustee in deeds dated 1759 and 1792, and in early records the same name frequently occurs in the accounts presented to the trustees. Further, in the minutes of a church meeting held on March 2nd, 1815, there is a record that Miss Elizabeth Bakewell was admitted to membership; and on a memorial stone now in front of the present church there is the following inscription:—

> "Sacred to the memory of Elizabeth Bakewell, who died April 4th, 1838, aged 77 years. She was the lineal descendant of the Rev. Thomas Bakewell, rector of Rolleston, who was ejected for Nonconformity in 1661, and for whose ministry the adjoining chapel was erected."

The fragmentary records extant shew the early history of the church to have been somewhat chequered. It has been stated that for 138 years there were no "church records," but that in 1799 the Rev. B. Holland was pastor. The earliest minute book in existence contains certain items of account (copied from an earlier book apparently destroyed), and from these it would appear there were a house and school connected with the chapel, which "with all the premises" were let to a Mr. Thos. Carver at the sum of £16 per annum. In 1806 (May and November) there appear payments by the trustees "to Mr. Robt. Cooper for use of Rev. McLean." Then there is a record of "a meeting of the Trustees of the Presbyterian Denomination, held at the 'George Inn,' Feb. 19th, 1807," and at this meeting it was, *inter alia*,

> "Resolved that the House, Tenement, and all the fixtures as above stated be offered to the Rev. Robt. McLean at the yearly rent of twelve pounds per annum on condition that he will quit the premises at three calendar months' notice when required by a majority of the Trustees.
> Resolved also that the chapel be offered to Mr. McLean at the yearly rent of two pounds under the same tenure."

A subsequent entry, in another hand, on Sept. 29th, 1807, says: "The Rev. Robt. McLean entered upon the house and premises and chapel at £14 per annum. N.B.—There is a seat belonging to the house in Burton church No. 2 middle aisle on the north side next the wardens' seat but was not let to Mr. McLean." Entries in 1808 and 1809 indicate that there was some dispute over the letting of this pew, and a postscript states that "S. Payne says the *late* Rev. B. Holland told his Father that part of the pew belonged to his house," from which we infer that the Rev. B. Holland died during his pastorate.

Mr. McLean seems to have vacated the pastorate in Nov., 1809, and to have been succeeded shortly afterwards by the Rev. George Betts, who remained about two years. The minutes of a church meeting held on Feb. 17th, 1810, shew an advance in the methods of conducting the affairs of the church, inasmuch as it was "Resolved that Wm. Carter be requested to procure two books—one as a Register for Baptisms and the other to record all things transacted at church meetings." Other resolutions refer to the fixing of periodical church meetings and to the election of two deacons.

If "all things" transacted at the meetings were recorded the records shew the business to have been very meagre, nor did the church meet at the regular periods resolved upon. In these minutes only one mention is made of Mr. Betts (the pastor), who appears from the accounts of the trustees to have left in October, 1811. In the following month (November 15th) a proposition was made to dissolve the church, but it was rejected and, the two deacons resigning, "S. Snelson and John Orpin agreed to take the books and the affairs of the church into their hands for the present." The society rented the chapel and house from the trustees at a yearly rental of £20, and during the next three years made overtures to several candidates for the pastorate, but they were all declined. At length, however, the Rev. Robert Neil, of Middlewich, became the minister, settling on Nov. 20th, 1814, but he only stayed one year, the church finding it "entirely impossible (under present circumstances) to raise the sum of eighty pounds annually for the support of Mr. Neil and family." In the course of a month the Rev. D. Morgan, of Somerton, accepted the pastorate, but he only stayed a few months, for the record of a church meeting on March 3rd, 1816, says: "Mr. Morgan not finding himself quite so comfortable as he wished gave notice thereof to the deacons (on the Saturday night) stating that they must not expect his labours on the following day."

In July, 1816, Mr. Samuel Blackburn was invited to serve the church for six months, at the end of which period he was unanimously invited to the pastorate, and was ordained on June 4th, 1817, but his short period of service was evidently an unhappy one, for we read that on Dec. 22nd of the same year his resignation was unanimously accepted.

Then follows an inexplicable interregnum. There are no church records until Feb. 17th, 1829; but a minute of a meeting of the trustees held at the Three Queens hotel on Nov. 29th, 1823, stated that it was

"Resolved that Mr. Harrison pay over to the Rev. R. Bromilley a gratuity of Ten Pounds—*viz*. Five Pounds at Xmas next and the remaining Five Pounds at Lady Day 1824, as a further inducement to continue his services to the communicants of the chapel."

When and under what circumstances Mr. Bromilley became the minister, and how long he continued, there is nothing to shew, except that in the trustees' accounts there are seen to have been periodical payments to him extending from July 24th, 1822, to April 10th, 1826.

For sixteen months in 1827 and 1828 the Rev. W. F. Buck, from Hoxton academy, ministered to the congregation, and then removed to Canterbury. Before his advent the church appears to have been dissolved, but in the early part of 1829 it was re-united under the Rev. John Wild, from the Blackburn academy; who in 1832 removed to Nottingham, where he ministered for 36 years. He was followed at Burton in 1833 by the Rev. T. Kennerley, from the college at Newport Pagnell; who removed to Mitcham, Surrey, in 1839. The Rev. W. F. Buck, who after leaving Canterbury spent some years at Harleston, Norfolk, then returned to Burton, and retained the pastorate until 1847. In his time the chapel was rebuilt. He was afterwards at Ross, Herefordshire. Next came the Rev. Thos. Arnold, from Rotherham college, whose ministry continued only to the end of 1850, when he accepted a call to Smethwick. He was afterwards for many years at Northampton, where he won deserved honour as a successful teacher of the deaf and dumb. After him came the Rev. D. Horscroft, from Hingham, Norfolk, in 1852; five years later he left for Bourne, Lincolnshire. Then followed the Rev. Alexander Mackennal (afterwards D.D.), from Hackney college, in 1858. At the end of three years he went to

Surbiton, and was afterwards at Leicester and Bowden. He was chairman of the Congregational Union in 1887. He was succeeded at Burton by the Rev. George Kettle, from Upminster, Essex, in 1862; he also remained three years, and went to Shrewsbury, where he laboured for 23 years longer. In 1865 the Rev. W. Aston came from Spring Hill college; his pastorate was likewise of three years' duration, after which he removed to Bodmin, Cornwall. He was succeeded by the Rev. Thos. Pearson, from Rotherham college; his ministry extended over twenty-four years, 1869-93. He afterwards ministered for a short time in Glasgow, and is now at Ware. Then followed the Rev. H. F. Walker, from Loughborough, 1893-1902. On his removal to Oakham an invitation was given to the Rev. Herbert G. Brown, of East Ham, who still retains the pastorate.

In 1887, owing to differences of opinion between the then minister and the deacons, principally upon questions of administration and procedure, the deacons, and with them a large proportion of the members, separated from the church and formed a new society, which obtained by purchase a small iron building in Guild Street, recently vacated by a Baptist church on removal to another part of the town. This new church called in 1889 as its first pastor the Rev. J. Bolton Petts, now of Bilston, and under his pastoral care, and by his energy and his judicious leadership, a considerable degree of prosperity was attained. From time to time efforts were made to bring about a reunion of the two churches, and much regret was felt that a scheme formulated in 1899 under the direction of the late Rev. J. A. Mitchell, then of Nottingham, proved abortive; the main difficulty being the provision of settlements for the pastors of the two churches. Upon the removal of the Rev. H. F.

Walker, of the High Street church, to Oakham, in 1902, the question of reunion again came to the front, and this time the negotiations, initiated by the officers of the Staffordshire Union, were successful; the main difficulty being overcome by the generous action of Mr. Petts in the resignation of his Guild Street charge "in the hope of furthering the happy and prosperous reunion of the two churches." The reunion was consummated in January, 1903, when the late esteemed secretaries of the Congregational Union (the Revs. W. J. Woods and J. A. Mitchell) were the special preachers. In November of the same year the Rev. H. G. Brown was called to the pastorate of the united church, and (as stated above) still retains the position. Mr. Petts had already settled at Bilston.

In connection with the Burton church it should be stated that a branch cause was established at the neighbouring village of Branstone in 1834, during the ministry of the Rev. T. Kennerley, and is now flourishing under the honorary pastorate of the minister at Burton. The neat little chapel, which occupies a conspicuous position in the main street of the village (with a separate Sunday school building on the opposite side of the roadway), has recently been enlarged and thoroughly renovated. This cause at Branstone had a very warm corner in the heart of the late Dr. Mackennal, who ever bore in kindly remembrance its faithful adherents. Of these perhaps the most noteworthy is Thomas Sturgess, a veteran who entered into the service of the school in 1836, and who yet, though verging upon his 99th year, is actively interested in the work.

October, 1906.   JOHN S. ILIFF.

Early Baptists in London

being a further extract from the Gould MS., see vol. ii. p. 352

NUMB : 2

An Old MSS, gieving some Acco^{tt} of those Baptists who first formed themselves into distinct Congregations, or Churches in London. found among certain Paper given me [*i.e. Benjamin Stinton*] by Mr Adams.

1633 — Sundry of ye Church whereof Mr Jacob & Mr John Lathorp had been Pastors, being difsatisfyed wth ye Churches owning of English Parishes to be true Churches desired dismifsion & Joyned togeather among themselves, as Mr Henry Parker, Mr Tho. Shepard, Mr Sam^{ll} Eaton, Marke Luker, & others wth whom Joyned Mr Wm Kiffin.

1638 — 1638. Mr Tho: Wilson, Mr Pen, & H. Pen, & 3 more being convinced that Baptism was not for Infants, but profefsed Beleivers joyned wth Mr Jo: Spilsbury ye Churches favour being desired therein.

1640 — 3^d Mo: The Church became two by mutuall consent just half being wth Mr P. Barebone, & ye other halfe with Mr H. Jessey Mr Richard Blunt wth him being convinced of Baptism y^t also it ought to be by diping ye Body into ye Water, resembling Burial & riseing again. 2 Col: 2. 12. Rom: 6. 4. had sober conferance about in ye Church, & then wth some of the forenamed who also ware so convinced: And after Prayer & conferance about their so enjoying it, none haveing then so so practised in England to profefsed Believers, & hearing that some in ye Nether Lands had so practised they agreed & sent over Mr Rich. Blunt (who understood Dutch) wth Letters of Comendation, who was kindly accepted there, & returned wth Letters from them Jo: Batte a Teacher there, & from that Church to such as sent him.

Early Baptists in London

1641 They proceed on therein, viz, Those Persons yt ware persuaded Baptism should be by dipping ye Body had mett in two Companies, & did intend so to meet after this, all these agreed to proceed alike togeather. And then Manifesting (not by any formal Words or Covenant) wch word was scrupled by some of them, but by mutual desires & agreement each Testified : Thóse two Companyes did set apart one to Baptize the rest ; So it was solemnly performed by them.

Mr. Blunt Baptized Mr Blacklock yt was a Teacher amongst them, & Mr Blunt being Baptized, he & Mr Blacklock Baptized ye rest of their friends that ware so minded, & many being added to them they increased much

The Names of all 11 Mo. Janu : begin

Richard Blunt	Sam. Blacklock	Tho Shephard ⎱
Greg. Fishburn	Doro. Fishburn	his wife ⎰
John Cadwell	Eliz. Cadwell	Mary Millifson
Sam. Eames	Tho. Munden	
Tho. Kilcop	William Willieby	
Robert Locker	Mary Lock	
John Braunson	John Bull	
Rich. Ellis	Mary Langride	
Wm Creak	Mary Haman	
Robt Carr	Sarah Williams	
Martin Mainprise	Joane ⎱ Dunckle Ann ⎰	
Hen: Woolmare	Eliz. Woolmore	
Robt King	Sarah Norman	
Tho. Waters	Isabel Woolmore	
Henry Creak	Judeth Manning	
Mark Lukar	Mabel Lukar	
Henry Darker	Abigal Bowden	
Eliz Jessop	Mary Creak	
	Susanah King	

*11th month understood as appears above! & this was Jany 9th.

41 in all

11.* January 9 added

John Cattope	George Denham
Nicholas Martin	Tho : Daomunt
Ailie Stanford	Rich Colgrave
Nath Matthon	Eliz Hutchinson
Mary Burch	John Croson
	Sybilla Lees
	John Woolmoore

thus 53 in all

1644 Those that ware so minded had comunion togeather were become Seven Churches in London.

1639   Mr Green wth Capt Spencer had begun a Congregation in Crutched Fryers, to whom Paul Hobson joyned who was now wth many of that Church one of ye Seven

1644   These being much spoken against as unsound in Doctrine as if they ware Armenians, & also against Magistrates &c they joyned togeather in a Confeſsion of their Faith in fifty two Articles wch gave great satisfaction to many that had been prejudiced.

See ye Notes at ye End of ye Confeſsion.

Thus Subscribed in y^e Names of 7 Churches in London.

Wm Kiffin
Tho : Patience
Geo : Tipping
John Spilsbury
Tho : Shepard
Tho : Munden

Tho : Gun
Jo : Mabbet
John Web
Tho : Kilcop

Paul Hobson
Tho : Goore
Jo : Phelps
Edward Heath

This print of the Meeting-house before its reconstruction is from a drawing made from a badly faded photograph—the only one in existence.

The Ancient Meeting-house at Ravenstonedale

THE village of Ravenstonedale, Westmoreland, is about a mile and a half south of the station bearing its name, and four miles and a half south-west of Kirkby Stephen. It is described as "a strange, straggling collection of cottages, medium-sized dwellings, farmhouses, &c."; but many of the cottages have been rebuilt within the last ten years. The village stands on a slope near the foot of Ash Fell, surrounded by mountains which rise to a height of 2,300 feet. Its mean elevation is about 850 feet above the sea level. The parish, formerly a chapelry of Kirkby Stephen, contains 16,400 acres, all pasture or moorland, which affords sustenance to thousands of sheep; and ponies of the Shetland variety are reared in large numbers. There is no arable land in the parish. The population (including the hamlet of Newbiggin, near the railway station) was 1,138 in 1801, but steadily declined throughout the last century; in 1901 it was only 838.

The parish church was built about the time of the Reformation, but was rebuilt in 1744. The registers commence in 1571. Thomas Dodgson was appointed to the benefice in 1634. He was strongly inclined to Presbyterianism; and in 1648 his name appeared, together with those of five or six elders,[1] in the certificate of a county committee which under the Long Parliament advised the formation of a classis "for the bottome of Westmoreland division." Reluctantly, and only after long hesitation, he submitted to the Act of Uniformity; and continued curate of Ravenstonedale until his death in January, 1673.

EARLY NONCONFORMIST MEETINGS.

Nonconformity in the dale originated in the labours of the Rev. Christopher Jackson, who in 1662 was ejected from the rectory of Crosby Garrett, a small village about five miles to the north. He

---

1 One of these, Anthony Fothergill, was the father of Elizabeth Gaunt, "the martyr of charity," who was burnt at Tyburn on 4th October, 1685, for "treason," committed by sheltering a fugitive from Sedgemoor—surely the crowning atrocity of Stuart misrule! She is believed to have been a Baptist. A window in the parish church commemorates her martyrdom. Her portrait was lately in the possession of Miss Fothergill of Brownber Cottage.

B

was the son of Thomas Jackson of Leeds, and was early apprenticed to some unspecified trade; but his studious habits excited the interest of friends, who sent him to Cambridge. He was admitted a pensioner at Magdalen Hall in June, 1652, at the age of 21; and commenced B.A. in 1655. Calamy calls him "a very pious man, of a holy life, and competent learning." On leaving the University he settled at some unnamed place in Yorkshire, whence he seems to have been outed at the Restoration. He then removed to Crosby, where his ministry was brought to an end by the Act of Uniformity. Having a little property in Ravenstonedale he retreated thither, living modestly—and it is to be feared scantily—on his own resources. To a conforming clergyman who gibed at his threadbare coat he replied, "If my coat is bare, it has not been turned." He held meetings for prayer and preaching in his own and other private dwellings, and does not appear to have been disturbed. Probably he enjoyed the protection of Philip, Lord Wharton—"the good Lord Wharton," as he was called—of Wharton Hall, about four miles distant, who was a great friend of the nonconforming clergy. Mr. Jackson married Anne Taylor, at Ravenstonedale, on 17th April, 1664; but how long he remained in the dale, and when and where he died, are unknown.

On the death of Mr. Dodgson, in 1673, Lord Wharton, as lord of the manor, had the appointment of his successor. He resolved on selecting a clergyman who would offer prayer, and not merely read prayers, in his family; and whose preaching should, on trial, be found acceptable to the parishioners. His choice fell upon Anthony Procter, who had been for ten years a Nonconformist. From 1651 he had been curate at Masham and Kirby Malzeard, and from 1655 vicar of Well, near Bedale, whence he was ejected in 1662. He obtained a licence under the Indulgence, to minister as a Presbyterian in his own house at Kirby Malzeard, on 20th November, 1672; but conformed on the withdrawal of the Indulgence, and was presented to the curacy of Ravenstonedale on 23rd October, 1673. Here he remained till 1689, when he removed to the rectory of Deane, in Cumberland, where he was buried 28th July, 1702. One of the same name, perhaps his son, was admitted to Frankland's academy at Rathmell, 7th April, 1670. He was evidently esteemed by the Nonconformists, who attended his preaching, though they could not tolerate the ritual of the State Church. In the account of the primary visitation of Bishop Nicholson of Carlisle, 12th July, 1703, it was stated that in Mr. Procter's time a small bell, called the "saints' bell," used to be rung after the Nicene creed "to call in the dissenters to the sermon." The "saints' bell," or as it was elsewhere called the "Sanctus bell," was a survival from pre-Reformation times; when in the Mass a bell was rung at the Sanctus, and again at the elevation of the Host.

Under Toleration.

We know but little more of Nonconformity in the dale until after the Revolution. When liberty of worship was secured by the Toleration Act, a house belonging to George Parkin became the usual meeting-place, and is believed to have been certified in 1692. Its location was a little lower down the hill than the present edifice. The first minister was Rev. Timothy Puncheon, who entered Frankland's academy on 19th February, 1688, when it was at Attercliffe. There is no record of his ordination; but he was associated with R. Frankland, O. Heywood, Jos. Dawson, and John Carrington, in ordaining five young ministers at Rathmell on 7th June, 1693. It is noteworthy that a marriage took place in the meeting-house on 4th January, 1693/4, and another on 24th August, 1697. Such marriages, though not very frequent, became illegal only in 1754. In 1693 Lord Wharton gave £100, the capital sum to be laid out in the mortgage of land, and the interest to be paid " to Timothy Puncheon, clerk, while minister at the house of George Parkin in Ravenstonedale, and his successors." This gift was the nucleus of what by subsequent benefactions has grown to a very respectable endowment. The indenture, dated 18th August, 1693, by which it is settled, is described as "the Purchase Deed of the Chapel premises and estate and Declaration of Trusts"; and is the only deed in existence of date prior to 1736. The following are the additional benefactions: by Mr. Pinder, a dissenting minister in London, to the said meeting-house, £30; John Thomson, hosier, of Kirkby Stephen, £20; Isabel Langhorn, £6; James and Mary Fawcett, £20; George Murthwaite, £10; all laid out in the purchase of land. There was also £100 in money contributed by Christopher Todd and others; £20 of it was lost, and the rest laid out at interest. Lord Wharton died 4th February, 1695/6, leaving a memory which is still fragrant by reason of his numerous charities and personal virtues.

It is not certainly known how long Mr. Puncheon remained at Ravenstonedale. Probably about 1712 he removed to Riveley in Northumberland, where he died in 1717. His successor was the Rev. John Magee, who was ordained 14th April, 1714. His appointment was unacceptable to a section of the congregation, who were perhaps inclined to the Arianism which was about that time gaining favour in many Presbyterian churches. A secession took place, encouraged by Thomas Dixon, M.D., minister at Whitehaven (1708-23), and founder of an academy there. James Towers, minister at Rathmell, wrote on 8th June, 1714, to Peter Walkden of Newton-in-Bowland that Dr. Dixon had administered the sacrament to the seceders; who in 1715 invited as their minister Rev. Jas. Mallison of Blennerhasset. He only remained a few months, and then removed to Howden in the East Riding of

Yorkshire, where he lived for nearly 30 years. How long it was
before the separation collapsed is uncertain, as we do not know
the *exact* date of Evans's List of Nonconformist Congregations,
written between 1717 and 1729, and preserved in Williams's Library.
Evans's account is: INDEPENDENT, " Russendale or Ravenstonedale,
f. John Magee. 300 (*hearers*). 3, (*county voters*). G(*entry*) 4, most
tenants under Lord Wharton."   PRESBYTERIAN, " Russendale *alias*
Ravingstondale, near Kirkby Stephen.   10 disc. James Malleson
1716 (rem.)" The "f" indicates that the church of which Mr.
Magee was pastor was aided by the Independent Fund; while the
later entry shews that after Mr. Mallison's removal about ten of his
adherents, calling themselves Presbyterians, continued to hold a
separate meeting, which seems to have lasted for several years.

MEETING-HOUSE ERECTED.

The present church building, or rather the greater part of its
walls, is believed to have been erected in 1726. According to a
document deposited in the archives of Orton vicarage and
supposed to be in the handwriting of Dr. Richard Burn, author of
the *Standard History of Westmoreland*, (also of the *Justice of
Peace, Ecclesiastical Law*, and other works), it was built on a
plot of ground sold by Richard Hewetson of Ellergill for six
pounds, of which he gave four towards the cost of the building.
It was registered at Appleby on 10th April, 1727. It had on the
eastern side two doors opening directly on the interior, which was
fitted up with fine old oak. There was an ⊏ shaped gallery at the
south end, and a three-decker pulpit with sounding-board stood
against the long side on the west. The floor was of stone; the
seats are said to have been uncomfortable, and the lighting
deficient. The portion southward of the bell-turret was a later
addition. Over the doorway admitting to the gallery was a brass
plate thus inscribed : " This gallery was built by the procurement
of the Reverend Mr. Ralph Milner, Anno Dom. 1731." This was a
kinsman of William Milner of Ashfield, one of the original trustees
of Lord Wharton's benefaction.

According to the parish register, a son of Mr. Magee was buried
2nd December, 1725, and his wife Eleanor, 11th February, 1733.
About this time, 1732 or-3, he seems to have resigned his pastorate;
but nearly ten years afterwards he was residing in the village, and
was referred to as minister of the church, as if he had resumed the
charge.

On 9th September, 1733, an invitation was given to the Rev. James
Ritchie, M.D., a Scotsman, educated at Glasgow University.
About a year after his settlement some of the trustees took ex-

ception to his Arminian teaching as contrary to the Westminster Confession of Faith, withheld his stipend, and evicted him from the meeting-house. He thereupon commenced a suit in Chancery against John Parkin and the other trustees; which after tedious delays, and the incurring of costs amounting to above £820, was decided in Mr. Ritchie's favour.[2] He thus recovered the arrears of his stipend and possession of the meeting-house. But long before this time he appears to have left Ravenstonedale; for by one account he was for thirteen years minister of the united congregations at Redwing, Cumberland, and Irshopeburn (?) in Weardale, Durham; and then for three or four years at Great Salkeld and Plompton, Cumberland. He repaired both the meeting-houses, travelling through several counties to collect the needful cost; and in 1753 removed from Alston to Mixenden, near Halifax. He was at this time an Arian, and was the author of two treatises on Jewish and other sacrifices.[3] The Mixenden congregation dwindled under his ministry, but he is said to have done much good as a physician. He died 15th October, 1763.

In an indenture dated 7th March, 1736, it is recited that the Ravenstonedale mortgage then amounted to £336, secured on the following properties, viz. :—"A messuage and tenement at the Townhead, barn, suitable peat-house and garth; one close called Hill, with a little bottome adjoining the same; one close called Low New Close; together with land lying on Town Croft, adjoining the ground late M. Atkinson's on the east side, with all edifices, &c." This trust deed was renewed from time to time on the appointment of new trustees. On a part of the property thus described the manse was built in 1854. Near by was a house, lately demolished, in which the minister formerly resided; it bore the inscription, I.A. 1728.

Frequent Changes of Pastorate, 1742-90.

The course of events after the removal of Dr. Ritchie is a little doubtful. An almost illegible memorandum among the papers of Joshua Wilson in the Congregational Library mentions one Welsh at "Russendale" in 1742. Nothing is known of him; he may have been Ritchie's successor, or he may have ministered to a secession. In a letter dated 1st July, 1743, the Rev. James Scott,

---

[2] Of these costs Mr Ritchie and his friends are said to have paid more than half. The balance of £365 16s. was apportioned among the trustees—of whom Rev. R Milner was one,—by the arbitration of Rd. Burn, LL.D.; a copy of whose award, dated 8th March, 1747, is in the library of New College.

[3] The titles were: *A Criticism upon Modern Notions of Sacrifice*, 1761; and *The Peculiar Doctrine of Revelation relating to Piacular Sacrifices*, 2 vols., 4to, published after his death in 1766.

minister at Horton-in-Craven, referred to a meeting at Ravenstonedale which Mr. Magee, minister of the place, "had engaged to call," but which had been deferred owing to that gentleman's illness. Two months later, Mr. Magee having died meanwhile (probably on a journey to Ireland), an urgent invitation was addressed to Mr. Scott to accept the pastorate. It was signed by John Perkins, John Bell, and James Fawcett, elders, and 34 other male members, one of them apparently a son of the late pastor. But Mr. Scott declined the invitation; removing a little later to Tockholes, and afterwards to Heckmondwike, where in 1756 he founded the academy now represented by the United Yorkshire College at Bradford.

Then followed in succession two students from the academy presided over by Dr. Caleb Rotherham at Kendal. Each held the pastorate for a very short time, and their order is uncertain. Probably the first was the Rev. Samuel Lowthion, a native of Penruddock, Cumberland, who removed to Penrith about 1745, and thence in 1752 to Hanover Square, Newcastle. There he ministered for 28 years, trained several young men for the ministry, died in May, 1780, and was buried in the north aisle of St. Nicholas church (now the cathedral). A handsome mural tablet was prepared to perpetuate his memory; but was not erected, because the incumbent insisted on the erasure of part of the inscription. In 1756 Mr. Lowthion had preached at the ordination of his old tutor's son and successor, Caleb Rotherham, junr., at Kendal. The sermon, which was printed, is a plea for unlimited freedom of speculation and utterance in the pulpit. Mr. Lowthion's fellow-student and probable successor[4] at Ravenstonedale was the Rev. John Blackburne; who *may* have been a native of the village. A Mr. Blackburn, said to have been born there, was among Rotherham's pupils, and was a probationer at South Shields in 1744. Not later than the beginning of 1747 Mr. Blackburn removed to King John's Court, Southwark. That congregation was dispersed in 1754, when he proceeded to Newbury, Berks., where he ministered till his death in 1762. He published two sermons, in 1749 and 1753; and also edited a posthumous work by Hopton Haynes, Esq., assay master of the Mint, entitled: *A Scripture Account of the Attributes and Worship of God, and of the Character and Offices of Jesus Christ.* As this book is uncompromisingly Unitarian, it is safe to assume that Mr. Blackburn held the same opinions.

There is still some difficulty in following the succession. Nightingale introduces the Rev. Richard Simpson, who entered Doddridge's academy at Northampton in 1745, and had a charge

---

[4] Mr. Nightingale in his *Lancashire Nonconformity* makes Lowthion to be the successor of Blackburne.

somewhere in Westmoreland. Nightingale thinks it was most likely at Ravenstonedale. He *may* have gone thence to Stainton, near Kendal, from which place he removed about 1763 to Warley, near Halifax, where he exercised a long and useful ministry, dying in 1795. His preaching was intensely evangelical; as may be seen in his posthumous volume of *Seven Practical and Experimental Sermons.* The next minister of whom we have any knowledge is the Rev. William Scott. He was a Presbyterian, in communion with the Established Church of Scotland. He was licensed by the presbytery of Dalkeith on 2nd December, 1760, ordained at Ravenstonedale by the Presbytery Class of Newcastle on 6th October, 1762, and removed to Abbot's Rule, near Jedburgh, in 1764.

The Agreement of the Presbyterian and Independent ministers in London in 1691 had been adopted in many parts of the country, and especially in the north of England. But seventy years later Arianism and Unitarianism were gaining ground to such an extent that the Cumberland Provincial Assembly, though professedly orthodox, were much more in sympathy with latitudinarianism— if not with downright heresy—than with evangelical truth. This was remarkably illustrated under the next pastorate. The Rev. Jas. Tetley was a student in the Heckmondwike academy in 1762. In 1767 he was at Ravenstonedale, but was "not in connection with the Cumberland Provincial." The pulpit at Cockermouth had been supplied for twelve months by a Mr. Selby Ord, who, not having been ordained, was thought incompetent to administer the sacraments. The people applied to the Provincial Assembly for assistance, but could only obtain the offer of service from ministers who were known to be heterodox, which they felt bound in conscience to refuse. They then applied to Mr. Tetley, who visited them, preached, baptized several children, and administered the Lord's Supper. (See Cockermouth church book, 5th April, 1767.)

Mr. Tetley was still at Ravenstonedale in 1774. His successor was the Rev. Jas. Somerville, a native of Pitmuir in Berwickshire. He had spent several years at Edinburgh University, and was licensed to preach by the presbytery of Lauder in December, 1771. For two years and a half, on the recommendation of Mr. Scott of Heckmondwike, he had supplied the congregation at Stainton, near Kendal, where he was the last resident minister. His first sermon at Ravenstonedale was preached on 28th May, 1775, from Acts x. 29; his ordination followed on 27th September, the officiating ministers being the Revs. Selby Ord of Cockermouth ; A. Allat of Forton ; and Luke Prattman of Cotherstone. He was highly esteemed by the people, but his stipend was only £40 a year. In 1776 the minister's house was repaired, and on 6th June, 1777, he married Jane Isabella Sprott in Scotland, and "started with his new house" in September. The chapel register, now at Somerset House, begins in 1777. It is recorded that the next year, 1778, there was an election of elders, and Anthony Fothergill was appointed clerk. In 1784 Mr. Somerville removed to Branton, Northumberland, where he died 8th July, 1808, aged 65. A Mr. Smith occupied the pulpit from 1784 to 1790; of him nothing further is known; he may or may not have been the James Smith who was at Keighley, 1749-53.

REVIVAL, 1790-1815.

The next minister was the Rev. John Hill. He was born in 1753, and trained at the Mile End academy under the Revs. Jos. Barber, S. Brewer, and John Kello. Leaving the academy in 1780 or-81 he ministered for short periods at Preston, Haslingden, and Carlisle (Lady Glenorchy's chapel). In August, 1790, "he was on a journey, and paid us an unexpected visit, when he preached on the Lord's day morning and afternoon; and after labouring among the people for some weeks he received a unanimous call." It was signed by 34 persons, whose names are given in the church book, the numbers of men and women being nearly equal. In 1793 Mr. Hill commenced a Sunday school, which he conducted himself. In 1802 a small piece of ground at the south end of the chapel was purchased, on which a room was built for Sunday school purposes; having dwelling rooms above, which were entered from the west side. The burial ground was also enlarged by pulling down a cottage which stood between the chapel and the roadway. The cost of these improvements was £250.

Mr. Hill was on terms of intimacy with Dr. Robinson, the minister of the parish church. Both were great smokers, and over their pipes they used to discuss the merits of different styles of preaching—Mr. Hill advocated and practised extempore utterance, while Dr. Robinson was accustomed to read his sermons. This Dr. Robinson was a remarkable man; besides being parish clergyman he was master of the grammar school, and received pupils from a distance, who boarded in his house. He was a strict disciplinarian and a splendid teacher; and it is said that as many as twenty of his pupils became clergymen, several of them with no other instruction than what he imparted.

Mr. Hill was accustomed to preach once a month in a barn at Dent, some 16 miles distant.[5] One result of these visits was the

---

[5] The only vehicles then used in the district were heavy farm-carts without springs. Mr. Hill is said to have first introduced the convenience called a "shandry"—a swinging seat with a back, suspended in the cart by chains. His shandry is still preserved as a memorial—converted into a garden seat.

The building in its present state is from a photograph taken by Rev. G. MANNING.

conversion of James Batty. A church was formed at Dent on 31st March, 1809; and in 1820 Mr. Batty became its second minister. In 1823 he began to preach at Sedbergh, and eighteen years later at Hawes, with the result that Congregational churches were formed in both these towns. Mr. Batty died 7th April, 1856, aged 77. His spiritual father, Mr. Hill, died 26th November, 1809, aged 56. His tombstone (erected by the church members in grateful recognition of his services), bears the following inscription :—

> Here lies interred beneath this stone
> A sinner saved by grace alone;
> Unmoved, uninjured, may his dust remain,
> Till the last trump shall bid him rise again.

The next minister was the Rev. Jas. Muscutt, who had studied under the Rev. G. Collinson at Hackney, and supplied for a short time at Darlington. He accepted the call on condition that the church should be reorganized, and put more strictly on the Congregational plan. It had been accounted Independent eighty years before; but there had been several Presbyterian ministers, and apparently the minister, elders, and trustees had managed things without much reference to the church members. Mr. Muscutt's terms were complied with, and he was ordained on 12th June, 1811, by the Revs. A. Carnson of Cotherston; James Jackson of Green Hammerton; W. Norris of Ellinthorpe; and W. Norris, junr., of Alston—all Congregational ministers. In 1813 Messrs. Richardson and Milner, two young men of the congregation, having often heard the minister complain of late and irregular attendance, collected money for a bell; for which a small turret or bellcote was erected. It was not very musical, but its usefulness made ample amends, and it still does regular service, and is as necessary as of old. Mr. Muscutt removed to Cockermouth in 1815, and died there 7th August, 1819.

TROUBLOUS TIMES, 1817-67.

His successor was the Rev. R. H. Bonnar, from the Idle academy. He was ordained 27th August, 1817, by the Revs. W. Vint of Idle; E. Stillman of Keld; and A. Carnson of Cotherstone. His ministry continued till 1835; but seems latterly not to have been prosperous. We find allusions to dissensions and litigation, and there was a separation led by a Mr. Benjamin Hewitson, which however came to nothing. A Rev. Wm. Hasell followed for a short time, and then, with a considerable part of the congregation, went over to the Wesleyans—for whom a chapel was built in 1839.

A paragraph in the *Kendal Mercury* of 6th February, 1836,

represents a deplorable state of things as then existing. The building is said to have been dilapidated, the windows smashed, the graveyard neglected and tombstones overturned, and the worshippers reduced to half a dozen. Full information is lacking as to the cause of the dissensions and litigation which had such unhappy results; but the personal element entered into it somewhat largely, complicated—it would seem—by doctrinal disputes; and it was in some way connected with the very inconvenient tenure of the chapel property. This now consisted of above 8½ acres of ground, with sundry buildings; and the custom of the manor did not permit conveyance on trust, nor that more than one person at a time should be admitted tenant of the same premises. It was therefore usual for one person to hold the whole on behalf of the church. This responsibility had been undertaken by John Hewitson; who by arrangement with the then lord of the manor, the Earl of Lonsdale, had enfranchised the property as far back as 24th June, 1808. At length, by indenture dated 26th May, 1836, Mr. Hewitson conveyed the whole to nine trustees, "to promote the advancement of the Protestant religion—as professed by Protestant Dissenters of the denomination of Congregationalists or Independents—whose doctrine is agreeable to the Assembly of Divines' Confession of Faith and Catechism." The minister was made liable to be removed for heterodoxy; and new trustees were to be chosen from time to time with consent of the members, male and female, who had been in communion for twelve months.

It was now found necessary to reconstitute the church. This was done at a meeting held on 5th August, 1838, presided over by Mr. Broadbent, then a student in Airedale College. Four women and two men formed the new society, Mr. B. Hewitson being chosen deacon. Soon after the Rev. Wm. Sedgwick, from Keld, undertook the pastorate, and removed to Dent in 1843. He was followed by Rev. J. F. Bryan, who had been a schoolmaster at Staleybridge, and laboured successfully to revive the decayed interest. But in 1846 he removed, to undertake the management of a new Ragged and Industrial school in Manchester, for the rescue of children of the lowest class from degrading and criminal associations. This work prospered exceedingly, and was reported on by H.M.'s. inspector as one of "the best managed and most effective" in the kingdom. It developed into the "Barnes Home" at Heaton Mersey, which was opened in August, 1871. On Monday, 11th December of the same year, Mr. Bryan died suddenly, having preached at Stockport the previous evening.

His successor at Ravenstonedale was the Rev. Walter Mathison, from Kendal; ordained 5th May, 1847. The ministers assisting were the Revs. D. Jones and John Ingless of Kendal; W. Brewis of Penrith; W. Palmer of Northallerton; J. W. Rolls of Hawes;

and W. Sedgwick of Dent. Mr. Mathison was accustomed to preach on alternate Sunday afternoons at the Baptist chapel at Crosby Garrett. During his ministry, in 1854, the present manse was built by public subscription. The old one, bearing date 1728, was pulled down in 1905, having become unfit for habitation. Mr. Mathison removed in 1856 to Market Drayton, and two years later to Australia, where he was still ministering in 1883.

For six years the church was united with that at Kirkby Stephen; but the arrangement proved unsatisfactory. The ministers of the united churches were the Revs. John Moses, formerly a Wesleyan, 1857-8; J. Barton, a Rotherham student, who had laboured at Bakewell in Derbyshire, 1858-9; and, on his removal to Wirksworth, Rev. Jas. Howard from Newtown, Montgomeryshire, 1859-63. Mr. Howard having removed to Hemel Hempstead, Herts., the union was dissolved, and Rev. Jos. Barnfather was called to the single pastorate. He removed to Dent in 1867, and afterwards to Parkhead, Cumberland.

MEETING-HOUSE RECONSTRUCTED, 1867.

The Rev. Robert Pool, from Parton, accepted the pastorate in 1868. His mother was a cousin of the celebrated Edward Irving. For five years he had laboured as agent of an undenominational mission on a salary of £60 a year, enduring no little persecution on account of his zeal for temperance. Bishop Villiers offered him £120 and a vicarage if he would "take orders," which as a conscientious Nonconformist he respectfully declined; and soon after, in 1862, he accepted a call to Parton at £80. At that time there were in the diocese of Carlisle 118 State Church "livings" under £100, the average being £83. Mr. Pool only remained about a year in Ravenstonedale, during which time the chapel, which sorely needed renovation, was dealt with in a manner which, though conducive to comfort, was on historic grounds very regrettable. The whole of the interior fittings were removed, except the beams of the gallery, under which a minister's vestry was contrived, and a lobby, entered by the southern door. The northern door and the old windows were built up, and six large circular headed windows substituted. A boarded floor was introduced, and an entirely new set of fittings; the fine old oak being sold for the ridiculous price of £2 6s, and providing a small fortune for the smart London purchaser. Mr. Pool raised the entire cost, about £200; but "on after reflection was inclined to think that he shewed more zeal than knowledge in the affair." He removed to Sedbergh in 1869; thence to Shelley, near Huddersfield, in 1874; and retired invalided in 1894. His life story has been admirably told by his son, the Rev. J. J. Pool, B.D., formerly of Rheims and lately of Peckham.

The Rev. Wm. Nichols, a Lancashire College student, followed Mr. Pool in 1869. He had held a pastorate at Kendal since 1862. He is the author of a *History and Traditions of Ravenstonedale*, from which several of the above named facts are taken. During his time, in 1871, an organ was placed in the chapel. He removed to Blackford Bridge, near Bury, in 1883; whence he retired in 1899. His successor was Rev. W. M. Fell, also of Lancashire College, who had held pastorates in New Zealand, Chorley, Portland, and Puddletown (Dorset). He came in 1884, and returned to New Zealand in 1887. About this time the dwelling-house adjoining the chapel was converted into a schoolroom, the lower room being adopted for a vestry and library.

The Rev. C. Illingworth entered on the pastorate at Christmas, 1887. For five years from 1849 he had been a successful town missionary in Bradford; in 1854 he was called to the pastorate of Westfield chapel, Wyke, where he laboured efficiently for 14 years, and afterwards for two years at Queensbury, near Halifax. In 1870 he became pastor of Lendal chapel, York; where for nearly 18 years he held the esteem of all classes by his religious and philanthropic activities. On removing from York he was the recipient of a testimonial which was presented at the Guildhall by the Lord Mayor, and to which Archbishop Thomson contributed. For eleven years longer he ministered in the Westmoreland village sanctuary, during part of which time he represented the parish as district councillor and guardian of the poor. Further improvements were made in the chapel on his initiative; amongst others, the reconstruction of the bellcote at the south end of the building. A stone over the schoolroom door bears the following record :— "This chapel roof was improved, and the belfry erected, in grateful remembrance of William Carver, Esq., of Kersal, near Manchester; who was called to his home in heaven on 25th day of April, A.D. 1889." Mr. Illingworth retired in 1898, and died on 9th May, 1903, in the 81st year of his age.

The present minister, the Rev. Geo. Manning, from the Yorkshire United College, Bradford, settled within a short time of Mr. Illingworth's retirement. His ordination took place on 18th May, 1899, the officiating ministers being the Revs. C. Illingworth, B. Dale (Bradford); A. Duff, LL.D., E. Armitage, M.A., and W. C. Shearer (United College); and G. Ledbury (Kirkby Stephen). In the same month the church received from John and Thos. Carver, Esqrs., the gift of a caretaker's house, and additional land for enlarging the burial ground. Recently Miss M. S. Carver bequeathed £500 towards the support of the ministry, but it will only be available on the falling in of an existing life. In 1905 a favourable opportunity offered for disposing of the lands and buildings which constituted the old endowment; they were therefore sold, and the money advantageously invested. Further improvements are under consideration, including a new organ, and the enlargement of the schoolroom.

A large marble tablet within the chapel contains a brief summary of the foregoing history, as follows:—

TO THE GLORY OF GOD.

This chapel was built and partly endowed by Philip, fourth Lord Wharton, lord of the manor, and others, for a congregation of Protestant Dissenters worshipping in a licensed house near this site in the latter part of the 17th century. The first stated minister was the Rev. Christopher Jackson, incumbent of Crosby Garrett, one of the ejected clergy, who preached here in 1662, and after many years of successful labour was followed by a number of able and faithful ministers of the Gospel. The present manse was built by subscription in 1854 during the ministry of the Rev. W. Matheson.

In the years 1894 and -5, the chapel, school and manse were restored and beautified and were furnished with a new heating apparatus; the burial ground was enlarged and other improvements effected in the property by two of the trustees, Thomas Carver, Esq., J.P., the Hollins, Marple; and John Carver, Esq, Greystone, Ealing, in loving memory of their mother, formerly Elizabeth Airey, who was a native of Ravenstonedale.

The tablet was erected in 1895 during the pastorate of the Rev. C. Illingworth.

The following statistics may be of permanent interest :—

Baptisms, from 1839 to 1906—267.
Burials, from 1844 to 1906—69.
Church members—at reconstitution in 1838, 6; in 1879, 23; in 1906, 46.

BRYAN DALE.
T. G. CRIPPEN.

Ebenezer Church, West Bromwich

(Revised and abridged from a paper by the Rev. W. Kelly, 1893)

THE following ministers in and around West Bromwich were among those who were outed at the Restoration, or for the sake of a good conscience and loyalty to God's Word left the State Church on 24th August, 1662 :—John Reynolds, of Wolverhampton ; Richard Hinks, Tipton ; H. Oasland, M.A., Bewdley ; Richard Baxter, Kidderminster ; W. Fincher, Wednesbury ; Thos.Byrdal, M.A., Walsall ; Anthony Burgess, M.A., Sutton Coldfield ; Samuel Wills, Birmingham ; William Turton, M.A., Rowley ; Thomas Badland (often called Baldwin), Willenhall ; and Richard Hilton, of All Saints', West Bromwich.

The two last names are inseparably connected with Ebenezer. Mr. Hilton had always been a hard student, and husbanded his time with judicious care. His mind was richly stored with knowledge ; he spent much time in prayer ; and on Sundays his spiritual zeal set fire to the discourses he had prepared. He was very judicious in everything he did ; his simplicity of manner and blameless life endeared him to his hearers ; his discourses were weighty and profitable, and even the worst of men were constrained to respect him. When he was silenced and ejected from the parish church many of his attached hearers came out with him ; and these formed the first nucleus of the Nonconformist community in West Bromwich.

The first minister of the "Old Meeting," the Rev. Thos. Badland (or Baldwin), was ejected from the incumbency of Willenhall at the Restoration, and from Clent by the Act of Uniformity. Worcester was his native place, and he made his way thither. Passing through West Bromwich he met with Mr. Hilton ; and remained a while to act as minister to the faithful few who were valiant enough to resist the demands of the State, and to come out from the parish church with their pastor Mr. Hilton. Mr. Badland reached Worcester some time in 1663, and formed the first Nonconformist church in that city. The present Congregational church in Worcester was founded in 1708, and rebuilt in 1858. Close by its pulpit is a marble tablet to the memory of the "Rev. Thomas Badland, a faithful and profitable preacher of the Gospel in this

Ebenezer Church, West Bromwich

city for the space of 35 years. He rested from his labours May 5th, A.D. 1698, Aet. 64. Mors mihi vita nova."

We are unable to discover any records to shew how the Protestant Dissenters of West Bromwich got along under the intolerance and ill usage to which they were subjected. We do not know whether Mr. Hilton was minister on the departure of Mr. Badland, and if so how long his ministry continued before he went to be private chaplain to Mr. Philip Foley. The church held its meeting in a room or private house, probably the house of one of Mr. Hilton's attached friends. Nor do we know in what year the first meeting-house was built; but we find that on 23rd Dec., 1699, John Lowe bequeathed a perpetual annuity (now known as "The Holyoak") of £2 10s. towards the support of the ministry of the Old Meeting. A deed (feoffment, which we understand to be a lease and release), dated 30th and 31st March, 1714, states the uses for which the then newly erected chapel was put up. The meeting-houses of the several denominations at that time (except those of the Quakers) were usually guarded by trusts of a general character, which neither specified the sect to which they belonged nor the doctrines which were to be preached. They were secured to the congregations of "Protestant Dissenters" worshipping in that place, who were allowed to choose such person as minister as a majority might elect. The deed of the Old Meeting states that the building "was and is intended for a meeting-house for the worship and service of God, and fitted for that purpose." The trustees were fifteen in number:—John Lowe, Josiah Turton, Richard Brett, Richard Wilton, Thomas Brett, Samuel Lowe, —Turton, Bailey, Brett, John Mayo, William Silvester, Edminy Weaver, Jonathan Clare, Richard Nock the elder, Thomas Nock the younger, and Richard Nock the younger. The trustees had power to expel any of their number who became scandalous or offensive, and to fill up vacancies so caused, by expulsion, or by death, or removal from the neighbourhood, up to the number of 15. Elizabeth Jesson appears to have given the land for the meeting-house, and the building was raised by subscription. We suppose this was the building referred to in Reeve's *History*, in which we are told that a lawless mob set fire to the Dissenters' meeting-house in 1715; and that a young man in the act of unroofing it was killed by slugs from Cornet Lowe's blunderbuss. For about a year the building lay in ruins, but was rebuilt by the Government in 1716.

Nine years after the rebuilding the Rev. Richard Wilton, M.A., was called to the pastorate; and for 40 years he preached the Gospel by lip and life, and with his people was a living protest against the interference of the State in matters of belief or modes of worship. As years enfeebled his strength he was obliged to find an assistant, in the person of the Rev. William Howell, who succeeded him in the full pastorate of the church in 1765. His ashes lie in the old portion of Ebenezer churchyard, close to the scene of his long and faithful work; the tomb is inscribed as follows:—" Here lie the remains of Richard Wilton, M.A., forty years pastor of this church. Justly esteemed and beloved for his cheerful and unaffected piety, his inflexible integrity, his open and benevolent temper, his faithfulness and zeal in the service of his Divine Master. He died Dec. 28th, 1765, aged 82 years."

In the same year two sacramental cups of hammered silver were presented to the church; they bear the following inscription:— " The gift of Elizabeth Brett, for the use of the Protestant Dissenting Society at West Bromwich, Staffordshire, 1765."

The Rev. W. Howell was sole minister from 1765 to 1776, in which year he passed behind the veil. For some unexplained reason he was buried in All Saints' churchyard. The only note we have seen respecting him is that on 15th March, 1752, he preached the funeral sermon of Mrs. S. Savage, taking as his text Daniel ii. 13. This Mrs. Savage was mother-in-law to the Rev. R. Wilton, and sister to the celebrated commentator, the Rev. Matthew Henry.

The four ministers who successively followed at the Old Meeting were the Revs. Joseph Ross, W. Robins, John Humphries, and — Braybrook. Little is known of them here beyond their names, which may perhaps be accounted for by the fact that the average length of their respective pastorates was only two years.[1] Whether the last of the four, Mr. Braybrook, removed or died is not clear; but in 1785 the Rev. G. Osborne was chosen to succeed him. It was placed on record that " having received a learned education with a view to the Christian ministry, he entered on the office of pastor to the Dissenting church at West Bromwich in the year 1785, from whence he removed to Worcester in the year 1792. He was highly esteemed as a preacher; his discourses were truly serious, judicious, and evangelical, calculated by their affectionate faithfulness to edify and improve all classes of his hearers. As a tutor he was eminently distinguished, and rendered highly useful to his pupils by his classical attainments and general knowledge, and by his unceasing anxiety to promote their interests. Blessed with a warm and benevolent heart, he entered at all times into every case of charity, with a generosity that will long be remembered by the poor. He had the honour to be one of the first promoters of Sunday schools (founded by Robert Raikes in 1780-81), and by the exercise of the most ardent zeal in that good work was the happy means of stimulating those exertions which have raised these institutions to their present high state of excellence and usefulness."

In 1793 the Rev. Mr. McGeorge was asked from Wolverhampton

---

[1] Mr. Humphries, removing to London, was for 35 years pastor of the Pilgrim Fathers' Church, which in his time removed from Deadman's Place to Union Street, Southwark; and was afterwards master of Mill Hill grammar school.

to take the oversight of the church. A scrap of paper in the Ebenezer safe, bearing the following memorandum, is the only record we have of Mr. McGeorge:—

"Journey to Worcester.

Walked to Birmingham			Hostler	...	0 1	No Dinner	...	0 0
Breakfast	...	0 6	Tea	...	0 8	Tea	...	0 6
Hostler	...	0 3	Turnpike	...	0 3	Coach	...	2 0
Horse Hire	...	12 0	Horse at Worcester		1 6	Coachman	...	0 3
Dinner	...	1 0	Breakfast	...	0 8	Mr. McGeorge's		
Wine	...	0 7½	Porter	...	0 2½	Expenses to	£1 1 4."	
Horse	...	0 7	Turnpike	...	0 3	Worcester		

At a church meeting on Wednesday, 4th March, 1794, the Rev. John Berry, "of Rumsey, was asked to become pastor at a salary of 70£ a year, which is 10£ more than has hitherto been raised for the minister of this place." Mr. Berry accepted the position, and laboured here from 1794 till 1797. On 13th January, 1796, John Addington and Bailey Brett made application to the clerk of Stafford County Court to have licensed "a House in the parish of West Bromwich, on the side of the road leading from West Bromwich Heath to Hill Top, and intended to be used as a place of meeting for Protestant Dissenters from the Church of England." At this time the Old Meeting was still described as "Presbyterian."

Mr. Berry was succeeded in 1797 by the Rev. Joel Maurice, of Stretton-under-Fosse, who was a man of grave and judicial character, an instructive and evangelical preacher, and well acquainted with Puritan theology. He died on 26th December, 1807; and a monument in Ebenezer churchyard marks the resting place of his dust. It bears the following inscription:—

"Sacred to the memory of the Rev. Joel Maurice, late Pastor of this Congregation, and also for upwards of 30 years over a numerous congregation at Stretton-under-Fosse, Warwickshire, where his labours will be remembered by many with affection and gratitude. Having borne honourable testimony to his Master's cause for a period of nearly 50 years, he could with truth exclaim in the words of the Apostle, II Tim. iv. chap. 7 & 8 verses (being the last from which he preached). He died Dec. 26th, 1807, in his 70th year."

On 24th April, 1807, at the age of 86, there passed away another notable personage, Mrs. Esther Bulkley, who was granddaughter to the celebrated commentator Matthew Henry. Before her death she gave her grandfather's *Exposition of the Old and New Testament*, in five large volumes, to the church, to be under the care of the pastor for the time being. Four of these volumes are in a good state of preservation in the Ebenezer safe.

In 1808 the Rev. James Cooper, born at Walsall, educated at Rotherham College, and for a short time minister at Wirksworth in Derbyshire, was chosen to fill the vacancy. His work was much

Ebenezer Church, West Bromwich

blessed ; and mainly through his exertions the old chapel, now too small for the purpose required, and dilapidated by over a century of use and abuse, was superseded by a more capacious and imposing structure—that which was afterwards for many years occupied by the schools. (The old chapel, it may be remarked, was where the caretaker's house now stands). The cost of the new building was £800. Mr. Cooper, after a ministry of 20 years, removed to another charge in 1829, and died at Norwich 27th May, 1863. In 1830 his place was filled by the Rev. W. Forster, who removed to London in 1834.

The Rev. Jas. C. Gallaway, M.A., a young man fresh from Highbury college, began his ministry in October, 1834 ; and during his nine years' stay great blessing and prosperity attended the Old Meeting. A remarkable religious awakening took place in 1840 ; the church grew, and a larger and more convenient sanctuary was erected, at a cost of £2,400, by the side of the present schools. For this purpose a piece of land measuring 33 by 24 yards was bought of Mr. Jesson. To the new building the name " Ebenezer" was assigned. Mr. Gallaway relinquished his charge in 1843, and became pastor at St. John's, New Brunswick (N. America). On his return to England he became the honoured and devoted secretary of the Chapel Building Society. His last years were spent on the spot endeared to him by the memories of his early ministry ; on 16th September, 1886, he " fell asleep," and his ashes lie peacefully under the shadow of the sanctuary he had built for God. In 1839 Mr. Gallaway received into the church a young man who was destined to take no small share in its Christian work. This was Mr. John Eld, who in 1841 was elected to the diaconate, and served in that capacity for above 50 years. He was for many years superintendent of the early morning adult school.

The Rev. William Henry Dyer was chosen to succeed Mr. Gallaway, and began his ministry in December, 1843. He was a man of grave disposition, of much logical and analytical power. On 28th April, 1853, he removed to Bath to fill the place vacated by the death of the Rev. Wm. Jay. He subsequently (1875) relinquished the ministry and became a barrister.

The pulpit was not long unoccupied, for in July, 1853, the church found a fit successor in the Rev. Wm. Cuthbertson, B.A., then a student at Spring Hill College, Birmingham. Mr. Cuthbertson commanded good congregations till his departure for Australia in 1856. He subsequently held pastorates at Bishop Stortford, and at Markham Square, London ; and was chairman of the Congregational Union of England and Wales in 1879. Crossing the Atlantic in 1882, he ministered successfully at Chicago, and at Woodstock, Canada ; and in 1891 returned to West Bromwich as pastor of the High Street Congregational church. In 1902 he removed to Dawlish, in South Devon. Mr. Cuthbertson was the first minister for many years who had taken office at Ebenezer, or the Old Meeting, without signing a " declaration of faith."

The Rev. John Whewell, of Belper, was chosen pastor in February, 1857. During the 11½ years of his ministry 126 members were received, a few by transfer, but mostly on profession of faith. It is on record that Mr. Whewell presided over 140 church meetings, "and in all the church's proceedings there was not a discordant note." In 1863 a dispute between the trustees and a neighbouring proprietor over damage done by mining operations was settled by arbitration ; the trustees received £229 10s. for encroachment, and £739 3s. 1d. for damage. Needful repairs to chapel and schools were effected, and a new organ was introduced. The total cost of repairs and improvements was £1,047 11s. 4d. The chapel was reopened in May, 1864, the opening sermons being preached by the Rev. J. C. Gallaway ; and at a subsequent meeting three of the old pastors—Messrs. Gallaway, Dyer, and Cuthbertson—were present. In October, 1868, Mr. Whewell removed to Coventry, and afterwards left the ministry.

The Rev. H. Luckett, of Gainsborough, was the next pastor. His ministry began 24th January, 1869. The early morning adult school was commenced on 17th April, 1870. This did excellent work for many years ; and as many as 640 men have been known to meet for instruction at 7.30 on a Sunday morning. The Pleasant Sunday Afternoon movement, which has been found singularly useful in many places, was initiated by Mr. John Blackham—one of the deacons—in 1875. Mr. Luckett returned to his former charge at Gainsborough at the end of 1877.

In September, 1878, the Rev. James Bainton, of Bideford, was called to the pastorate. Pew rents were abolished in January, 1880, and the church's finances improved under the weekly offertory system. In the year 1884 as many as 90 members were added to the church, largely as the result of two special evangelistic missions which were held in April and December. On 1st January, 1886, a testimonial was presented to Mr. Timothy Hartland on his retirement from the post of choirmaster, which he had held for the long term of 50 years. Mr. Bainton resigned on 12th September, 1886, having accepted a call to Heywood, Manchester.

The Rev. W. Kelly, a student from New College, London, was invited to succeed him. His ordination took place on 30th March, 1887. The Rev. C. A. Berry, D.D., of Wolverhampton, offered the ordination prayer ; the Rev. S. Newth, D.D., of New College, delivered the charge ; and eight neighbouring ministers participated in the service. The school building being out of repair, and condemned by the authorities as unfit for teaching purposes, was replaced at a cost of £1,600. Mr. Kelly removed to Sheffield in 1893 ; and was succeeded the following year by the present pastor, the Rev. O. L. Morris, from the college at Brecon.

Puritans and Presbyterians in the Channel Islands

A very short paper on this subject, by E. le Brun, Esq., of Jersey, appeared in *Transactions*, vol. I., pp. 406-7. The following somewhat fuller memoir, by the same esteemed contributor, has additional interest as the author's legacy to our Society; having been written within two months of his lamented death, which took place in July of last year.

SITUATED between two great nations, and enjoying their own free institutions, the Channel Islands have been for centuries a place of refuge for religious and political exiles. Many illustrious personages have found a shelter there.

It is very possible that some of the Lollards and followers of Wycliffe came to the islands and prepared the way for the Reformation. In 1547, Daniel le Vair, Martin Langlois and Thomas Johanne, came from France and preached the Reformation. In Jersey the gentry seem to have become generally favourable, and it was easily established. In Guernsey it was not received so easily, some of the leading families remaining for a time faithful to their ancient faith.

During the reign of Queen Mary Catholicism was of course re-established, and two women were burnt in Guernsey; but on the accession of Elizabeth in 1558 the Reformation movement was continued. In 1563 William Marise, Seigneur de la Ripeaudière, came from Anjou to Jersey, and organised a church in St. Helier according to the

Genevan form, and the leading families gathered around him. In Guernsey William Beauvoir, a distinguished native, who had fled to Geneva during the reign of Queen Mary, obtained from Calvin the minister Nicolas Baudoin, who is described as an able and learned divine. He established a church at St. Peter's Port on the Genevan or Presbyterian plan.

Helier de Carteret, head of the most distinguished family in the Channel Islands, went to Queen Elizabeth and solicited the official permission to establish churches organized according to the form used in France and Geneva. As French was then the only language generally known in the islands, it was desirable to obtain a French minister, duly qualified. De Carteret succeeded, and obtained in August, 1565, orders in council authorizing the establishment at St. Helier in Jersey, and at St. Peter's Port in Guernsey, of churches with preaching and organisation similar to those of the French church in London; but it was ordered that in the country parishes of both islands the prayer book and forms of the Church of England were to be followed. But the churches in the towns being settled with able ministers, it was to be expected that their example and influence would prevail. In fact, so it did; and the governors of the islands and other authorities supported the Puritan and Presbyterian discipline.

Already on June 28th, 1564, a synod composed of representatives from all the islands was held in Guernsey, and a full organisation existed. Afterwards these synods were held regularly; yet perhaps some divergence of opinion existed on one point, for the celebrated Cartwright and Snape were invited to come and give their advice. They came in 1576 and remained about one year. Snape resided in Jersey and became chaplain of the governor. Cartwright resided at Castle Cornet, in Guernsey, and served as chaplain of the governor of that island. They were present at the synod held that year and helped probably to complete the organisation of the churches. Twenty years later Cartwright revisited Guernsey, and spent about two years in that retirement.

This state of things continued during the reign of Queen Elizabeth. At the beginning of the reign of James I. some disputes arose in Jersey, and the then governor, Sir John Peyton, took advantage of it to favour the Church of England. After some years of struggle an episcopal dean was named; he was an Italian by birth, but had married an English lady. In 1623 a code of ecclesiastical canons for Jersey was sanctioned by the king in council, and these are still the law. In these remain some traces of Presbyterian times.

In Guernsey Presbyterianism remained until the restoration of the Stuarts. The first episcopal dean was named in 1662; a number of ministers refused to conform: Le Marchant, Perchard, Morehead, De la Marche, Herivel refused. The first was imprisoned in Castle Cornet and afterwards in the Tower of London. The dean met so much opposition that he asked the aid of a company of soldiers, and the churches were deserted.

A great opposition seems to have been made both in Jersey and Guernsey to the prayer book and the episcopal forms. It is only from the middle of the nineteenth century that some of the particular usage, vestments, and words have been introduced into Jersey.

A thoroughly good and trustworthy history of those times, 1540—1670, would be desirable. The leading facts are known, and various authors have given accounts of them; but they are all incomplete, and the original sources of information are difficult to reach.

From the gleanings of a rather extensive literature a fair and interesting history can be compiled. The historians of Jersey and Guernsey, particularly Le Quesne's *Constitutional History of Jersey* and Tapper's *History of Guernsey*—these two are trustworthy guides as far as they go. Lelievre in his *Historie du Methodisme dans les Îles de la Manche* has also written a very interesting account.

As to the original documents I will name only a few:—*Le Registre des Collogues des Eglises de Guernesey*, MS. in Guille-Alles, Guernsey. *Le Registre des Collogues de Jersey*, MS. in the library at Cambridge. *La Discipline Ecclesiastique*, revised in 1597, was printed in 1885; a MS. of the *Discipline* is in the Bibliothèque de l'Arsenal, Paris. *Les Chroniques de Jersey*, an old MS. printed in 1832 and 1858. Probably some documents might be found at the British Museum, or in the Bodleian. The public and the ecclesiastical records of the several islands could also be searched. I must also mention Peter Heylin's *Full Relation of Two Journeys*, the one into the main land of France, the other into some of the adjacent islands: London, 1656.

E. LE BRUN.

Jersey, May, 1906.

Some Penry Dates

IT is not clear where Waldegrave first set up his secret press, after his gear was seized on April 16th, 1588, during the printing of Udall's *Diotrephes*. The case of type which he smuggled away to Mrs. Crane's house in Aldermary he apparently left there till about midsummer, when he removed it to Molesey. But in April, towards the end of the month, he printed Penry's *Exhortation vnto the Gouernours and people ... of Wales*. This, in its first edition, is a pamphlet of 66 pp., and contains no reference to R. Some's *Godly Treatise*. Some's work, in its first form, is dated May 6th, and perhaps issued from the press a week later. But a second edition of Penry's *Exhortation* has now been discovered by Sir John Williams, Bart., (see *Transactions*, Oct. 1906), containing the statement: "Master D Somes booke was published this day"; the date of which we can therefore fix with sufficient exactness. A third edition followed. It consists of the original *Exhortation* "set downe ...word for word as it was in the former impressiō," but now printed in a smaller type and occupying only 40 pp. It is followed by an addendum, in which Penry argues syllogistically, that they can be no true "ministers at all, good or bad, to whom the Lord neuer said go and preach: Matt. 28. 18. 19." This finishes on p. 65 and is signed IOHN PENRI. Then follows: "To the Reader. I haue read Master D. Somes booke, the reasons he vseth in the questions of the dumb ministerie. . . . . . The weaknes of his reasons, shalbe shewed at large God willing....." In fulfilment of this promise, when Waldegrave set up his press at Mrs. Crane's house at Molesey about the end of June, he printed for Penry *A Defence of that which hath bin written*. This has apparently only come down to us in a mutilated form, without title page, and without the invariable introductory "epistle," which would have occupied sig. A i.-iv. The signatures run regularly B to I in fours, and the leaves are paged 1-63. The tract ends: "Thus M. Some I haue run through those points in your book that concerned me."

The appearance of the *Defence* compelled Some to issue a second edition of his *Godly Treatise*, containing a supplement, dated Sept. 19th, 1588, replying to Penry's arguments; chiefly as stated in the *Defence*, but with references also to the *Exhortation*.

Penry's next work was *A View of some part of such publike wants*, &c., which Waldegrave printed on the Marprelate press, when it was lodged at the house of John Hales at Coventry. From Henry Sharpe's evidence we learn that it was in circulation before March 9th, 1588-9. It was always known contemporaneously as *The Supplication* from its running headline: "A Supplication vnto the High Covrt of Parliament."

WM. PIERCE.

The Taunton Communion Plate

BY the courtesy of the pastor and deacons of Paul's Meeting, Taunton, we are enabled to present a print of the old and highly prized communion plate belonging to that church. The flagons are comparatively modern, and are not specially noteworthy; but the cups are of much historic interest. The tall cup, of ecclesiastical pattern, is traditionally reported to have belonged to the Rev. George Newton, the ejected vicar of St. Mary Magdalene's, and first pastor of a Nonconformist fellowship in Taunton. The central cup with handles, bearing a chased figure of a bird, is believed to have been presented by Rollin Mallock, Esq., by whom the site of the meetinghouse was also given to the congregation in 1668. The other two cups of similar form were given, about 1713, by John and Elizabeth Coles. The two outermost, of a more modern shape, were presented in 1751. We have not been furnished with particulars as to size, weight, or hall marks; except as to the cup inscribed "The gift of John Coles to Taunton Church." This, the second from the right hand, is $4\frac{3}{8}$ inches broad at the top, $2\frac{3}{4}$ broad at the bottom, and $3\frac{1}{2}$ inches high; the date mark is 1689.

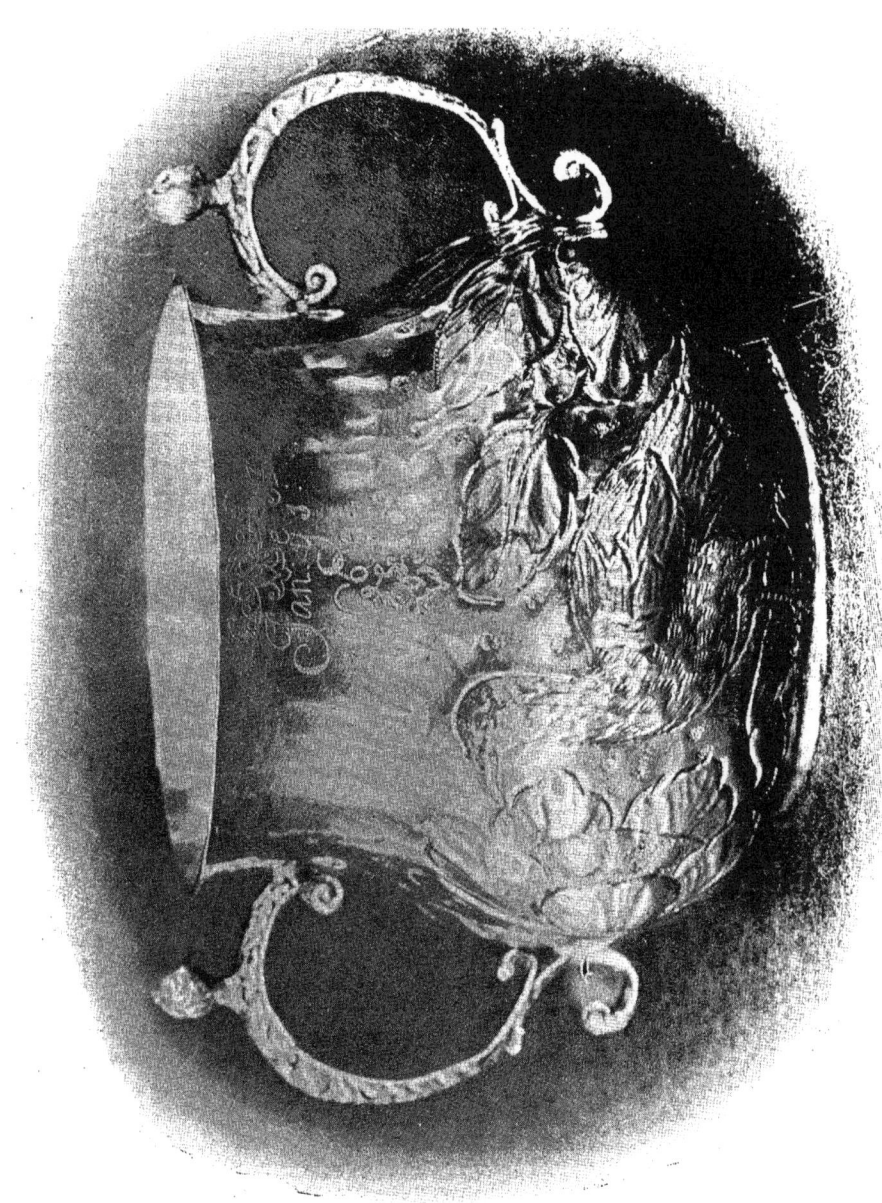

TAUNTON COMMUNION PLATE—THE MALLOCK CUP.

THE TAUNTON COMMUNION PLATE.

Bury Street Chapel

The following is an exact transcript of a MS. in the possession of C. W. Toms, Esq., of Putney, treasurer of the Bury Street Trust :—

AN ACCOUNT OF Yᴱ TRANSACTIONS THAT RELATE TO Yᴱ BUILDING OF Yᴱ NEW-MEETING-HOUSE IN BURY-STREET, & OF Yᴱ METHOD OF DISPOSING OF THE PEWS & PLACES.

Upon yᵉ Report made by Mr Humphrey Stevenson, one of the Deacons of yᵉ Church, that there was a peece of Ground in Bury-street proper to build a Meeting-house. The Members of yᵉ Church after some Consultations there[upon] subscribed about 300£ toward the building

Some of yᵉ Members being deputed agreed with Mr Charles Great for ground to build a meetinghouse on part of his garden in Burystreet (*viz*) 40 foot front & 50 foot deep, at 20£ per an. ground rent, for a lease of 50 years. The Trustees named in yᵉ Writings were these 9, Mr I. Watts yᵉ Pastor for yᵉ time being, Mr Wm Pickard, Mr Danl Scott, Mr Humfrey Stevenson, Deacons; Mr Thomas Pickard, Mr Jonathan Joyner, Mr Nathanaell Barton, Mr Andrew Holts, & Mr Thomas Hort.

Thro the great Care of our Deacons Mr Danll Scott & Mr Humfrey Stevenson yᵉ Meetinghouse was built very conveniently & finished by Michaelmas 1708. & thro yᵉ Skill & Integrity of Mr H Stevenson who assisted Mr Andrews yᵉ Undertaker in this Work, The whole Charge amounted to no more than 650£ : which was gratefully acknowledged by yᵉ Pastor & the Church.

Generall Notice was giv'n to all yᵉ Members of ye C[hurch] yᵗ had subscrib'd 10£ and upwards towards yᵉ Meetinghouse [that] they were desir'd to meet together att Amsterdam Coffee-house Thursday Sept. 23ᵈ att 5 in yᵉ afternoon to agree upon a method for yᵉ disposing of Pews and Places.

Note. There were 8 Persons present : Of wᶜʰ Number 4 were yᵉ

Deacons of y⁰ Church & 5 of them were Trustees for y⁰ Meeting-house, who according to y⁰ Original agreem⁺ of y⁰ Subscribers are capable of determining all affairs relating thereto.

Agreed without any Contradiction on all y⁰ Articles following. (*viz.*)

1. That y⁰ great Design of their Subscription being for y⁰ conveniency [&] Increase of y⁰ Church, and Encouragemt. of Hearers, they would not insist upon ingrossing so many Seats as their Subscriptions will purchase according to any proposed Rates.

   Another Reason of this Agreemt was y⁺ there might be [a] great Number of Seats left for others to purchase in order [to] defray y⁰ remaining Charge of y⁰ Building.

2. That each Person chuse their Seats in [*MS. mutilated and illegible*] their Subscriptions. And among those who have subscrib'd equal The Elder Members of y⁰ Church chuse first.

   The Reason of this Article was y⁺ after all other M[ethods] of chusing had been propos'd they could find none y⁺ would give less Offence than this.

3. That all who have subscrib'd 20£ have 4 Seats assign'd them wheresoever [they] chuse. And if any of them have more than 4 persons in their present family they shall have One or 2 Seats more according to y⁰ number of the family.

   The Reason of this was because most of those y⁺ subscrib'd 20£ had but small familys, and they were not willing to give themselves y⁰ liberty of possessing Seats to admitt their Friends into, y⁺ so others might not expect it. And they hoped this Self-denying Agreemt. of theirs would prevent all y⁰ lesser Subscribers from complaining of these Rules.

4. That Every Subscriber have their Household Servants accomodated with Seats. (*viz*) The Apprentices in y⁰ 3ᵈ Rank of Gallerys nearest y⁰ Pullpit, The Maid Servants in y⁰ Same Rank nearest y⁰ Doors.

   The Reason is because y⁰ Apprentices are esteem'd [to be] in a Station above others, & y⁰ Subscribers would willi[ngly] have all their Servants encouraged to hear y⁰ Word.

[5] That the Places assign'd to Subscribers [&] Purchasers be register'd thus (*viz.*) The use of one or m[ore] Places in a particular Seat made over to them for their Conveniency in public Worship during their personall attendance there: And if they Dye [or] absent themselves longer than six

months their Interests therein to be void, & those places to fall into yͤ hands of yͤ Trustees.

There appear'd to be Great Reason for such an Article as this, Because where yͤ Seats themselves have been made over to any Persons, they have sometimes become troublesome afterwards, and pretended a Claim to yͤ Boards & Materials, & to yͤ Spott of Ground on wᶜʰ yͤ Seats stood. And where yͤ meer Use of a Seat has been made over to them without any limitation of yͤ Time of their Life or personall Attendance, they have given it away to Successors, or sold it as they please to persons yᵗ wᵈ be Injurious to yͤ Church. And yͤ Church could never reap further Benefitt thereby.

[6] That Whosoever has any place or places assign'd to them in a Seat yᵗ has more places in it than they possess, shall be willing to admitt other Subscribers or Purchasers into yͤ Same Seat; Unless they please to purchase those vacant places themselves.

The Reason [is] because 'twas Impossible to Contrive [the?] Seats So as just to suit yͤ Number of every Family. Yet if any Family of yͤ Subscribers or others desired more places than they us'd att present, they should have yͤ Liberty of purchasing for themselves a Seat without admitting other Company.

[7] That yͤ Several Members of yͤ Church in low Circumstances who are not capeable of purchasing, Some who are aged or honourable & others of meaner Character shall have places assign'd them gratis suited to yͤ Respect due to them.

[8] That Saturday Sept 25th att 2 afternoon all yͤ Subscribers of 10£ and upwards be summon'd to meet att yͤ Meeting-place & agree upon yͤ Several Seats and Places they desire to be assign'd to them according to yͤ foregoing Rules.

Accordingly on Saturday they mett and such places as they chose were appointed to them.

Agreed then yᵗ Wednesday afternoon Sept 29 yͤ Rest of yͤ Church who have subscrib'd less than 10£ meet and have places assign'd them according to yͤ foregoing Rules. But if any of those Subscribers desire places yᵗ are more in Number & more valuable than their Subscription amounts to, they may add to their Subscriptions & so may purchase what places they please before yͤ Rest of yͤ Church or Hearers are [ad]mitted to purchase.

Accordingly they mett and fixed upon several places wᶜʰ were register'd as theirs.

Because several yᵗ are not Members but constantly attend on yͤ Ministry of our Church desire to purchase places for themselves, it was agreed yt on Tuesday afternoon Octr 5th yᵉ rest of yᵉ Church yt are not provided of places meet together & yᵉ Deacons & Trustees of yᵉ Meeting-place will attend there to dispose of Seats to them before others are admitted to purchase. Public Notice was given of this to yᵉ Church just after yᵉ Evening Worship, Octor 3d.

Agreed also yt whereas yᵉ Building of a Convenient place for worship was judged necessary for yᵉ Church, and yᵉ Mony rais'd by Subscription wd scarce defray above half yᵉ Charge, All yᵉ Members of yᵉ Church should be putt in mind of this Expense, & should be earnestly exhorted to assist yᵉ Paymt. of yᵉ Remainder by purchasing places for themselves & familys according to yᵉ necessary Rates agreed on by yᵉ Trustees; or att lest to do towards it what their Circumstances will admitt off. But those who are not able to give anything shall have places assign'd them as before agreed.

These agreements were putt in practice, & several members of [yᵉ] Church procured places for themselves accordingly.

After this there was private Notice given to those of the Church yt were in meaner Circumstances, that if they pleased to attend at thee Meeting-house on a day appointed, they should have places assigned to them gratis.

After yᵉ Members of the Church were fixed in seats, there was publick notice Given on two severall Lords-days to yᵉ Auditory, that there would be attendance given on days appointed to dispose of Places to them for their Accommodation in publick worship: And severall of the Hearers came accordingly & purchased places for themselves & familys.

Agreed by yᵉ Trustees, that whatsoever alteration for Conveniency or Ornament any persons made in the Seats they had purchased, should be entirely at their own Expense. And that no Such Alteration should be made as might Deface the present form of the pews without particular permission of the Trustees.

Jan: 30th 1709/10 Mr John Rolleston & Mr William Theed were chosen Trustees in the Room of Mr Wm Pickard & Mr Jonathan Joyner Deceased.

Whereas the Debt remaining for yᵉ Building was Considerable, The members of yᵉ Church had lately Subscribed anew, & most of them had [paid] their Subscriptions, & reduced the Debt to Sixty or Seventy pounds. The new Subscribers were desired to chuse for themselves each a place or two more for themselves or familys if they pleased, ffriday Feb 18th: wch was done.

Agreed by yᵉ Trustees, that whereas they were forced at first to rate the Seats at a little higher price in order to diminish the debt (tho' the prices were lower than in most New meeting-houses), Yet now the payment is almost finished, they think it equally necessary for the Encouragement of the Auditory to sink yᵉ prices of the

Seats : & have reason to believe y^t the Church or ye auditory will not take it amiss, Since The Trustees themselves have been The Chief Subscribers, & at far more Expense than their Seats would have been at the highest rates : & since those y^t have bought places before have now enjoyed them almost a year & a half.

It was also desired that ye Members of ye Church that woud provide themselves of new or more places according to ye lower prices would attend on ffriday Feb 10th. Which was done.

Agreed that public Notice should be given to the Auditory that ye Trustees had rated ye seats at lower prices, & that there would be attendance given to accommodate them. This Notice [was given pub]lickly after Sermon Lds day May 14th 1710, & attendance Tuesday afternoon for this purpose.

Note, in ye Conveyance of a property in these seats to the Subscribers or purchasers, the form is this—(*viz*)

That the use of one or more places in a particular seat is assigned to them for their conveniency in public worship during their personall attendance there. And if they dye or Absent themselves above 6 months, their interest therein to be Void, & fall into ye hands of ye Trustees.

Jany : 30th : 1709/10   The Rates now Sett on ye Pews are
In the Ground-floor.

(*Names cancelled in the MS. are indicated by square brackets [thus].*—ED.)

Numb.	Places	Price		Numb.	Places	Price	
1	6	15s. 0d	Mrs Styleman Mrs Snook Mr Jno King. 1. Mr Hawes family	9	6	25.	Mrs Han. Westall [Mr Causton 2] [Mr More] [Mr Bingham 2] Mr Wm Towle 3
2	6	15.	Mr Hackshaw. 2.				
3	6	17.6	[Mr Wm Ashburn] [Mrs M. Veale] Mr Hawes family	10	6	25.	[Mrs Joyner. 2] [Mrs Fitzwilliams 2] [Mrs Claridg] Mrs M Charleton Mr Sanderson 2. Mrs Foster 1
4	6	17.6	Mr Hackshaw 2. [Hanna Bur] [Mr Hawes 3] Mrs Moore & Mrs FitzWilliams Mr Streafield with No. 6	11	5	30	[Mr Hinks 1] [Mr Nat ffield 2] [Mr ffeilde Isaac] [Mr Wm ffeilden and the other place att Mr Hincks decease] Wm Wood [Mr Page 2] *Something illegible.*
5	6	20.0	Mrs Holman. Mr Tingey. 2. Mrs Bridgwater. Mrs Veale. Mrs Pankhurst. 1.				
6	6	20.	Mrs Budgen [Mrs Panckhurst] Mr Streatfield & Family	12	6	30.	[Mrs Berry] [Mr Collet 2] [Cap. Fry 2] Mr Boddicott 1, Mrs Morsen 1.
7	6	22.6	W Fyfe.1 : Mary Wickam 1				
8	6	22.6	Mr Hilton. 3. Mr Hilton 1				

Bury Street Chapel

Numb.	Places	Price	
13.	6	35.	Mrs Abigl Hawksworth 1, Mr Hoole 2, Mr Bently 2, Mrs Ann Brown 1.
14.	6	35.	[Mrs Great] [Mrs Edwards 2] [Mrs Powell.] [Mrs Sharp 1] Mrs Price. Dr Porter 2 [Mr Roffey 2] Mr Wagner 2
15	4		[Mr Bernard] Mrs Atwood Mr Bates [Mrs Abney 2] [Mr Feast 1]
16	4	40.	Mrs Gerrard. Mr Basnets family
17	4	40.	[Mrs Loaves 2] Mrs Feast 1 Mr Gishurst 3. all
18	4	40.	Mr Bellamy 2
19	4	40.	Mr Pickard 4
20	4	40.	Mrs Hazell 4
21	4	40.	Mr Pickard 4. Lady Abney 2 in Mr Pickards seat
22	4	40.	[Mrs Charleton] [Mr Skinner 3] Mrs Mason
23	4	40.	[Madm Harris] 4 Mr Smith &c.
24	4	40.	Mrs Byfield [Mrs Bellingham 2] [Mrs Heath] Mrs Smith Mrs Woodward. Mrs Bullom. Mrs Gerrard Mrs Brown
25	4	40.	Mrs. Ellicott
26	4	40.	Illegible. Mrs Chaukley Mrs Lewis. Mrs Lewin Mrs Woodward. Mrs Bullock, Mrs Gerrard, Mrs Brown.
27		40.	[Mr Watts senr 2] [Dr Chancy] [Mrs Steers] Mr Grub
28	7	40.	[Mr Barton senr 5] [Mrs Fleetwood 2] Mr Sadler 1, Mr Morrison 2
28†			Mr Roffey
29	8	40.	Sr John Hartopp 6. Mrs Gould 1, Mr Fleetwood 1
30	5	30.	[Mr T Pickard jnor 2] [Mrs Brett 3] Mr Fields family
31	6	35.	[Mrs Winnock senr 4] [Mr Winnock 2] Mrs Hannah Pettitt, Mr Fields family 4. Mr Hort 2
32	5	25.	[Mrs Blount 2] [Mrs Ouldham 1] [Mr Gouldsmith 1] [Mr Watts 2. Mr Causton 2
33	6	30.	[Mr Stevenson 2] [Mrs Harris 1] Mrs Bosworth 1. Mrs Jacobson 2. Mrs Ashurst 1. Mrs Abney 1.
34	5	20.	
35	6	25.	Mr ffrance
36	6	25.	[Mrs Wilson] [Mr Terry's Servt] Mrs Lamb Mrs Fyfe Mr Parish's family
37	7	30.	Mrs Watts. Mrs Bassnett 2. Mr Scott. Mrs Planner 2 Mrs Gill
38	6	20).	[Mrs Palmer] Mr Dix family
39	7	25.	Mrs Tull 2. Osmond 1

THE TABLE

	16	40.	Mr Rolleston, Mr Theed Mr Scott, Mr Terry, Mr Warner, Mr Durvill, [Mr Cooper], Mr Stevenson. Mr Hazell. Mr Bosworth Mr Vanderplank

IN THE GALLERY

Numb.	Places	Price	
1	5	7.6	Eliz Knowles
2	5	7.6	
3	5	12 6	[Mrs Wint 3]
4	5	12 6	Mrs Hogsflesh
5	5	17.6	Mr North 1, Mr Parker 1
6	5	17.6	Mrs Hogsflesh 2, Mr Clod? 2 Mrs Biggs 1
7	6	40.	Mr Gough 2 [Mr Beazley 2] [Mr Stone 3] Mr Porter & Family
8	6	40.	Mrs Rolleston 5. Mrs Hopkins. Mr Sherwin 2
9	7	30.	[Mrs Arnold] [Mrs Ruck] [Mr J Bowes] [Henry Elgin] Illegible. Mr Woodcock 2 Mr Brackstones 2
10	7	30.	[Mr Bowes 2] [Mr Saml Bowes] Mr Wm Tong [Mr Dent] Mr T Crisp 1. [Mr Bates] [Mr Pugh] [J Ellicott Junr 1] [Mr Pettit 2] Mr Brown 2 Mr Berry 1
11.	7.	15-	Mrs Jones 1 Mr Weed 1
12.	7.	15-	Mr Scot 1
13.	7.	10-	
14.	7.	10-	
15.	6.	12.6	[Mrs Ann Denman] illegible.
16	6.	12.6	
17	6.	17.6	Mrs Ann Denman 1 Mrs Owen 1. Chapman 1, Edmonds 1
18.	6	17.6	[Mr Hort 2] [Mr Smith 2] Mr Dix 2. Mr Ward 1
19	7	35.-	[Mr Lamb 3] [Mr Sanchey] [Mr Streatfield 2] [Mr Porter 2] Mr Bingham 2. Mrs Hayter 1 Mr H Crisp 1. Mrs Marcrof(?) 1 Mrs Miller 1
20	7	35.-	Mr Scott. 3 [Mr Theed 3] [Mr Wm Watts] dec. Mr Ashburn 2
21	8	40-	[Mrs War.... 2] [Mrs Stevenson] [Mr Leal] illegible [Mrs M Win] Mr Watmore 3 [Mr Sage 2] [Mr Roffey] Mr Roberts 1 Mr Twells 1
22	8	40-	[Mr Bart—the rest illegible]
23	7	20-	Mr Fitzwilliams. Mr Burl
24	7	20.	[Mr Holt 4] Mr Norris 2 Mr Steene 1
25	7	15-	
26	7	15	[Mr N. Field 2]

Bury Street Chapel

The arrangement will be clearly understood from the annexed plans, which are reproduced from the MS.

Sir John Hartopp's pew was No. 29, Lady Abney's No. 21, Dr. Chauncey's No. 27, and Mr. Terry (the aged ejected minister) sat in the table pew.

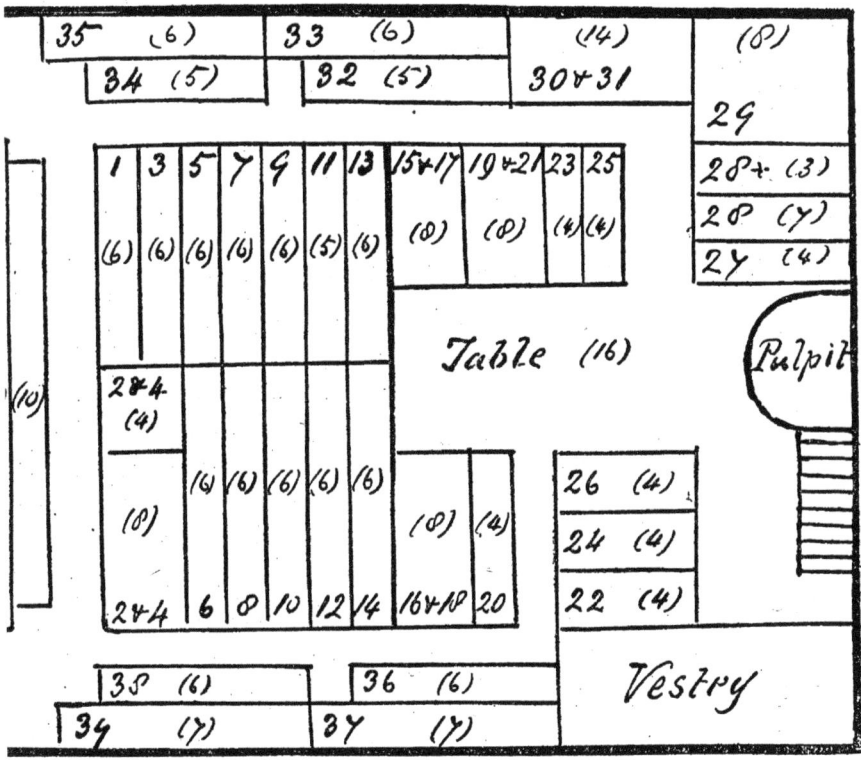

PLAN OF GROUND FLOOR, BURY STREET MEETING HOUSE, 1708

Plan of Gallery, Bury Street Meeting House, 1708

The following memoranda, in a similar but smaller handwriting, and evidently at a later date, are written on a blank page of the original document :—

Lease date 28 April 1708 from 25 March 1708 for 50½ years. Mr Great not to build but within 18 ffoot on the North side & within 10 ffoot on the North East side. [*Qy. Is not* "*but*" *an error ?*]

Bury Street Chapel

Trustees Names		
Revd Mr Isaac Watts Pastor		⎫
†Mr Thos Pickard	dec^d	⎪
†Wm Pickard	dec^d	⎪
†Jona Joyner	dec^d	⎬ Originally
†Nath Barton	dec^d	⎪
†Danl Scot	dec^d	⎪
†Humphr Stevenson	dec^d	⎪
†Andrew Holt	dec^d	⎭
Thos Hort		

	In the room of
30 Nov 1710	
†John Rolleston dec^d	W Pickard dec^d
†Wm Theed, Decd,	Jona Joynes dec^d
9 Nov 1715	
Rev. Mr Samuel Price, coPastor	T Pickard dec^d
†Nath Barton dcd	N Barton dec^d.
†Jno Ellicott decd	H Stevenson decd
Nath Field.	Wm Thied dec^d.
1 May 1724	
†Jn Warner dec^d	John Rolleston dec^d
Robt Grubb decd	And Holt dec^d
26 Oct 1730	
†Wm Ashburn decd	D Scot decd
Wm Field	Jn Warner dcd
30 May 1735	
John Woodcock	Jno Ellicott decd.
27 June 1740	
James Jacobson	Nath Barton dcd
Nicholas Crisp	Wm Ashburne dec^d
March 1741	
Wm Roffey	Robert Grubb decd

(All the names marked † are scored through).

At a meeting of ye Trustees 24 Febru 1737 on repairs of y^t Meeting occasioned by the Fire on the 27 Janu. last agreed to pay as follows, viz—

	£	s	d
Mr Niblett & his Wife attending to cleang &c	2	12	6
P^d his bill for help & Wood	1	10	—
Mis Barnett & her Daughter Mary Daniel	—	15	—
Several for Help, Expences, & Engine (3 *illegible*)	2	5	6
Glazier (Mr Oakes) Bill	10	14	.
Plasterer, Mr Mills	5	—.	—
Smithy	1	6	—
Carpenter (Mr Biggs)	2	19	—
& a guiney for attendance &c	1	1	—
Painter	5	5	—
Bricklayer	2	2	—
	35	10	—
Allow'd by ye Insurance Office	9	9	—
	26	1	—

The Meeting house shut all the Month of April 1746. The Trustees agreed to pay y^r following bills for repairs, viz—
Bricklayers bill for new Tiling all the top &c
Plaisterers bill for white washing &c
Carpenters bill
Painters
Glaziers bill
Plumbers
Smiths

(*The amounts are not stated.*)

Robert Browne and the Achurch Parish Register

THE first volume of the Achurch parish register is a parchment book measuring 11 inches by 8, consisting of 21 leaves, and covering the period from 1591 to 1669. Robert Browne commenced the register immediately on taking up his duties as rector; for he was instituted in September, 1591, and the first entry occurs on December 22nd, 1591. The last entry in his handwriting is dated June 2nd, 1631. Between these two dates there are 560 entries, *viz.*, 296 baptisms, 75 marriages, and 189 burials. With the exception of the critical year 1616 [see facsimile No. 2] the authorship of the entries is indisputable. From 1591 to June, 1616, Browne enters 177 baptisms, 46 marriages, and 127 burials. From June, 1616, to March, 1616-7, there are entered 6 baptisms and 3 burials; concerning whose authorship I am doubtful. From June 17th, 1617, to Jan. 18th, 1625-6, Arthur Smith and John Barker enter 70 baptisms, 20 marriages, and 33 burials. From April 9th, 1626, to June 2nd, 1631, Browne enters 43 baptisms, 9 marriages, and 26 burials.

From the first entry to the very last, nearly forty years later, Browne's writing is remarkably clear and well shaped. The names are almost invariably printed in old English text of a large size. A glance at either of the accompanying facsimiles will confirm all that has been said by various writers concerning the admirable care and labour Browne bestowed upon this duty of his. The present writer has inspected only about a score of

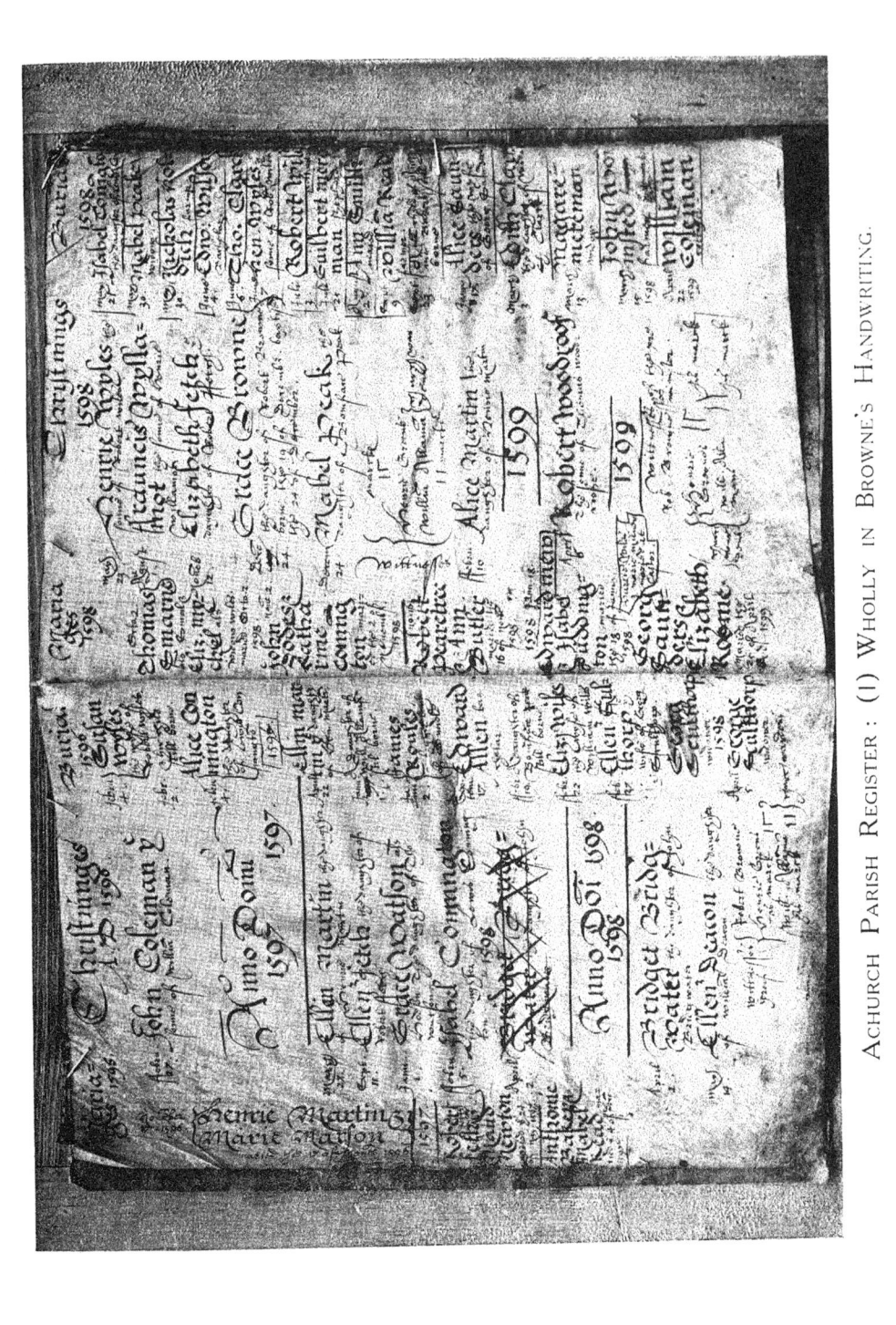

Achurch Parish Register: (1) Wholly in Browne's Handwriting.

parish registers, but Browne's stands by itself in striking contrast to all the others for distinctness and legibility. The mistakes made—in wrong column or before new date is entered—are all corrected and could be counted on one hand. According to the ordinance issued October 25th, 1597, by the Convocations of Canterbury and York, and confirmed by Queen Elizabeth, each page was to be attested by the signature of the incumbent and churchwardens. This ordinance was carefully observed by Browne, and specimens of such attestation may be seen on both of the accompanying plates. Thrice there is a very full attestation, in Browne's hand, *e.g.*: " 1602 Nouember 17. the churchwardens of Thorp Achurch namely Lawrence Austen & John Smith do subscribe that the Register above written sense the 25 of March last past is true & perfect read in the church & kept according to law & order   By me Robert Browne

> Lawrence Austen his marck |X|
> John Smith his marck || "

Browne evidently desired to give all the information necessary to the identification of the person whose name he enters. Thus we find in the marriage column the place of residence of the contracting couple, especially if either happens to be from some other locality. In the burials column most frequently we are informed of the relation in which the deceased stood to some person presumably known. It is to this commendable purpose of identification, and to the possession of a heart touched by the pathos of human life, that we are to look for the explanation of the unusual comments which Browne so frequently appends, and concerning which such unfavourable judgements were formed by Dr. Dexter and others who followed him. Below are to be found almost all of the "unusual" entries. It is thought to be unnecessary to give every instance of certain classes of comment. It would occupy too much space, and not add to our knowledge, to reproduce every entry of "stillborne" children, or all the innocent comments such as "widdow," "bachelar," "farmer." Specimens only, and the number of occurrences, of these well defined classes will be given; otherwise every unusual entry is reproduced.

And they speak for themselves! How any one closely acquaintanced with this register could say that the compiler was mad, passes the writer's comprehension. One could wish to be infected with the same madness! Such scrupulous care and excellent workmanship, such rare method, so intimate an interest in each parishioner, and so quick an eye for the tragedy of life, ill accord with the theory of a disordered mind. Whatever other arguments may be adduced to support the theory that Browne was not in his right mind (and I fancy Mr. Champlin Burrage has demolished them), at least his parish register cannot be urged. In fact, the author of that theory, Dr. Dexter, to whom we all owe so much, must have given but a cursory glance at the register, or he would not have made such a number of mistatements concerning it. The remarks cannot be deemed "uncalled for"; certainly they are not "severe." Moreover, they are not confined to the years neighbouring his disappearance, but are equally distributed throughout his whole incumbency, including even his first entry and his last. In the writer's judgement they are a remarkable testimony to Browne's thoroughness, good sense, and warm heart.

The "schism" entries form a separate class, and are still an unsolved problem. The authorship of the 1616 entries is uncertain. Dr. Dexter takes them to be from Browne's hand. The present writer has pondered over that page for hours during the last eighteen months, and has submitted it to the inspection of several persons competent to judge, some having considerable experience in the handwriting of the 16th and 17th centuries, but with no clear result. The first judgement is certainly against Browne's authorship. The change from 1615 to 1616 is startling. The regular bold old English text gives place to an irregular small hand. The alteration in the original is even more striking than in the facsimile (plate 2), for the colour of the ink is different; and in the year 1616 itself the ink again changes; perhaps the entries of that year are not all from the same hand. Only this can be said with certainty—that Browne's usual style ceases with the entry "Anno Domini 1616"; that a new hand appears with the entry "Anno Domini 1617"; and that the intermediate entries are possibly by Browne, but probably not.

The authorship of the "schism" entries of 1629-1631 is certain. They are by Browne. In a future paper the writer will quote extracts from the Peterborough records which will shew Browne and most of these "schism" people pitted against one another in the ecclesiastical courts. They formed a party against the old man and absented themselves from church apparently because of a certain amount of nonconformity on the part of Browne.

One more strange fact must be mentioned. Although these "schism" baptisms and burials take place chiefly at Lilford, there is no record of any of them (either in 1616 or the later period) in the Lilford register, which was carefully kept by the rector, Edmund Johnson. Evidently then the baptisms were not at the parish church. But I hope to return to the whole subject in my next paper.

I cannot close these introductory remarks without acknowledging my great obligation to the present rector of Thorpe Achurch, the Rev. H. C. Holmes, M.A., who most courteously and willingly has allowed me the freest of access to all the registers in his keeping, and has facilitated my research in many ways. It is a pleasure also to report that Mr. Holmes has ensured the preservation of Browne's register by having it bound (cover and all, untampered) in stout and handsome vellum boards).

LIST OF THE "UNUSUAL" ENTRIES.

1591. Burials December 22. Annice Sickson, widdw [sic]
1592. Burials. Septe 26 Elizeth Noy, widdow
Oct° 14 Margaret Bridgwater, widdow of John Bridgwater
Februa 1. Thomas Smith, baby
Februa 21 Annice Watson, widdow
1594 Christnings Oct — Lucie Worm ... bastard, the reputed daughter of John Worm
1595 Burials, Nouem 20 Alice Bates, a servant of ours & formerly from...brought ...a rare......William... [Undecipherable]
1596 Burials, Februa 4 Susan Wyles the wife of Robert Wyles
Februa 2 their child still born.
1597 Burials. Janu 1 A daughter of Will. Allaman still borne.
[There are eleven similar entries in the register.]
Janu 2 James Roules, a beggar boy of Oundle.
Septem 17 Edward Allen bachelar
[There are four similar entries in the register.]
1598 Burials April 5 George Sculthorp widower
May 30 Mabel Peake widow
May 30 Nicholas Holdich, farmer
Juli 3 Robert Wyles cottager
Juli 25 Guilbert Mereman shepherd
[There are twelve similar entries, giving the occupation of deceased.]

1599. Burials. Sept 30 Guilbert Pickering, Gentlemā my L. Burghleys officer, buried at Titchmarsh.

[This may be the Guilbert Pickering who married Robert Browne's sister Dorothy. If so, that would account for his mention here. Bridge tells us that this Guilbert Pickering "possessed employments of Trust and Credit under the Lord Treasurer Burleigh by which he considerably improved his fortune." See further, Congregational Historical Society's *Transactions*, vol. II., p. 154.]

Decem : 23 A′ man child of Anthony Peake still borne.

1600. Burials. July 16 Elizabeth Mew a nourse child of one Mew of Barnwell.

Nouem 28 Edmond Smith brother of John Smith a stranger who came frō Waddenho & died at his brothers house.

1601 Burials June 16 Elenor Pickering, gentlewoman & widdow.

[Possibly widow of the above mentioned Guilbert Pickering.]

Nou 5 Elizabeth Faustex, seruant.

1602 Burialls Juli 20 Susann Adams gentle, the wyfe of Mr Tho Adams.

1603 Christnings Nouem 26 Añ Dawkins saied to be the daughter of one Williā Dawkins of unknown dwelling.

Dec 11 { Clement, Marie & Ellen } Smal āls Smerne yᵉ children of Tho Smal or Smerne born all at one birth.

[The same entry appears in burial column dated Dec. 25th.]

1603 Mariages Feb 25 Edward Wells of Stoke Doyle & Annice Clarck of Castor in North. maried with license by Mr Wells preacher.

[Probably Robert Browne's curate.]

Nou 14 Robert Wakemā & Elizabeth Martin maried here by Mr Edm Johnson

Robert Wane & Elizabeth Marson of Lilford maried here by Mr Edm Johnson.

[In the Lilford register there occurs this entry: "1599 Edmund Johnson is minister." He also married a couple at Achurch in 1614.]

1603 Burials Dec 2 Añ Dawkins y⁰ child of a sorowing womā called Juda Stāley alias Dawkins

[" Sorowing "; possibly because the putative father had left the poor woman to bear her shame alone. See above entry, Nov. 26th.]

1604 Christnings June 3 Wylliam Deacō the sonne of Robert Deacon a Londoner.

1604 Burials. Sep 25 Marie Smith a sojourner with John Smith hir brother.

1605 Burials April 25 William Browne servaunt of Robert Browne.

1606 Burials Julie 18 Marie Hobson an ould poore maied the daughter of ... Hobson.

Octo 12 A child of Robert Wane imperfect & still borne.

1608 Burialls. December 15 Thomas Draper base borne as he saied before his death, a boy seruant of Henrie Willamot, ran away from his maister & was intertained & kept by Henrie Willamot contrarie to his maisters will, & surfytted in haruest in Henrie Willamots worte & was turned out of him being sick & afterwards received againe & kept by him in his sicknes tyll he died.

1609 Burialls Nouemb 25 Henrie Burie a nurse child of Mr Burie of Tichmarch.

Decemb 19 Thomas Harbert an aged man.

1610 Burialls April 10. Robert Smith, laborer, a maried man.

1612 Burialls April 24. 1612 Georg Meakins, seruaunt.

Maie 25 Robert Austin bachelar & seruaunt.

March 2 Alexander Deacon Millner.

1613 Burialls Febr 8 Geoffrey or Jeffrey or Gaifry Drawwater, laborer.

March 16 Robert Willamot a maried man.

[There are ten similar entries in the register]

Achurch Parish Register

1614 Burialls June 25. 1614 Bridget Goarge, lately maried, came to Achurch from Warmington & then died at Achurch.

June 26 Georg Marson a maried mā & a poore laborer.

1615 Mariages Nouemb 20. 1615 Anthonie Brooks of Winwick And Annice Willamot of Thorp Achurch took two certificates from both ye parishes & were maried els where—without licence.

1615 Burialls Sept 17 1615 Edward Mew, Husbandmā buried Sept 17

Oct 19 1615 Henrie Woodroof ye sonne of Tho Woodroof, Shoemaker.

The authorship of the following entries is doubtful :—

1616 Christnings August 11. 1616 Joane Greene the daughter of Syluester Greene baptized in schisme at Lilford.

August 25. 1616 Thomas Saunders the sonne of Thomas Saunders bapt at Lilford.

[Inserted in Marriage column. See facsimile.]

Sept 22. 1616. Ann Meakins ye daughter of Tho. Meakins baptized at Lilford in schisme.

Febru 12 Ffrauncis Holdich the sonne of James Holdich baptized . . . . . . at Lilford.

[The words "in schisme" were in the original entry and have been scratched out.]

Burialls March 16. 1616 Richard Denis buried in schism at Lilford.

The following are in the hand of Smith or Barker :—

1617 Christninges Feb 8. 1617 Marie Wakefeeld the daughter of a stranger one Marie ye wife (as she said) of Peter Wakefeeld of Water-well next Wishetry, Glasse-varrier.

Marriages June 17. 1617 Robert King & Katherine Cowper both of this towne.

[The expression "of this towne" is used fifteen times, and "of this parish" four times, by Smith and Barker between 1617 and 1626. Browne never once uses the former; yet Dexter (p 124) speaks of "his Brownistical way of calling the parish of Achurch the 'towne'"!]

Burialls Oct 18. 1617 Mirrian Wormerted, widdow

1618 Christenings Feb 28. 1618 Elizabeth Smith ye daughter of Arthur Smith curate of this towne at that tyme

[A similar entry occurs in 1620.]

1619 Buriells March 27. 1619 Richard Woodruffe a Bachelor.

1621 Burialls March 10. 1621 Silvester Pinnis a poore & lame boy kept of ye towne.

1622 Baptizings Oct 2. 1622 William & Christopher ye sonnes of Antony Browne borne both at a birth & another at ye same time still borne.

1625 Marriages Nou 15. 1625 Thomes Woolfall, clerke & Elizabeth Oliver, both of this parish.

The following are all in Browne's handwriting, which reappears in the register on June 25th, 1626:

1626 Marriages Julie 13, 1626 Thomes Browne widdower & Dorcas Lenton maied, maried by license at Brigstock.

Burialls Julie 12, 1626. Annice Adams alias Randol, widdow.

Januari 1626 Elizabeth Read ye wyfe of John Read, sometyme widow Wane.

1627 [at the end of the baptizings, with no date.]
A child of Edmond Quinsey baptized els where & not in our parish church.

[The child was baptized at Lilford, as the following entry from the Lilford register dated 1627 shews: "Edmund the sonne of Edmund Quincey was baptized the tenth day of Julie." A writer in *Notes and Queries*, 1860, states that Quincey-Adams, the American statesman, was descended from this Edmund Quincey. The names Quincey and Adams frequently occur in the Achurch and Lilford registers.]

1627 Mariages Januarie 31. 1627 Clement Weston & Alice Wyles maried by licence at Thrapston.

Februarie 16. 1627 John Burns & Denice Harbert both of this parish

[Twice elsewhere, in 1630 and 1631, Browne uses this phrase.]

Buriells April 25. 1627 Elizabeth Wilson, widowe.

1628 Mariages June 10. 1628 Allen Greene & Marie Law maried at Hitching in Hertfordshire June 10. 1628.

1629. Christnings October 25. 1629 Allen Greenes child baptized in schisme at Lyllford named John.

December 13. 1629 Williem Osbaston's child baptized at Lillford in schisme named Marie.

December 20. 1629 Likewise Thomas Saunders his child baptized at Lilford named Elizabeth.

Buriels April 25. 1629 John Cranfeald seruaunt of Tho [*undecipherable word*] who liued, dyed & was buried in schisme.

October 31. 1629 Allen Greens child buried in schisme.

1630. Christnings. Octob^r 17. 1630 Mary Greene the daughter of Allen Greene & James Connington ye sonne of James Connington baptized at Stoke October 17. 1630.

[This entry is much smeared as though it were written over an obliterated entry.]

Nouember 7. 1630 A child of my ungracious godsonne Robert Greene baptized els were in schisme.

Buriels. Septemb^r 24. 1630 Annice Dust, widow.

Octob^r 24. 1630 An Irish youth dying in ye manour house porch for want of succour & buried Octob^r 24. 1630.

Januarie 1. 1630 Robert Stephens borne at Wansworth & sent to Bythorne in Huntingtonshire dyed & buried at Achurch Januarie 1. 1630.

Februarii 8. 1630. Edward Greene an ould & lame Bachelar buried Februarii 8. 1630.

Februarii 13 1630 Margaret Bridgwater ye wife of Boniface Bridgwater dying in childbed & buried Februarii 13. 1630.

March 30. 1630 Annice Hartwell widdow buried March 30. 1630.

1631 Burials May 8. 1631 A child of Jame Connington baptized & buried by by [sic] him self in schme [sic] maie 8.

June 2. 1631 Marc ye daughter of a wanderer.

F. IVES CATER.

Oundle.

List of Members

Hon. Members marked *H*, Life Members marked *L*.

Adeney, W. F., Rev. Prof., M.A., D.D.
Anderton, W. E., Rev., M.A.
Andover (U.S.A.) Theological Seminary
Astbury, F. T., Rev.
Atkinson, S. B., Esq., M.A., M.B., B.Sc
Avery, John, Esq.
Baptist Union, The
Bartlet, J. V., Rev. Prof., M.A., D.D.
Basden, D. F., Esq.
Bate, Frank, Esq., M.A.
Bax, A. Ridley, Esq.
Beaumont, E., Esq.
Boag, G. W., Esq.
Bragg, A. W., Esq.
Brown, J., Rev. Dr., B.A.
H Brown, W. H., Esq.
Brownen, G., Esq.
Burrage, Champlin, Esq.
Campbell, R. J., Rev., M.A.
Carpenter, J. Estlin, Rev., M.A.
Carter, W. L., Rev., M.A.
Cater, F. I., Rev., A.T.S.
Chevalier, J., M.
Clapham, J. A., Esq.
Clark, J. H., Esq.
Clarkson, W. F., Rev., B.A.
Claydon, George S., Esq.
Cocks, J., Esq.
Congregational Library, Boston, Mass
Cribb, J. G., Esq.
Crippen, T. G., Rev.
Dale, A. W. W., Esq., M.A.
Dale, Bryan, Rev., M.A.
Davies, J. Alden, Rev.
Davis, C. H., Rev.
Davis, J. E., Esq.
Davy, A. J., Esq.
Dawson, E. B., Esq.
Didcote, C. Page, Esq.
Dimelow, J. G., Esq.
Dixon, H. N., Esq., M.A., F.L.S.
Dixon, R. M., Esq.
H Dore, S. L., Esq., J.P.
L Ebbs, A. B., Esq.
Ebbs, W., Rev.
Ellis, C. W., Rev.
Evans, A. J., Esq., M.A.
Evans, G. Eyre, Rev.
Evans, Jon. L., Esq.
Evans, R. P., Esq.
Firth, C. H., Prof., M.A., LL.D.
Flower, J. E., Rev., M.A.
Forsyth, P. T., Rev., Dr.
Friends' Reference Library
Galloway, Sydney V., Esq.
Gasquoine, T., Rev., B.A.
Glasscock, J. L., Esq.
Gordon, A., Principal
Gosling, Howard, Esq.
Green, Joseph J., Esq.
Green, T., Esq.
Grice, T. E., Esq.
Grieve, A. J., Rev., M.A., B.D.
Groser, W. H., Esq., B.Sc.
Hall, C. W., Rev.
Hall, W. H., Esq.
Harris, W. J., Esq.
Harrison, G. W., Esq.
Harwood, W. Hardy, Rev.
Hawkins, F. H., Esq., LL.B.
Henderson, A. D., Esq.
Hepworth, Frank N., Esq.
Hepworth, J., Esq.
Hepworth, T. M., Esq.
Heslop, R. Oliver, Esq., M.A., F.S.A.
Hewgill, W., Rev., M.A.
Hills, A. M., Miss
Hitchcock, W. M., Esq.
Hodgett, C. M., Esq.
Holt, Edwyn, Esq.
L Hounsom, W. A., Esq., J.P.
Huckle, Attwood, Esq.
Iliff, John S., Esq.
Jackson, S., Esq.
James, Norman G. B., Esq.
H Johnston, W., Esq.
Jones, A. G., Esq.
Keep, H. F., Esq.
Kenward, Herbert, Rev.
Key, James, Rev.
King, Jos., Esq., M.A.
Knaggs, J., Rev.
H Lancashire Independent College (Goodyear, C., Esq)
Lawrence, Eric A., Rev.
Layton, F. J., Rev., A.T.S.
Lester, E. R., Esq.
Lewis, D. Morgan, Prof., M.A.
Lewis, Geo. G., Esq.
Lewis, H. Elvet, Rev., M.A.
Lewys-Lloyd, E., Esq.
Lovatt, J., Esq.
Low, G. D., Rev., M.A.
Luke, R., Esq.
Macfadyen, D., Rev., M.A.
Mackintosh, R., Rev. Prof., D.D.
Massey, Stephen, Esq.
H McClure, J. D., Dr.
McCrae, A., Esq.
Minshull, John, Esq.
Mottram, W., Rev.
Muir, W., Esq.
Mumford, A. A., Esq., M.P.

List of Members (continued)

Musgrave, B., Esq.
H New College
    (Staines, Howard, Rev.)
Nightingale, B., Rev.
H Palmer, C. Ray, Rev. Dr.
Palmer, W. M., Esq.
Parnaby, H., Rev., M.A.
Pearson, S., Rev., M.A.
Pierce, W., Rev.
Pitt, Walter, Mrs.
Powicke, F. J., Rev., Ph.D.
Poynter, J. J., Rev.
Pugh, Mrs.
Rawcliffe, Edwin B., Rev.
Rees, J. Machreth, Rev.
Richards, D. M., Esq.
Ritchie, D. L., Rev.
Robinson, W., Rev.
Rollason, Arthur A., Esq.
Rudge, C., Rev.
Rutherford, J., Esq.
H Rylands, Mrs., D.Litt.
Scamell, J., Esq.
Serle, S, Esq.
Shaw, H, Rev.
Silcock, P. Howard, Esq., B.A.
Simon, D. W., Rev., D.D.
H Smith, W. J., Esq., M.A.
Smyrk, C. Watt, Rev.
Souter, Alex., Prof., M.A.
H Spicer, Albert, Sir, Bart., M.P.
H Spicer, George, Esq., M.A., J.P.
Standerwick, J. W., Esq.

Stanier, W. H., Esq.
Sykes, A. W., Esq.
H Thacker, Fred. S., Esq.
Thacker, Henry, Esq.
Thomas, D. Lleufer, Esq.
Thomas, John, Esq., J.P., C.C.
Thomas, Wm., Rev.
H Thompson, J., Esq.
Thorpe, F. H., Esq.
Titchmarsh, E. H., Rev., M.A.
H Toms, C. W., Esq.
Turner, G. Lyon, Rev., M.A.
Tyson, R. G., Esq.
U.S.A. Congress Library.
Wallis, R. B., Esq., J.P.
Walmsby, L. S., Esq.
Watkinson, J., Esq.
H Webster, Isaac., Esq.
L Whitley, A. W., Esq.
Wicks, G. H., Esq.
H Wilkinson, W., Esq
Williams's Library.
Williams, Mrs.
Williamson, David, Esq.
Williamson, David, jr., Esq.
Windeatt, E., Esq.
Wing, Lewis, Esq.
Winterstoke of Blagdon, Baron
Wontner, A. J., Esq.
Wood, Leonard B., Esq., M.A
Woodall, H. J., Esq.
Young, Hugh P., Rev.

OFFICERS OF THE SOCIETY.

President	Rev. Dr. John Brown, B.A., Hampstead, London, N.W.
Hon. Treasurer	Rev. G. Lyon Turner, M.A., Crescent Lodge, St. John's, London, S.E.
Hon. Auditor	Mr. John Minshull, Memorial Hall, London, E.C.
Hon. Editor & Librarian	Rev. T. G. Crippen, ,, ,, ,,
Hon. Secretaries	Rev. T. G. Crippen, ,, ,, ,,
	Mr. Henry Thacker, ,, ,, ,,

CONDITIONS OF MEMBERSHIP.

(a) LIFE MEMBERS, paying twenty guineas in lieu of annual subscription.
(b) HONORARY MEMBERS, paying an annual subscription of one guinea or more.
(c) ORDINARY MEMBERS, paying an annual subscription of five shillings.

Subscriptions should be made payable and remitted to the Hon. Treasurer, as above; and are due *in advance* on January 1st in each year.

New members are entitled to all the publications issued by the Society in the year they join.

Transactions

Vol. III., No. 3]   [SEPTEMBER, 1907

Contents

Editorial	139
Congregational Historical Society : Balance Sheet	144
Memorials of Dr. Doddridge	145
Historic Communion Plate	153
Hanover Chapel, Peckham	155
T. G. Crippen	
The Centenary of Mill Hill School	171
N. G. B. James, M.A.	
The Last Years of Penry	182
T. Gasquoine	
John Asty and the Fleetwoods	187
Stanley B. Atkinson, M.A.	
The Religious Condition of London in 1672	192
G. Lyon Turner, M.A.	
List of Officers, &c.	206
List of Members	207

Can be obtained direct from the Book Saloon, Congregational Union of England and Wales, Inc., Memorial Hall, London, E.C.

Printed for the Society by
Fred. S. Thacker, 3 Dyers' Buildings, Holborn, London.

EDITORIAL

The AUTUMNAL MEETING of our Society will be held at Blackpool on Wednesday, 16th October, at 4.30 p.m., in the Wesleyan Lecture Hall, Adelaide Street. A paper on " Early Nonconformist Churches in Lancashire " is expected from the Rev. J. H. Colligan, Presbyterian minister of Lancaster, and opportunity for discussion will be afforded.

Our Society has sustained a grievous loss by the death of the Rev. Bryan Dale, M.A., of Bradford, which took place on 30th July. Mr. Dale was a Cornishman, having been born at Cury, near Helstone, on 22nd February, 1832. In his youth he was a member of the Wesleyan Association, now merged in the United Methodist Church, but having adopted Congregational principles he entered the Western College, then seated at Plymouth, at the age of 18. His first pastorate was at Coggeshall, Essex, the church founded by Dr. John Owen ; where he was ordained in 1855, and ministered about seven years. During that time he contributed materially to the success of the local bicentenary commemoration of the ejected ministers, and wrote *The Annals of Coggeshall*, which is of permanent value. In 1863 he removed to Sion Chapel, Halifax, where he exercised a fruitful ministry for over 23 years, during which time two new Congregational churches were established in the town. Retiring from pastoral work in 1886 he became secretary of the Yorkshire Congregational Union, in which capacity he served the churches to the end of his life. His life of *The Good Lord Wharton* takes rank as a standard biography ; and by his untiring efforts the perversion of that nobleman's " Bible Charity " was in large measure —though not altogether—rectified. He wrote a number of papers on antiquarian topics, some of which were issued as separate pamphlets. But, next to his pastoral and secretarial duties, his favourite pursuit was investigating and recovering the history of Yorkshire Nonconformity. It has been said that "what Mr. Dale did not know of the churches of Yorkshire was not worth knowing." His MS. collections fill numerous volumes ; and it is hoped that arrangements will be made to render generally accessible the result of his researches. Mr. Dale was present at our annual meeting in May, when his bodily feebleness was painfully evident. His character is happily summarized in a newspaper obituary:—" A strong, true, and tender friend and Christian; in every respect an able minister of the New Covenant."

An interesting communication from Principal Gordon, of Manchester, corrects two inaccuracies in the account of Richard Frankland and his Academy, vol. II., pp. 428-9. He informs us that Joseph Boyse was not a Baptist but a Presbyterian; who "was for infant baptism not only in his practice but in his polemics." He further says that the John Piggott who was Frankland's pupil was living at Bolsover in 1726. The Baptist minister in Little Wild Street was another person of the same name.

A. J. Davy, Esq., of Torquay, furnishes some interesting facts relative to Rollin—or more correctly Rawlin—Mallock, the donor of the richly chased cup figured in our account of the Taunton communion plate. His father, Roger Mallock of Exeter, merchant and silversmith, is nominated a life member of the city council in the charter granted to the city by Charles I. in 1627. He was sheriff of Exeter in 1631, mayor in 1632, and again in 1636. His house, still standing in Gander Street, afforded lodging to the judges in 1640 and 1646. In 1648 he was ejected from the council for his resistance to their order to deface an inscription on the wall of a churchyard recording its consecration about 11 years before. The inscription, however, was not defaced, for it still remains. Evidently Roger Mallock's sympathies were not with the Puritan party. In 1654 he bought from Sir Wm. Cary the house and manor of Cockington, which was rebuilt by his son. The latter, Rawlin Mallock, J.P., was M.P. for Ashburton from 1677 to 1679, and for Totnes in 1689-90. He died in 1690, or soon after, leaving the house and manor to his son of the same name, then a child about 9 years old. His descendant and namesake was the Tory member for Torquay division in the last Parliament.

In our account of the ancient church at Ravenstonedale (III., 91), the origin of Nonconformity in that neighbourhood is ascribed to the labours of the Rev. Chr. Jackson after the Restoration. N. Penney, Esq., of the Friends' Library, reminds us that George Fox, Francis Howgill, and other Friends visited the district as early as

Editorial

1652, when several were "convinced," and a meeting established which continued until 1709, and probably later. See *First Publishers of Truth*, pp. 248, 272.

Mr. Penney informs us that several of what for convenience we have called "canting names" are found among early Friends in Great Britain and Ireland ; *e.g.*, William Edmundson, the Quaker apostle of Ireland, called a son "Trial" in 1700. Still later in America are to be found Consider Merritt (man) 1766, and Thankful Collins (woman) 1798. The name Offspring Blackall was inflicted in 1652 on a child who lived to be Bishop of Exeter. Reverting to an earlier time, a correspondent calls our attention to the commencement to Penry's farewell letter to his children (1593) "To my dear and tenderly beloved daughters ; Deliverance, comfort, safety, and sure hope." This phrase has usually been understood as a benediction ; but the fact that one of them, probably the eldest, was named Deliverance (she was married in 1611, aged 21) suggests that the other words were also names—Comfort, Safety, Sure-hope. Comfort as a woman's name is not unknown in America ; Grace and Mercy, names of the same class, are fairly common, and Hope is still occasionally met with. Only a few years ago some amusement was caused by the appearance of a Mrs. Virtue Innocent at a police court on a charge of which she was honourably acquitted. And the editor has personally known two women who were afflicted with the names Temperance and Obedience. Evidently " canting names " were not peculiar to the generation of Praise-God Barbone.

*

The *Axminster Ecclesiastica* has been for some years out of print. It is much to be wished that this instructive record of troublous times may soon be replaced on the list of current literature. Meanwhile the Rev. F. B. Wyatt has printed, in a small pamphlet, *A Brief History of the Church of Christ of the Congregational Order in Axminster*, which contains numerous extracts from the ancient MS.

*

Another small publication to which we accord a hearty welcome is *Wem : History and Guide*, by Rev. H. Merchant, M.A. It contains a concise account of the local Nonconformity ; which claims among its worthies Andrew Parsons (the ejected rector), Richard Latham (the first dissenting minister), Peter Edwards, the elder Hazlitt, and Sir John Bickerton Williams. It would be well if similar local histories were published of many small towns where faithful men served their generation by the will of God and are now all but forgotten.

＊

We have received from our esteemed treasurer, the Rev. G. L. Turner, M.A., a critique on Mr. Boseley's book on *The Independent Church of Westminster Abbey*, the severity of which compels abridgment. Mr. Turner writes :—

"To a reader with Nonconformist sympathies and an entirely uncritical spirit, this book may prove interesting or even enlightening . . . . But to one who knows anything of his Calamy or Wilson's *History of the Dissenting Churches of London*, and has read Dr. Vaughan's *English Nonconformity*, and vol. III. of Dr. Stoughton's *History of Religion in England*, what there is in this goodly volume of plain historic fact will seem strangely familiar ; and its redundancies, needless repetitions . . . . [and] irrelevant excursions into topics only in the remotest fashion connected with the subject . . . . [are] irritating . . . . and disappointing." [*After reference to preliminary announcements*] " We regret to say, however, the expectant student will look in vain for anything fresh or new, or for any evidence of original research, except perhaps the leaf from the parish register of St. Bartholomew's, which shews that Hogarth was baptized in the church in the purlieus of which the Independents worshipped who had migrated from the Westminster Abbey church of Commonwealth days."

[*The reviewer proceeds to notice a number of serious inaccuracies* :—] " On p. 103 we are told that the Rev. W. Strong was buried in the south transept of the Abbey, near his Presbyterian predecessor. His Presbyterian predecessor was the Rev. Stephen Marshall, B.D. (p. 71), who did not die—we are told on p. 72—till November 19, 1655 ; whereas William Strong was dead and buried on July 4, 1654, which is more than 16 months before. . . . . Hardly less a chronological error is the reference to Sir Harbottle Grimstone as Speaker of the House of Commons in the year of the Great Plague (1665). Sir Harbottle Grimstone was a member of the House at the time, for he stood for Colchester in the five successive Parliaments from 1660 to 1685 ; but it was only in the *first* of these— what has been called 'The Healing Parliament'—which recalled Charles the Second—that he was Speaker. The Plague happened in the *second*, when Sir Edward Turner was Speaker.

" But the worst of all is the laboured reference (covering six pages, 179-185) to Sir Walter Mildmay as connected with the priory church of St. Bartholomew . . . . Sir Walter Mildmay according to our author " lived in the reigns of Henry VIII. and Edward VI. rendering most eminent service to the state when Elizabeth was

Editorial 141

queen" (p. 179). Quite true, it was in Elizabeth's reign that he died, in the 77th year of his age, in the year 1589. But that being the case, how could any man write on the self-same page of this Sir Walter Mildmay, 'While the Independents continued to worship in this Priory Meeting-house' there was one 'in public authority whose sympathies were entirely with them,' when he has told us that they did not begin to meet there till after 1660; and proceed to dilate on the stirring thought that he would not infrequently worship with them, when he had died more than 70 years before?

"It .... surely wounds the *amour propre* of any intelligent Independent to think that a volume so ..... defaced by bad mistakes should have been presented to the King, and accepted by him as a sample of Nonconformist scholarship! We can only hope that he has not read it, and that it has not fallen into the hands of any Court ecclesiastics with a gift for 'higher criticism.'"

[It is only a matter of simple justice that Mr. Boseley should have the right of reply.—EDITOR.]

CONGREGATIONAL HISTORICAL SOCIETY

FINANCIAL STATEMENT from May 11th, 1906, to May 8th, 1907.

RECEIPTS.

	£	s.	d.
Balance in hand - -	95	3	3
Annual Subscriptions - -	69	15	0
Sales—			
C.H.S. *Transactions*, etc. 11 9 7			
Burrage's Booklet - 2 8 0			
	13	17	7
	£178	**15**	**10**

PAYMENTS.

	£	s.	d.
Printing *Transactions* - -	78	17	0
Burrage's Booklet - -	4	5	0
Hire of Room, Memorial Hall	1	1	0
Cash Journal - -	1	7	6
Annual Subscription — Friends' Historical Society -	0	5	0
Postages, Stationery, Printing and Sundries - -	5	6	5
Balance at Bank - -	87	13	11
	£178	**15**	**10**

Examined and certified correct,

JOHN MINSHULL.

July 2nd, 1907.

Memorials of Dr. Doddridge

IN the *Transactions* of last January the secretary requested information respecting autographs or relics of Watts and Doddridge. Several correspondents have supplied welcome contributions, including unpublished letters of *both* these eminent divines, which it is hoped will be printed next year. Meanwhile, we have pleasure in giving a list of *all* the Doddridge relics and autographs which we have been able to locate. Personal memorials of Dr. Watts appear to be much more rare. We shall be glad to receive and utilize further communications on the subject.

I.—Doddridge Relics in the possession of the church at Castle Hill, Northampton.

Church Book, containing entries in Doddridge's handwriting.
Various notes of sermons in his handwriting.
Chair, table and mirror used by him in the chapel vestry.
His black skull-cap.
The *Northampton Mercury*, containing an account of his death.
A quarto volume containing letters written to Doddridge by Count Zinzendorf and others.
† The cover or "table-carpet" of the communion table, which was in actual use when Colonel Gardiner received the sacrament for the last time at the hands of Dr. Doddridge.
A jacket of white serge, with white satin front and cuffs; worn by Dr. Doddridge on the day of his death, 26th October, 1751.
Two other coats worn by Dr. Doddridge.
A pair of large plated shoe buckles worn by him.
A jewel cabinet, covered with tapestry representing scenes from the book of Esther; it was inherited by Doddridge, and was in his house at Northampton when he died.
A tapestry representing "The Judgement of Paris"—figures in 17th century costume. It was inherited by Doddridge, and was treasured by his descendants as an heirloom until, with other relics, it was transferred to the custody of the church.

A pair of high-heeled shoes, embroidered in silk, worn by Mrs. Doddridge at Court.

Portions of a ball dress worn by Mrs. Doddridge and believed to have been presented to her by Frederick, Prince of Wales.

A brass lantern, capable of being folded flat. It is said to have been used by Mrs. Doddridge on her way to and from the chapel after Dr. Doddridge's death.

Copy of the first edition of Doddridge's hymns; presented by the transcriber, Job Orton, to Doddridge's widow. Orton has headed the hymns with the dates when they were written, and in some cases the events by which they were suggested. Bound up with the book are 28 of the hymns in Orton's handwriting.

Probate of the will of Dr. Doddridge.

Probate of the will of Mrs. Doddridge, dated 1771, and witnessed by the Rev. Caleb Ashworth.

Two Bibles, Sir John Doddridge's *History of the Principality of Wales &c.*, an early seventeenth coat, two pairs of richly-embroidered gloves, and several pieces of fine needlework and old lace. All these were held as heirlooms in the family; though there is no certain evidence (whatever the probability) that they were actually used by Dr. and Mrs. Doddridge.

[All the foregoing from † downward were sold to the church in 1904 by the Rev. Frank Doddridge Humphreys of Honiton; now residing at Handsworth, Sheffield.]

II.—Doddridge Relics and MS. at New College.

(a.) *Miscellaneous Relics and Memorials.*

Portrait (in Council Room) ascribed to John Russel, R.A., by whom it is said to have been painted posthumously from three original portraits. It cannot have been painted from life as Russel's age was only 15 when Doddridge died.

Portrait bust (in library). Artist unknown.

Portrait in alto-rilevo, modelled from family portraits by John Doddridge Humphreys, a grandson of Dr. Doddridge.

Doddridge's study table, his walking-stick, and a quadrant *supposed* to have belonged to him.

Dr. Watts's catechisms, presented by himself to Dr. Doddridge.

The Assembly's Catechism Explained, by D.S. (David Some); presented to Doddridge by the author. With notes in Dr. Doddridge's shorthand.

Doddridge's New Testament, interleaved, with many of his notes in shorthand.

A leaf of his Bible, with notes in shorthand on the margin.

Doddridge's ordination certificate, with ten signatures, dated 19th March, 1729/30. Mounted in the first volume of his *Family Expositor*.

Memorials of Dr. Doddridge 147

(*b.*) *MSS. chiefly or wholly in Doddridge's handwriting.*

Doddridge's draft of a letter to the church at St. Alban's, requesting admission to its fellowship. Holograph, unsigned; with two lines of shorthand at the foot.

Shorthand volume in Doddridge's hand: *Notes on the Harmony of the Evangelists, Part I. From the beginning to the cure of the Paralytick.*

Bundle of shorthand notes on the Epistles to the Romans and I. Corinthians.

Shorthand MS.: *Theorems of Archimedes and Rules of Syllogism Demonstrated;* and *The General and Speedy Rules of Syllogism Demonstrated from the first Principles.*

A case containing the following, all in shorthand, viz.:—(1) Lowman's *Civil Government of the Hebrews*, abridged; (2) *Lectures on Anatomy;* (3) Mr. Hanbury's MSS., *Conic Sections;* (4) Addenda to *Conick Sections* from Mr. Hanbury's MSS., altered; (5) Mr. Eames' *Conick Sections: Of the Ellipse*, and appendix of several carefully drawn diagrams; (6) a few rough notes on plain trigonometry.

Seven cases full of shorthand notes on sermons.

Shorthand MS.—Rough draft of the *Family Expositor* on the Epistle to the Romans.

Shorthand MS.—Preparatory notes for expositions at family prayer.

MS. exposition of the system of shorthand used by Doddridge.

MS. of *The Family Expositor* in shorthand.

MS. revised translation of the minor prophets, in shorthand; completed by Doddridge just before his last illness.

Two MS. volumes of notes on the Hebrew text of Ezekiel, Daniel, and the minor prophets. The chapters and verses are indicated by a system of spacing, and the notes entered from time to time in shorthand.

Two similar MS. volumes of notes on the Greek text of the Epistles and Revelation; shorthand on the same plan.

Shorthand volume—*Critical Lectures on the Book of Acts.*

Shorthand volume—*Critical Notes on the Epistles, Rom. to ii. Cor.*

Bundle of shorthand notes on the Greek text of the New Testament: Romans to Hebrews.

Volume of above 40 autograph letters of Doddridge to his friend Dr. Clark of St. Alban's, 1723-50.

Bundle of original MS. sermons.

MS. volume of 100 sermons.

Commonplace book, shorthand: Hints on Books Read.

Commonplace book, shorthand: Theological References, contracted.

Commonplace book, shorthand: Theological extracts from numerous writers.

Commonplace book, shorthand: Lengthy extracts on various topics.

Private diary in three volumes: 4th September, 1738, to 6th November, 1743.
Records of housekeeping expenses, 3 volumes: 1732-5, 1735-9, 1740 flg.
Two other cash books: 1739-41 and 1743-50.
MS. book, *partly* in shorthand: list of widows and orphans needing relief.
MS. preface for the second part of Watts's *Improvement of the Mind*, to be published by Doddridge from the original MS.
Constitution, Orders, and Rules relating to the Academy at Northampton, agreed upon by the Tutors and the several members of it in Decr 1743. 16 pp., 4to. Doddridge's holograph, with 64 autograph signatures.
Latin MS. *Theologiae sive Pneumatologiae et Ethicae, Pars ii.* 2 vols.
Shorthand MS.: Miscellaneous lectures on various subjects, *viz.*:—
(1) *The Initiation of the Ancients*; (2) *Antiquity of the Hebrew Points*; (3) *Conduct of Ancient Philosophers*; (4) *Date of the 1st Epistle to Timothy, and its Inspiration*; (5) *Confucius's Notion of a Deity*; (6) *Celsus's Testimony to the New Testament*.
Lectures in Pneumatology &c. Shorthand.
An Abstract of our Pneumatological References. Shorthand.
An Abstract of the References in our Lectures on Logick. Shorthand.
Lectures on Civil Government. Shorthand.
Lectures on Jewish Antiquities. Large 4to. vol., shorthand. (Used by Dr. Caleb Ashworth.)
Treatise on Arithmetic and Algebra. MS. in longhand.
Lectures on Anatomy, and on Logic. Shorthand.
Shorthand MS., *Eames's Anatomy, Contracted*.
MS., *Mr. Eames's Conic Sections.*
MS. containing algebraic problems.
Plan of the meeting-house (roughly drawn with pencil); and account of the seats. (The figures on the plan are Doddridge's; the "account" is in shorthand.)

[It is possible that *some* of the foregoing MSS. may not be *wholly* in the handwriting of Doddridge, as it is not easy to distinguish the shorthand of different writers.]

(c.) *Of the following, which are among the Doddridge MSS., the handwriting is uncertain* :—

Four volumes of shorthand notes of sermons by various preachers.
Quarto vol. in shorthand: *Lectures on the Evidences and Doctrines of the Gospels, given by P. Doddridge, D.D., 1742.*
Shorthand MS., *Abridgment of References in Doddridge's Lectures.*
A Treatise on Arithmetic and Algebra, larger than the one mentioned above. (I do not think the hand is Doddridge's.—T.G.C.)
Bundle of miscellaneous shorthand notes of sermons, lectures, etc., not arranged.

(d.) *The following are certainly* not *in the handwriting of Doddridge.*

Hymns (84) on several occasions, composed chiefly for the use of congregations under the author's care. Transcribed from the author's own copy, 1742. (Shorthand MS. presented to the Coward Trustees by Mrs. Joshua Wilson)

Shorthand MS. *Abridgement of References in Doddridge's Lectures.*

Shorthand notes on lectures on anatomy. Shorthand remarks are *added* in Doddridge's hand.

MS. notes of sermons by Doddridge ; probably taken by one of his students.

Three volumes of shorthand notes of sermons by Doddridge and others.

Two volumes of *Contractions of Pneumatological References* in Doddridge's lectures. Written in shorthand by Caleb Ashworth.

Several bundles of replies to questions on religious topics, which seem to have been propounded by Doddridge to his students or hearers. All are endorsed in his handwriting. Some are written in full, some in shorthand ; and some bear names which afterwards became famous. They might probably repay examination.

A letter to Doddridge, in French, commending the *Family Expositor.* Signed P. J. Courtonne, Amsterdam, 1748.

A confession of faith in shorthand ; memorandum attached, " I am coming to the conclusion that this is Steffe's Confession, not Doddridge's." With it is a confession, partly written in full and partly in shorthand, signed " Tho. Steffe."

Three small volumes, uniformly bound, of which I. and II. bear Doddridge's signature :—

  I. (partly in the handwriting of J. Jennings, Doddridge's tutor at Kibworth) contains : (1) *Cursus Academicus ;* (2) *Libri ab Academicis emendiant transcribendi ;* (3) *Exercitia aliqua primi Anni ;* (4) *Questiones Logicae, et innuenda objectionum ;* (5) *Prologi, Epilogi, et Interludia* (eight in English : one of them also in Latin) ; (6) *Dramata* (brief summaries of 14 comedies)..

  II. *Prolegomena Critica, Sive Apparatus ad S. Scripturae Lectionem ; in usum Juventutis Academicae :* by Samuel Jones, interlined here and there with notes in Doddridge's hand.

III.—*Arithmetica Universalis et Numeralis.* (Looks like Jennings's hand.)

Mosheim's preface to the German edition of Doddridge's *Rise and Progress,* Hanover, 1750. "Attempted in English by P.H.O."

Engraved tract ; Rich's shorthand, improved by Dr. Doddridge : edited by Rev. S. Wood, B.A. London, 1830, price 2/6.

Narrative, by Rev. S. Clark, of a remarkable dream of Doddridge's.
Copy of the will of John Doddridge, of Bromridge, Devon; dated 20th January, 1658; proved by Judith Doddridge, widow and executrix, 20th July "1769"—error for 1679 or 1669.
Letter of Philip Doddridge, jun., to his mother. Tewkesbury, 12th May, 1764.
Poem on the death of Doddridge by H. Moore; with autograph of Mercy Doddridge, jun. "Gift of the Author."
The Northampton yearly bill of mortality for 1770, with a hymn by Doddridge.

(e.) The Doddridge Correspondence.

Nine large folio volumes, in which are arranged above 1600 letters and documents relating to the Doddridge family, from 1728 to the death of Celia Ann Doddridge (the doctor's youngest daughter) in 1811. They include:—
    125 letters of Dr. Doddridge addressed to his wife.
    11 letters of Dr. Doddridge addressed to his daughter.
    2 letters of Dr. Doddridge addressed to other persons.
    6 letters written *to* Dr. Doddridge by his wife.
    151 letters written *to* Dr. Doddridge by various persons.
    Letter of Mrs. Doddridge to her children on the death of Dr. Doddridge.
    The call addressed to Dr. Doddridge from the church at Northampton, February, 1728.
    Documents relating to the will of Thomas Ekins (15th September, 1744) of which Dr. Doddridge was executor.
    List of books purchased by and presented to Dr. Doddridge on 19th September, 1749.
    Proposal for printing the *Family Expositor*, with subscription signed "Caleb Ashworth."

III.—Doddridge MSS., etc., in the Congregational Library.

Lectures in Pneumatology, Ethics, and Divinity. 5 volumes in Doddridge's own shorthand MS.
Memorandum book, containing accounts of receipts and payments of money, students' indebtedness, etc., 1731-32; above 120 pp. in Doddridge's handwriting.
Doddridge's *Algebra*, written out by Rev. Jas. Follett.
Doddridge's lectures on Pneumatology, etc., written down in shorthand by one of his students, probably D. Baker, of Kettering, whose name is on the fly leaf.
David Brainerd's *Mirabilia Dei inter Indicos*, with Doddridge's autograph on title page.

Memorials of Dr. Doddridge

Printed sermon on Genesis v. 24, with "Mrs. Doddridge" on the title page, in Dr. Doddridge's handwriting. Some other words have been obliterated.

Funeral sermon for Col. Gardiner, 2nd edition ; with "Mrs. Doddridge" on the title page in Dr. Doddridge's handwriting.

Sermon, 25th April, 1749 ; bearing Mrs. Doddridge's autograph.

Letter of Selina, Countess of Huntingdon, to Dr. Doddridge, undated.

The arms of the family of Doddridge, painted on canvas.

IV.—Letters in the possession of the Congregational Church at Market Harborough.

1. From Dr. Doddridge to the deacons at Market Harborough, in reference to an invitation given to the Rev. Job Orton.
2. From the Rev. S. Wood of Rendham to Dr. Doddridge, explaining why he declines an invitation from Market Harborough.

V.—Doddridge Relics and MSS. in Private Custody.

(1) *Rev. F. D. Humphreys retains—*
   A Family Bible, dated 1689, in which a register of the family has been carefully kept until the present time.
   The old armorial bearings which formerly hung in Dr. Doddridge's study.
   A watch—imperfect.
   A flint and steel.

(2) *Rev. Dr. Chapman, of Western College, Bristol, possesses—*
   An eight-day clock with square brass dial, made in Northampton, and presented to Dr. Doddridge by the congregation at Northampton on the occasion of his marriage, 1736. Dr. Chapman says : "The case is a good specimen of the early enamel work introduced into this country about that time. The clock keeps time most accurately."

(3) *The Rev. G. Eyre Evans, M.A., of Aberystwith, has—*
   A volume containing "Two Funeral Sermons : one on Dr. Samuel Benion, and the other on the Reverend Mr. Francis Tallents, Minister of the Gospel in Shrewsbury. London, 1709." On the title is in a neat boyish handwriting, " P. Doddridge"; and on the front fly leaf, "*Ex dono Clarissima Sororis ejus*, 1717," and below " *E libris* Ph. Doddridge."

The following Doddridge relics are missing; any clue to their whereabouts is desirable.

1. A set of family portraits, including Sir John Doddridge, Dr. Ph. Doddridge, and others. They were sold by J. D. Humphreys to Sir Charles Reed in 1858 ; enquiries respecting them since the death of the latter have yielded no result.

2. Luther's German Bible in two volumes, and a leather belt with romantic associations, once the property of Dr. Doddridge's maternal grandfather, John Bauman. These were in the possession of the same J. D. Humphreys in 1850; but it is not known what became of them.
3. A very dilapidated trunk, leather, bound with iron clamps and studded with nails forming the device "P.D. 1701." It was sold in Honiton in 1905.

The Rev. Frank Doddridge Humphreys, of Handsworth, Sheffield, has kindly furnished the following genealogical record, taken from a Bible which has been in the possession of the family above 200 years.

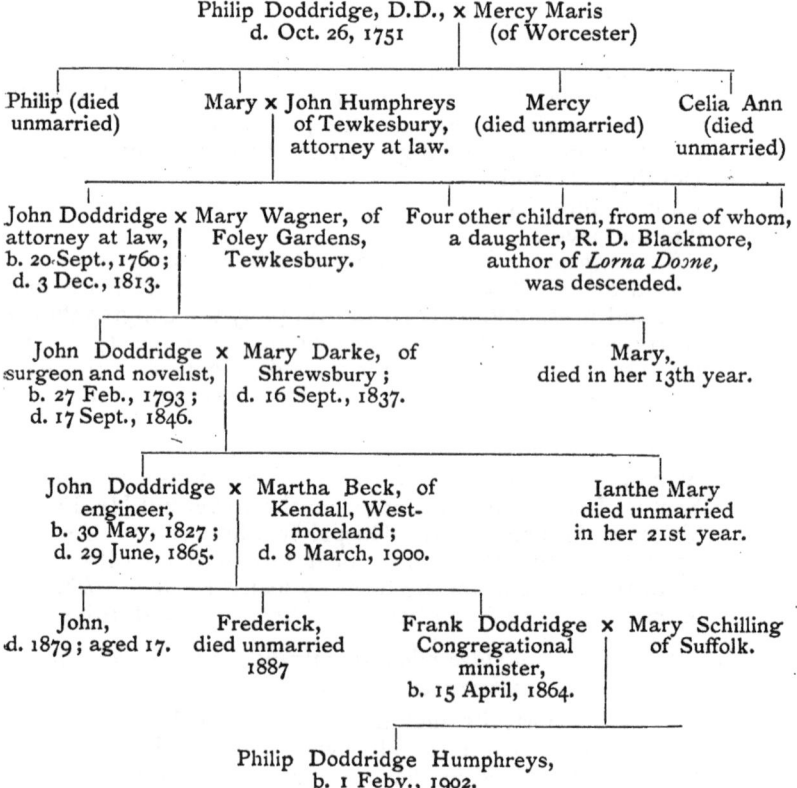

THE FLAVEL CUP.

Historic Communion Plate

1.—The Flavel Cup

A PHOTOGRAPH of this interesting relic—the property of Prince's Street church, Devonport—has been kindly furnished by the Rev. E. W. Bickley, together with an account of it written by a former pastor:—

> The cup differs from the rest of the communion vessels in being shorter, broader, and of simpler workmanship. It has characters engraved on it, thus:
>
> 1663
> . D .
> . I . F .
>
> The cup was given to Prince's St. church by the Rev. Andrew Kinsman [*the first pastor, 1763-1793*]. There is no doubt it was the property of the Rev. John Flavel of Dartmouth. Mr. Flavel was one of the ejected ministers. This cup was used by him and his congregation when observing the Lord's supper in the dark days of persecution when they worshipped in the roads, in barns, in houses secluded, and in the old Independent chapel at Dartmouth. These facts were not known to many until a short time ago, when an old member happened to be with us, made enquiries about the cup, and gave us the above information.
>
> *Signed*   THOMAS HOOPER.
>
> August 2, 1886.

2.—The Pilgrim Church Beakers, etc.

Of this interesting group a photograph has been contributed by the deacons of the Pilgrim Fathers' church, Southwark. The most important part consists of the four silver beakers, which were given to the church by a former pastor, the Rev. Jonathan Owen, in 1694. Their special importance is that they furnish a material link in the chain of evidence which connects the present church with that ministered to by Wadsworth in 1669 (before the Indulgence); and so *presumably* with the Paedobaptist remnant of the church gathered by H. Jacob in 1616.

There are two sets of patens, four of each. The deeper ones are of pewter, and were used by the church when it met in Deadman's Place (1690-1788); the others are plated and belong to the earlier years of the last century.

The candlesticks are traditionally reported to have stood in the table of the meeting-house in Union Street (1788-1820), when candles were the only means of illumination. The snuffers were their indispensable attendants.

The flagon is modern, and of no historic interest.

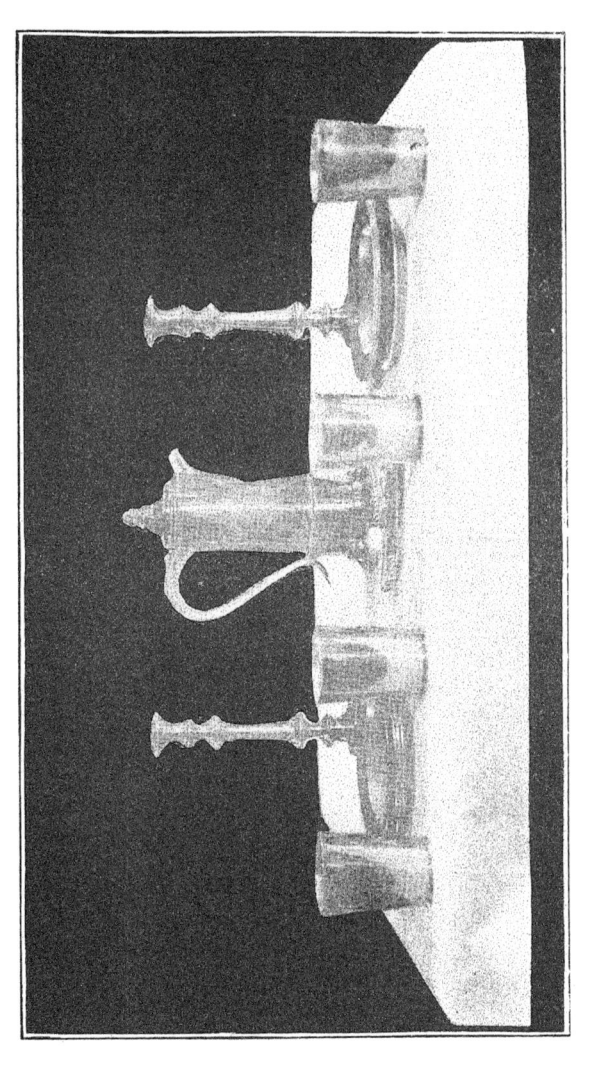

Communion Plate, etc., at the "Church of the Pilgrim Fathers," Southwark.

Hanover Chapel, Peckham

(Compiled at the request and with the assistance of the deacons)

THE early history of this congregation is somewhat obscure; but there seems no reason for rejecting the tradition that it originated in 1657, in connection with the labours of the Rev. JOHN MAYNARD.

On 11th August, 1643, the vicarage of Camberwell was sequestrated from Peter Danson (who figures discreditably in White's *Century of Scandalous Priests*) to Alexander Gregory. On 26th May, 1646, Mr. Gregory was "certified as fit for Lambeth."; but does not seem to have been removed thither, as afterwards we find a payment of £75 from the sale of bishops' lands made to his use as minister at Cirencester. The date of his removal is not given; but John Maynard succeeded him at Camberwell, in the same year 1646.

About a year later Surrey was divided into six "classical presbyteries," having their centres at (1) Godalming, (2) Dorking, (3) Guildford, (4) Kingston, (5) Croydon, (6) Reigate. The "Croydon classis" comprehended most of what is now accounted metropolitan Surrey; the presbytery consisted of five ministers and ten lay elders, among whom were the Rev. John Maynard and Messrs. Johnson and Webster of "Camerwell."

Mr. Maynard was M.A. of Queen's College, Oxford; he sat in the Westminster Assembly, preached twice (in 1644 and 1646) before the Long Parliament, and in 1654 was an assistant to the Commissioners for removing Scandalous Ministers. His puritanism seems to have made him unpopular with some of his parishioners, who "petitioned the committee for displacing improper ministers to remove him, he having a living in Sussex, but they did not succeed."[1]

In a pamphlet written in 1651 by Richard Culmer of Harbledown, entitled *The Minister's Hue and Cry*, there is a story how certain farmers in Camberwell were accustomed to defraud the minister of his tithes. "At last," they say, "he was glad to pack away from us, after an agreement made for his tythe by which we

---

[1] Manning's *History of Surrey*, from a MS. in the Bodleian.

got above a hundred pounds. We wearied out the Roundhead, and had our wills of him, for all his Tythe-laws and Committee-orders." The farmers are mentioned under fictitious names, and the name of "the Roundhead" is not given; but there can be little doubt that Maynard is intended: local tradition speaks of him as having been "forced by religious intolerance to resign the vicarage of Camberwell," and his successor seems to have been appointed in 1653. He thereafter took up his abode in what is now called Meeting-house Lane, and is said to have preached for some time in his own house; and afterwards, in 1657, to have erected the old meeting-house which gave name to the thoroughfare. Later, but when we are not informed, he seems to have left Peckham.

The "living in Sussex" which Mr. Maynard held together with his vicarage of Camberwell, was Mayfield, about 8 miles south of Tunbridge Wells. To this he was appointed in 1625 and was ejected in 1662. Necessarily this rural cure was served by a succession of assistants, the last of whom was ejected with him. Notwithstanding his frequent non-residence he seems to have been highly esteemed by his Mayfield parishioners, amongst whom he died 7th June, 1665, and was buried in Mayfield churchyard. On his tombstone is a Latin inscription, in which he is said to have been "the Light and Ornament of the parish for 40 years." Besides the sermons already mentioned he was the author of three treatises, which were only published after his death:—*The Beauty and Crown of Creation*, 1668; *A Memento for Young and Old*, 1669; and *The Law of God Ratified by the Gospel of Christ*, 1674.

There is also much uncertainty as to the few years immediately following Mr. Maynard's death. Local tradition affirms that he was followed by the Rev. BARTHOLOMEW ASHWOOD, the ejected rector of Axminster, Devon. He is said to have come to Peckham in 1664, and preached there for some years. But this tradition cannot be accepted as wholly correct. Ashwood in 1660, while still rector of Axminster, organized among his parishioners a Congregational church which subsists to this day. The records in its ancient church book were published in 1874 under the title of *Ecclesiastica; or a Book of Remembrance*. From this we learn that, in spite of ejection from his rectory, in spite of persecution and imprisonment, Ashwood retained his pastorate at Axminster until his death in 1678.[2] The church often had to meet in woods and fields and secret places, and persecution often drove the pastor from home; so that there is nothing unlikely in the supposition that he visited Peckham and preached there in 1664, and on subsequent occasions. But there is nothing of this in the

---

[2] The mistake is no doubt due to the compiler of a biographical dictionary, quoted in Manning's *History of Surrey*, who says that Ashwood "lived the remainder of his life" at Peckham, "dying a little before the Revolution." The writer evidently confounded Bartholomew, the father, with John, the son.

Ecclesiastica, nor was it known to Calamy or the editor of the *Nonconformists' Memorial*; and any continuous ministry at Peckham is out of the question. It is a noteworthy fact that in Sheldon's *Return of Conventicles*, 1669, there is no mention either of Peckham or of Camberwell; nor was any meeting-place in the parish licensed under the Indulgence in 1672. It would therefore seem that Maynard's meeting-house was for the time disused, and that whatever Nonconformist worship was carried on in Peckham was in secret, and probably intermittent. Whether Maynard had organized a regular society, and if so whether through these troublous times it maintained corporate continuity, are matters about which we have no information. However, we may accept it as a fact that Bartholomew Ashwood had *some*—though it is uncertain *what*—connection with Peckham Nonconformity between 1664 and 1678. Of his writings, published after his death, we have *The Heavenly Trade, or the Best Merchandizing*, 1679, and *The Best Treasure—a Discourse on Ephes. iii. 8*, 1681.

The next minister mentioned is the Rev. JOSEPH OSBORNE. He had been appointed to the vicarage of Benenden, Kent, in place of one who had been removed for incompetence. He was highly appreciated there, and after trial by Cromwell's commissioners his appointment was confirmed. At the Restoration he was strongly urged to conform; and the patron of the living, a hearty Royalist, refused to present anyone in his place. But Osborne replied that "faith and a good conscience would stand him in more stead than a hundred livings." After his ejectment in 1662 he still persisted in his Nonconformity, though the Dean of Rochester offered him a better benefice than that of which he had been deprived. After several removals he took up his abode at Brighton, where on 8th May, 1672, he was licensed under the Indulgence as an Independent preacher, and ministered to a settled congregation for nine years. In 1681, being again harassed for his Nonconformity, he came to Peckham, where he continued to preach till 1689. He then removed to Ashford in Kent, and afterwards held pastorates at Tenterden and Barsted. From the latter he retired on account of infirmity, and ended his days at Staplehurst on 28th December, 1714, at the age of 85.

All the above named were of the noble band of confessors who sacrificed home, status, and means of livelihood because they could not declare their "unfeigned assent and consent to all and everything contained and prescribed in and by" the Book of Common Prayer; which had been revised for the purpose, not of removing passages offensive to scrupulous consciences but, of casting out Puritanism from the Church, and if possible from the soil, of England. The succeeding ministers were for the most part Dissenters by birth, training and conviction.

The first of their number was Rev. JOHN BEAUMONT. He had been a student in Morton's academy, Newington Green; and was privately ordained with several other ministers in London in 1689. He came to Peckham soon after and remained till 1698, when he removed to Battersea. Thence he was called to Deptford, where he ministered for 32 years, and died in 1736. One tradition is that the Peckham church was first organized by "Beaumont of Deptford"; but, although there seems to be no definite record of the date, we may be pretty sure that its formal organization took place years before his time.

His successor was the Rev. JOHN ASHWOOD, son of Bartholomew Ashwood of Axminster. He was born in the same year in which the meeting-house was built; and studied under Theophilus Gale in his academy on Newington Green. For some time he was a schoolmaster at Axminster and Chard. In consequence of persecution he purposed, about 1683, to emigrate to Carolina, but was hindered by sickness. His brief memoir, written by Thomas Reynolds, refers to some great deliverance which he experienced, the particulars of which we are not told, but the facts are believed to be as follows:—Several members of the Axminster church were concerned in the ill judged enterprise of Monmouth in 1685, and one of them, at least, was slain in battle. Ashwood was charged with treason for sheltering some of the fugitives, and was sentenced to death by Jeffreys; but "was saved from execution by the influence usually employed in such cases at the needy Court." Whatever be the truth of this story he certainly suffered imprisonment in connection with the affair. After his release he became pastor of a church in Exeter. Thence, about 1695, he came to London, and for two or three years he preached in Hoxton Square and Spitalfields. In 1698 he undertook the pastorate at Peckham, where he died 22nd September, 1706, aged 49. He does not appear to have published anything in his lifetime, but to his memoir, printed in 1707, are appended two discourses under the title of *A Minister's Legacy to Fatherless Children*.

From the death of John Ashwood there is a chasm in the history which we are unable satisfactorily to fill. But from Dr. John Evans's list of meeting-houses in England, compiled about 1717 or soon after, we learn that the pastorate had been held by one GEORGE DAVY, who in 1716 removed to Prince's Street, Upper Moorfields. Whence he came to Peckham, and when, we have no information.

He was followed by the celebrated Dr. SAMUEL CHANDLER, who was the son of a minister at Hungerford (afterwards at Bath). He studied first under John Moore at Bridgwater, and afterwards under Samuel Jones at Gloucester, leaving the latter academy about the time when it was removed to Tewkesbury. There he formed lifelong friendships with two fellow-students named

Butler and Secker, both of whom conformed to the Established Church, and became, one, Bishop of Durham, and author of the immortal *Analogy of Religion*, and the other, Archbishop of Canterbury.

Chandler spent some time at the University of Leyden; and in 1716 was chosen pastor of the church in Peckham. The next year, the lease of the old meeting-house having expired, the congregation removed to a new edifice on the site now occupied by Hanover Chapel. Three years later Mr. Chandler suffered a serious misfortune; it was the year of the notorious South Sea Bubble, in which he was induced to venture the whole of his wife's property, and every penny of it was lost. He thereupon endeavoured to supplement his rather meagre stipend by opening a bookseller's shop in the Poultry; which business he carried on, conjointly with his pastorate, for several years. During this time he was associated with Dr. Nathaniel Lardner in a weekly lecture at the Old Jewry meeting-house on the evidences of natural and revealed religion. He afterwards delivered a second course on the same subject, which he printed in 1725 under the title *A Vindication of the Christian Religion, in two parts*. He presented a copy to Archbishop Wake; who, not suspecting that the author was other than a bookseller, wrote to him as follows:—"I cannot but own myself surprised to see so much good learning and just reasoning in a person of your profession; and do think it a pity you should not spend your time in writing books rather than in selling them."

The next year, 1726, he was invited to become assistant to the Rev. Thomas Leavesley, the minister at Old Jewry; and for about three years he was accustomed to preach there on one part of the day, and at Peckham the other part. At length, being elected co-pastor with Mr. Leavesley, he finally discontinued his ministrations at Peckham in 1729.

It was not till after Chandler had left Peckham that he became prominent in connection with the efforts which were made for the repeal of the Test Act. He it was who, after the failure of those efforts in 1738, headed a deputation to Walpole on the subject, and fairly cornered that shiftiest of Whig politicians. Reminding him of his frequent assurances of good will, qualified by the evasive addition that "the time had not yet arrived," he asked him bluntly "when that time would come," and received for once the straightforward answer "Never."

Chandler was a man of exceptional learning, and is said to have been able to write in Greek as readily as in English. Of his very numerous works the following (besides his *Vindication of the Christian Religion*), were issued while he was at Peckham:— *Paraphrase and Critical Commentary on the Prophet Joel*, 1725;

Hanover Chapel, Peckham

Reflections on the Conduct of Modern Deists, 1727; *Discourse on the Nature and Use of Miracles,* 1727; *Vindication of the Antiquity and Authority of Daniel's Prophecies,* 1728; and some sermons. It is not necessary to notice at length his later works, some of which were against the Deists, some against the Church of Rome, some in defence of religious liberty, and some dealing with theological controversies; but his *Life of David, Paraphrases on the Epistles to the Galatians, Ephesians and Thessalonians, History of the Inquisition,* and *History of Persecution,* deserve special mention. His theology was evangelical, though not Calvinistic; but in his printed sermons there is said to be a lack of warmth, of doctrinal clearness, and of practical application. His learning and literary abilities were appreciated by the Universities of Edinburgh and Glasgow, each of which conferred on him a diploma of D.D.; he was also a Fellow of the Royal Society, and of the Society of Antiquaries. He died 8th May, 1766, in the 73rd year of his age, and was buried in Bunhill Fields.

The Rev. THOMAS HADFIELD, M.D., who had been educated for the medical profession, followed Dr. Chandler. According to W. Wilson's MS. in Williams's Library he came from Midhurst. He was ordained, seemingly as co-pastor, on 19th October, 1726; the officiating ministers being the Revs. John Beaumont, Jos. Hill, and Thos. Reynolds. His *Confession of Faith* was printed; it is evangelical and trinitarian. In 1729 he became sole pastor, and exercised a useful ministry until his death, at the age of 46, on 21st February, 1741. Dr. Chandler preached his funeral sermon.

During Dr. Hadfield's pastorate, in 1737, a Mr. W. Tomkins endowed the church with £375 South Sea annuities, on condition that sermons should be preached yearly on Christmas Day, Easter Monday, Whitsunday, and the 1st day of August—the latter probably in commemoration of the death of Queen Anne, which frustrated the last Jacobite plot against religious freedom. (Other small endowments were given, by Mrs. Plunkett in 1762, Mr. Shanks in 1795, and Mrs. Hyardahl in 1831; but the capital value of the whole falls below £1,200.)

The next pastor was the Rev. JOHN MILNER, D.D. He is believed to have been a Somerset man, and was educated under the Rev. John Moore at Bridgwater. His wife was a daughter of one of the Taunton maids who in 1685, under the direction of the patriotic schoolmistress, Miss Blake, embroidered the Monmouth banner. Fortunately for her, she was removed from the school before the actual presentation. The location of Dr. Milner's first pastorate is not known, but in 1722 he ministered to a congregation at Yeovil, where he also kept a grammar school. While there he published three educational works which were much esteemed in their day; a Latin grammar in 1729, a Greek grammar in 1732, and a treatise on rhetoric in 1736. He took part in the ordination of Dr. Amory at Taunton in 1731, and in an ordination at Bridport in 1739. The sermon he preached on the latter occasion was expanded into a treatise having the title *Religious Liberty Asserted*. He accepted an invitation to Peckham on the death of Dr. Hadfield in 1741, and set up a boarding school in Meeting-house Lane. As a teacher of youth he had a high reputation. Towards the close of his life he had as an usher for a few months that erratic genius Oliver Goldsmith, who at his table first met Griffith the publisher, a meeting which had important literary results. Another of his ushers was Dr. Hawkesworth, a literary man of note in his day, now best remembered as the author of the stately morning hymn " In sleep's serene oblivion laid."

Dr. Milner was a popular preacher, and gathered around him as hearers many persons of social standing, culture, and influence. Among them was Chief Justice Copeland, who contributed liberally towards the necessary enlargement of the meeting-house. He was the author of a volume on *The Nature, Obligation, and Benefit of Public Worship*, 1748 ; *Instructions for Youth, in six Sermons*, 1751; *The Honour and Happiness of the Poor—Three Sermons, with Prayers and Hymns*, and a number of fast, thanksgiving, ordination, and funeral sermons. One of these was on the battle of Culloden, one on the death of Dr. Watts, and one on the Lisbon earthquake His preaching was thoroughly evangelical, so far as regards the mediatorial work of Christ; but vague as to His Person, suggesting an inclination towards the then popular Arianism. He died 24th June, 1757, aged 69, and was buried in Camberwell churchyard.

He was succeeded in August, 1758, by the Rev. SAMUEL BILLINGSLEY, son of Richard Billingsley, pastor at Whitchurch, Hants., and grandson of Nicholas Billingsley, who had been ejected by the Act of Uniformity from Weobly, Herefordshire. He was ordained at Marlborough in 1725 ; removed thence to Ashwick, Somerset, where he continued 18 years ; thence to Bradford-on-Avon, where he ministered for 10 years. At Peckham he was greatly beloved for his wisdom, zeal and kindness of heart. In 1770 he retired to Bath, where he ended his days.

On his retirement there were two candidates for the vacant pulpit ; one, the son of the retired pastor, and the other the Rev. RICHARD JONES, late minister of the church in Crosby Hall, which had been disbanded the previous year on the expiry of the lease. The choice of the church fell on the latter. Mr. Jones had been a pupil of Dr. Doddridge, and before going to Crosby Hall was for some time pastor of a Presbyterian church at Cambridge. He entered on his ministry at Peckham on 13th February, 1770. He is described as a ripe scholar, a fine preacher, and a saintly man ; yet his pastorate was, on the whole, a failure. He is understood to have been an Arian ; certainly his views as to the Person of

Christ were not such as are usually deemed orthodox ; while on the inspiration of Scripture and the future state he held opinions in advance of his age, though probably not such as would be severely criticised in the present day. During his pastorate the freehold of the building was secured, the lease granted in 1717 having been only for 60 years ; and the property was put in trust. But the congregation steadily dwindled, and towards the end the members could be counted on one's fingers. Mr. Jones died on 30th September, 1800, in the 73rd year of his age. His chief publication was *Friendship with God ; an Essay*, 1772.

A new era began with the new century. Shortly after the death of Mr. Jones the church officers, failing to obtain a supply elsewhere, sent to Homerton College for a student. He came—a lad in his 19th year ; and, as he afterwards wrote, " well knowing the kind of doctrine which had obtained during thirty years, he resolved to avail himself of the only opportunity that might be afforded to assert the divinity of our Lord and Saviour Jesus Christ," from Heb. I. 10-12. Contrary to his expectation, this visit was the commencement of a ministry that lasted 53 years, and was one of the most remarkable London pastorates of the century.

WILLIAM BENGS COLLYER was the son of a builder at Blackheath, and was born on 14th April, 1782. As a boy he was noted for his fluency of speech ; at the age of 13 he is reported to have addressed a cottage meeting, and about that time was permitted to attend classes at Homerton College. At the age of 16 he was admitted a theological student, his tutors being the Revs. J. Fell, S. Berry, and for a short time J. Pye-Smith. His visit to Peckham was followed by requests to supply again and again ; the congregation rapidly increased, and an invitation to the pastorate speedily followed. Mr. Collyer was ordained on 17th November, 1801, the officiating ministers being Drs. Fisher, Hunter, Winter, Messrs. Berry, Brooksbank, S. Morrell, and Urwick. The young pastor's confession of faith was uncompromisingly evangelical.

At the first communion service, January, 1802, five new members were added to the ten who previously formed the entire fellowship. Improvement was rapid : a public prayer meeting was at once instituted, soon followed by a Wednesday evening lecture ; and in a year's time the congregation numbered 500. A Sunday school was commenced in 1804, and two years later a day school on the Lancastrian plan. About this time Mr. Collyer preached a course of sermons on "Scripture Facts," which excited much interest. They were published in 1807, with a dedication to Lord Chancellor Erskine ; and no less than three bishops' names appear on the list of subscribers. This was the first of a series of seven volumes, which together constituted a valuable course of Christian apologetics.

Peckham Meeting-house: 1717-1817.

In 1808 an anonymous writer published a malicious book entitled *Hints on the Nature and Effects of Evangelical Preaching; by a Barrister*, which was designed to prepare the way for the attempt, made later in Lord Sidmouth's notorious bill, to restrict religious liberty. Mr. Collyer promptly replied in *An Appeal to the Legislature and the Public in Answer to the Hints of a Barrister &c*; and thus rendered effective service in frustrating the conspiracy.

It was about this time that Mr. Collyer attracted the notice of some members of the royal family. The circumstances have never been clearly explained; but acquaintance grew into a warm personal friendship with the Dukes of Kent and Sussex, especially the former. It is a notable fact that these only of the sons of George III. were free from gross personal vices. In 1808 Mr. Collyer received from the University of Edinburgh a diploma of D.D., which is said to have come " through the hands of H.R.H. the Duke of Kent." It is a pretty safe conjecture that it was conferred at H.R.H.'s suggestion: the bestowal of such a degree, however well deserved, on a young man of 26 is so unusual as to invite some explanation. Dr. Collyer afterwards received the degree of LL.D., and was admitted a Fellow of the Society of Antiquaries. In the same year, 1808, the chapel was enlarged by the erection of side galleries.

It may be convenient here to name the remaining volumes of Dr. Collyer's Apologetic series, with their dates and dedications :—

2. *Lectures on Scripture Prophecies*, 1809 ; dedicated to the Countess of Glencairn.

3. *Lectures on the Miracles*, 1st February, 1812; dedicated to H.R.H. the Duke of Kent. The author refers to "my intimate acquaintance with your character."

4. *Lectures on the Parables*, 1823 ; dedicated to H.R.H. the Duke of Sussex, with a reference to the Duke's interest in Biblical studies.

5. *Lectures on Scripture Doctrines*, 1817 ; dedicated to William Wilberforce, Esq.

6. *Lectures on Christian Duties*, 1819 ; dedicated by permission to the Duchess of Kent.

7. *Christianity Compared with Mohammedanism, Hindooism, Ancient Philosophy, and Modern Deism*, 1818 ; dedicated to Prince Leopold of Saxe-Coburg, afterwards King of Belgium.

Contemporary critics took care to make known abroad the fact that Dr. Collyer was not wholly free from personal vanity. It was scarcely surprising, in view of the many distinguished personages—including princes, a lord chancellor, and at least six bishops, whose names appear in his subscription lists. But his dedications are remarkably free from adulation, and have about them a manly tone which is in the highest degree honourable to all concerned. At a later time the volumes were issued in a consecutive series, in the order indicated by the figures prefixed above.

In 1812 Dr. Collyer published *Hymns, partly Collected and partly Original*, a book of unusual merit for its day. It contained nearly 1,000 hymns by at least 90 authors; of which above 100 were previously unpublished, nearly 60 being the compiler's own productions. Later publications contain about 100 more of Dr. Collyer's hymns, many of them for special occasions. Most are of a meditative character, and though often of singular beauty are not well suited for public worship. Only a few are found in modern hymn books, but two of them are destined long to survive; one, partly translated from the German, beginning "Great God, what do I see and hear?" is universally popular; the other, as embodying the Gospel call, has rarely been equalled. What can surpass the tender persuasiveness of a verse like this?—

> "Return, O wanderer, return!
> Thy Saviour bids thy spirit live;
> Go to His bleeding feet, and learn
> How freely Jesus can forgive!"

In January, 1814, with the full approval of the Peckham congregation, Dr. Collyer undertook the Sunday afternoon services at Salter's Hall, Cannon Street; an ancient Presbyterian church with a remarkable history, which originated before the Revolution. The ministers had long been Arian, if not Unitarian, and the congregation was reduced to a mere handful. Here, as at Peckham, Dr. Collyer's ministry led to both numerical and spiritual revival. In 1821 he was violently assailed by some of the Unitarian party in a pamphlet entitled *Some of Dr. Collyer's Errors Stated and Corrected*. In June, 1825, he found it necessary to restrict his labours to Peckham; after his withdrawal the Salter's Hall congregation again declined, and in a few years the place was closed.

In 1817 the Peckham meeting-house, which had been built just a hundred years before, gave place to the present more commodious structure. Hanover Chapel, as the new building was called in compliment to the royal family, was opened on 17th June, Dr. Collyer preaching in the morning, and the Rev. W. Jay of Bath in the evening. The Duke of Sussex was present at both services. The organ is understood to have been presented by the Duke of Kent. The two princes are said to have worshipped at "Hanover" on several occasions; and, as was to be expected under the circumstances, the place was frequently crowded by a

Hanover Chapel, Peckham

fashionable congregation. It must be remembered that at this time both Peckham and Camberwell were villages completely detached from the metropolis and from each other. Among the worshippers at Hanover Chapel at this time was the distinguished philanthropist, Thomas Thompson. He was born in 1785, and was an intimate friend of Dr. Collyer. In 1818 he established the first floating chapel for sailors; in the following year the Sailors' Society; and soon afterwards the first Sailors' Home. In 1819 he initiated the Home Missionary Society, of which for forty years he was treasurer. Though only moderately wealthy, for many years he sent a yearly anonymous donation of £100 to the London Missionary Society; and his gifts for the benefit of sailors totalled at least £3,000. While he attended Hanover he lived at Brixton, whence however he removed in 1829; and in his later years resided at Poundsford Park, Somerset, where he died in 1865. His daughter Jemima, known to the world as Mrs. Luke, was born in 1813; and to the end of a long life retained grateful memory of spiritual help from a sermon of Dr. Collyer's on Luke xxii. 61, which she heard when ten years old. About 1839 she had fully arranged to proceed as a missionary to India, but was prevented by failure of health. Two years later she wrote her ever popular children's hymn, "I think when I read that sweet story of old." In 1843 she married the Rev. Samuel Luke, and after a long widowhood died early in 1906.

Many stories are told of Dr. Collyer's intimacy with the royal dukes, which are probably apocryphal. There seems, however, to be some authority for the statement that, during a visit to Kensington Palace in 1819, the infant princess, afterwards Queen Victoria, was placed by her father on the doctor's knee; and that in somewhat later childhood she was an occasional playmate of his only daughter. It is said that he was once invited to enter Parliament; a safe seat for a pocket borough being offered him, but declined. And there can be little doubt that, if he would have conformed to the Established Church, the highest ecclesiastical rank would have been within his reach; but, notwithstanding courtly associations, he steadily adhered to the principles of evangelical Nonconformity. He was an Independent by conviction, but scarcely a Congregationalist; indeed he was somewhat inclined to be autocratic, and had no liking for church meetings. Up to this time the Peckham Dissenters had always been reputed Presbyterian, though since the Restoration there had been no Presbyterian Church courts, and the churches so called had always been practically Independent. The management, however, had been entirely in the hands of the church officers, and in Dr. Collyer's time affairs were directed by the trustees and a committee of management.

By the time Dr. Collyer attained the age of 50 his activities were much restricted both by the state of his health and by his personal idiosyncrasy. An appreciative obituary notice in the *British Banner* says of him :—" Soft, gentle, refined almost to effeminacy . . . his popularity became a burden to him, consuming his time by endless and hurtful attentions which were paid him almost to the extent of persecution. . . . He became weary of popularity, and considered that God's work was best advanced by steady, regular, organised labour." He was a man of warm affections, kind and gentle to an extreme ; "his heart and purse ever open to the cry of the needy." In his later years he published little except a number of sermons. Two volumes, however, demand notice. When the Dissenters' Marriage Act was passed, in 1838, he put forth a *Manual* of liturgical forms for baptism, marriage, burial, etc., judiciously adapted from the Book of Common Prayer, and accompanied by about 90 hymns for sacramental and ceremonial occasions, and for the use of the sick. At a later time he was deeply interested in efforts for the conversion of the Jews ; and in 1848 published a little volume of *Hymns for Israel*, which illustrate at once the strength and weakness of his muse. Before this his increasing feebleness necessitated an assistant, who was found in the person of the Rev. H. J. GAMBLE, from Margate. He commenced his duties as co-pastor on 8th November, 1846 ; about which time the chapel was considerably enlarged. On entering upon the 50th year of his ministry Dr. Collyer preached a remarkable sermon from Acts xxvi. 22,23. In this he solemnly appealed to any who might have been present at his ordination, and to all who had at any time attended on his ministry, whether in one single instance he had swerved from the doctrine then laid down, and the profession then made. " I have learned no other way of salvation. . . . I have found no other refuge for my own soul ; but I am persuaded that the Saviour is all sufficient, that this hope will not make ashamed, that this foundation can never fail."

In March, 1850, the church presented to Dr. Collyer, as a mark of esteem and affection, a portrait of himself painted by H. W. Pickersgill, R.A. In October, 1852, Mr. Gamble removed to Clapton, much to the regret of the senior pastor; who, however, though in great bodily weakness, took part in the recognition service. (It may be noted that Mr. Gamble died in 1887, at the age of 65.) His place at Peckham was supplied by the Rev. ROBERT WYE BETTS, from New College, who entered on the duties of assistant minister on 1st May, 1853. Mr. Betts bore striking testimony, in a funeral sermon, to the affectionate relations which subsisted between himself and his venerable senior. Dr. Collyer preached his last sermon on 11th December, 1853, and died on Sunday, 8th January, 1854, in his 72nd year. He was buried in Nunhead cemetery, where a conspicuous monument records his virtues.

Mr. Betts was a native of Portsea. While at college he was a popular supply, and an effective open air preacher—a form of Christian service in which he greatly delighted. It is said that when he received Dr. Collyer's invitation to become his assistant he had already written, but not sent, his acceptance of a call from another church. Within a few months he succeeded to the sole pastorate, and was soon confronted with serious difficulties. While many were edified by his ministry, some were offended, and spoke of him as too young for the position. Such opposition only made him the more zealous to overcome evil with good, and the church was crowded with an appreciative congregation. About this time, or soon after, the Congregational order was fully adopted, and deacons first appointed. But other difficulties arose from the personal jealousies of cliques within the church; and ultimately some withdrew "who might not have profited so well had they remained." An opportunity for their withdrawal was afforded by the erection of Linden Grove church, which was needed to meet the claims of an increasing population, and was opened in May, 1857. The first sermon was preached by the Rev. Jas. Sherman; Mr. Betts was present, and afterwards preached there on many occasions.

Somewhat later a small chapel at Hatcham was rented, where preaching was commenced and a Sunday school established. It was long hoped that this might become the nucleus of a new church, but these hopes were not realised. The mission was carried on, with varying fortunes, for many years; but at length, by resolution of the church, it was discontinued in 1906.

Greater success attended another effort. The school accommodation at Hanover was very defective, and Mr. Betts projected a building which might serve for school and social purposes, and at the same time be a memorial of his revered predecessor. The project was happily realized; and in 1862 Collyer Hall was opened and paid for.

Another successful enterprise, which owed its inception to Mr. Betts, was the Surrey Congregational Union; the first meeting of which was held at Weybridge on 9th June, 1863. He was also a leading promoter of the united open air mission services on Sunday afternoons on Peckham Rye.

These and other labours were carried on in much bodily weakness; and twice Mr. Betts found it necessary to seek relief in a milder climate for several months. He died, after much suffering, on Tuesday, 1st December, 1868, in the 44th year of his age. His published works are a volume for the young, entitled *Words in Season*, and five or six sermons.

A brief memoir of Mr. Betts was written by the Rev. Thos. Ray, LL.D., a retired minister who at the time kept a school at Peckham, and rendered occasional aid during the pastor's illness.

Mr. Betts was followed, after an interval of above a year, by the Rev. GEO. B. RYLEY, who, after leaving Cheshunt College in 1866, had held a four years' pastorate at Bocking, in Essex. He came to Peckham in 1870, and remained till 1889. During this time the environment of Hanover was undergoing a steady change, which seriously affected the character of the congregation, and the methods of Christian work adapted to the new surroundings. The strain was probably increased by the erection, in 1899, of the church in Dulwich Grove.

The years of Mr. Ryley's pastorate were marked by the accomplishment of much useful work. In 1870 Collyer Hall was improved by the addition of a gallery, classrooms, and a smaller hall with a separate entrance, at a cost of £1,100. A working men's club was initiated, but this only lasted about four years. A literary society was formed in 1874, which still subsists. For several years a Christmas dinner was given in the large hall to some hundreds of poor children and aged people. This afterwards gave place to a soup kitchen, and this again to a daily meal for poor children, at the nominal charge of a halfpenny, but in many cases quite gratuitous. This continued until 1892.

Mr. Ryley was a hard worker and a good organizer, and was much esteemed for his efforts on behalf of the poor. During the later years of his pastorate he was a member of the London School Board, and did good service on its committees. After 19 years he removed to Christ Church, Addiscombe, and four years later to Bow. At length, in 1897, after more than 30 years' not unfruitful ministry in the free atmosphere of Nonconformity, he condescended to accept." orders" in the Episcopal Church!

Three short pastorates ensued. The Rev. Henry Barron, a student of New College, had in the course of fourteen years held pastorates at Portsmouth, Basingstoke, and at Batley (Yorks). While at Basingstoke he had been secretary of the Hants Congregational Union, and had honourably distinguished himself as a champion of religious liberty when the municipal authorities attempted to suppress the meetings of the Salvation Army. He accepted the call of Peckham in 1890, but somehow the situation proved uncongenial, and he only remained about a year. From 1891 to 1896 he ministered at East Finchley, and then retired in infirm health. He latterly resided at Tooting, where he organized the local Free Church Council. He was a man of genial disposition, high public spirit, and fine literary taste. He died, after a long and painful illness, on 27th August, 1902, in his 55th year, and was buried in Nunhead cemetery.

The Rev. JOHN WILLS, from Handsworth Wesleyan College followed from 1892 to 1894. He then removed to West Croydon, where he long exercised a useful ministry. He was succeeded by the Rev. J. W. BOWMAN, M.A., B.D., a student of Lancashire

Hanover Chapel, Peckham 169

College, who had ministered for five years at Newcastle. He came to Peckham in 1895, and resigned in 1900. Since then he has held a charge at Rothbury, (Northumberland), and is now at Whitby.

By this time it was evident that new conditions required new methods. The chapel was renovated, the electric light introduced, and "evenings for the people" instituted—where secular topics were dealt with in a religious spirit, and emphasis was laid on the fact that the Kingdom of God is concerned with the things of this life as well as the future. In 1901 the pastorate was undertaken by the Rev. JOHN JAS. POOL, B.D., son of the Rev. Robert Pool of Sedbergh. After studying at Sedbergh grammar school and Rotherham College, he had ministered for a short time at Todmorden, and then for six years at Union Chapel, Calcutta, and for ten years at the English Congregational church, Rheims. Under his guidance measures were adopted to increase the spiritual efficiency of the church by work on social lines. Men's Own and Women's Own meetings were instituted; a friendly At Home was arranged once a month, after the evening service; a Social Institute was founded, where encouragement was given to harmless recreation; and various departments of Congregational work were assigned to committees, not consisting exclusively of church members, which occasionally met in general council. In this work invaluable aid was rendered by Mr. WALTER J. J. FRANKS, formerly a lay preacher in the Methodist New Connexion, who in 1906 became assistant minister. The result of these efforts was seen in large accessions to the fellowship of the church, especially of the young. Meanwhile, however, the erection of Herne Hill church in 1904 led to some depletion of the congregation, and diminution of financial resources. Another cloud has lately arisen, in the retirement—through failing health—of the pastor. At first it was hoped that a sea voyage and a few months' rest would effect his restoration. But about Christmas, 1906, under urgent medical advice, he tendered his resignation, which was regretfully accepted, and a few weeks later he sailed for America. He is the author of several interesting works, of which *Woman's Influence in the East*, and a delightful memoir of his father, are the most noteworthy.

Mention must here be made of two members of the church who, under the auspices of the London Missionary Society, have gone forth to preach the Gospel in the regions beyond. Miss ANNE KEET, in 1823, became the wife of the Rev. W. Campbell, of Bangalore; who after his retirement from foreign service held a pastorate at Croydon. The Rev. CHAS. THOS. PRICE, after a course of study at Cheshunt College, laboured in Madagascar from 1875 to 1882. He has since held pastorates at Lenham and Buckingham, and is now at Ross. Rev. BENJ. THOS. BUTCHER, also a Cheshunt student, was appointed to New Guinea in 1904, and is labouring there on the Torres Straits station.

The 250th anniversary of the church was held on 14th April, 1907, and succeeding days. Memorial sermons were preached by the venerable Jas. Guinness Rogers, D.D., and a series of enthusiastic meetings followed on several evenings, inspired by gratitude for the past and hope for the future.

T. G. CRIPPEN.

Mill Hill School.

The Centenary of Mill Hill School (1807-1907)

THE history of education among Nonconformists has yet to be written, but it may be said with certainty that when undertaken it will prove to be a most interesting field of research. Of the two thousand ministers who were ejected by the Act of Uniformity the greater number had been educated at Oxford or Cambridge. The two Universities themselves were governed by Puritans during the Commonwealth, and not the least famous of Oxford's vice-chancellors was the Independent, John Owen. No less eminent for learning than for piety, these evicted parsons in many cases set up schools of their own in spite of the penalties of the Clarendon Code. Among the private schools thus established was that of the Rev. Richard Swift, the vicar of Edgware until 1662. He was one of the few ejected ministers who had not been educated at the University, but he seems to have been a good classic notwithstanding.

The village of Mill Hill in which he started his school was "right off the high road" in every sense of the word, and was a fairly safe place of retreat for a persecuted dissenter. While Richard Swift was at Mill Hill, Richard Baxter was taking refuge at Totteridge, the adjoining village, and the two were subsequently still nearer neighbours when they were confined in Newgate for holding conventicles in their own houses. Swift had great difficulties with his school when the plague broke out and carried off several of his boys, but he ultimately recovered his numbers, and died in

1701, a moderately prosperous schoolmaster, in the 86th year of his age. Of the actual work done in his school we have no exact record; but we can gather from descriptions of similar seminaries that it was by no means a narrow curriculum, including Greek, Latin, logic, metaphysics, natural and moral philosophy, rhetoric, theology, and Biblical criticism. "The history of such schools," says a well known writer, "would be the finest record of education, outside of the ancient Universities of Oxford and Cambridge. It is not improbable that in the early eighteenth century their academies afforded an education even superior to the contemporary Universities, superior if not in book learning at any rate in the culture of the finer virtues of life."

During the latter half of the eighteenth century, however, there was a marked decline; and the need for a school on more adequate lines was very much felt among the Nonconformists of London. At a time of strain and stress, when the great shadow of Napoleon was still darkening the map of Europe, a meeting of prominent dissenters was held at the New London Tavern, Cheapside, with Mr. Samuel Favell in the chair, to found a school "for affording the best means for a sound, learned and pious education." The day chosen was June 18th, 1806, a day destined to become world renowned nine years later by the battle of Waterloo. It was not, however, until a full year afterwards, in June, 1807, that the school was an accomplished fact. The list of founders deserves to be given in full as a tribute to the strength of purpose and magnificent faith of a body of men who could venture to erect a school on such broad foundations at such an inauspicious time. The committee consisted of seven ministers and twenty laymen: The Revs. John Atkinson (of Homerton College, Mill Hill's first headmaster), John Clapton, junr., (of the Weigh House), John Humphries (afterwards headmaster), Joseph Hughes (one of the founders of the Bible Society and its secretary) John Savile, John Pye-Smith (Fellow of the Royal Society and principal of Homerton College), John Townsend (founder of the Deaf and Dumb Asylum); and Messrs. W. Alers Hankey, W. Barnard, J. Benwell, J. Bunnell, Isaac Buxton, M.D., John Fowell Buxton, James Collins, Samuel Favell (the first treasurer), John Fenn, Joseph Fox, James Gurney, J. Gutteridge, E. Maitland, J. Page, W. Sabine, W. Savill, E. Stonard, E. Tompkins, H. Waymouth, W. Whitwell, J. Wilson. It is a remarkable fact that the foundations of Mill Hill should have been so extremely broad, seeing all the educational disadvantages under which Nonconformists had suffered for a century and a half. It was only a hundred years before that a Bill had been passed through both Houses of Parliament forbidding any to teach in a school without a licence from a bishop; who would be most unlikely to grant one to a Nonconformist. Another sixty years was still to elapse before the Universities would be opened to Nonconformists. And yet in founding Mill Hill it was distinctly stated that "while the school was intended mainly for dissenters, sons of Episcopalian parents would be very welcome, and no attempt would be made to proselytize—such a thing being entirely foreign to the catholic foundation of the school."

The school was commenced in Ridgway House; an old Jacobean mansion in which had lived a succession of Quakers — Jeremiah Harman, a descendant of one of Cromwell's Ironside colonels; Michael Russell, and his son-in-law Peter Collinson. The latter was an eminent botanist, and is believed to have planted many of the trees still standing on the school estate. He was a friend of Benjamin Franklin, and of Linnaeus, who during a visit is said to have planted some cedars in the grounds. The successive headmasters at Ridgway House were (1) the Rev. John Atkinson (July 1807-Dec. 1810), (2) the Rev. Maurice Phillips (Jan. 1811-Dec. 1818), (3) the Rev. John Humphreys (April 1819-July 1825), and (4) James Corrie, M.D. (July 1825-Dec. 1827). How well these gentlemen acquitted themselves in their office is to be seen in the names of the eminent men who during these early years of the history of the school were among their pupils; such as the Rev. R. W. Hamilton, (1808-10) LL.D., of Leeds, chairman of the Congregational Union in 1847; Sir Thos. Noon Talfourd (1808-10), Justice of Common Pleas, friend of Lamb and Dickens, and author of *Ion* and other dramas; Henry Shaw (1815-), "father" of the city of St. Louis, Missouri, to which his benefactions amounted to about a million sterling; James Fraser (1816-19), founder of *Fraser's Magazine*; the Rev. Jas. Challis (1818-20), M.A., senior wrangler 1825, Fellow of Trinity College, Cambridge; and the Rev. H. Mayo Gunn, Congregational minister of Warminster, a notable champion of religious liberty.

The present schoolhouse, designed by Sir Wm. Tite, was commenced in 1825, and finished in 1827, at a cost of £25,000. Of the old boys who passed from the old house to the new the most noteworthy are the eminent church musician, the Rev. Thomas Helmore, M.A., "priest in ordinary" at the Chapel Royal, St. James's, editor of the *Hymnal Noted* and other works of the same class; and the Rev. Thos. Rawson Birks, M.A., Fellow of Trinity College, Cambridge, and Professor of Moral Philosophy.

During the next seven years no less than three headmasters followed in quick succession: (5) the Rev. George Samuel Evans, M.A. Glas. (Dec. 1827-July 1828); (6) the Robert Cullen (Dec. 1828-May 1831); (7) the Rev. Henry Lea Berry, M.A. Glas., an old Mill Hill boy (May 1831-Sept. 1834). To this period belong some of the most distinguished alumni of the school, *e.g.*, the Rev. Robert Gandell (1829-30), M.A., Fellow of Hertford and Queen's Colleges, Oxford, and Laudian Professor of Arabic; the Rev. Edward White (1829-32), of Kentish Town, author of *Life of Christ*, &c., and chairman of the Congregational Union, 1886; Sir Samuel Davenport (1830-33), LL.D., K.C.M.G., one of the earliest settlers in South Australia; and the Right Rev. W. Jacobson, D.D., Fellow of Lincoln College, Oxford, and Bishop of Chester.

The next headmaster was (8) Thomas Priestley, (Oct. 1834-Sept. 1852). He was grandnephew of the famous natural philosopher and Unitarian divine, the Rev. Joseph Priestley, LL.D. With him began what was long regarded as the school's golden age. During his administration, with the Rev. Wm. Clayton as chaplain, the number of boys rose to 134. It is a noteworthy fact that in 1838, the second year in which it was possible to achieve such a distinction, a Mill Hill boy, William Ridley, matriculating in London University, took the first place in honours for natural history and chemistry. Mr. Priestley's most eminent pupils were Benjamin Scott, F.R.A.S., for many years Chamberlain of the City of London; the Very Rev. Thomas Edw. Bridgett (1837-9), rector of St. Joseph's R.C. Theological College, Teignmouth; Thomas Barker (1840-43), J.P., D.L., editor of the *Daily News*; Horatio Nelson Lay (1841-45), C.B., Chinese Secretary to Lord Elgin's special mission to China, 1858, Inspector General of Customs for the Chinese Government, 1859-67 ; the Right Hon. Lord Winterstoke (1842-7), formerly M.P. for Coventry and Bristol, now chairman of the court of governors of the school; Thomas Scrutton (1844-), member of the first London School Board, and remembered for many benefactions ; Albert Henry Bamfield (1844-6), Lieut.-general, distinguished for military service in India ; Philip Henry Sandelands (1844-7), Major-general ; Sir Alfred George Marten (1845-6), M.A., K.G., Fellow of St. John's College and M.P. for Cambridge ; Sir Wm. Roberts (1845-6), M.D., F.R.S., Professor of Medicine in the University of Manchester ; Honble. Alfred Peach Hensman (1846-8), Attorney-General of Western Australia, afterwards a judge of the Supreme Court.

The next headmaster was (9) the Rev. **Philip Smith**, B.A., Lond., an old Mill Hill boy and brother of the more famous Sir William Smith, of *Dictionary* renown. He ruled from December 1852 to July 1860. "None of the headmasters more successfully embodied the twofold idea with which the school was founded, scholarship and broad Evangelist Christianity," nor has any more adequately fulfilled the requirements of the school motto : " Et virtutem et Musas." Among his pupils may be mentioned Alexander Crum Brown (1853-4), D.Sc., M.D., F.R.S., Professor of Chemistry in Edinburgh University ; Philip Henry Pye-Smith (1854-6), B.A., M.D., F.R.S., Vice-Chancellor of London University ; Sir Alfred Tristram Lawrence (1854-9), M.A., LL.B., Camb., K.C., Judge of the Supreme Court ; Sir Ernest Mason Satow (1856-59), K.C.M.G., H.M.'s Minister successively at Tangier, Tokio, and Peking ; Sir Albert Spicer (1858-60), Bart., M.P., chairman of the Congregational Union, 1893 ; and the Rev. Walter F. Adeney (1859), M.A., D.D., principal of Lancashire Independent College.

On the retirement of Mr. Smith several changes were made in the administration; and this fact, together with deficiency of funds, made the position of the next three headmasters extremely difficult. These were (10) the Rev. Wm. Flavel Hurndall, M.A., Lond., Ph.D. Heidelb., (July 1860-July 1863); (11) the Rev. Philip Chapman Barker, M.A., LL.B. Lond., (July 1863-July 1864); (12) the Rev. George D. Bartlett, M.A. Aber. (July 1864-July 1868). These all made earnest efforts to save the school from decline, but their efforts were unavailing, and in 1868 it was decided to close the school. Mr. Thos. Scrutton, however, succeeded in enlisting the sympathies of several prominent men, especially Samuel Morley, M.P., and the Rev. H. Alford, D.D., Dean of Canterbury. It was the time when the great battle for the abolition of tests in the Universities was being fought and won; and the governors of Mill Hill, being thus encouraged, resolved to continue the school on a broader foundation, and with an atmosphere from which the dominance of any particular sect should be carefully excluded. A new scheme was approved by the Court of Chancery; the property of the school was placed under the management of a newly elected court of governors, and all surplus income was directed to be applicable only to the improvement of the school. The new foundation was too late for Mill Hill to be recognized under the Public Schools Act of 1867; but it is only from the date of its reconstruction that it can claim really to have been a public school in the modern acceptation of the term.

The new headmaster was (13) Dr. R. F. Weymouth, M.A., the first D.Lit. of London University, (Sept. 1869-July 1886). He was able to gather around him an exceptionally efficient staff including the Rev. Robert Harley, F.R.S., Dr. Fred.

Stock, D.Lit. Lond., and Dr. J. A. H. Murray, editor of the great *Oxford Dictionary*. A long period of prosperity ensued, and many University and other distinctions were won by those who were educated in the school. Even during the preceding years of depression the honour of Mill Hill had been upheld by men like the Rev. H. Arnold Thomas (1861-) M.A. Lond. and Camb., chairman of the Congregational Union in 1898; and Alfred Cort Haddon (1867-8), M.A., Sc.D. Camb., F.R.S., F.Z.S., Professor of Zoology at Cambridge: and within a few years from the reconstruction of the school it sent forth Thos. Edw. Scrutton (1870-73), M.A. Lond. and Camb., LL.B. Lond., K.G., Fellow and Professor of Constitutional Law in University College, London; Thomas McKinnon Wood (1871-2), LL.D. St. And., chairman of London County Council, 1898; Owen Seaman (1874-8) M.A., Camb., Professor of Literature in the School of Science, Newcastle, and since editor of *Punch*; the Rev. S. Lavington Hart (1876-), M.A. Camb., D.Sc. Lond., Head of the Walford Hart Memorial College, Tientsin, China; George Kemp (1877-81), colonel and M.P.; and Herbert Fitz-Edwin Ward (1877-), African explorer. During Dr. Weymouth's headship Burton Bank was erected (1875) as a boarding house for 34 boys, the sanatorium and swimming bath were built, a school magazine and natural history society were founded, and the Old Millhillians' Club was inaugurated. The climax of this period was the distribution of prizes on "New Foundation Day" 1879, by the Rt. Honble. W. E. Gladstone, shortly after which the school's number reached the then unprecedented total of 180. After this the school entered on another period of depression, and in 1886 Dr. Weymouth resigned.

Shortly before this Dr. Murray had retired. For his convenience in working on the *Dictionary* he

RIDGWAY HOUSE
(original habitation of Mill Hill School).

had erected a wooden and iron building which was called the Scriptorium ; which on leaving he presented to the school for use as a reading room. It was unfortunately burnt down in 1902 ; but was rebuilt on an improved plan, from the design of Mr. T. E. Collcutt, F.R.I.B.A., in the following year.

From July 1886 to July 1891 the headmaster was (14) Mr. Chas. Vince, M.A. 'Camb., who subsequently sought fame as secretary of the Tariff Reform League. At his retirement the number of boys had fallen to 61.

A new era of prosperity began with the advent of his successor, (15) J. D. McClure, M.A., LL.D. Mus.B. Trin. Col. Camb. He at once threw his whole heart and soul into the development of the school, with a success which may be in some degree measured by a numerical test. In his first term the number of boys rose to 75, in May 1898, it was 185, and to-day it has reached the splendid total of 260. Under his direction the playing fields have been enlarged and levelled, the gymnasium rebuilt, the sanatorium enlarged, and a new museum and music rooms built. A headmaster's house was erected in 1897. The following year a new chapel was built from designs by Mr. Basil Champneys, and was formally opened for worship on New Foundation Day, 1898, by the Rev. Dr. Fairbairn ; the old chapel being transformed into a "big school." In 1899 a new block of class rooms and a chemical laboratory were added, largely through the generosity of Mr. Herbert Marnham. 1904 saw the erection of "Collinson House," with accommodation for 40 boys, from the designs of Mr. T. E. Collcutt; and since then Lord Winterstoke, to whom the new chapel was largely due, has crowned his many gifts by adding to them a new library. Meanwhile Mill Hill has held its own alike in the fields of sport and in competition for scholarships at the Universities, in Class Lists and Triposes.

The achievements and prospects of the school were well summed up the other day in a speech delivered by the present headmaster. "Our hopes for the future must needs be founded on the experience of the past. The fact that there has been in the last few years a steady and continuous growth in the numbers attending shews that the school supplies a distinct want. The same period has witnessed a growth in the efficiency of the school and in the development of that *esprit de corps* which every great school invariably and inevitably inspires. It has been made clear that boys and masters trained under widely different condition, and belonging to different churches, can and do live in mutual helpfulness and respect united by the strongest of ties—a common loyalty and a common faith.........In a few years at most the secondary schools of the kingdom will be of two types, (1) those supported wholly or in part from the public funds; (2) those which rely entirely on their own endowments and fees. There cannot be the least doubt as to which class Mill Hill must belong, for to accept State aid would be to destroy her very *raison d'être*. For Mill Hill is, in truth, a great religious foundation; great, not in the magnitude of endowment nor in the numbers gathered within her walls, but great in the work she is called upon to do, and in the principles of which she is the living embodiment. To support such an institution is not merely an act of loyalty to a beloved *alma mater*, but an act of loyalty to cherished convictions—an act of faith in a great principle. The school begins its second century of existence under happy auspices. Never has its equipment been so good; never have its numbers been so great; never has the school spirit been so strong; never has the faith in the future been so firm; never has the ideal which Mill Hill imperfectly realises been so clear in the minds and hearts of her sons. We claim that in the past the school has stood for unity and comprehensiveness. In the future it must be our aim that Mill Hill continue not as an *un*-denominational (for she exists not for negations, but for the assertion of a positive truth) but rather as an *inter*-denominational school, second to none in equipment, character and teaching. Boys educated under the influence of such ideals, learning sympathy from differences, unity of spirit through diversities of training, must needs grow into large hearted, generous, tolerant yet earnest Christian manhood, and form no unworthy part of the true aristocracy of character which constitutes the real wealth of every nation."

The Centenary of the school was celebrated on 5th July of this year; the prizes being distributed by the Rt. Hon. Sir H. Campbell-Bannerman. No less than seven Mill Hill boys are at this time members of the House of Commons; of whom several were present at the celebration.

N. G. B. JAMES, M.A.

The Last Years of Penry

IT has been customary with the modern historians of the life of Penry, from Waddington onwards, to refer distinctly to his return from Scotland, to which he had fled on the seizure of the wandering press, as having taken place in the autumn of 1592. Earlier writers, such as Neal (*History of the Puritans*) and Fletcher (*History of Independency*), the latter of whom wrote only a few years before Waddington, without any explanation, and in evident ignorance of depositions which make it clear that Penry was in London at all events in November, give the early part of 1593 as the date for the return. But no writer, so far as I have discovered, seems to have been observant of the strong grounds for believing either of these dates to be inaccurate. Of the general time of the flight into Scotland, as having followed shortly after the seizure of the press and the arrest of the printers in August, 1589, there is no doubt; and there are points in the examination of Udall, minister at Newcastle-on-Tyne, which seem to make it almost absolutely certain that it took place in October of that year. If he returned in September of 1592, the date commonly given, there are three years of life in Scotland to be accounted for, and Mr. Grieve in his interesting and valuable introduction to the recent republication of the *Aequity* has the reflection which one might like to believe true: " It is pleasing to think that the devoted wife who so bravely shared the vicissitudes of her husband's course, and who in 1593 was left a widow with four little daughters, had one period of comparative freedom from anxiety and settled home life." But is it after all so clear that Penry did remain in Scotland till 1592, or has there been some confusion between the time when he reached London, or at all events finally settled there, and the date of his leaving Scotland?

First of all there is the distinct record in the Calendar of State Papers for Scotland after various entries referring to James VI.'s edict of banishment against him: "Dec. 18, 1590, Penry departed." Mr. Sidney Lee, in his article on Penry in the *Dictionary of National Biography*, makes no reference to these State papers, but has the remark that "James told Elizabeth, Penry had left. But as matter of fact he had not." As, however, he gives no authority for this singular statement, it is allowable, perhaps, to put it down to surmise. If we can believe that Penry was somewhere in England, possibly in different places, carefully screening himself from undue observation, mingling here and there with "Brethren of the Separation" or the more advanced Puritans in Northamptonshire; in St. Alban's, that hot bed of Puritanism and Separatism, where there is definite testimony that at the time he was a welcome guest; or in "Norfolke and Suffolke," where his comrade, the writer of *Hay any Worke for Cooper?*, acknowledges that he has friends, and in whom, as bent on exile, we know from Penry's letters that he had deepest interest; then the suddenness of his action according to the previous view in joining the brethren in London immediately after long fellowship with the Presbyterians of Scotland passes away. Without dwelling on the direct testimony in depositions which make it perfectly plain that Penry was in and out of London during the closing months of 1592, a habit

which might easily have been adopted earlier;
or turning to some indirect allusions, such as his
references to his papers first roughly made in
Scotland bearing on Queen Elizabeth, which to my
own mind seem clearer on the supposition that
Penry had left Scotland a year or two previously,
and had since been somewhat of a wanderer, but
which might affect other readers differently; there
is one unqualified statement of Penry's which
seems to make it absolutely clear that Penry was
not living in Scotland after the close of 1590. In
the letter written from " close prison " " this 10th
of 4th month of April, 1593 " to his four daughters,
to be read " when they came to years of discretion
and understanding," he reminds them: " Shew
yourselves helpful and kind unto all strangers,
and unto the people of Scotland, where I, your
mother, and a couple of you, lived as strangers,
and yet were welcome, and found great kindness
in the name of our God." As we read the letter
there must be no rash guess that Penry and his
wife had left their two elder children behind, and
that the two younger children were born in Scotland. The exigencies of time forbid this. Earlier
in the letter Penry says: " The eldest of you is not
yet four years old, and the youngest not yet four
months." The youngest therefore was born shortly
before Christmas, 1592, the oldest not earlier than
April, 1589; and, as the way of speaking of her
would seem to imply that the birth was not very
long after that time, it may be regarded as certain
that the eldest was an infant in arms when the
parents took their flight in October of that year.*

---

* Remembering the incidents which gathered about the birth of this child, there is for us a peculiar significance in the Christian name (as shewn in the Amsterdam register of marriages) given to her by the parents—Deliverance. Then when we find this appearing as the first note of a fourfold benediction sent to the four daughters at the beginning of the letter—"Deliverance, Comfort, Safety, and Sure Hope," one may begin to wonder if the names of the other three daughters are hidden in the three other notes. Dare we venture to suggest as names, after the Puritan fashion, Consolation, Salvation, and Hope? In the marriage register, May 14, 1611, Deliverance is entered as "orphan," aged 21. This accords with the date given above.

Further, it can scarcely be doubted that the second child was born in 1590. It is clear that the other two were born out of Scotland.

It is just possible that the keen eyed legalist, so naturally found in an Historical Association, might be ready to remark the possibility of a double birth for the two younger children of Penry during the six or seven months commonly allowed for Penry's last days in England; there thus being possible, if one wished to argue it, a longer stay in Scotland than to the close of 1590, without its being hindered by the intruding birth of Penry's other children. It is certain that these two were not twins, for Penry refers to one as distinctly "the youngest." So the birth of the two has to be distributed in the two years after 1590.

Only one point may seem to prevent some difficulty—The translation of *Propositions and Principles of Diuinitie propounded and disputed in the vniuersitie of Geneva*, written by Penry when in Scotland, was published in Edinburgh, 1591. But it would have been quite possible for Penry to make the translation in 1590, and when the edict of banishment at last impelled flight for it to be published in his absence. In the same way the depositions during the Marprelate examinations and trials make it quite clear that Penry's *Appellation* was in the hands of the printers in Rochelle whilst Penry was in Northamptonshire in 1589, and that it was published in March, 1589-90, after he had made his flight to Scotland.

One other suggestion might without unfairness be made; and if any definite references to Penry's presence in Scotland at any time after 1590 could be found, it would have to be made. Just as in the succeeding century, after the ejectment of 1662, there were some who, like the devoted John Shuttlewood of Sulby, found some security from the special district of their labours being in two contiguous counties, such as Leicestershire and Northamptonshire, so that magisterial action for one portion did not reach the other; so Penry, hunted in Scotland, and endangered in England, might have been in and out of either; even as in the closing months he was in and out of London, sometimes as far from it as Derby. If his friend John Udall, on whom he called in his flight to Scotland, was still in Newcastle-on-Tyne, this might well have been; but he had already entered on his long and unjust lingering in the Marshalsea prison of London.

One distinct reference there is, of course, in the examination of Penry before Mr. Justice Young, (dated April 5, 1593): "He sayth he came out of Scotland about September last in the company of John Edwards," and Edwards confirms this statement, substituting, however, November for September. One visit to Scotland, therefore, there was—probably a brief one—after what I would venture to call the definite return of December, 1590.

Is it not clear then that Penry's quiet rest in Scotland has to be shortened in our estimation by two years; and that in return we may think of him as in different parts of England, having ever closer fellowship with the scattered Brethren of the Separation, till in the autumn of 1592 he is prepared for full fellowship with them?

T. GASQUOINE.

John Asty and the Fleetwoods

IN Vol. II. No. 4 of these *Transactions* a brief account is recorded of the foundation of the Ropemakers' Alley (Little Moorfields) meeting-house. For twenty years John Asty was pastor; his association with the Fleetwood family, as is that of Isaac Watts with the Abneys, is noteworthy. The facts below are collected mainly from the earliest minute book of the church (now meeting at Latimer Chapel, Mile End Old Town), from John Asty's diary (which the present writer has not seen), and from *The Protestant Dissenter's Magazine* for 1799.

Asty, or Aste, was an East Anglian name. In 1612 Susan Knapp married Francis Asty of Bury. In 1672 (May 2) Robert Asty was licensed to preach at the house of Susan Adams, Halter Street, Bury. John Asty, who was born in 1667, was probably the second son of Robert Asty, who was then settled in Norwich. In 1675 (September 12) John Asty was received into Dr. Collinge's family; he remained there until 1683 at the expense of Samuel Smith of Colkirk; then he went to the academy of Thomas Rowe at Newington Green, where Isaac Watts was also a pupil. In 1695 (Nov. 18) he "came to live in the family of Smith Fleetwood, Esq., of Armingland Hall, near Norwich, to perform the work of the ministry as a chaplain in his house." This was the seat of the late Lieutenant-general Fleetwood, near Oulton.

On April 16, 1700, a letter was addressed to John Asty urging him to accept the vacant pastorate at

Amsterdam: he declined, retaining his private chaplaincy until 1710, when he preached on the last three Sundays in May at Ropemakers' Alley meeting-house. "I removed from Mr. Fleetwood's family about one year and three-quarters after his death, and came to London (October 14, 1710) being called to the pastoral office by the Church of Christ in Ropemaker's Alley. I was set apart April 4, 1711. The ministers were Mr. Trail, Ridgley, Foxon, Watts (preached), Mr. Collings, Clarke (prayed), and myself concluded the work of the day." On December 28, 1710, the church minutes record: "to Mr. Asty a gift at the Black Swan £10." The following names occur on the church roll of that year and the next: Lady Rich, Doctor Pack, Mrs. Moore, Madame Crouch (who on February 7, 1714, left a legacy of £100 to the funds), Madame Gibon or Gibbons (who on September 11, 1717, gave £100 to the church). There follows an entry: "pd. for 100 nominal stock in South Sea Company £112 5s." (September 13). Although there is evidence that John Asty stayed much with the Fleetwoods at Stoke Newington we find these entries in 1711 (October) " to sundry tradesmen at fitting up ye house viz £13 . 4 . 10 "; (July 17) "to Mr. Asty 2 Qua Sallary to 24 June last"—an amount which shews he was in receipt of £50 a year with a manse. In 1712 Madame Fleetwood is found among the members; several of that family were members of the Bury Street congregation at this time.

The diary records: "A memorable day was June 23 1714, observed in our church by fasting & prayer for this nation, and the whole interest of God's church which were apprehended, not without cause, to be in the greatest danger. It was a day of fervent prayer: a very visible & mighty assistance did run through the whole work of the day, minister & people exceedingly affected." In 1716 the minutes record several items of interest: Mr. Asty for River Water, 5/-; King's Tax for the Meeting House, £2 . 10 . 8 ; Mrs. Sarah Stanton receives £4, that being her annuity out of the Halliford Estate. In 1717: "pd Brother Jones for Tobacco for Br Hilliard 18/-"; on the previous October 21, "pd for a Load of Coles for Mr. Hilliard 15/-." On June 29, 1718, John Asty occupied the pulpit of Martin Tomkins of Stoke Newington, although a year later at the Salters' Hall conference he opposed the latter's views on the Trinity. The diary ceases in 1719 with a reference to the great drought and to the excessive sickness during the summer of that year.

The " Charge of Renewing the Lease & Repairing the Meeting House & dwelling House in Ropemaker's Alley. Ano 1722 " which included a "Fine to the Citty of London for a lease of 21 years £170 . 0 . 0," was £536 . 19 . 6. Among the subscribers to the fund were Isaac Watts, a guinea; Madame Elen Fleetwood, three guineas, and her step-daughters: Mrs. Elizabeth Fleetwood, one guinea, and Mrs. Jane Fleetwood (who survived until 1761, and contributed to the funds of the church as late as 1758 ; she was " buried in linen " and left a legacy to the poor of Stoke Newington); Madame Richards ; Madame Alice Bateman ; Madame Cooke ; Joseph Alleine, £5; John Duck, £10 ; John Thompson, £5—the last three then being deacons.

In 1723 Congregationalists and Presbyterians separated ; a year later the roll of this church numbered 33 men and 68 "sisters," among whom were Elen Fleetwood, Elizabeth Fleetwood, Mary Carter, and Hannah Paul (who died while still a member, in 1783, at the age of 85 years).

In 1727 (September 25) John Asty was in the

chair at the original meeting, which numbered 35 members, of "The Board of Independent Ministers resident in and about the Cities of London and Westminster." In 1728 (June 23) he preached a funeral sermon on Mrs. Elizabeth Fleetwood, spinster, of Stoke Newington, who was "buried in A velvett Coffin in the church" there. Her will was proved August 28, and under it John Asty benefited. This sermon, based on Job ix. 12, was published. Next year Smith Fleetwood (the second), her brother, died, leaving John Asty £5. John Asty died 1730 (January 20). Six days later he was buried in Bunhill Fields, his funeral being attended by Revs. Ridgley, Hall, Rawlings, Wilcox, Newman, and by Dr. J. Guyse, who preached the sermon, which was subsequently published. A final minute records: "1732. June 9. £35 towards Mr. Asty's funeral." Ellen Fleetwood died July 23, 1731, and was buried in a velvet coffin at Stoke Newington. She was the second wife and widow of Smith Fleetwood (the elder); among her lapsed bequests were: "To Mr. Asty, minister of the Gospel, a wainscot press & some of the books therein & £10 to the deacons of his church for the poor," a codicil, dated Nov. 25, 1728, left John Asty £10 in addition had he survived.

John Asty edited in 1721 *A Complete Collection of the Sermons of John Owen &c.*" Wilson (1799) refers to "remarks in the famous Dr. Owen's Life, which was drawn up by him & printed with a large volume of the Doctor's works. He (John Asty) was a serious preacher but not popular." He is spoken of in *The Bunhill Memorials* as "a worthy son of a pious father."

Peter Goodwin, from Great Yarmouth, succeeded John Asty. "N.B. I came with my family to London Sep 2. 1730 and was set apart to the pastoral office in the — Sep 24." "N.B. I was chosen a lecturer at Pinner's Hall in the room of the Revd. Mr Jno Hurrion deceased Feb 3 1731/2. The numbers being as followeth :

> First balloting : Mr Guise 35, Goodwin 32, Rawling 16, Gladen 10, Jolly 3, Wood 3.
> Second balloting Mr. Guise 37, Goodwin 59."

W. Wilson, quoting in 1799 from a document dated 1731, gives the dimensions of the Ropemakers' Alley meeting-house as "fifteen squares"; there were three galleries with four seats each.

STANLEY B. ATKINSON.

The Religious Condition of London in 1672 as reported to King and Court

by An Impartial Outsider

THIS is contained in what I imagine is really a *State Paper*, though preserved, not in the Record Office, but in the MS. Department of the British Museum.

It is part of Vol. 186 of the Stowe Collection. It has no name attached to it; and the library authorities judge it to be only a careful (and quite reliable) copy of the original paper, which should be preserved elsewhere. It is composed of three parts—

> I. The first gives an account of the Lord Mayors and Sheriffs of London for the years immediately preceding this year, 1672, with the state of things in which it is the object of this Report to deal: (1) The Lord Mayors from 1669; and (2) The Sheriffs from 1668.
>
> II. The second part is headed "The Present State of the Nonconformists, 1672"; and
>
> III. The third is entitled "An Account of the Church of England Churches and Clergy in London, 1672."

Though the subjects are distinct enough—and at first glance the first section seems to have little or nothing to do with the second and third—the mode of handling them suffices to make them simply three sections of one and the same report.

Its writer had evidently been commissioned to ascertain as accurately as possible the attitude of the city towards the person of Charles II., or, more exactly, towards the Stuart monarchy, with a view to determine how far the several elements or classes of the citizens might be relied upon to support the monarchy in any policy it might adopt in domestic or foreign politics, on which differences of judgement might arise. And what gives the paper such interest and importance to us is that the religious attitude of the civic officials and of the different classes of society is regarded as of serious and grave political importance. The Episcopalians of the Church of England are reckoned safe—as pledged to the monarchy—and bound to be loyal to the Court policy, whatever it may be; and those outside it are, *ipso facto*, "doubtfuls." So that it has been deemed wise, as far as possible, to get reliable information as to the relative strength of the loyalists and doubtfuls in both the civic and religious life of London city at that time.

In the first part of his report, therefore, he passes in review the chief citizens of London who, through their recent tenure of high office (whether as sheriffs or mayors), have had or possessed at that very time special influence over the general body of the inhabitants; and in the other two sections forms a comparative estimate of the several sections of the *religious* public, and of their recognized and official leaders, whether outside the Church of England or in it.

He deals at first with those *outside*, and at much greater length, and thereby gives unconscious testimony to the importance of the Nonconformist element in the life of the city at that period.

Nonconformity in the city was undoubtedly of greater strength, proportionally, than it is easy, or even possible, for a London Nonconformist of these degenerate days to conceive, much less to realize. The great mass of the city population—

clerical and lay—was Puritan when Charles returned to such a delirious welcome on the 29th of May, 1660, a welcome which in its madness was the prototype of Mafeking day in our own sad times. And though, under the baneful guidance of Clarendon, Parliament had been doing its utmost—as the tool of the anti-Puritan party in the Church of England—to *crush* out the Puritan section, all it had succeeded in doing was to *drive* out its best and purest and noblest, to form a Nonconformity in character and ability stronger than itself. The wavering fringe of the population — always, alas! too large — who had no intensity of spiritual life, and no strength of religious or ecclesiastical conviction, had no doubt been reduced to submission, or at any rate frightened out of "the opposition" by the penal statutes successively passed (Act of Uniformity, the First Conventicle Act, the Five Mile Act, and the Second Conventicle Act), but in London the three last had been to a large extent a dead letter, so large and influential a section of London's population being resolutely opposed to their execution. Nor had the Church of England gained ground—rather had they seriously lost it —in connection with the two great calamities that had overtaken the city in 1665 and 1666, the Great Plague and the Great Fire. The magnificent opportunities which had been thus offered to the Church of England clergy of gaining a hold of the desolated population by an exhibition of self-denying devotion to the sick and dying in the one, and the homeless and churchless in the other, had been utterly neglected by their selfish panic-flight in the Plague time, and their indolent and impotent waiting for State help to rebuild their parish churches after the Fire; and the unselfish zeal and Christlike activities of the Nonconformists in both emergencies had established them still more firmly in the respect and affection of the people.

It is only natural, therefore, that this "Royal Commissioner" should report on the Nonconformists before he touched upon the Church of England.

Of course, he makes the best he can of the Church of England, and the worst he can of the Nonconformists ; but he uses the whip of scorn pretty impartially. Though doubtless an adherent of the State Church, he is more a "man of the world" than a man of the Church. His religious nature is not very quick nor fervent, but his eyes are very keen to see the foibles of others, and he delights to shew the shrewdness of his judgement in the case of all conduct which is capable of being construed as under the play of mixed motives, and the result is a delightfully spicy account of the various sects among Dissenters and the different clergy in the Church of England.

Stowe 186. I.

Lord Mayors of London, 1672

1669. S! William Turner—a person esteemed zealous for the Church, until the year of the Mayoralty. Then he espoused the interests of the Non-conformists. Under him they first gained the confidence of meeting openly ; which confidence, as it had its original from his courting of them, so it hath since encreesed (*sic*) to the dayly affronting his Majesties Authority. About 3 months before his mayoralty expired, there were frequent consultations at his house with the heads of the nonconformists about continuing him Lord Mayor another year, which designe they brought upon the stage on Michaelmas day, and carried it on with such arrogance and tumult that the peace of the City was in great hazard, and if the modesty of the Royal party had not been very great, it might have been a bloody Michaelmas Day.

Sir John Lawrence and S! William Turner have now no

considerable Interest in London: no, not among the Dissenters; for what they gained by their treacherously complying with that party (suffering them to break the Laws) that they have lost by their imperious & insolent behaviour towards almost all persons they have had to doe with.

But it is judged by knowing persons, most pernicious to his Majesty to suffer inferior Magistrates to grow popular by giving indulgence, and it is wish't the Liberty some Lord Mayors of London have largely given to the Sectaries hath not in a great measure brought about the fatal necessity upon his Majesty of tolerating now—to the great disturbance of many of his ancient Loyall subjects.

1670. Sr Samuel Starling, when he came to be Lord Mayor, put in Execution the Laws vigerously (*sic*) against the Phanaticks. Herein he found greater difficulty and opposition, because his immediate predecessor(s) Sir William Turner had given them all manner of Liberty. Ever since he hath been branded by them with all the marks of infamy. He is a person of good Learning: a solid judgment, & great courage, contemning all Danger for the safety of his Majesty's government.

1671. Sir *Richard Ford* succeeded him in the Chair. He suspended the Execution of the Laws against the Nonconformists by which he gained the applause of all that partie, though they had used all the villanous arts imaginable to keep him out of the Government. He is a man of excellent parts, and may do his Majesty excellent service in the City.

1672. Sr George Waterman, the present Lord Mayor, a person almost void of understanding, but not of will. He is very weake in the one, but most Perverse in the other. He employs abundance of time, but does no business. He for a while was guided by Sr John Lawrence who Ledd (*sic*) him astray, but he begins to hearken now to the Court of Aldermen, who dispatch their business with great Quiet since the Evill spirit of Sr John Lawrence is departed from them.

1673. Sr Robert Hanson is a person (who) heartily Loves the King's interest, and will next year make a better Lord Mayor than the present, he having a better understanding & a better conscience.

Sheriffs.

1668. *John Forth* is a hasty, passionate person; no lover of the Church of England, but makes it his business to cast reproach on those that are so. It is concluded by very many—that his Loyalty consisteth much in his Excise farms, and the profitt he makes by them. He rarely sees the inside of a Church, and therefore it cannot be said how he behaves himself there. He hath a Consecrated Chappell in his own house, but that is all of Conformity that he hath. A Nonconformist & a Brewer officiating there, when he is at Leasure on a Sunday to heare. He is a man of no reputation for keeping his word.

1670. *Daniel Forth* is a person that hath much more command of his passion than his Brother; hath a greater care of his words, and a man of greater abilitys in business, but as to Church affairs of the same principle with his brother. He hath good interest in some considerable Nonconformists.

1670. Patience Ward hath had a wife many years, but whether they were ever married is a question unless it were according to the directory of the Quakers. He is a very considerable merchant. What interest he hath is among the Nonconformists, and that is not much.

1671. John Moore; brought in as Alderman by S: John Lawrence & S: William Turner ... to bring in such a party into the Court of Aldermen, favourers of Nonconformists, as might be an Overballance to the Loyall Church party, & to strengthen themselves.

S: John Lawrence & S: William Turner did put affronts and indignities upon some of the younger Aldermen by which they were almost totally discouraged from appearing in any publick business; but the case is now altered.

As to Alderman Moore, there is very good ground to believe that he will prove a very good magistrate.

II.

The Present State of the Nonconformists, 1672.

The Protestant Nonconformists make up a considerable part of the nation; they are divided into *four* parts.

The *Presbaterians* (sic), The *Independants* (sic), The *Anabaptist*, The *Quakers & 5th Monarchy* men.

The Danger to the Monarchy of England, may be, is not alike from all of these

" 1. The Presbaterians, so called, are Least to be Feared, many of the most considerable of them, both Ministers and People, being heartily affected to the Government, both Civill and Ecclesiasticall, and if the renouncing of the Covenant, and a Ceremony or two, had not stuck so fast in their consciences that they could get them neither up nor down, they had not now stood in need of indulgence; but had been of the Church, and had had their share of the preferment of it.

"The Pastors and People of this sort, generally frequent the Church and the service of it. That they are true friends of the Civill government appears by their vigerous endeavours to bring in the King from his Long Exile, and their joy when it was accomplished. Besides, many of those now alive, and who have a great interest in that Party, had no hand in the Late rebelleous (*sic*) warr, nor in the mischiefs of it : they being either at school or young students in the University at the beginning and during the continuance of the warr.

"They are a party devided (*sic*) among themselves, some being for three-quarters conformity, some for half, some for a Quarter, & a few of them for none at all; and those few, it is doubted, are something akin to the Jesuits. The one giving the Pope power of Excommunicating & deposing Kings, the other the same power to their Presbiterian consistory.

"These are of the right Scotch breed who would bring the King to the stool of repentance, when ever they shall judge that he hath transgrest. These will never own his Majesty's Supremacy in matters Ecclesiasticall unless it be now, in the business of indulgence.

"Setting aside some of the best preachers of the Presbaterians, the rest will hardly gett a living by toleration, for their people are generally covetous, and are not willing to pay their tithes and contributions too. Plurality of Church payments is as troublesome to them as plurality of Livings. It hath been known within two or three years that a Minister (with ten children) hath preacht a week day Lecture to a large conventicle within two miles of London, and for a year's pains hath not received above 9 pounds.

"The most popular men of this party are : D[r] *Bates*, D[r] *Seaman*, D[r] *Manton*, D[r] *Jacombe*, D[r] *Annesley*, M[r] *Jenkins*, M[r] *Wattson*, M[r] *Calamy*[1], M[r] *West*[2]; and M[r] *Bull*, M[r] *Mays*, M[r] *Stancliffe*, all three partners in one great brewhouse, but men of great interest in their party, and good preachers : M[r] *Senior*[3], one much cried up by the women, & M[r] *Woodcock*[4], an excellent schollar (*sic*), M[r] *Baxter*[5] (the greatest person among them), and a

---

[1] *Mr. Calamy* is Edmund Calamy the second; was ejected from Moreton in Essex, gathered a congregation in his father's house in Aldermanbury, afterwards (1672) being licensed to preach at Curriers' Hall, Cripplegate.
[2] *Edward West*, ejected from Whitenham, Berks; his meeting-house was in Ropemakers' Alley.
[3] *Thomas Senior*, lecturer in the house of Alderman Ashurst, in Hackney.
[4] *Thomas Woodcock*, ejected from St. Andrew Undershaft (Leadenhall Street), preached in Hackney; and afterwards with Dr. Bates. He was Fellow of Jesus College, Cambridge; and Proctor of the University.
[5] The great *Richard Baxter*.

few more. There are some others that draw great numbers after them, from whome his Majesty cannot expect any continued peaceableness, neither will they themselves finde their congregation to continue to them. Before the Act of Uniformity these men were so inconsiderable that they did almost preach to their Church walls; and it is possible it will be so again, now that the penalty of the Laws is suspended, and the terrible thing called persecution laid asleep—the only thing that gave them a reputation: among these there is Mr Doolittle[6], the two Mr Vincents[7], Mr Barrum[8], &c.

2. "The *Independents* are the next considerable party, and in some respects more considerable than the former, if not for number, yet for their unity among themselves, & from the danger that may arrise (*sic*) from their evil Principles. They are perfectly united among themselves. There's no devision (*sic*) between their Churches, nor in their Churches, between the particular members thereof.

"There (*sic*) Pastors have an absolute dominion, for a maid or a widow cannot make honest provision for the flesh in the Honble way of Matrimony without their consent. Once upon a time, not long ago, a Marchant who had lived many years beyond the sea, and returning rich to his own country, spyed an independent virgin beautifull and rich, and was immediately wounded to the very heart. He humbly implores the help of the maid, who told him she could not marry without the consent of her spiritual guides. Love directs the Languishing Lover to him, who questions with him what Church he was of. He told him, Of the Church of England. 'Why then,' quoth he, 'you must get a Church of England mistress. But if you will become a member of my Congregation, make confession of your faith openly, and enter into our spiritual Church-covenant, I will then undertake to melt down your fair enemy to a complyance with your desires.' Oh powerful & mighty Love! the Lovesick man accepts the conditions, studies a confession of faith, reads it openly to the People, is admitted a member, and so gains a free use both of his own members and commodities. By this means, 'tis not to be imagined how many persons of Estates are brought to joyn with them. But they are careful that they admit few or no poor ones to come in among them: for they worship the Golden Fleece, and their Ministers are very rich. The same power the Pastors have over the persons of their people, the same they have over their Estate. Among their Evill principles, this is the worst. They hate Monarchy; and that his Majesty would find, if they had but a fitting opportunity. The

---

[6] *Thomas Doolittle*, ejected from St. Alphage's, London Wall; conducted a school (or academy for students for the ministry) in Moorfields.
[7] *Thomas Vincent*, ejected from St. Mary Magdalen, Milk Street; and *Nathaniel Vincent*, ejected from Langley Marsh, Bucks (of Southwark).
[8] *Andrew* or *Arthur Barham*, ejected from St. Helen's, Bishopsgate; of Hackney.

heads of this party now alive are : D[r]. *Goodwyn*[9], D[r]. *Owen*[10], M[r]. *Phillipp Nye*[11], M[r]. *Joseph Caryll*[12], M[r]. *George Griffiths*[13], M[r]. *Thomas Brookes*[14], and M[r]. *Meade*[15], who hath that Congregation that was M[r]. *Greenhill's* at *Stepney*.

"Carril and Goodwin were in the late times called the Apostles of Cromwell. These several persons never exprest the least trouble, sorrow, or repentance for that Horrid act of Murdering Charles the first, nor for any other of the detestable Villanies committed in the Late times, but promoted, approved, and applauded them. When they have been beseecht to speak a few words to the Usurper to spare some of the King's party condemned to slaughter, as in the case of D[r]. Hewet & others, they would profess they could not in conscience shew mercy to any of the enemies of God & his people.

"One very considerable person, an Independent now alive, and powerful among them, but now minister, when the news was brought to the Exchange that the Fatal Stroke was struck, and that the King was murdered, pulled off his hat, &, lifting up his hand to heaven, cryed 'Thanks be to God, that Great tyrant is fallen.' These things, it is hoped, will prevail with his Majesty, though he indulge them, yet to keep a strick (*sic*) eye over them, and a strong Guard upon them."

Parallel

Presbaterians
The Presbaterians are more in number by much
  ,,   ,,   are generally for Government by Bishops.
  ,,   ,,   are weak in their *Politicks* & open in their councills.
  ,,   ,,   had by their rebellion gott all power into their hands

Independants
The Independents are *more* united
  ,,   ,,   are for *no government*
  ,,   ,,   are cunning, subtile persons, secret & close in their designs
  ,,   ,,   cheated them out of it, & made fools of them ever after

Both parties are rich & have great interest in trade, and have made it their great designe to cast all the reproach of Ignorance, Lazyness, and immorality upon the conforming clergy, that they

---

[9] *Dr. Thomas Goodwin*, ejected from the Presidentship of Magdalen College, Oxford; preached to a congregation in Cripplegate.
[10] *Dr. John Owen*, Dean of Christ Church, Oxford, and Chancellor of the University; retired first to Stadham, then to London.
[11] *Philip Nye*, ejected from St. Bartholomew, Exchange; preached in Cherry Tree Alley, Bunhill.
[12] *Joseph Caryl*, ejected from St. Magnus, London; ministered in Leadenhall Street.
[13] *George Griffith*, ejected from Charter House, London; ministered in Addle Street, Wood Street.
[14] *Thomas Brooks*, ejected from St. Margaret's, Fish Street Hill; ministered in Lime Street.
[15] *Matthew Mead*, ejected from Shadwell; settled at Worcester House, Stepney; went to Holland, and had just returned to Stepney.

The Religious Condition of London in 1672

might take off the esteem of the people from them, which hath in a great measure succeeded.

3. The *Anabaptists* are not so numerous as the former parties : yet they are a large Body. Some of their chief teachers are *Capt. Kiffen*[16], M[r]. *Knowles*[17], M[r]. *Harrison*[18], M[r]. *Gosnold*[19], M[r]. *Northcott*[20]. Their not baptising their children, and their rebaptising, is judged an opinion not dangerous to the Civil authority. Very many of them were active Vigilant men in the Late times, and were good soldiers & officers under the Commonwealth & Oliver; but they were most zealous for a Commonwealth, ánd so they are to this day. His Majesty's Indulgence puts them & some of the Independant Churches into as good a Condition as to their conscience &, in some other regards, as they were in before his Majesties restoration. The Independants & Anabaptists, with some few of the fiercer Presbyterians, are proud & censorious;—quakerlike they will denounce judgments both upon Kings—and Kingdom, upon any pretended miscarriage they do, but hear of. These are great frequenters of Coffee-houses, & great improvers of any little matter that is but whispered against the Court or the Government.

These with some hypocritical Loyallists (*sic*) take pains to divulge any thing that may cast reproach upon the King, and to disperse any scandalous verses of which many have been abroad of late. Whitehall is belyed if this be not done also there. These are busy in State affairs, and crying out upon taxes and burdens[21]; never considering the vast priviledges (*sic*) England enjoyes, above any Nation upon earth, so that it is most heartily and earnestly deprecated by the true lovers of the King that they do not joyntly turn head against the King, if his Majesty should be brought to straits by his foreign warr. How farr the *indulgence* may prevent this, time will show, but it is a great prudence to provide for the worst.

4. The *Quakers* most truly deserve the character of rude, saucie, unmannerly, with all the ugly names that belong to an illbred person; it is no wrong to them to say they are mad, & fitter for Bedlam than sober companie. 'Tis impossible to give account of their Teachers, they being all so; both men and women. Their places of meeting were lately these : one at *Ratcliffe*, one at *Wheeler Street;* these by the industry of S[r]. John Robinson were broaken to pieces.[22]

---

[16] *Alderman Wm. Kiffen*, "a gentleman of note among the Baptists, and of interest at court."—*Neal : Pur.* III, 391

[17] This can be none other than the venerable *Hanserd Knollys*

[18] *Edward Harrison*, licensed to preach in his own house in *Petty France*, July 25, 1672 (a second licence for himself September 5, 1672).

[19] *John Gosnald*, educated at Cambridge, chaplain to Lord Grey, and licensed for Little Moorfields.

[20] Not identified.

[21] This paragraph calls to mind a letter from Sir Thomas Player to Williamson, written July 6, 1671 (*S.P. Dom. Car. II.* 291, 143). Could Sir Thomas Player be the author of this?

[22] Sir John Robinson was Lieutenant of the Tower. Ratcliff and Wheeler Street were in the Liberties of the Tower (or Tower Hamlets).

One at Devonshire house without Bishopsgate : one in St. John's Street, one in Westminster : one in Southwark, two within the walls of London, viz! one in Gracechurch Street & one at the Bull and Mouth within Aldersgate. There are among them many rich men that drive very considerable trades and are, as to the affairs of the world, as wise in their generation as any person whatever ; in their Traffick they will tell you they will make but a word, but 'tis great odds if at that word they do not Cheat you. Though they seem mortifyed, yet they are intollerable Lovers of the flesh &c. Their greate deluding Maxime which flatters many people into a good opinion of their innocency is they cannot fight, that they are peaceably to suffer all wrongs, & to revenge nothing ; but at the same time, they will curse you from the beginning of the bible to the End of the Revelations, even from making Caen a Vagabond to the binding of the Red Dragon and casting him into the Bottomless pitt. And there's no question if the Spirit (that is Advantage or Opportunity) did but move, they themselves would be the inflictors of all the punishments and plagues mentioned in that Sacred Book, and that with all imaginable Cruelty. But notwithstanding the pretence of not fighting, they have in the time of warr fought, and that desperately. They tell you Likewise, as they will not fight against you, neither can they pay any taxes, or find any Armes for fighting ; no, not against the Great Turk or the Pope, if they should come to fight us. But there is a good cure for this very ill principle, in the Law, viz. "Distraining," which severity makes them very angry. But they restrain it for fear it should be discovered that the Old Man is stirring in them.

They are but *Fifth Monarchy* men *disguised ;* and they would be found such, but that at present they consult their own interest. They are very carefull of their poor, & very diligent in increasing their party, ready to assist one another upon all occasions. They hate all other Nonconformists as much, if not more, than they hate a Church man. —Captain Mead,[28] now a Quaker, a person of great Estate & great Trade, he hath been a Presbaterian & Independant, & what not. If he may be believed, the Presbaterians & Independants are knaves, dangerous persons, ready to do any mischief : when he was one of them, he professes he was ready to do so, and he is confident his Majesty cannot be safe from any of the Dissenters but the Quakers. They are no very great party, but they are stout, and able to endure hardshipp. While the Laws were executed upon them, and their Meetings broke up by force, they had many spectators, and some compassionate ones, & this made the world believe they were numerous, but since they have hansome (*sic*) Liberty, no body concerns themselves about them.

---

[28] ? William Mead who with William Penn had been accused of holding a tumultuous assembly in the public streets, and at the trial in August, 1670, was acquitted by the jury, but was still fined and imprisoned (Dr. Stoughton, *History of Religion in England*, III., 390.)

The Religious Condition of London in 1672

If there be any sharp or severe reflections in the foregoing papers they are not to Exasperate his Majesty or to discourage him in his begun indulgence, for very many understanding persons, conformists and nonconformists, do highly applaud his Majesty's prudence & Clemency, and there is none displeased but a fue (*sic*) waspish Churchmen : but they are only to excite the King for his own safety, nor to trust these people with any Civill or Military Employment, And to have continually such a force in pay, beside of his trained bands, as may be able to suppress any tumults that may arise.

III.

An Account of the Church of England Churches and Clergy in London, 1672

And now it were most passionately to be wished that the Clergy of the Church of England, who, ever since his Majesty's most happy return, have enjoyed the honours & proffits of that Church to a greater degree than any of their predecessors, had been but as industrious in a Right and Legall way, as the Nonconformists have been in a wrong and unlawfull way.

But notwithstanding what hath been said, it may be proved that London, and the parts about it, were never furnisht with more able, pious, Learned, ingenious, gentile ministers, not since there was preaching than before the plague and fire. Those two dreadfull callamities seperated Ministers and people, not only in place, but Affection, and many of them are not yet returned to a good understanding one of Another.

The Persons of Greatest reputation, and that have the greatest Interest among the people are These that follow :

St. Andrew Undershaft—Mr Grove
All Hallows Steyning—Mr Holland
St. Botolph's Bishopsgate—Dr Bagshaw, a man of excellent Learning, A most ingenious preacher, one that hath a very great congregation & great command over them.
St. Andrews Holborn. Dr Stillingfleet, one that needs no character, only he is greatly admired by all Learned men, and greatly beloved by all good protestants.
St. Bartholomew the great—Mr Burgess.
St. Olive's, Hart Street—Mr Mills
St. Bartholomew the Less—Mr Orme

The Three Last are good Schollars, good Preachers, & have a good interest in their parishes.

D: Arden, minister of St. Botolph's, Algate (*sic*), a very great parish, he is a gentile Clergyman, and well beloved by his people

D: Mason, minister of St. Peters the Poor, an ingenious person, but not very popular

D: Lewes of All Hallows the Wall—a sober, honest minister.

Lothbury—M: Flower
St. Ethelburgugh—M: Clark
St. James, Duke Place,—M: Harrison
} These are men of no reputation, neither in their Parishes, nor in London.

D: Tillotson preaches a Lecture every Tuesday morning in St. Martin's Church, not farr from the Exchange. A great number of the Clergy, & of considerable merchants resort to it. He is a Person of very great Esteem

Dr. Horton is minister of St. Helen's, he hath a very great congregation of half conformists, in whom he hath very great interest. he is a man of very good Learning, and a constant, Laborious preacher.

St. Botolph, Aldersgate—D: Wells. An Excellent person, greatly valued by all sorts about him.

St. Dunstans in the West—M: Thomson, one highly conceited of himself, but very few beside are.

The parishes forenamed escaped the Fire.

St. Christopher's—A Church, almost furnisht—M: John Hall, a good preacher.

St. Dunstan's in the East—M: Giffard, Divinity reader at Gresham Colledge, an excellent minister, a most Laborious person in his work, by which he hath a very great Audience, & but few Nonconformists in his parish.—From his person it may be observ'd that Learned, constant, preaching would cure a great deal of Nonconformity & prevent a great deal more : his Church was first furnisht since the Fire, & is Adorned with a handsome Organ

St. Mary Aldermanbury will be finisht this year. D: Ford, minister, a worthy man, an ingenious Poet, & very good preacher, a man of very good interest. he preaches yet in a Hall till his Church be finisht.

St. Stephens, Coleman Street.—M: Neast, minister, very well beloved by his parish, unless by a few, froward, ill-conditioned phanaticks : a painfull person in his employment, preaches in a Tabernacle, as the people call it.

St. Sepulchers—a very Large Church, built since the fire—D: Bell, minister, a person who, by his great Charity, and constant Laborious preaching, hath very much gained the affections of that great people committed to him.

St. Margaret, Milk Street annexed to St. Lawrence, Jewry—D: Withcheott minister, a man of great Learning, and of a very great interest among the Considerable people of London :

The Religious Condition of London in 1672

he preaches every Sunday in the Afternoon to the Lord Mayor and Court of Aldermen, in their Chappell at the Guildhall.

St. Magnus,—Mr Ivory ⎫ men of good repute with their
St. Margaret Pattens—Dr Hicks ⎭ people
St. Mary Woolnoth—a beautifull Church with an Organ. Suddenly built after the fire by the great bounty and care of Robert Vyner—Mr Crispe parson
St. Mary Hill—Mr Thomas White
  Both these Last popular preachers, and well beloved
St. Mildred's Poultrey—Dr Perenchaife, a great schollar, very well approved by his people.
St. Mildred's, Bread Street—Mr Durham, a most excellent preacher, constant among his people, one that hath great power with them.

There are some others, persons that deserve for their parts, Learning, and sober Carriage, a very good Esteem, but their Churches not being built, they are strangers to their people, and their people hardly know them. And there are some, by reason of their mean parts, or no good behaviour, have no Love in their parishes, unless among the worst and most inconsiderable. There are others whose Learning deserves honour and Esteem, but their nonresidency spoils their reputation and interest; as Dr Bridoke, Parson of St. Bartholomew behind the Exchange, Prebend of Windsor, Dean of Salisbury, & rector of Stands in Lincolnshire.
Dr Hodges, Parson of St. Peters, Cornhill, Dean of Hereford, and parson of Kensington in Middlesex
Dr Cartwright, Parson of St. Thomas Apostles, Prebend of St. Paul's, & parson of Barkin (*sic*) in Essex.
Dr Pritchard, Vicar of St. Giles Cripplegate, one of the greatest parishes in England, Prebend of St. Paul's, and hath another Living by Uxbridge, which so takes him off from his very great charge at St. Gilles (*sic*) Cripplegate, that he preaches there but one sermon in Three Weeks, his Church being then well filled.

G. LYON TURNER.

OFFICERS OF THE SOCIETY.

President	Rev. Dr. John Brown, B.A.,	
	Hampstead, London, N.W.	
Hon. Treasurer	Rev. G. Lyon Turner, M.A.,	
	Crescent Lodge, St. John's, London, S.E.	
Hon. Auditor	Mr. John Minshull, Memorial Hall, London, E.C.	
Hon. Editor & Librarian	Rev. T. G. Crippen, ,, ,, ,,	
Hon. Secretaries	Rev. T. G. Crippen, ,, ,, ,,	
	Mr. Henry Thacker, ,, ,, ,,	

CONDITIONS OF MEMBERSHIP.

(a) LIFE MEMBERS, paying twenty guineas in lieu of annual subscription.

(b) HONORARY MEMBERS, paying an annual subscription of one guinea or more.

(c) ORDINARY MEMBERS, paying an annual subscription of five shillings.

Subscriptions should be made payable and remitted to the Hon. Treasurer, as above; and are due *in advance* on January 1st in each year.

New members are entitled to all the publications issued by the Society in the year they join.

List of Members

Hon. Members marked *H*, Life Members marked *L*.

Adeney, W. F., Rev. Prof., M.A., D.D.
Anderton, W. E., Rev., M.A.
Andover (U.S.A.) Theological Seminary
Astbury, F. T., Rev.
Atkinson, S. B., Esq., M.A., M.B., B.Sc.
Avery, John, Esq.
Baptist Union, The
Barrett, Geo. S., Rev., B.A., D.D.
Bartlet, J. V., Rev. Prof., M.A., D.D.
Basden, D. F., Esq.
Bate, Frank, Esq., M.A.
Bax, A. Ridley, Esq.
Beaumont, E., Esq.
Boag, G. W., Esq.
Bragg, A. W., Esq.
Brown, J., Rev. Dr., B.A.
H Brown, W. H., Esq.
Brownen, G., Esq.
Burrage, Champlin, Esq.
Campbell, R. J., Rev., M.A.
Carter, W. L., Rev., M.A.
Cater, F. I., Rev., A.T.S.
Chevalier, J., M.
Clapham, J. A., Esq.
Clark, J. H., Esq., J.P.
Clarkson, W. F., Rev., B.A.
Claydon, George S., Esq.
Cocks, J., Esq.
Congregational Library, Boston, Mass.
Cribb, J. G., Esq.
Crippen, T. G., Rev.
Dale, A. W. W., Esq., M.A.
Dale, Bryan, Rev., M.A.
Davies, J. Alden, Rev.
Davis, C. H., Rev.
Davis, J. E., Esq.
Davy, A. J., Esq.
Dawson, E. B., Esq.
Didcote, C. Page, Esq.
Dimelow, J. G., Esq.
Dixon, H. N., Esq., M.A., F.L.S.
Dixon, R. W., Esq.
H Dore, S. L., Esq., J.P.
L Ebbs, A. B., Esq.
Ebbs, W., Rev.
Ellis, C. W., Esq.
Evans, A. J., Esq., M.A.
Evans, G. Eyre, Rev.
Evans, Jon. L., Esq.
Evans, R. P., Esq.
Firth, C. H., Prof., M.A., LL.D.
Flower, J. E., Rev, M.A.
Forsyth, P. T., Rev., Dr.
Friends' Reference Library
Galloway, Sydney V., Esq.
Gasquoine, T., Rev., B.A.

Glasscock, J. L., Esq.
Gordon, A., Principal
Gosling, Howard, Esq.
Green, Joseph J., Esq.
Green, T., Esq.
Grice, T. E., Esq.
Grieve, A. J., Rev., M.A., B.D.
Groser, W. H., Esq., B.Sc.
Hall, C. W., Rev.
Hall, W. H., Esq.
Harris, W. J., Esq.
Harrison, G. W., Esq.
Harwood, W. Hardy, Rev.
Hawkins, F. H., Esq., LL.B.
Henderson, A. D., Esq.
Hepworth, Frank N., Esq.
Hepworth, J., Esq.
Hepworth, T. M., Esq.
Heslop, R. Oliver, Esq., M.A., F.S.A.
Hewgill, W., Rev., M.A.
Hills, A. M., Miss
Hitchcock, W. M., Esq.
Hodgett, C. M., Esq.
Holt, Edwyn, Esq.
L Hounsom, W. A., Esq., J.P.
Huckle, Attwood, Esq.
Iliff, John S., Esq.
Jackson, S., Esq.
James, Norman G. B., Esq.
H Johnston, W., Esq.
Jones, A. G., Esq.
Keep, H. F., Esq.
Kenward, Herbert, Rev.
Key, James, Rev.
King, Jos., Esq., M.A.
Knaggs, J., Rev.
H Lancashire Independent College (Goodyear, C., Esq)
Lawrence, Eric A., Rev.
Layton, F. J., Rev., A.T.S.
Lester, E. R., Esq.
Lewis, D. Morgan, Prof., M.A.
Lewis, Geo. G., Esq.
Lewis, H. Elvet, Rev, M.A.
Lewys-Lloyd, E., Esq.
Lloyd, J. H., Esq.
Lovatt, J., Esq.
Low, G. D., Rev., M.A.
Luke, R., Esq.
Macfadyen, D., Rev., M.A.
Mackintosh, R., Rev. Prof., D.D.
Manchester College, Oxford
Massey, Stephen, Esq.
May, H. A., Esq.
H McClure, J. D., Dr.
McCrae, A., Esq.
Minshull, John, Esq.

List of Members (continued)

Mottram, W., Rev.
Muir, W., Esq.
Mumford, A. A., Esq., M.P.
Musgrave, B., Esq.
New College, Edinburgh
H New College, Hampstead, N.W.
    (Staines, Howard, Rev.)
Nightingale, B., Rev.
H Palmer, C. Ray, Rev. Dr.
Palmer, W. M., Esq.
Parnaby, H., Rev., M.A.
Pearson, S., Rev., M.A.
Pierce, W., Rev.
Pitt, Walter, Mrs.
Powicke, F. J., Rev., Ph.D.
Poynter, J. J., Rev.
Pugh, Mis.
Rawcliffe, Edwin B., Rev.
Rees, J. Machreth, Rev.
Richards, D. M., Esq.
Ritchie, D. L., Rev.
Robinson, W., Rev.
Rollason, Arthur A., Esq.
Rudge, C., Rev.
Rutherford, J., Esq.
H Rylands, Mrs., D.Litt.
Scamell, J., Esq.
Sell, W., Esq.
Serle, S., Esq.
Shaw, H, Rev.
Silcock, P. Howard, Esq., B.A.
Simon, D. W., Rev., D.D.
H Smith, W. J., Esq., M.A.
Smyrk, C. Watt, Rev.
Souter, Alex., Prof., M.A.
H Spicer, Albert, Sir, Bart., M.P.

H Spicer, George, Esq., M.A., J.P.
Standerwick, J. W., Esq.
Stanier, W. H., Esq.
Sutton, C. W., Esq.
Sykes, A. W., Esq.
H Thacker, Fred. S., Esq.
Thacker, Henry, Esq.
Thomas, D. Lleufer, Esq.
Thomas, John, Esq., J.P., C.C.
Thomas, Wm., Rev.
H Thompson, J., Esq.
Thorpe, F. H., Esq.
Titchmarsh, E. H., Rev., M.A.
H Toms, C. W., Esq.
Turner, G. Lyon, Rev., M.A.
Tyson, R. G., Esq.
U.S.A. Congress Library.
Wallis, R. B., Esq., J.P.
Walmsby, L. S., Esq.
Watkinson, J., Esq.
H Webster, Isaac, Esq.
L Whitley, A. W., Esq.
Wicks, G. H., Esq.
H Wilkinson, W., Esq
Williams's Library.
Williams, Mrs.
Williamson, David, Esq., J.P.
Williamson, David, jr., Esq.
Wilson, T., Esq.
Windeatt, E., Esq.
Wing, Lewis, Esq.
Winterstoke, The Rt. Hon. Lord
Wontner, A. J., Esq.
Wood, Leonard B., Esq., M.A
Woodall, H. J., Esq.
Young, Hugh P., Rev.

Transactions

[Vol. III., No. 4]   [FEBRUARY, 1908

Contents

...torial	209
...conformity in Cumberland and Westmorland	212
J. Hay Colligan	
...e upon the Map	229
...Jessey Church, 1653-1678	233
W. T. Whitley	
...Watts's Tomb	240
...Unpublished Letter of Dr. Watts	241
...nd Lane Chapel : Martock, Somerset	244
John Scamell	
...Ancient Meeting-house at Wattisfield, Suffolk	251
...es of Aparant Church	257
...of Members	266
...of Officers, &c.	268

...be obtained direct from the Book Saloon, Congregational Union of
England and Wales, Inc., Memorial Hall, London, E.C.

Printed for the Society by
Fred. S. Thacker: 3 Dyers' Buildings, Holborn, London

EDITORIAL

Our usual Autumnal Meeting was held in the United Methodist lecture hall, Coronation Street, Blackpool, on Wednesday, 16th October, 1907 : the Rev. Dr. Brown in the chair.

Prayer having been offered by the Rev. W. Mottram, the minutes of the Annual Meeting, being already printed, were taken as read.

The Rev. J. H. Colligan, M.A., minister of Trinity Presbyterian church, Lancaster, having been introduced by Mr. E. B. Dawson, read an instructive paper on " Early Nonconformity in Cumberland and Westmorland." After discussion, in which the Revs. B. Nightingale, T. Gasquoine, and others took part, an unanimous and hearty vote of thanks was accorded to Mr. Colligan for his paper ; and he was requested to place it in the hands of the Secretary for publication.

It was resolved on the motion of the Rev. W. Mottram " That this society places on record its sense of the irreparable loss it has sustained in the lamented death of the Rev. Bryan Dale, M.A. ; and the Secretary is hereby commissioned to express the same to the surviving members of Mr. Dale's family."

*

We are glad to give place to a suggestive paper by the Rev. Dr. Whiteley, Baptist minister of Preston. The writer directs attention to several facts which, though printed fifty years ago, seem to have been totally overlooked. On the general question of the historic continuity of the Pilgrims' Church, however, it could scarcely be expected that Mr. Fitten and his adherents, when reorganizing the church on a Strict Baptist basis, would recognize any division ; in their view the Paedobaptist members would be regarded as excluded for neglect of what the majority esteemed a divine ordinance. In the absence of church rolls it is, of course, impossible to *prove* that the minority formed the nucleus of the church that worshipped in Deadman's Place in 1672 ; but the difficulty of otherwise accounting for that assembly strongly supports the usual tradition.

While there can be no doubt that Neal confused the Jacob-Jessey church with that of Hubbard and More, a link connecting the former with the south side of the Thames appears to have been generally forgotten. It is well known that Lothrop, Barbone, and others were arrested in Blackfriars in 1632; but an entry quoted by Waddington from the records of the High Commission, dated 12th June 1634, mentions "John Lothrop of Lambeth Marsh."

On the subject of Canting Names (see *Transactions* III, pp. 78 and 141), Mr. H. N. Dixon calls our attention to Waylen's *House of Cromwell*, pp. 337 fg., where it is stated that among 17,280 names in Besse's *History of the Quakers*, though many unusual classical names are found, the only canting names that appear are *five, viz.*, Faith Sturges, Mercy Chase, Provided Southwick, Shunamite Pack, and Temperance Higwell. (The first, second, and fifth of these are not yet quite obsolete). Three daughters of Sir John Danvers of Culworth were named Temperance, Justice, and Prudence (Prudence was occasionally met with in the last century). Waylen also mentions the following as authentic.—Hate-evil Nutter, a New England elder and great persecutor of Quakers; Gracious Franklyn,* master of Heytesbury hospital; Consolation Fox, a captain in Fairfax's last army; Pious Stone and Manna Reeve, two of Cromwell's early troopers mentioned in the *Squire* papers; Sir Faithful Fortescue,* a parliamentary officer "who proved very unfaithful at Edgehill"; Accepted Frewin, Archbishop of York, and his brother Thankful Frewin; Increase Mather,* a well known New England divine; and Livewell Chapman, a bookseller rebuked in *Mercurius Aulicus*, 9th August, 1660, for vending a book of fanatical anecdotes. (The three marked * were noted on p. 78).

We hoped to give in this issue the final result of Mr. Cater's inquiries into the later life of Robert Browne. But Mr. Cater informs us that he has discovered some new facts which require further research before coming to definite conclusions. He hopes to have these in readiness for our next issue.

We are glad to present the last instalment of the *Wiggenton MS*. We should be obliged to any friend who is familiar with the writings of early Separatists, and who would express a definite opinion as to the authorship of the anonymous tract now printed for the first time. Possibly a clue may be found in the peculiar and twice repeated phrase "word of message."

We give with this issue a print of the ancient *thatched* meeting-house at Pound Lane, Martock, Somerset. The still more ancient edifice at Horningsham is well known. We should be glad to hear of any more old thatched meeting-houses still in use or existence.

Editorial

Personal memorials of Isaac Watts are so rare that the following communicated by Rev. G. Eyre Evans, M.A., is of interest :—

In the copy of Baxter's *Directory* at the Presbyterian meeting-house, Middletown, Delaware Co., U.S.A., is this inscription—

> 30 Jany. 1735 Given by the Rev. Isaac Watts, of London, for the use of the Middletown Meetinghouse, that people who come from far & spend their whole day there, may have something proper to entertain themselves with, or talk of to one another between the Services of Worship, morning & afternoon.

*

It is well known that there was a Separatist church in the west of England as early as 1600, some members of which were among the exiles at Amsterdam. A very vague tradition ascribes this early evolution of Puritanism to the influence of the Scottish workmen who built and worshipped in the chapel at Horningsham. It would be interesting to know if there are in that region any families of Scottish origin who can trace their *local* ancestry to the days of Queen Elizabeth.

*

We should be glad to have some particulars of the history of the old Baptist chapel at Cote, Oxfordshire.

*

Some time before 1810 a small congregation with their pastor, Mr. McNeeley, who had temporarily worshipped at Monkwell Street, united with Mr. Brooksbank's people at Haberdasher's Hall. On 27th April, 1821, the "Rev. Stephen Mummery and church" reopened Dr. Watts's old meeting-house in Bury Street, which had been closed for a few months. Mr. Mummery's church possessed one of the "Dorset" endowments, which had formerly been enjoyed by Mr. McNeeley's congregation. Information is earnestly desired as to the course of events from 1810 to 1821.

*

We would earnestly appeal to our friends to use their personal influence to obtain an increase of membership in the society. Many works of historic importance could be reprinted if our income were adequate to the work.

Members are requested to note the new address of our treasurer— "Wheatham Hill, Hawkley, Liss, Hants."

Nonconformity in Cumberland and Westmorland

THE subject before us to-day is so extensive, that the following paper can only be described as a sketch of an important field of northern Nonconformity. Leaving out the Baptist movement, which appears as early as 1652, and the convulsive origin of Quakerism, there remains the history of seventeen congregations. The registers and records of these congregations are very imperfect. Not one congregation has original registers, and, with the exception of Cockermouth, the registers were begun when the stress of the storm was over. In several cases the Presbyterian ministers from Scotland originated the records, while in other cases, such as Penruddock and the joint congregations of Great Salkeld and Plumpton, there is not a vestige of official record.

Before giving an outline of the history of each congregation we shall indicate the position we take up on the whole subject. The origin of Nonconformity in the two counties must be traced to the Puritanism among the clergy of the Established Church. Long before the Act of Uniformity there were Puritan vicars and rectors, who, generally speaking, developed into Presbyterians. About ten years before 1662 we find a group of men in the parish churches of these two counties, wholly intent upon preaching an evangelical doctrine. In the greater number of the parishes we find "churches" existing inside the parish, the ministers being pastors of the churches and parsons of the parish. The Act of Uniformity put an end to this, and with the ejection of the ministers various groups of the parishioners became Nonconformists also. The ejected ministers appear to have left the counties, and to have laboured elsewhere, while several conformed. The work was carried on by two or three silenced ministers, who had never held livings, but who would probably have done so had not the Bartholomew Act prevented them. Of these Anthony Sleigh, M.A., of Penruddock, and George Nicholson, M.A., of Kirkoswald, are two fine examples.

From 1662 to the Act of Toleration was the heroic period of Nonconformity in the two counties, for the Indulgence did not bring much relief. Then came "the meeting-house era" (1690-1710), and the groups of nonconforming folk began to creep out of their secret meetings in farmhouses and barns, and to erect those plain structures that here and there remain. The first generation of Nonconformists was fast passing away at the beginning of the eighteenth century, and a diminution of zeal is already noticeable. Anthony Sleigh's son, of Penruddock, applied to Bishop Nicholson for deacon's orders. Richard Gilpin's son conformed, and became recorder of Carlisle, and the sons eased in their adherence as the times had eased in their intensity.

After the decease of the ejected and silenced ministers the academy students took their places, and here a word may be said about these institutions. Every one knows the work of Richard Frankland, M.A., who carried on his ministry and at the same time educated the youth of the nonconforming homes. His great service was in Yorkshire and Westmorland. In the latter county his residences were at Natland, Dawsonfold and Hartbarrow. This last place, near the south end of Windermere, offered an escape from a writ, from either Westmorland or Lancashire. The purity of his message and the splendour of his sacrifice cannot be too highly appreciated.

The academy of Messrs. Chorlton and Cunningham, of Manchester, was not drawn upon by Cumberland and Westmorland[1]; but Cunningham, when minister of Penrith, did a private work in educating several of the youth of the neighbourhood.

The practice began about this period of obtaining supply from Scotland. As far as we can gather these men, having passed through the divinity halls of the various universities, were licensed and set free to wander. Apparently no oversight was taken of the licentiate, and of course there was no jurisdiction over the congregations in England. At a later period, when the secession churches arose in Scotland, discipline was maintained over their ministers, as is seen in the cases of Francis Rattray of Blennerhasset and James McQuhae of Kendal; but even then there was no jurisdiction over the congregation from Scotland. For a period of about seventy years a number of the congregations in Cumberland—Independent and Presbyterian alike—were supplied from the Church of Scotland. The rest of the congregations were supplied from the academy of Dr. Caleb Rotheram in Kendal. He, himself a native of Great Salkeld, had the confidence of the Nonconformists of Cumberland and Westmorland. Though it is to be feared that his method was too rationalistic to be safe, he was on the whole an excellent minister, an esteemed tutor, and a man whose outlook was—in a modern phrase—that of a progressive theologian. In the later stages of their careers a number of his students became 'advanced,' but the temper of the times was as much to blame as their training, and Rotheram's academy can scarcely be held responsible. The stream that came from Scotland was strongly Calvinistic; while the

---

[1] William Pendlebury, of Kendal, was trained partly by Frankland and partly by Chorlton. Samuel Audland, of Penruddock and Kendal, is the only instance of supply from this academy, and he was a native of Westmorland.

Rotheram stream was Arminian. An important cross current in the tide of rationalism was introduced by the arrival of James Scott at Stainton, who afterwards became the founder of Heckmondwike academy.

Towards the close of the eighteenth century the causes throughout the two counties were near the point of extinction.

In the beginning of the nineteenth century several of the churches became Independent, under doubtful circumstances, and others attached themselves to secession presbyteries in Scotland. These afterwards entered into that union which formed the United Presbyterian Church in 1847; and in 1876 they returned to their early English connection, by helping to form the Presbyterian Church of England.

It is from this point of view that the following accounts are given. Looking at the group of Independent congregations in alphabetical order, we find:

Alston (Garrigill)

This cause did not originate in an ejected congregation, or through an ejected minister. The influence of Nathanael Burnand, M.A., the ejected vicar of Brampton, was felt in his itinerant ministry. The first minister, Thos. Dawes, was possibly a student of Frankland's, and appears, later on, to have been minister of Kirkoswald. He was probably connected with Dr. Dawes the vicar of Barton, Westmorland, who had a nephew named Thomas. The next minister, Mr. Turner, was probably connected with the ejected vicar of Torpenhow.[2] The third minister was Mr. Dickinson, who was probably the Thos. Dickinson who entered Frankland's academy in 1689. He was followed by Adam Wilson, from the Church of Scotland. He formed a cause at Neshopeburn, and worked the two congregations together. The next minister was James Richie, M.D., who is referred to under Ravenstonedale. The sixth minister was Thomas Smith, and the record of his ordination is in the minutes of the Penrith congregation, where the Provincial met in 1753. He returned to a charge in Scotland. He was followed by Mr. Dean, who was probably Adam Dean of Kirkoswald.[3] The last minister whom we need mention is Timothy Nelson, M.A., who was there for 38 years. He had previously been at Penruddock, and when he retired from Alston, in 1800, he took charge of the congregations of Great Salkeld and Plumpton, he being a native of the former village. He died there in 1829, having lived a long and honoured life in the service of Cumberland Nonconformity.

---

[2] It is possible that "Mr. Turner" may have been Thomas Turner the ejected vicar, but Calamy has no particulars beyond the name.

[3] Our surmise is that Dean, while minister of Kirkoswald, supplied Alston pulpit. He is found earlier than the above date, and later also, at Kirkoswald, &c.

Cumberland and Westmorland

He was the first historian of local dissent, but unfortunately most of his papers have been lost. His descendants are still connected with the meeting-house of Great Salkeld.

Blennerhasset

The particulars of this congregation consist of two names in Evans' list. The first is James Mallison, who may easily have belonged to the Penruddock family of that name.[4] We have no record of his Blennerhasset pastorate. In 1714 he ministered to a secession of 10 disciples at Ravenstonedale, and in 1717 removed to Howden, Yorks, where he was in 1722. The late Mr. Bryan Dale says he was there for nearly 30 years.

The other name is that of John Seyer (or Sayers), who was probably at Keswick before he went to Blennerhasset. Nothing further is known of him.

There is no date upon the old meeting-house. In appearance it is like several houses in the village that are dated 1760, so that originally it was probably a cottage. The modern history of this congregation is associated with Sir Wilfrid Lawson and his son, the late Sir Wilfrid.

An interesting fact in Blennerhasset Nonconformity is the ministry of Francis Rattray, a preacher from the Secession Church of Scotland, who was in 1789 called to Whitehaven. He remained there a year, itinerating as far as Kendal. Afterwards he was at Mixenden and Sheffield, and finally at Blennerhasset, where he left the Secession Church, and became a Baptist minister.

Cockermouth

Cockermouth was established through an outside influence, although Puritanism of a pronounced type is found in the adjacent parish of Bridekirk as early as 1616. The Rev. Thos. Larkham, M.A., who visited the county in 1651, was the means of founding the Cockermouth church, 11 years before his ejection from Tavistock, Devonshire.

The first minister was George Larkham, M.A., the son of Thomas, who was inducted into the parish of All Saints, Cockermouth. At that time the two counties had Puritan vicars. It was quite consistent, because there was no Act of Uniformity. That Act was, in a subsidiary sense, an attempt to unify the types of doctrine and the forms of service then existing throughout the parish churches. There was no episcopal ordination, nor was it desired; for Cromwell's commissioners had taken the place of the bishops in

---

[4] In 1672 Miles Mallison was married at Greystoke. This may easily have been the grandfather of the above minister. If so, this would connect him with a well known Nonconformist yeoman, John Noble of Penruddock.

ecclesiastical matters. The questions of using the buildings that political fortune had put them in possession of, exercising the advantages of the parochial system, and, above all, of supplying the religious needs of the parish, were the practical aspects that absorbed the thought of the Puritan preachers. Accordingly when George Larkham was appointed by the commissioners to the living of All Saints, Cockermouth, he proceeded to form "a church" in the parish. He was ordained by the presbyters Thomas Larkham, M.A., Gawin Eaglesfield, M.A., and George Benson, M.A., on December 28th, 1651. From the year 1660 matters became acute in the State Church. In that year—to use Larkham's own words —"the afflictions of the churches began to tumble in upon them, heaps upon heaps." In 1659 the last church meeting was held at Bridekirk. In 1660 George Larkham ceased to preach at All Saints. On August 27th, the day after this cessation, the inhabitants of Cockermouth gave him a call in public to be their minister, *nem. con.* Sir George Fletcher disregarded this memorial, and Larkham was formally ejected. Three days afterwards he took leave of his people. In 1661 the church had several meetings in "parts and parcels," some meeting on one side of the river Derwent, others on the other side. For a portion of the year 1661 he had to cease his labours in public. Two months before the Act of Uniformity had come into operation the Cockermouth church had kept a day of prayer and conference on the subject of conformity. They decided that they "would not own the present generation of ministers," but those of the Puritan type "might be heard accidentally (occasionally) even though they did read Common Prayer. It was, however, considered an unlawful thing for the Church to read Common Prayer, for several reasons."

It was not until 1687 that a site was secured for a meeting-house: "after 26 years' compulsory exile, the Church met in a place prepared."

This is as far as we require to trace the Cockermouth history at present. In his volume on this church the Rev. W. Lewis has given full particulars. In the later stages of its congregational life it appears to have had the general experience of the Cumberland causes. One of its ministers was suspected of doctrinal declension, and one other minister, at least, was from the Church of Scotland.

Keswick

This cause evidently arose through the ministrations of James Cave (*vide* Calamy). He was ordained in the parish church of Crosthwaite in 1656, for general work, apparently. In 1657, the churches of Keswick and Cockermouth met at Thornthwaite, near Bassenthwaite Lake, and the two parsons preached; "the meeting was comfortable." Cave removed from the county after his

Cumberland and Westmorland

ejectment, and ultimately was a minister in London, where he died in 1694.

There is a gap between 1662 and the first name on Evans' list, but probably there was a close connection between Keswick and the other churches. Notably Cockermouth and Kirkoswald.

From the traces we have of several ministers, we find that the pulpit supply was either from the native element, or from Scotland.

Kirkoswald

This church has had the normal history of the other congregations of Cumberland. It is difficult to distinguish between the work at Huddlesceugh, Parkhead and Kirkoswald, but they were all fed from the same source. So also, we surmise, were Great Salkeld and Plumpton, until about 1700. The two personal forces in the Eden valley, in the early nonconforming period, were George Nicholson, M.A., and Simon Atkinson. The former only entered the county a short time before the Bartholomew Act; but the latter appears to have been vicar of Lazonby, from which he was ejected. Both were evidently working in the district at the same time. Nicholson died in 1697, and Atkinson in 1694. Particulars of their service are given in Calamy. This is a church where the registers have been lost. They were begun by the Rev. Caleb Threlkeld, M.A., M.D., (1702-1713) in existence in 1824 (*Home Missionary Magazine*). From the fragments that remain we see that the cause was founded in 1658, with aid from Cockermouth, and that afterwards it follows the normal course of having for its ministry the native element, then the Scotch element, and at the beginning of the nineteenth century a pronounced Independent.

Ravenstonedale

Our remarks here differ in several particulars from the sketch of this church written recently by the late Mr. Bryan Dale and the Secretary of your Society. It is hardly necessary to cover that ground, except to remind you that the influence of "the good Lord Wharton" was potent in this district, and that even after the Restoration there was in the parish church a strong Low Church influence. In the incumbency of Anthony Proctor, M.A., (1673-1689) "the saints' bell[5]" was rung after the Nicene creed, to call the Dissenters to sermon. Mr. Proctor had been a Nonconformist for ten years before he was selected by Lord Wharton, who chose him knowing he would be acceptable to the parishoners.

The doctrinal troubles of this congregation began early. In 1714 a secession took place, encouraged by Dr. Dixon of Whitehaven (a

---

[5] The saints' bell was probably the old sanctus bell, but was distinct from the sanctuary bell, which was a little distance from the church.

native of Ravenstonedale). We think that were it as Messrs. Dale
and Crippen suggest, a question of Arianism, it would be a
remarkably early date; but the probability is that it was the
question of Arminianism *versus* Calvinism. The sermon of Joseph
Dodson of Penruddock, in 1719, entitled "Moderation and Charity,"
shews that many minds were becoming centred on this great
doctrinal problem. Dr. Dixon administered the sacrament to the
seceders, who were the first to secede on any question in the two
counties. The minister was James Mallinson[6] of Blennerhasset.
He was possibly one of Dr. Dixon's students. He remained at
Ravenstonedale until 1717, and then went to Howden, Yorks.

Before the secession took place the minister was James Magee,
who was ordained there in 1714, and remained with the original
congregation until about 1732.

The particulars in the sketch by Messrs. Dale and Crippen concerning James Ritchie, M.A., M.D., the next minister, are somewhat
deficient. Another account of him appears in the article on Great
Salkeld meeting-house, published this year in the Cumberland and
Westmorland Antiquarian Society's *Transactions*. Ritchie appears
to have been able, and somewhat advanced, but there is no proof
that he ever became an Arian. The elaborate inscription to his
memory at Mixenden weakens the statement that the congregation
there "dwindled under his ministry."

It is impossible to examine in detail this congregation's history,
but our theory is that Mallison was the progressive man; and if he
came from Penruddock, Dodson's Arminian views would have their
effect upon Mallison. Upon his departure about 1717 the seceders
(numbering only ten at the beginning), returned to the old congregation, which resumed its Presbyterian and orthodox character.

Magee's successor appears to have been Samuel Lowthian, a
native of Penruddock, a child of good lineage and great hopes.
After a seven years' ministry at Ravenstondale he removed to
Penrith, and from thence to Richard Gilpin's old church at Newcastle, where, we fear, he was caught in the rationalism, if not in
the heterodoxy, of the times.

The next minister was (according to Dale and Crippen) John
Blackburn. We have gone carefully over the sketch, (which is
admittedly uncertain here), and think that the particulars given refer
to two men of the same name. In fact we cannot find any reason
for concluding that Blackburn was ever at Ravenstonedale. An
examination of the names of those attending the Provincial at this
time makes us hazard the suggestion that a Mr. Saunders was at
Ravenstonedale, from about 1753 to 1756.

The next name introduced is that of a Richard Simpson. This
is placed here because it is on record that he had a charge in

---

[6] There are two forms of the name, Mallison and Mallinson.

Westmorland. Mr. Nightingale suggests that it was Ravenstonedale, but we are inclined to think it was Stainton, where a Richd. Simpson was minister, 1749 (?)-1763, at the same time acting as Dr. Rotheram's assistant.

At this period there are several ministers from the Church of Scotland, and one from the newly founded academy at Heckmondwike. In the above mentioned sketch the congregation's life at this stage is inadequately represented. About 1780 Ravenstonedale, like the other congregations in Cumberland, was *in extremis*, and it was not until 1790, upon the settlement of John Hill, from Mile End academy, that the cause began to revive. Mr. Hill carried on a good work until his death in 1809.

The next minister, James Muscatt from Hackney, took a bold step. He accepted the call on condition that the church " should be re-organised and put more strictly on the Congregational plan." The sketch says that it had been accounted Independent 80 years before (there is only the reference in Evans' list to justify this, and even that might be explained), " but," continues the sketch, " there had been several Presbyterians, and apparently the minister, elders and trustees had managed things without much reference to the church members." This, we venture to submit, was not irregular procedure, since the constitution, character, and endowments of the congregation were Presbyterian. As to the legality of Mr. Muscatt's action, we must leave that question to the judicial mind.

There were several youths from this meeting-house who afterwards became Nonconformist ministers:

(1) The Rev. Thos. Dixon, M.D., Whitehaven, who kept an academy from which a number of students were sent out to supply pulpits.

(2) The Rev. Ralph Milner. His people were well-to-do statesmen in the dale. He was a student of Dr. Dixon's. His first charge was Wantage, Berks., in 1726. By his " procurement" the gallery of the meeting-house was built at Ravenstonedale, in 1731. His other charge was Yarmouth (Old Meeting) where he ministered, 1731-1761. In the closing period of that ministry he had as assistant John Whiteside, a native of Lancaster, and previously minister of Great Salkeld.

(3) The Rev. James Alderson. He was a native of Westmorland, and as the name is found in Ravenstonedale the strong probability is that he belonged to this meeting-house. His first charge was Great Salkeld, from which place he removed to Lowestoft, where he died in 1761. His son Robert was minister of the Presbyterian church at Norwich, but conformed and became recorder of Norwich. It is from this family that the well known judge Baron Alderson was descended, who was the father of the late Marchioness of Salisbury.

Stainton

The beginning of the cause at Stainton is obscure, but probably the influence of Gabriel Camelford, the ejected vicar of Staveley, was felt in this neighbourhood. The meeting-house was built in 1697, and in the churchyard there is the gravestone of Roger Dickinson (1676-1762). This may have been the son, or grandson, of Roger Dickinson the elder, of Beetham parish church, in the classis for the barony of Kendal.

The list of ministers is imperfect. The first one is John Atkinson, 1722. There were several persons of that name, and according to Mr. Nightingale one appears to have been at Crook, while the other was at Stainton. Although the thread is complex at present we are inclined to identify the John Atkinson, who wrote the reply to Joseph Dodson of Penruddock, and who undoubtedly was at Stainton, as the John Atkinson who appears in 1696 as schoolmaster of Motherly, Penruddock. After this there are several names, including John Kirkpatrick, (Kilpatrick) and the well known James Scott, afterwards of Heckmondwike, both of whom were from Scotland. In 1772 James Somerville from Scotland was settled there; but the cause was so poor that he was not able to receive ordination until he was called to Ravenstonedale in 1775. He was afterwards at Branton, Northumberland, where his ministry as an evangelical one was very successful. Somerville was the last minister at Stainton, and when the Rev. George Burder, of Lancaster, visited the place in 1779, he found the cause almost deserted. At the present time weeknight services are held in the old meeting-house, conducted by the members of the Lowther Street Independent church at Kendal.

Turning now to the group of congregations in connection with the Presbyterian Church of England we draw attention to :

Brampton

The particulars of this congregation are fully given in the article in the Cumberland and Westmorland Antiquarian Society's *Transactions*, vol. iii, N.S., and in the *Monthly Messenger* of the Presbyterian Church.[7] The registers are complete from 1712. There is still in existence in this congregation a large board displaying the royal coat of arms, which was put up by the authority of the Privy Council at the close of the seventeenth century. This public declaration of the congregation's loyalty to the crown was demanded only from the perverse congregations, and in itself tells the story of this Border cause. There are only two or three of these boards throughout the kingdom.

---

[7] Both of these accounts are written by Mr. Henry Penfold, an office-bearer of the Brampton congregation.

Cumberland and Westmorland

The course of the congregation's history need not detain us. It originated through the ejection of Nathanael Burnand, M.A., vicar of Brampton. The ministry has been supplied mainly from the Church of Scotland, although in the eighteenth century the provincial meeting of Cumberland and Westmorland performed the ordinations. Upon the removal of the ministers to parish livings in Scotland their ordination was acknowledged by the Church of Scotland.

Carlisle

The history of Nonconformity in Carlisle is obscure in its beginnings. There was no ejected minister from any of the parish churches. The bishop at the Restoration was Richard Sterne, but the see had been previously offered to Richard Gilpin, the ejected vicar of Greystoke, who declined it. His relative Bernard Gilpin had been unable to accept the same honour in Queen Elizabeth's reign. Gilpin purchased Scaleby Castle, near Carlisle, and it is probable that among the Nonconformists who gathered in the large kitchen of that Border fortalice, the Puritans of Carlisle were to be found. In this cathedral city the Five Mile Act would be rigidly enforced. The first minister of Carlisle is Thomas Dickinson, who was there in 1712. Then follows, as far as we can trace, the usual development with the unique climax, for Cumberland, of a Unitarian congregation. In 1778 a Secession cause was formed, and after various fluctuations Presbyteriansm of a Scotch type was planted, and continues to thrive. Little of the old English Presbyterianism remains.

Haltwhistle

This cause probably originated through the influences of Gilpin of Scaleby Castle and Burnand of Brampton (brothers-in-law).

In Dr. Evans' time (1717-1729) it was at Wardrew (near Gilsland), for the water-drinking time, and the services were carried on by twelve ministers jointly. The first trust deed of Haltwhistle is dated 1744. The ministry has been mainly Scotch. The cause has always been Presbyterian, and there is nothing abnormal in its history.

Kendal

Kendal is the home of many schisms. The particulars are well known, as there have been several chroniclers. A book will be published this year by Mr. Francis Nicholson, entitled *Kendal Unitarian Chapel*. It will deal with the early records, which are in no sense Unitarian, but contain much valuable material for studying the early history of Kendal Nonconformity. The name of Richard Frankland is inseparably associated with Kendal, for in addition to his pastoral charge he started an academy at Natland, which from 1674-1684 was most serviceable to northern Dissent.

Two other important names are those of the Rev. Caleb Rotheram, D.D., and the Rev. Caleb Rotheram, junr., whose united ministry lasted 76 years. A few years after the settlement of Caleb Rotheram, junr., (1763) a petition was sent to the Associate Presbytery of Edinburgh for supply of sermon. This was granted, and the Rev. James McQuhae was ordained in 1764. McQuhae took part in an independent ordination, and brought himself under the discipline of the Secession Church in Scotland. Mr. Nightingale tells the story (p. 284 Westmorland vol.).

McQuhae refusing to submit became an Independent, and was minister of Tockholes, Lancs., in 1771; but a certain party detached themselves from the Presbyterian (Secession) congregation, and ultimately, in 1781, Lowther Street Independent chapel was built. In addition to these shades of Dissent in Kendal particulars are found of Unitarian Baptists (or Dippers), Inghamites, Sandemanians and Universalists.

During the long ministry of the Rotherams the original Presbyterian cause had been changing, and in the pastorate of the Rev. John Harrison (1796-1833) the congregation became decidedly Unitarian.

Penrith

The cause originated in the ejection of Roger Baldwin from St. Andrew's church. The Five Mile Act was evidently enforced, and this probably explains the strength of Nonconformity in the Eden valley. The congregation at Penrith has had an unbroken history from the Act of Toleration. The ministers have been mainly from the Church of Scotland, but Samuel Lowthian and Samuel Threlkeld were natives of the district. The history of the congregation is entirely English. In 1799, through the decay of Dissent, Penrith applied to the Secession Church of Scotland, and received a minister from that denomination. After becoming part of the United Presbyterian denomination it eventually, in 1876, returned to its original English Presbyterian connection. It is impossible to give further particulars here, but its traditions equal, if not exceed, those of Cockermouth.

Penruddock

The story of this cause has been told by the present writer in the Cumberland and Westmorland Antiquarian Society's *Transactions*, vol. v. N.S. That sketch is inaccurate in several particulars, but the outline is unalterable.[8] We shall only add the following fresh information.

In the *Transactions* article a reference was made to the parish list of Penruddock. We have since been able to examine the documents, and have made a rich discovery. The papers themselves do not contain many direct allusions to the religious aspect of the struggle, but it is evident that it is a fight between Puritan and Roman Catholic on the one hand, and Puritan and Episcopalian on the other.

The first group of documents relate to a law case between the tenants and Andrew Huddlestone, lord of the manor of Hutton John. Before the manor came into the possession of the Huddlestons it had been occupied by Thomas Hutton. In his time the tenants had kept the Borders for king and baron, and upon the lordship of the Huddlestons claimed special privileges in their tenements for this Border service. The fight began in 1628, and in the year 1635 the tenants sent a petition to Charles I., which was presented at Newmarket. In 1637 Baron Trevor decreed for the tenants; but for 70 years afterwards the struggle went on, until the House of Lords made the final award in favour of the tenants. The matters in dispute related to the amount of fines they should pay, and boon services they should render; but beneath these disputes there was the feudalism of the baron, who insisted that they were only tenants at the will of the lord, and the Puritan spirit, that, as free men in Christ, demanded freedom from intolerant and unfair claims.

The other case related to an excessive tithe the Puritan rectors had received, 16 gallons to the bushel measure. The Restoration rectors increased the tithe until it reached 22 gallons; but the tenants appealing, the case was tried in 1672 at Carlisle, Appleby and Lancaster, when it was settled in favour of the tenants.

In these two cases the Puritan attitude towards authority is seen. It was not antagonism to the lord of the manor, or to the parson of the parish, that prompted the people to appeal. They disliked the tyranny of the one, and the doctrine of the other; but they fought the lord and the parson on the injustice of their charges. In this respect the Puritans differed from the Quakers, who refused both to acknowledge authority and to pay the tithe. It is perhaps worth remembering, in these days when authority is distasteful to the Nonconformist conscience, that the Puritan revolution was never anarchical.

The men who carried on these two battles were members of the

---

[8] The name of Richard Gilpin, that great Puritan, will always be associated with Penruddock. He was the rector of the parish of Greystoke, and it was his congregation there that afterwards formed the Penruddock meeting-house. His predecessor was Mr. West (or Weston) whose doctrine was "effectual upon many." He was buried there September 15th, 1654 (Greystoke Register and John Noble's Funeral Sermon, 1708).

Penruddock meeting-house, and in 1685 were excommunicated by the rector of Greystoke.

Penruddock is without a line of official history; yet the cause there is one of the rarest pearls in the coronet of churches in Cumberland.

Great Salkeld and Plumpton

These congregations have been worked under one minister from an early date, probably before 1737. The full story of these causes appears in an article in the Antiquarian *Transactions* this year. Its ministry is almost identical with that of Penrith. Several important families were connected with this congregation, among others being the Rev. George Benson, D.D., the two Caleb Rotherams, the three Threlkelds (the Revs. Caleb, M.A., M.D., Samuel, and Thomas), the Lowthian family (the Rev. Thomas Lowthian, born at Great Salkeld; the Rev. Samuel Lowthian, born at Penruddock), and the Nelson family (the Rev. Timothy Nelson; M.A.).

Whitehaven

Although Whitehaven is some miles from Cockermouth, yet the early Nonconformists of Whitehaven were dependent upon the ministry and ordinances of the latter place. The first reference in the Cockermouth registers to Whitehaven is in 1660. Between that date and the Indulgence a common friendship existed, while occasionally meetings of the Cockermouth church were held at Whitehaven. In 1675 the Whitehaven church appears, from a reference in the Cockermouth registers, to have become a separate church; but its connection with Cockermouth is found as late as 1692, when George Larkham baptised several children of the Whitehaven church. In 1695 a deed was drawn up for Protestant Dissenters " whether Presbyterian or Congregational according to their way or persuasion," but no mention is made of a minister until the name of Thomas Dixon, M.D., occurs in the 1711 deed as minister of Market Place. During his pastorate the cause was influential, and Evans' list states that five of the members were merchants having a joint fortune of £36,000. The same authority also mentions that the Dissenters of Whitehaven had such influence in the elections at Cockermouth, that these two congregations were able to return whom they pleased. The names of several English ministers follow that of Dixon, and in 1773 a Church of Scotland minister appears. This denomination supplied the ministry until the disruption of 1843, and at that period the congregation allied itself with the Free Church of Scotland. In 1876 the Whitehaven congregation became part of the Presbyterian Church of England. In the eighteenth century a second cause had been formed. In 1775 twenty-seven Scotch residents applied to the Secession Church (Presbytery of Sauquhar) for "sealing ordinances." This was the formation of High Street congregation, which continued until 1895 when it united with Market Place.

Crook

This congregation is now extinct. The ministry of Gabriel Camelford, the ejected vicar of Staveley, was probably exercised in this neighbourhood. The names of several ministers who were at Crook are known, one being Samuel Bourn (1711-1720) whose son became prominent in the Arian movement. The last name we can trace is that of Abraham Ainsworth, who was there in 1729.

II

THE IMPORTANT QUESTION OF POLITY can only be briefly considered. Perhaps it will suffice for the present if we state the positive side of the case.

The prime document is the Agreement of the Associated Ministers of Cumberland and Westmorland in 1656. Their churches are the parishes on the Congregational model or are "churches" within the parishes. The Articles of Agreement were drawn up by Richard Gilpin, who followed the lines of Richard Baxter in the Worcestershire Agreement.[9] The document is a perfect example of Christian charity towards each other, in men who differed in "the power of the keys" and polity, both of which were inflammatory subjects in those days.

Dr. Drysdale in his valuable work on English Presbyterianism says that the Articles reflect the genius and spirit of Presbyterianism. This is especially true from the view of modern Presbyterianism, but the document was clearly a compromise and a constitutional basis for two types of polity.

The incontrovertible fact, as "the explication" shews, is that while it was not Presbyterian it was not Independent. Discipline was exercised by the Association, not only in the cases of ministers but in grave cases in the congregations. On the subject of "sins of ancient date" the advice of the Association had to be asked. At ordination of ministers the Association appointed trials, and if satisfied they set the candidates apart. Similar instances of over-

---

[9] The Agreement of the Associated Ministers of Essex in 1658 acknowledges its obligation to other agreements, and in many passages resembles the Cumberland agreement.

sight could be quoted from this document, but these will suffice to prove that the Association was more than a federation and that it had internal executive power.

The Association agreed to meet once a month at Carlisle, Penrith and Cockermouth; occasionally they met together, and this is evidently what is meant by a general meeting.

At a general meeting at Keswick in 1685 Richard Gilpin preached his sermon on "The Temple Rebuilt." It deals with the differences, entirely ecclesiastical, of these Puritan vicars who were still in their livings.[10]

After the Act of Uniformity we hear nothing of the Association for a long time. This is not surprising considering the state of things between 1672-1689. When the meeting-houses began to spring up in the two counties the Association was revived, probably on the London model of 1691, under the name of the Provincial meeting. The first trace of it is in 1709, when they ordained James Campbell, a Scotch Presbyterian, to the English congregation of Brampton, Cumberland. The latest trace of it is in 1783 when they ordained Richard Paxton to Penrith. That meeting is called "the Provincial of Cumberland." There were only two surviving causes in Westmorland at this period, those of Kendal and Ravenstonedale. The defection of the former had taken place and the latter may have attached itself to Yorkshire, or, which is more probable, may have become isolated. A Mr. Smith was there 1784-90, but nothing is known of him.

The existence of the minutes of the Provincial has been a matter for conjecture. Our theory is that there were no separate records, and that the minutes of their meetings were inserted in the registers of the congregations at the places where they met.

With regard to the individual congregations we find that no restriction whatever was placed upon their freedom. They were allowed to develop as they chose. In the first half of the eighteenth century the tendency of the Provincial was to become less presbyterial in its procedure, and that of the congregations to become more independent in action; but the Provincial maintained its authority on the subjects of ordination and admission into the ministry, as is seen in the case of Caleb Rotheram, junr. It was only when the congregations became so weak as to be unable to support ministers (1780-1800) that the Provincial ceased to exist; and it was the dissolution of that Association that threw the congregations into isolation and sheer Independency.

The question of the polity of each congregation is a complicated

---

[10] A passage on p. 30 upon government and ordinances clearly shews that Gilpin believed in "confederacy or combination." Whether it is more than Association "confederacy" is not stated, but he is not in favour of action by congregations separately. The sermon met with the fullest approval of the Association, who ordered it to be printed. A few weeks afterwards, however, George Larkham left Cockermouth to attend the Independent Conference at the Savoy.

Cumberland and Westmorland

one, and would require to be dealt with at great length. Dr. Dale in his posthumous work, recently published, says that the characteristic of the Presbyterian congregations was that of trustees and office bearers, in distinction to that of Independent congregations which was that of the church meeting.

By this test a good claim could be made to-day by the English Presbyterians for several buildings that are not in their possession; but we are not disposed to press this rigid test as far as Cumberland and Westmorland are concerned.[11] There is little doubt that while the strong tendency was Presbyterian[12] that element became weaker as each period passed, and was almost obliterated at the close of the eighteenth century; but that fact does not alter the early and marked characteristics of the congregations, nor does it conceal the truth that among several congregations Independency appears in the decadent stage of the congregational life.

III

THE QUESTION OF DOCTRINE though important need not detain us long. From the fact that no Warrington students are to be found in the pulpits, the only two congregations that became Unitarian are Carlisle and Kendal. The latter was through the influence of the Rotherams, particularly the son. A landmark in the history of the Provincial is the ordination of Caleb Rotheram, junr., in 1756, when grave doubts seem to have arisen from this step.

The academy men who filled the pulpits of the counties were natives, and though several of them appear to have moved from the old position their heterodoxy is at a late stage in their ministry and after they had left the counties. The congregation, as a whole, retained the Westmorland Confession of Faith (modified), and the *Shorter Catechism*. The ministerial supply from Scotland in the eighteenth century brought a fresh vitality to these English documents, and there is strong evidence that the Calvinism of Scotland saved the meeting-houses of Cumberland and Westmorland from the fate of Lancashire in the second half of the eighteenth century.

The last thing that need be said to-day is that had it not been for James Scott, a man trained in a Presbyterian divinity hall, many meeting-houses in Lancashire and Yorkshire could never have striven against the Latitudinarianism of the time. He it was who

---

[11] The harmony between the denominations (if they may be described as such at this early stage) is heard in the remarkable clause of the Whitehaven trust deed.

[12] With the exception of Cockermouth which, beginning in a pronounced Presbyterian atmosphere, sent its ministers to the conference of Independents at the Savoy Palace in 1685.

started the reaction and founded the Heckmondwike academy, which, in spite of "the Rational Nonconformist" and Warrington academy, was successful in saving the meeting-houses by turning them into independent congregations and making them citadels of the evangelical faith. It will perhaps be put down to the credit of Scotchmen, who are often charged with mercenary motives for invading England, that your own denomination had a great deliverance through the Berwickshire man who preferred the Calvinism of the seventeenth century to the Rationalism of the eighteenth, yet who saw below creeds and beyond polities into the evangelical verities of the Christian faith.

J. HAY COLLIGAN.

Note upon the Map for "Cumberland and Westmorland" Article

IN constructing a map to accompany Mr. Colligan's instructive paper it seems desirable to make it so far comprehensive as to illustrate the whole history of seventeenth century Nonconformity in the two counties. The map therefore locates the "Bartholomew" ejectments of 1662, the licences under the Indulgence of 1672, the few Baptist churches that were founded within the century, and the Friends' meetings that were constituted before the Revolution. The authorities are Palmer's *Nonconformist's Memorial*, the Calendar of State Papers, Dom. Ser., 1672-73, Evans's List in Williams's Library, and Mr. Norman Penney's valuable work *The First Publishers of Truth*.

1.—Ejected Ministers, 1662: Cumberland.

ADDINGHAM.—Daniel Broadley.
ANISTABLE.—George Yates (afterwards conformed).
BOLTON.—John Forward (afterwards conformed).
BOWNESS.—John Saxton.
BRAMPTON.—Henry (?) Burnand, afterwards minister at Harwich.
BRIDEKIRK.—George Benson, afterwards of Kellet, Lancashire.
BROOMFIELD.—A minister whose name is not recorded.
CALDBECK.—Richard Hutton.
CARLISLE.—Comfort Star, M.A., afterwards pastor at Lewes, Sussex.
COCKERMOUTH.—George Larkham, M.A.
CROGLIN.—John Rogers, M.A., afterwards ministered in Teesdale and Weardale.
CROSBY.—John Collyer.
CROSSTHWAITE.—James Cave, afterwards pastor at Daventry.
EDENHALL.—Thomas Tailor, afterwards preacher at Alston Moor, etc.
EGREMONT.—Mr. Halsell.
GREYSTOCK.—Richard Gilpin, M.D., afterwards of Newcastle.
HUTTON.—John Jackson.
ST. JOHN'S CHAPEL.—James Carr.
KIRKANDREWS.—Thomas Courtney.
KIRKLINTON OR KIRK-LEAVINGTON.—Mr. Hooper.

LAMPLUGH.—John Michael or Myriel (afterwards conformed).
LAZONBY.—Simon Atkinson.
MELMERBY.—William Hopkins.
NEWKIRK.—Mr. Cragg (afterwards conformed).
PENRITH.—Roger Baldwin, afterwards of Eccles.
PLUMLAND.—Gawen Egglesfield.
SOWERBY.—Peter Jackson.
THURSBY.—John Carmichael, afterwards in Scotland.
TORPENHOW.—Thomas Turner.
WETHERHALL.—Mr. Wilcox.

Westmorland.

ASKHAM.—Christopher Langborne.
BARTON.—Timothy Roberts.
CROSBY-ON-THE-HILL.—Christopher Jackson, afterwards at Ravenstonedale.
HUTTON CHAPEL, KENDAL.—Mr. Greenwood.
KENDAL.—John Wallis.
KIRKBY STEPHEN.—Francis Higginson (afterwards conformed).
ORTON.—George Fothergill (afterwards conformed).
RAVENSTONEDALE.—James Dodson (afterwards conformed).
SHAP.—John Dalton (afterwards conformed).
STAVELEY CHAPEL.—Gabriel Camelford, afterwards pastor in Furness.

2.—Licences granted under the Indulgence, 1672: Cumberland.

ALLONBY.—House of Richard Egleshold, Presb. 16th July.
ALSTON MOOR.—John Davy, Congl., at house of Reginald Walton. 29th June.
BRAMPTON.—(Misspelled Branton and Brantam) Nathaniel Burman, Presb., General. 5th Sept.
House of William Atkinson, Presb. 5th Sept.
BRIDEKIRK.—George Larkham, Presb., at his own house at Hames Hill, 2nd May; the house licensed 26th July.
House of Edward James, Presb. 30th Sept.
CARLISLE.—House of Barbary Studholm, Ind. 3rd Feby., 1673.
COCKERMOUTH.—House of Richard Lowry, Presb. 16th July.
CROSFIELD.*—House of Wilson (no initial or description). 30th Sept.
CROSTHWAITE.—House of Gawen Wrenn, Presb. 16th July: corrected as Gawden Wreen, Cong. 5th Sept.: and again corrected as Gawen Wrenn, Cong. 18th Nov.

---

* Crosfield—not located—was probably about 5 miles E.S.E. of Whitehaven.

Note upon the Map

DEARHAM.—Gavin Eaglesfield, Indpt., at his own house. 9th Decr.
EMBLETON.—House of John Casse, Presb. 16th July.
GREYSTOCK.—Anthony Sleigh, Presb., at house of John Noble. 15th June. (?)
HESKETT.—Simon Atkinson, Congl., house of W. Sanderson. 29th May.
HOLME CUTTRAM.—House of Thos. Barnes, Indept. 9th Decr.
KIRKOSWALD.—Giles Nicholson, Congl., general. 22nd July.
   House of William Jameson, Presb. 5th Sept.
   House of Thomas Therkeld (no description). 28th Oct.
PENRITH.—(Misspelled Penrick): house of Thomas Langhorne, Cong. 19th Nov.
TORPENHOW. — House of Thomas Younghusband, Presb. 16th July.

Westmorland.

HEVERSHAM.—House of Edward Bridges, Presb. 28th Oct.
   House of John Hinde, Presb. 28th Oct.
KENDAL.—Thomas Whitehead, Presb., house of John Garrett. 13th May.
   George Benson, Presb., at his own house. 16th July.
   House of William Syll, Presb. 22nd July.
   House of John Gernet, Presb. 5th Sept. (misspelled Rendal).
   House of James Atkinson, ⎫ (mispelled Kendle; ⎫ no
   House of James Cook, ⎭ description) 9th Dec.
WHINFIELD.—House of William Warriner, Presb. 22nd July.

3.—Baptist Churches in Cumberland.

BROUGHTON.   EGREMONT.   OULTON.

(None in Westmorland).

4.—Friends' Meeting-houses: Cumberland.

ABBEY HOLME, soon after 1653.   PORTINSCALE, 1653.
ALLONBY, 1656.   CROSFIELD, 1677*   SCOTBY, before 1661.
BIRKER.   ISELL, 1653.   SOLPORT, 1673.
BOLTON, 1653.   KIRKBRIDE, 1653.   SOWERBY, 1653.
BROUGHTON, 1653.   KIRKLINTON, 1672.   WIGTON, 1653.
CALDBECK, 1653.   MOSEDALE (Grisdale How), 1653.
CARLISLE, 1653.   PARDSHAW CRAGG, 1653.
COCKERMOUTH, 1688.   PENRITH.

---

* See previous footnote.

Westmorland.

GRAYRIGG.	PRESTON PATRICK.	UNDER BARROW.
HUTTON.	RAVENSTONEDALE.	DENT (Yorksh.), 1680.
KENDALL.	SHAP.	SEDBURGH (Yorksh.) 1652.
	STRICKLAND HEAD.	

5.—Academies.

FRANKLAND's temporarily at Natland, Dawsonfold, & Hart Barrow.
DIXON's at Whitehaven.
ROTHERHAM's at Kendal.

The Jessey Church, 1653-1678

THE church founded in 1616 by Henry Jacob, and ministered to afterwards by Lathrop and Jessey, has attracted attention in recent years owing to the discovery of some of its early documents. The papers known in Baptist circles as the Jessey Records and the Kiffin MS. were copied in 1711 by Benjamin Stinton. His *Repository*, misused by Neal and condensed by Crosby, came into the hands of George Gould of Norwich, whose transcript was recently published in the *Transactions* of the Congregational Historical Society. The authenticity of these papers had been challenged in America, where it had been defended by Geo. A. Lofton, by Champlin Burrage, and by the present writer, who then proceeded to write the story from 1616 till 1645 from these contemporary papers, tracing nine of the churches into which the original foundation separated. This was published in the *Baptist Review and Expositor* for January, 1906.

Some letters from the Jessey church in 1653 and 1654 to the Baptist church at Hexham, now at Rowley and Blackhill or Hamsterley, were printed in 1854 by the Hansard Knollys Society. Seven years earlier the same society had printed more correspondence of this church with the Baptist church at Broadmead, Bristol, from 1669 till 1678. The information in these two sets of letters has been overlooked of late, and deserves to be analyzed, in order that the history from original sources may be continued for another generation.

The Jessey Church

First, as to the place where the church habitually met. The letters to Hexham are subscribed from "the church meeting at Swan Alley in Coleman Street." This agrees with the colophon to Jessey's *Storehouse of Provision* published in 1650, and dated from the same place.[1] We must distinguish this from the Particular Baptist church of Hanserd Knowles in Coleman Street itself, and from the great general Baptist church of Thomas Lamb in Bell Alley, parallel with Swan Alley. Not one of the three was reported in the bishop's enquiry of 1669; in 1672 only Lamb's people applied for a licence, this time in White's Alley, and met with a refusal for reasons obvious to those who know their militant disposition. At this time Vavasour Powell calls our church small,[2] so that it might easily escape notice, and in fact, while it was certainly existing in 1669, it is not reported from any quarter. The place in 1672 is uncertain, but there is nothing to suggest a change. An idea has grown up that the church met in Southwark; this seems due to Neal's confusion with the ancient church of 1592 and also with the 1621 church of Hubbard Canne More and How. It is true that Jessey on Sunday morning preached at St. George's in Southwark, but he also lectured at All Hallows, and preached at Anchor Lane, besides ministering to his own church in the afternoon. The documents of the church give no hint of any removal, or of any meeting being held south of the Thames: in 1663 Jessey's funeral started from Woodmongers' Hall,[3] just off Coleman Street; in 1669-1678 the Bristol correspondence never mentions Southwark, but styles this a church in London.[4]

Next, as to the continuity of the church.

---
[1] *Fenstanton Records*, pages 345, 347, 349, 349.
[2] *Broadmead Records*, page 108.
[3] Crosby, vol. I, page 320.
[4] *Broadmead Records*, pages 104, 115, 155, 157, 158, 203, 383, 384.

The Jessey Church

Vavasour Powell vouched for this in 1669, calling it "the church brother Jessey belonged to."[2] And a letter of October, 1670, is endorsed by Mr. Terrill of Bristol, the recipient, "Letter from the church of Jesus Christ in London, that formerly walked with our beloved brother Henry Jessey, now deceased."[5] On this point there can be no doubt, and it is instructive to note how completely the membership could change in a few years. Stinton has preserved the names of several members between 1633 and 1640, but in 1653 the Hexham letters mention none of these, while George Baggott, Thomas Shefold, Matthew Strange, George Waddle, George Ware, are now prominent, with George Barret as teacher alongside Jessey.[6] In 1669 every one of these has disappeared, and we find in the next two years John Abbot, John Buckmaster, Samuel Buttall, Thomas Chappell, Nathanael Crabb, Thomas Dawson, Michael Dunwell, Nathanael Hall, Thomas Hardcastle, John James, William Nuttall, John Smith and Richard Woollaston.[7] As Powell calls the church "but small," there were perhaps few other men.

As to the integrity of the church, there is no sign in these letters that any further division had taken place. Powell and the church itself regard this group not as part of Jessey's church but as Jessey's church complete. Some of the 1640 members may be traceable elsewhere, but that could be due to their transfer separately; some of the 1653 members may be traced to another community, but there is no hint here that any had seceded or had been dismissed to form another church, as had happened down to 1643. The 1669 people are regarded and regard themselves as the

---

[5] *Broadmead Records*, page 117.
[6] *Fenstanton Records*, pages 345, 348.
[7] *Broadmead Records*, pages 102, 104, 120, 125, 140, 155.

same church which in 1637 called Henry Jessey, and these letters carry on their story as an undivided whole until 1678.

We can note the succession of pastors. From now 1616 till 1622 Henry Jacob was chief, 1624 till 1634 John Lathrop, 1637 till 1663 Henry Jessey; all three ex-clergymen. In 1670 John Abbot, ejected from Fishborne in Sussex, was a prominent member, but not the elder; Thomas Hardcastle, late vicar of Bramham in Yorkshire, was on trial for that post.[8] Before the church decided, the Broadmead church at Bristol invited him, and he went, to the unappeasable indignation of the London church. Seeing that he was beyond reach, they called James Fitten, an old friend and fellow-sufferer of his, who is found in office by 1674.[9] He was helped for a short time by Henry Forty, who in 1675 went to Abingdon.[10] Fitten lived till 1676 at least, when he visited Trowbridge, and was asked to ordain Hardcastle, a request he evaded.[11] He soon died, and the church called a fifth pastor, whose name is unfortunately not given. He also died soon, and the church then made another vain attempt to get Hardcastle back.[12] At this point information fails.

The evolution of the church is carried a step further than was generally known. In 1616 it was indeed a separate church, but on very good terms with some Puritan clergy, and in 1630 it still accepted members from the Establishment, only stipulating for a verbal covenant. But questions were rife whether baptism by the State clergy could be recognized, and though these were hushed by the secession of many doubters, Jessey in 1642 followed the example set by some of these, so far as to return to the legal method of baptism:

[8] *Broadmead Records*, pages 108, 111, 140, 155.
[9] *Broadmead Records*, pages 111, 383, 198, 203.
[10] *Broadmead Records*, pages 198, 203.
[11] *Broadmead Records*, page 359.
[12] *Broadmead Records*, pages 383, 384.

immersion. It would appear that he still administered this to infants, but in 1645 he abandoned this practice. And then he conceded that baptism in the State Church was null and void, and was himself immersed. This however, was the limit of his progress : a Baptist confession had been framed in 164¾, it was revised in 1646 and republished in 1651 ; Jessey never signed it, though Henry Forty did. In 1653 the Hexham correspondence shews that Jessey strongly advocated mixed communion,[13] and in 1670 and 1671 the church corresponded with Broadmead, also of this type,[14] without any hint that a change had occurred. But the installing of Fitten seems to have made a difference, and the Bunyan meeting at Bedford, another church of the same liberal type, refused to transfer a member hither on this express ground. Henceforth Fitten is found co-operating with Strict Baptists, such as Thomas Collier of Wilts, Nehemiah Cox of Petty France, Captain Richard Deane, Henry Forty, Major and Alderman William Kiffin.[15] Presumably then, the church had at last evolved into a regular Baptist church. There is no sign in the letters of any secession or division, but on the contrary of new members being added.[16]

Various traditional stories about this church seem to be negatived by these letters which have been so long disregarded. Thus the position of Forty has been misunderstood, while his senior James Fitten has been quite forgotten, as also an ephemeral successor. Then it has been held that the Paedobaptist members in the church at 1663 carried on the corporate life into the fellowship disclosed in 1669 under Wadsworth and Parsons in Globe Alley, Maid Lane, Southwark: these

[13] *Fenstanton Records*, pages 348, 349.
[14] *Broadmead Records*, page 360.
[15] *Broadmead Records*, page 359.
[16] *Broadmead Records*, pages 203, 383.

letters give us no reason to connect the church at any time with Southwark, but fix it in Swan Alley, close to London Wall and Moorgate Street; they give no sign of any disruption after 1663, and shew that the whole church was associating with Strict Baptists in 1678. However many ancient churches unite their threads in the present Pilgrim church on the New Kent Road, no strand has yet been discovered passing from the Jessey church. And on the other hand, whereas it was also supposed that on Forty leaving for Abingdon in 1675 the Baptist members joined their cousins under Kiffin, this also proves a double misconception: the church held together at least three years longer, and had two more pastors. Moreover, the ancient books of Kiffin's church have no record of any fusion with Jessey's church, nor do they contain the name of a single one of the members of this church, even as joining individually.

Four members of the church are recognized in four different Baptist churches as representatives at the assembly of 1689: Barret at Mile End Green, Buttall at Plymouth, Crabb at Shad Thames, Dawson at Horsleydown. As the church is not to be identified with any of the London churches, every one of which is known, the probability is that the little band had either merged into some other, or had given up its corporate existence. If a guess may be hazarded, the false tradition that the church joined Kiffin suggests the enquiry whether it really did join William Collins and Nehemiah Cox at Petty France, for this church did presently move to Devonshire Square and absorb the members of Kiffin's disbanded church*;

[*This statement, though verbally correct, is liable to misapprehension. The Petty France church, the smaller of the two, had a substantial endowment. When it removed to Devonshire Square, the older church, though numerically larger, was formally disbanded, and its members at once enrolled in the immigrant brotherhood that the endowment might be preserved. The whole business was merely prudential, and did not really affect the historic continuity of the Spilsbury-Kiffin church, which has survived from 1633 to this day. EDITOR.]

unhappily the records of this famous body, known to Ivimey in 1812, are at present mislaid.

The name of Nathanael Crabb affords material for another conjecture. Stinton notes at the head of documents 1, 2, 4 in his repository that they were from papers given him by Richard Adams. Now Adams and Crabb were members of the same church in 1689, Crabb was a member of the Jessey church from 1670 till 1674 at least. It is therefore conceivable that he was the person who handed over to Adams the early documents, including " several sheets containing ye names of ye members of ye said congregation and ye time of their admission," which unfortunately Stinton did not think worth copying.

These two suggestions may perhaps be disproved; but the facts here summarised, and available in print for more than fifty years, make it plain that there is more need for co-ordination of studies, and for scholars to address themselves to the materials at hand, both that false legends may be exploded, and that true stories may be reconstructed.

PRESTON. W. T. WHITLEY.

Dr. Watts's Tomb

The following receipt for payment in relation to the repair of Dr. Watts's tomb in 1809 may be of some interest.

1809 ——Chatteris Esqr.
to Thos. Waller
110 Shoreditch.

	£	s	d
May 31.—To taking off Black Marb. Ledger from the Tomb of Dr. Isaac Watts & refacing do.	1	15	0
To No. 735 letters (Deep cut) on do. at 3^d	9	3	9
To Refixing Do. in Bunhill F^{ds} Bury^l Ground	0	9	0
1810 July 21.—To taking down Old, Clearing away and Erecting a new strong $Port^d$ Tomb, Cramps, Lead, &c.	30	0	0
To Working up Brickwork to do., 1500 Bricks and 33 hods $Moit^r$ & Men 2 Days	5	19	3
	£47	7	0

Rec^d Feby. 29th 1812 of ——Chatteris Esqr the sum Forty Seven Pounds Seven Shillings for Stone Tomb and Brickwork to D^o in Bunhill fields Burial Y^d over Dr. Isaac Watts

Impressed Stamp, 8d.

for Thos Waller
Hy Waller

£47 : 7 . 0

An Unpublished Letter of Dr. Watts

THE following letter has been contributed by Mr. R. W. Dixon, of Sandal Heath, Salisbury. The Rev. Henry Francis, to whom it is addressed, became pastor of Above Bar Independent church, Southampton, in 1726; and was succeeded in 1765 by the Rev. W. Kingsbury, M.A., who retired in December, 1809.

LONDON, *March 19th, 1728/9.*

DEAR BROTHER FRANCIS,

Your last is now before me with all the long detail of discouragements which you enumerate there. I own many of them to be just & the future prospects of the Dissenting Interest in Southampton after the Lives of some few persons is fomew^t unpleasing & afflictive, if we look meerly to appearances. But I have a few things to offer which will in some measure, I hope, reconcile your thoughts to a long continuance among them.

1. Consider how great things God has done for the difsenting Interest in Southampton by your means, even more than have ever been done by any minister whatsoever. Theres a new & larger Meeting-house built for you: There's a great number added to the Church more than ever were in so few years time (I believe) since I was born, or perhaps long before.

2. There are some persons in whom God has begun a good work, & will (I hope) Carry it on by your means. Oh do not think of forsaking them who live by your ministry.

3. There is scarce any people in England who love their Minister & honor & esteem him more than yours do you: This Voice of the people is the Voice of God, generally, if not always. You know not what wounds you make in the hearts of those who love you when you do but speak of leaving them, or intimate your discouragements & uneasiness in any measure so as to look towards a departure.

4: When you sometimes think another must be the person whom God will honor in carrying on his work in that Town, Where will you find him? Where is the man who is better qualified for this service or is likely to be so much beloved as you are? And 'tis this affectionate respect of the people that is the chief foundation of usefullness so far as reason & probability go. So that if you leave them, you cannot do it with any other prospect than in leaving them like sheep in the Wilderness to be scattered, languish & dye, which I am sure will have no pleasing influence on the heart of one so sensible as Mr Ffrancis.

5. Jf you leave them, whither will you go? I have continual complaints from the Country as well as in the City that the case is the same in many places as it is with you, & much worse. No additions to the Church, Declenfions of the Auditory, Sinking of the Subscriptions & the Support of the Minister to a great Degree, The deaths of members and their posterity leaving the Towns or leaving the Difsent so that your Case, tho. not universall yet 'tis very common. You may leave Southampton & make a much worse exchange.

6. Consider dear Sir, whether this be not a Temptation thrown in your way to discourage you in your work and weaken your hands. 'Twas a kind providence that has enabled you to weather the Storm which W : F : had raised : and will you raise Storms & Clouds in your own breast to make your work drag on heavily?

7. Let us remember dear Brother that we are not engaged in a work that depends all upon reasonings, & prospects and probabilities & prefent appearances, but upon the hand & Spirit of God. If he will work who shall hinder? He can work in unforseen ways & rayse his Israel tho. it be small, & can make a stone become a great Mountain : Read Esa. 54.2,3. Esa. 56.8 Esa. 49.19-21. Prayer can give accomplishment to promises.

8. Think again Dear ffriend, You are not under the perplexing & overwhelming Cares about the support of a family. Suppose your own discouraging prospects should come to pass in a great measure ; you can Live Comfortably tho. not save so much ; now you well know that grandeur or prosperity or encreasing Circumstances in the World are not the things we propose when we become Dissenting ministers. If we can but feed the flock of Christ & keep it from sinking, by becoming instrumentall to add such a succession of members as may support it in the World, this is well worth living for. But I hope better things than this tho. I thus speak. I hope not meerly for a continuance of the church by your ministry but an honorable encrease : & if not of the rich, yet of the poorer or lower sort, whose souls may join to make a large & glorious Crown for you in the Day of the Lord Jesus.

ffarewell Dear Bro : Meditate on these things ; Turn your

thoughts to the Objects which are more joyfull & the Occasions you have for thankfullness. Prayse & Thanksgiving are Springs to the Soul & give it new Activity. May Grace and Peace be with you in abundance. Pray for us under our discouragements, who add not half so many to our Church as you do. Once again ffarewell from Your affectionate Brother & humble servt.

J. WATTS.

[In Dr. Watts's autographs, as was common in those days, capital I and J are used at hazard.—ED.]

Pound Lane Chapel : Martock, Somerset

THE influence of Lollardy was early manifested in Somerset. From Trevelyan's *England in the time of Wycliffe* we learn that at Langport in 1447 "the tenantry of the Earl of Somerset drove their priest from his office, stopped all his services, buried their dead for themselves, refused to do penance, beat the bishop's officers when they interfered, and rid themselves of all ecclesiastical influence and jurisdiction." After the Reformation we find early indications of Puritanism and Separatism in the county. F. Johnson, pastor of the exiled church at Amsterdam (1593-1618), refers to " a church... professing same faith with us " in the west of England ; and among the marriages of English people recorded in the public records of Amsterdam—a large proportion of whom were members of the exiled church—at least ten names are associated with places in Somerset.

When the Long Parliament entered on the work of a more thorough reformation, Somerset was one of the counties which adopted the Presbyterian system in its entirety. It was divided into four "classes" ; the names of the ministers and elders for each parish are given in Shaw's *The Church under the Commonwealth.* The ministers and elders who accepted this arrangement subscribed the Solemn League and Covenant, binding themselves to uphold the Presbyterian system, and use the Directory in public worship.

Martock is a small market town in south Somerset, about halfway between Somerton and Crewkerne. Its population in 1801 was 2,102 : in 1891 it had increased to 2,848. When the Presbyterian organization was constituted in 1646 it was included in the Ilchester and Ilminster classis, which embraced 97 parishes.

In 1642 the House of Commons appointed Puritan lecturers for many parishes where the character or preaching of the incumbent was unsatisfactory, but without dispossessing the latter unless in cases of gross misconduct or incompetence. These lecturers were to have the use of the church and pulpit on one portion of the Lord's day, usually the afternoon, and one day in the week, for the purpose of preaching a lecture. On June 3rd of that year a Mr. Gundrie was appointed lecturer at Martock. The vicar at that time was Mr. Walrond, who appears to have remained there till 1645. But when the Parliamentary ordinance was published in 1646, establishing the Presbyterian system, the name of the minister

Pound Lane Chapel: Martock, Somerset

was given as Mr. Debancke or Debank, who had been approved by the triers as a suitable minister. This implies that Mr. Walrond had been removed as unsuitable. The elder for Martock was James Burford. Another Martock worthy, William Strode, lord of the manor and founder of the grammar school, was elder for Charlton Adams, a village about eight miles distant. The Presbyterian form of worship was maintained in Martock parish church from 1646 to 1662.

Mr. Debank, as minister of Martock, received on 25th December, 1649, the sum of £60 from the sale of dean and chapter lands. He died apparently in the spring of 1653/4. Calamy speaks of him as "the worthy and pious Mr. Debank; who on his deathbed lamented the little success he had met with amongst the people."

He was succeeded by the Rev. James Stephenson, who was presented to the benefice by Thomas Oliver, clerk, the patron, and approved by the triers 20th October, 1654. In 1655 an augmentation of £60 was granted to the minister of Martock by the "trustees for the maintenance of ministers. . . . they being already approved by the commissioners for approbation of public preachers." Of Mr. Stephenson Calamy says "he was a native of Scotland, and educated in the University of Glasgow; but went to Ireland in 1627, and was ordained both Deacon and Priest by Dr. Downham, Bishop of Derry, and—it seems—without subscription (*i.e.* to the Prayer Book)." After a copy of his ordination letters Calamy continues: "He left Ireland in 1641 when the Rebellion broke out, and the papists designed to put all the protestants to the sword. He saw so much of the true spirit of the Romish religion when there that he left behind him in Ireland property to the value of £2,000, which he might have recovered had he returned, but rather chose to lose it than live among such people."

He first came to Bristol, and afterwards settled at Tormarton in Gloucestershire. His name is attached to the "testimony" of the ministers of that county in 1648. After that he went to Holland for a time, and on his return to England was presented to the vicarage of Martock. Calamy says: "the inhabitants of this place were an ignorant sort of people: Mr. Stephenson therefore took a great deal of pains with them in preaching and catechizing their young ones in public, and others in private, and other ministerial services. And the parish being great (for it is a Hundred in itself, containing nine tithings) he was the more assiduous in his endeavours to spread knowledge and piety among them, and his labours were rewarded by their success. After the death of his son, who was a physician, he practised in that faculty himself, and met with great encouragement. The vicarage, with an augmentation of £50 per annum, was worth to him about £100 a year, but he was ejected by the Act of Uniformity (1662), and removed to an estate he had in the parish. But though he was silenced in public, yet he continued his ministry in private, both before and after the Oxford Act. This last Act obliging him to leave Martock, he removed to Crewkerne [about six miles distant]. There he preached in his own hired house, and continued to do so though he had many enemies, and some that threatened to burn his house down."

Murch says that Mr. Tomkins, ejected from Crewkerne in 1662, was afterwards tempted to conform. But some of his people were less pliable ; and adhering to the principles of Nonconformity had the ministerial services of Mr. Stephenson from 1665 to 1667.

" After two years' absence," says Calamy, " Mr. Stephenson returned to Martock, and preached there in a licensed house upon Charles II.'s Indulgence (1672), not having above £8 a year from his people. At length he, with some other ministers, were convicted of a conventicle, upon the information of two women of ill fame. The sum to be levied on him was £40 ; but such precautions were taken that he lost less than was expected. Sir G. Horner made him an offer of what was much more considerable than what he had left in the church if he would conform ; but he could not satisfy his conscience to do so. He was a man of great integrity, and often said that his heart should not reproach him as long as he lived. He continued to preach after the Indulgence was withdrawn, and died 15th July, 1685, aged about 80."

In Sheldon's *Return of Conventicles*, 1669, " Martocke " is found under the heading " Archdeaconry of Wells." No house or denomination is mentioned, but the number of conventiclers is given as 300, and the teacher's name is Henry Butler. This shews the strength of Nonconformity at that date, and that in time of persecution there was no lack of a teacher or minister ; also that all could not meet in Mr. Stephenson's house, but must have gathered in different places, and probably with different teachers.

At the time of Mr. Stephenson's death, 1685, there was evidently an organized congregation meeting in a dwelling-house, and ministered to by the Rev. Thos. Budd of Lambrook (3 miles distant) and a Mr. Bishop. Mr. Budd kept a register of baptisms for both Lambrook and Martock, in the same book but in separate lists. This book is now in the Non-parochial Registry, Somerset House. The Martock list contains 79 entries (besides one incomplete) ; the first being dated two days before Mr. Stephenson's death, viz. : " 1685. Saml. Budd, son of John Budd and Elizth his wife, was born June 13th and baptized July 13th 1685." The last complete entry reads " 1697. Elizth Moore daughter of Ambrose Moore of Hurst and Elizth his wife, was born Nov. 27th and baptized 3rd December, 1697." The following curious entry occurs under 1695 : " Memorandum that from the first day of May, 1695, a Tax was laid upon Births for five years."

There are also four marriages entered in the book, two of which

Pound Lane Chapel: Martock, Somerset

relate to Martock and shew the close connection that existed between the Lambrook and Martock congregations:

"1691. Anthony Field of Stapledon and Mary Goodden daughter of Andrew Goodden of Newton, both of the parish of Martock, were married the second day of February 1691 at Middle Lambrook meetinghouse: Their purpose of marriage being first published at Martock meetinghouse three several Lord's days, and the consent of her Father being first declared."

1694. William Lawrence the younger and Susanna Matravers (*i.e.* Cunmer [?]) both of Newton in the parish of Martock were married the Twenty third day of March 1694 at Middle Lambrook meetinghouse: Their purpose of marriage being first published at Martock meetinghouse three successive Lord's days, and their parents' consent being first sufficiently made known."

A MS. book in Dr. Williams's Library, written in 1774, and containing histories of several old congregations, confirms and throws more light on this relationship. Under "Martock" it says: " This congregation of Protestant Dissenters was first formed about the time of the Revolution in 1688. They first met in a licensed dwellinghouse, but had no pastor of their own for several years. The people being partly Calvinistic and partly otherwise, at first two ministers of neighbouring churches supplied them by turns, each once a fortnight. These ministers were Mr. Budd and Mr. Bishop, who continued in this connection for some considerable time." As the last entry in Mr. Budd's register is dated 1698, that would probably be about the time when the arrangement ceased. Mr. Budd must then have been an old man, as he was appointed minister of Kingsbury by the Parliament in 1646. No particulars are given of Mr. Bishop, and nothing further is known of him.

The MS. continues: "The people at Martock, thinking it necessary to have a settled minister, at length united in inviting Mr. Hallet, who was looked upon as a moderate Calvinist." He continued in that relation for upwards of 30 years; but "at length some differences arising between him and a principal family that attended on his ministry, he resigned his charge, and left Martock some years before his death." His name appears as minister at Martock in Dr. Evans's list of ministers between 1717 and 1729, and he is also named in a later list of 1735 as still at Martock, with a congregation of 400. He is described in these lists as an ordained Presbyterian minister.

There can be little doubt that the chapel in Pound Lane was built during his ministry, or just before its commencement. The land on which it is built was granted, with adjoining land, by William Strode, lord of the manor and son of him who founded the grammar school (both of whom were Nonconformists), on lease to Andrew Westcott in 1679; and by him to his son John Westcott in 1715. John sold the lease to Amos Pittard in 1719, and then purchased the fee simple. Amos Pittard, "with the approbation, advice and consent of the said John Westcott," sold a part to Drury Royse and John Royse for the trustees " of a meetinghouse there late erected" ; Amos Pittard junior being one of them. The deed of release in fee, dated 7th March, 1722, contains this curious clause : " In trust nevertheless for the use benefit and behalf of the Presbyterian meeting of Protestant Dissenters there assembling for the Worship of God continuing in the pure and uncorrupt Faith of the Gospel and to no other Use Intent or purpose whatsoever which Meeting should it be suppressed by the Lawes of this Realme or through or by any other Cause or Causes whatsoever be discontinued the House shall never be converted into a Mansion or Dwelling House or let to any Tenant to use and occupy the same for any Trade Work or Merchandize whatsoever but shall by those in whom the property is now or at such Time shall be invested be disposed of by them or either of their Successours in some other way as to them shall seem meet and convenient."

At the same time William Judoe, another of the trustees, executed a deed of rent charge on "Four Acres of Arable land at Guildings" to trustees for securing " One Annuity or Rent Charge of forty shillings out of the same unto the use behoof and benefit of such Teacher or Teachers Preacher or Preachers of and unto the Presbyterian Congregation of Protestant Dissenters that shall for the time being be assembled at Martock for the worship of God." Nothing is known of any subsequent appointment of trustees, though at the foot of the original deed is written in another hand "Survivor—Perran, 1760."

This William Judoe died in 1724, and was buried in front of the chapel. The rent charge appears to have been paid up to 1862. But an attempt to recover it in 1903-4 failed, as the present owner of the land pleaded the Statute of Limitations, and the Charity Commissioners declined to contest it.

After Mr. Hallet's withdrawal the people at Martock were supplied for two or three years by Mr. Lane and Mr. Baker. Some time before 1754 the latter was chosen pastor, and continued to preach at Martock a considerable number of years. It was during his pastorate, in 1760, that another small rent charge of thirty shillings was granted on five acres of meadow land in Martock Mead and Southey by John Westcott (probably another of the first trustees) to the " Minister or Pastor " of this congregation. This has not been paid since 1870, and, as the land cannot now be identified, is probably irrecoverable.

There is a tradition that, during Mr. Baker's pastorate, George Whitefield preached at Pound Lane : (see *Somerset Congregational Magazine*, January, 1891). It is certain that some preachers of Lady Huntingdon's Connexion came into the neighbourhood about 1773 or-4, and having fitted up a house at South Petherton, about

Pound Lane Chapel, Martock, built about 1720

Pound Lane Chapel: Interior

Pound Lane Chapel: Martock, Somerset

two miles off, attracted many of Mr. Baker's people. In consequence the Pound Lane congregation was considerably diminished. The number in 1774 is given as "upwards of 100, and about 20 communicants." Soon after this time Mr. Baker left; but lived till 1799, dying at the age of 86.

The preachers above referred to must have been the Revs. Richard Herdsman and Christopher Hull. Mr. Herdsman was the first student from Lady Huntingdon's college at Trevecca, and became the first pastor of a new congregation at South Petherton; which in 1775 seceded from the older society because of the Arian tendencies of its minister, Rev. J. Kirkup (see *Transactions*, vol. III, p. 25). Mr. Hull left the Connexion in consequence of having accepted the doctrine of universal redemption; he settled at Bower Hinton, in Martock parish, and founded the congregation which still flourishes there. The chapel was built in 1791. During the preceding three years Mr. Hull had itinerated between Bower Hinton and Bridport.

The Rev. Nicholas Shattock, from the academy at Daventry, was minister at Pound Lane in 1780. He removed to Ilfracombe in 1784.

The next minister of whom we have any knowledge is the Rev. S. R. Pittard. In 1798 he wrote the *Address from the Ministers of the Somerset Association*, a tract which was highly commended in the *Evangelical Magazine* of that year. On 11th January, 1799, he took part in the reopening of the old Presbyterian chapel at Somerton, which had long been disused.

The Somerset Congregational Union was formed at South Petherton in 1796; the Rev. R. Herdsman being the first secretary. The fourth meeting was held in Pound Lane in 1799; the speakers were the Revs. Toller, Bond, and Hey, but no details of the meeting are recorded. Other meetings of the Union were held there in 1809 and 1824.

All registers and records of the Pound Lane congregation between the first quarter of the eighteenth century and the middle of the nineteenth appear to be irrevocably lost. The only known documents are the original trust deeds of 1722, and appointments of new trustees in 1754, 1789, 1817, and 1857; the two deeds of rent charge; and a mutilated register of baptisms, marriages, and burials, containing entries early in the nineteenth century. The names of the following ministers are given in connection with baptisms:—

John Brick, no date ("Here in Sept., 1815" J. Wilson's MS.)
James Trego, to 1824 (he died at Brighton in 1865, aged 87)
Ebenezer Smith, 1824 to 1828
William Croome, 1828 to 1832

Pound Lane Chapel: Martock, Somerset

S. R. Pittard, 1832 to 1834 (Mr. Pittard had been for some time minister at Lambrook, but seems to have retired and been living at Martock).
P. H. Hannaford, 1834 to 1837
Wm. Hyde, 1837 to 1842

Mr. Hyde seems to have been the last regular minister. He was living in London in 1857.

After his removal the pulpit was sometimes supplied by Mr. Price, the Baptist minister of Montacute : and subsequently a Mr. George Paul, a Baptist layman, was chosen pastor—not without a vigorous protest, as is shewn by letters dated 1856 and 1857, and now in the present writer's possession. He held the pulpit until about 1876 or -7, by which time the congregation had become very small, most of the old families having withdrawn and attached themselves to the church at Bower Hinton. Mr. Thomas Walker, of North Street, whose family had long been connected with the place, and whose father appears to have been appointed a trustee in 1817, told the writer that Dr. Stuckey, who lived at the manor house, once told him that he knew he ought to pay something out of his property to the minister at Pound Lane ; but did not do so, because he thought the persons in possession were not legally entitled. Mr. Paul once made an attempt to recover the rent charges after they were refused, but failed. Clearly he, as a professed Baptist, could not claim endowments settled by deeds which distinctly specify that the "Teacher or Pastor" must be of the "Presbyterian Discipline," which provides for infant baptism. Probably if the trustees appointed in 1857 had then exerted their legal powers Mr. Paul would have been removed, and the endowments would not have been lost.

After Mr. Paul's retirement the pulpit was supplied for a time by Mr. John Story of Norton-sub-Hambden, Mr. Chas. Benson of Martock, and others who were strict Calvinists ; until Mr. Benson took the sole charge, preaching at Norton in the morning and Pound Lane in the evening. But no church organization was kept up, nor sacraments administered. This went on till 1906, when age and increasing infirmity compelled Mr. Benson to discontinue the evening service, at which often only six or eight attended. He then asked the Rev. W. J. Harris of Bower Hinton, to take the matter in hand and provide for services.

All that has yet been done is to arrange for a Tuesday evening service once a fortnight, which is sometimes well attended. Meanwhile, in 1901, new trustees were appointed, of whom the present writer is one ; and it is hoped that means may be devised to revive this ancient interest.

JOHN SCAMELL.

THE MEETING-HOUSE AT WATTISFIELD, SUFFOLK; BUILT 1706, DEMOLISHED 1876.

The Ancient Meeting-house at Wattisfield, Suffolk

A FULL history of the Congregational church at Wattisfield, organized on 14th September, 1654, is given in Browne's *History of Congregationalism in Norfolk and Suffolk*, pp. 466-476. Browne, however, does not give the "Profession of Faith," drawn up and agreed to at the first constitution of the church. This we are enabled by the kindness of the present pastor, Rev. C. E. Chandler, to lay before our readers; together with prints of the ancient meeting-house erected in 1706, which had unhappily become so dilapidated after 170 years that repair was out of the question, and its demolition was a regrettable necessity.

The Wattisfield church-book is one of the most important documents of its kind in existence, containing a large amount of historical matter; much of it set down by the learned Thomas Harmer, who ministered to the congregation for 54 years, and died 27th November, 1788.

Covenant adopted by the *Wattisfield Congregational Church*, "on the 14th of y⁰ 7th Month in the Year 1654."

"Wee doe Covenant or Agree in the Presence of God, through the Assistance of his Holy Spirit, to Walke together in all the Ordinances of our Lord Jesus, so far as the same are made clear unto us: indeavouring the Advancement of y⁰ Glory of our Father, The subjection of our Wills to the Will of our Redeemer, and the mutual Edification each of other in his most holy Faith and Fear."

"THE PROFESSION OF FAITH AS IT WAS DRAWN UP AND AGREED TO BY THE CHURCH FROM THE FIRST."

1. We believe the Lord our God to be one God blessed for ever, and that He is but One in essence though yet distinguished by Relative Properties into Three Persons, that is to say, Father, Son & Holy Spirit : & that this distinction doth not suppose three several Essentialities, but three several ways of subsistence & diverse ways of His manifesting Himself to us.

2. We believe that each of these Relations is God, Infinite, Eternal, Immortal, Invisible, Holy, Just, Almighty, Omniscient, Omnipresent & every way absolutely perfect & blessed ; & therefore the only Object of all Spiritual & Divine Worship.

3. We believe that of, from, and by this God were all things made & created that are in Heaven, Earth & under the Earth : & that at the beginning or at the Creation everything was very good in its kind : & amongst these, those unclean Spirits (though now most miserably wretched in their fall by their not keeping their first station) were according to the order of their creation holy & good. So man also in his first estate was created in the image of God, but by reason of the mutability of his nature & though the subtlety of the Temptation he was easily carried away in the transgression & through that fall of his not only lost that blessed image in his own soul, but likewise forfeited & utterly lost the same to all and every other person that was to proceed out of his loins (excepting only our most dear & precious Saviour). And now instead of that blessed image of God which consisted in holiness, knowledge, purity & rectitude of his mind & will unto God, have succeeded all that miserable & worse than Egyptian darkness that is now upon his understanding with that enmity & rebellion that is in his nature, that perverseness & obstinacy that is upon his will, with all that froward disorderliness that is in his affections ; so that every one of his faculties is now depraved ; and Death which before had no existence is now begotten & brought forth into the world.

4. We believe that God who from all eternity foreseeing the miserable Defection of man, did yet notwithstanding purpose & decree within Himself to advance not only the Glory of His rich & free Grace in the recovery of some of those persons which were thus lost through Adam's sin ; but in that way of Salvation which the Lord in His wisdom hath now ordained the glory of every other of His attributes do most eminently shine forth, as of His Wisdom, Holiness, Power, Righteousness, yea & Justice itself : all which now become most gloriously propitious unto man in that great design & mystery of His will in Effecting our Salvation.

5. Which mystery we believe, in the fulness of time, God manifested & brought forth before the sons of men, to wit, in the manifestation of Christ : Who though equal to the Father as touching His Godhead yet took upon Him the form of a servant & became man like unto us : & was clothed with our whole nature of infirmities (sin only excepted) : & in that estate He died & dying fulfilled the determinate counsel of His Father & likewise satisfied Divine justice, & thereby paid the price & purchase of salvation for all the Elect of God.

WATTISFIELD MEETING-HOUSE, 1706-1876 (FRONT VIEW).

6. We believe that for those the Lord Jesus Christ is become an Everlasting Mediator & Advocate with the Father : for those He became incarnate, died & rose again, & is now ascended unto the right hand of Glory, there to make intercession for them.

7. For those he is appointed of the Father to be King, Priest, Prophet & Lawgiver. As King to lead, govern and protect them. As Priest to make atonement for them & to intercede for them. As Prophet & Lawgiver to enlighten, teach counsel & instruct them. And therefore He is anointed not only above His fellows but above all measure with the spirit of wisdom, understanding,

counsel, knowledge & the fear of the Lord, and thereby is become a most fit Head to govern so great a body as the Church.

8. And that they might have a perfect Rule of Righteousness both for faith, Knowledge & Obedience, He hath given them the Holy Scriptures, which are a Rule so absolute in themselves that they are able to make the man of God perfect, thoroughly furnished with all good works without man's traditional additions, which Scriptures (as they are vulgarly distinguished into the Old & New Testaments) for that spirit of Holiness that breathed in them, the profoundness & immensurableness of their wisdom, with that wonderful heartsearching property that is in them we own for the very word of God & that the pen-men of the same were inspired & directed by that infallible & Holy Spirit of God.

9. We believe that the Lord Jesus Christ is become Author of Life & Salvation only to so many as believe in His name. And that true Justifying Faith, whereby Jesus Christ with all His benefits is effectually apprehended & applied, is the special & proper gift of God, given particularly to the Elect: And that He worketh this faith in their hearts by the effectual & lively operation of His own Spirit upon their souls: And that we are to wait upon the Lord for the dispensation of that Spirit in a faithful & constant use of those means which Himself hath appointed to that end: as, searching the Scriptures, hearing the word preached, with attendance upon all other ordinances for that purpose.

10. For Ordinances we own, as of our Lord's institution, the two Sacraments (vulgarly so phrased) that is to say, Baptism & Breaking of bread; praying in the Spirit; preaching of the Word: singing of Psalms: communion of Saints; administration of the Censures, to wit,—Admonitions both private & public, Excommunication, with Sanctification of the Lord's Day.

11. We believe that the Lord Jesus Christ hath a Spiritual Kingdom here on Earth, which though it be not of this world, yet is in this world. And that therein He doth exercise the power of His Headship amongst His saints; & that the subjects of this Kingdom are all true believers of what nation, condition or relation so ever.

12. Yet more especially we believe that a company of Believers called by the word & Spirit of Christ, separating from the world's worship & joining together by mutual consent to walk in the faith & order of the gospel are more visibly owned & attested by Christ for a Church of Christ: unto whom He hath committed many special privileges which without apparent breach of gospel-order cannot be enjoyed but by believers so separating from the world & conjoining themselves in gospel fellowship.

13. We believe that the Essential matter whereof such a Church of Christ is to be constituted is of right, & ought to be of none others but such as are Saints by calling, sanctified by Christ, made partakers of His Spirit & that they have union & communion with Him their head.

14. Yet do we believe that in the purest Churches many graceless spirits, & cunning hypocrites may notwithstanding there crowd in & shroud & shelter themselves there; but then they are not known or discovered to be such. And if upon discovery by clear evidence that church does not labour to purge out such as leaven from amongst them, we believe it is that church's sin.

15. We believe that to a Church so constituted, Jesus Christ hath committed the Seals of the Covenant, the power of the keys, to wit, of receiving in & casting out; the dispensation of all ordinances, with power to elect & choose all her own officers with special promises of His presence, blessing, protection & favour towards them.

16. For matters dubious we are persuaded thus to judge—That seeing we know but in part & much of the vail is still upon our hearts which keeps us from seeing the things of our peace. And therefore are we waiting for the rising of that Day-star still in our hearts: that where doubts remain upon any of our spirits we are to yield each to others all christian forbearance that may stand with our walking orderly in love & inoffensively to a brother's conscience.

17. Where Christ hath purchased a freedom for us we are not to bring ourselves into bondage; yet with that Christian prudence to make use of our liberty, always looking where the glory of God may lie most, & the expediency of our practice most for the peace of ourselves & others.

18. We believe a Civil Magistrate to be an Ordinance of God set up to be a terror to evil doers & for the praise & encouragement of them that do well: Whom we are bound to pray for & to be subject to in well doing, & that, not only for fear, but for conscience sake.

19, We believe a Resurrection of the dead: and that a day is set (which is only known to the Lord) when all shall arise that either now are or hereafter shall be asleep in the dust: and that all shall come to judgment, when the Lord Jesus Christ, unto Whom is committed all judgment from the Father, shall take vengeance on all those that have not obeyed His gospel, punishing them with everlasting destruction from His presence. But then His sheep shall be separated from the goats & shall inherit the Kingdom prepared from the foundation of the world.

20. Which appearing of Christ we ourselves do await, expect & pray for: resting with some confidence in our own spirits, that these vile bodies of our sinful flesh, which must be turned into dust, except prevented by the coming of Christ (and then they shall only be changed) shall yet be raised up at that great day & made like to His own most glorious body: that so we may receive the fulness of that Everlasting Redemption; therein to admire & adore Him for ever, singing that new song of Moses & the Lamb. . . . . Great & marvellous are Thy works Lord God Almighty, just & true are Thy ways Thou King of Saints. Who shall not fear Thee O Lord & glorify Thy Name!

We hope at some future time to illustrate the valuable communion plate of the church, part of which was presented as early as 1678.

Profes of Aparant Church

THE following is the remaining document—as yet unpublished—from the "Wiggenton MS." in the Congregational Library: see *Transactions* vol. ii, p. 147. It is the fifth piece in the volume, occupying pp. 41-52, and is in the same handwriting as Barrowe's treatise and Greenwood's *Pastoral Epistle*, a hand which certainly is *not* Wiggenton's. There is no clue known to me as to either the author or the copyist. The erratic spelling suggests that it may have been written by some illiterate person from dictation. The point of view is that of an extreme Separatist; and the bitterness of tone is painfully conspicuous. [ED.]

PROFES OF APARANT CHURCHE.

1 The churche of christ is his Kingdom; therfor wher the kyngdom of christ is not his church is not. Wher christ Doth Rull & Rayne Ther is he kyng; but wher rull and rayngn is taken out of his hand, ther is he dispossed of his Ryght, of his Inheritance, which is his kyngdom. But your ministers, or rather tymservors, confes y^t they have not the true church govñment; y^t is as much to say christ his regiment & septer: therfor they have not his kingdom, & therfor not his church aparant.

2 Yf they answer that the whol world is the kyngdom of christ, & y^t he ruleth every whair, the Question is not of that Rulling y^t he, being god equall with his Father, ruleth & governeth all things; but to him being man, his heavenly father hath geven him the inhertaunce of mount sion, which is his church, as it is written I have sett my King upon Sion my holly mountayn; also the lord hath chosen sion, & loved it, & to dwell in it, saing this is my Rest for ever, ther will I mak the horne of David to bud, for I have ordeyned a light for myne anoynted./ this Sion is the church; this horne of David is the strength of his septer, and of the kyngdome of christ.

Psalm 132

D

3   Yf they answer yt in som part they have this govm̄ent, because as they say they preach the word, which is the septer of the kyngdom of christ: first mark well they are faine to call back again yt wch they before have preached, yt church govn̄ment is wanting. Allso I demannd of them yf ther be any partting or halting with the lord, or if they may yowk an oxe and an asse to gether in the lords tillage; or what agrement is betwext god & belyall. for what peace or felowship hath the scepter of christ with the septer of antichrist, that they shold Joyn to gether in govn̄ing? The lord our god is a Jelous god, & will not suffer his honour to be geven to another.

The 4 below should have been placed here. *Lastly, I answer yt the word which is his septer of his kingdom is his word of messag preached with power and auctoritye by them which ar sentte, which preach with governing & govrn with preaching, how they do itt shall

2   apear afterward.

4   When the chifeste & heiest ecleseausticall autoritie is in the hands of antichrist, ther is not the church of christ; for christ hath geven this auctoryty to his own servants: but in the *Evidently error for "ministers."* churches of these miisters* The lordly byshops, deanes, chaneslors, archdeacons, comisaryes, & such lyck being the popes basterds, these have chefer autoritye then his servaunts, & these straunge (?) prelasy execut domin̄on over them, & they sufer that yoak of bondag; they therfor have not the church of christ among them aparante.

3   In the church of christ every man may executte yt which our savior christ hath com̄anded as in the 18 of Mathew, conserning of bringing of dew complaints unto the church, in these words 'tell the church,' but in the churches of these ministers this cannot be executed; no, not when a wolf is thrust upon
Mat. 18.17. the people in stead of a shepard, or any other most grose & horryble inequitie is donne among them. they cannot Complayn to the church, except they will call the byshop the church; & he is alwayes the chefe workmaster of that messechefe of sending of woulfes & dome Dogs unto them. therfor they have not the church of christ aparant among them. lett them answer wherever they did know yt this commandement of our Savior christ cold be put in pracktys amonge them, which in the church of christ may be pracktysed Dayly.

4   Also in the church of christ ther be Keyes of the kyngdom of heaven to bynd and to lowsse in outward goūmente: but in the churches of these ministers they have not this auctorytie, but they must fetch it from the comisaryes cortes or other chapell cortes, which ar contrary to christ & therfor antychristian & against christ. therefor they have not the church of christ among them aparant.

5   They which being put in offyce by a kyng, & they geve over

Profes of Aparant Church 259

ther offyse & auctorytye into the hands of a straunge kyng, ar becom traytors to ther true kyng; & have not kyngdom amongste them. but these ministers have betrayed the keyes of the kyngdom [of] heaven which ar comitted to them & to the church into the hands of lord byshops, comesaryes, & such lyke, which ar strange maiestrats; therfore they ar traytturs to christ, & have spoylled his kyngdom; therfor they have not his kyngdom nor his church aparant among theme.

6   The church of christ is sanctyfied & mad glorious without spot or wrinckell or grose pollutions y^t ar retayned and mayntained when they be ownse manyfested in daungering the statte of the church. but in theyr churches they confes ther be many and gret pollutions, and ar bothe mayntained & retayned. therfor they have not the church of christ aparant.

7   We acknowledge ther be many pollutions in the mañers of men; but being secrett, & not known openly indangering the statte of the church govment, ar then left to god. but yf they be manifeste & openly known, in Daungering the statt of the church, ar then becom such spottes & wrinckells as declar the church not to be glorious nor santyfied to christ, & therfor to be none of his.

8   Know ye not y^t a letell levene leveneth the wholle lomp as the apostell pall speaking to have on evell member cutte of.
1 Cor. 5 6.

Yf then one wicked man worthie excommunication not being reconsiled tendeth to the savouring (?) of the whole lomp which is the church, how much mor shall so many wicked offyces, & so many wicked men which use them, and so many wicked gyedg (?) which submitt them selves to them, & so many people some Ignorant & some wilfull y^t ar holden captyve by these gyudes (*sic*) in those ofyces contynewing after this sorte not onlye mak sower but also mak to stynck the wholl lompe of the church in the nost^r of god. therfor such churches be not the churches of christ, Seing they ar all corupt & have donne y^t y^t is abhominable.

but this is the comendacions of the church by the mouth of the pfitts the people shall be all ryghteous, the grafe of my planting shall be the work of myne own hands y^t I may be glorified; meaning that outward inyquitey must be fare from the children of the church. / and those children which be planted, they be the lords plants, and the profitte speaking saing a litell on shalbe a thousand and a small one a strong nation; as we see this day that the wicked bandes of the lords enimies cant not stand agaynst the power which god hath geven to a small on speaking in his name to the confounding of them all.
Isai. 60 21.

Also the pfytte speaketh thus of the church of christ; y^t is violence shall be no mor hard of in the land, neather disso-

   latione nor distruction in the bordars; but thou shalt call
<small>Isai. 60 18</small> salvatione thie walls & peace thy gaets. but in these
   churches whosoever desyreth to live godly in christ Jesus,
9 & to keep a good contiones, in the true worship & service of
  god without bondage of red prayers in popishe wyse, and a
  number of other corupt begerlye serimonies, those his people
  must sufer violence bothe of ther wicked guides themselves
  and also of the byshops withe others; & those abhomyna-
  tions of desolations thrust into the people instead of christs
  true worship; and all the mynisters must use them, & the
  Reste of the people must Joyne with them & so confyrme them,
  & so altogether with the lawe add to the bonds of those y^t
  suffer for a wittnes against them. Ye, they styll cry for the
  cevill maiestrats sword, & so crave for more violence against
  the children of god unconvinced or uncondemned, and therfor
  not his church.
10 The harlot which hath not taken away her fornications out
   of her syght and her adulteryes from between her brests
<small>Hosea 2 2.</small> is not the spouse of christ, yea, though she hath byne the
   mother church; as yeat is writen, plead with thie mother,
   plead with her, y^t she is not my wyf. but to chang the
<small>* (?) are,</small> true church offices with false antychristian offices, or*
   spirituall fornications & adultyes, which in the church of
  these ministers ar not yeat taken away: therefor they be but
  harlots, & not the churches of christ.
11 In the church of christ the horn of David doth bud, & his
   crown florish upon him. bute in ther churches the horn of
<small>Salm 132
17, 18.</small> antychrist Doth not onlye bud but also florish; & the
   crownes florish upon her heads of byshops, chaunsslers,
  comissaryes, plants y^t the heavenlye ffather hath not planted,
  & must be pluckt op by the Rowtes before the horn of David
  cane spring. therfor they have not the church of christ
  aparant.
12 In Sion, which is the lords church the prestes ar clothed with
<small>Salm 132, 16.</small> salvation: but in ther churches the ministers ar clothed
   with distruction, for most of them ar blynd gydes & dome
  dogges, destroyers and murderers of sowles; & the rest, which
  sem to have knowledg ar malyshsious & envious & obstinat
  against the lords howse building, and will not build them selves
  nor suffer them that wold: so distruction & not salvation
  cometh both to them selves & others. therfor they have not
  Sion, which is the church of christ, aparant among them.
13 In the church of christ they may easilye be deserned who ar
   within or who ar without; as it is writen for what have I
<small>1 Cor. 5 12.</small> to doe to Juge those that ar w^thout, doye not Judge those
   that ar within. but those churches or pishes ar all on
  felowship; we see not who ar within or who ar without, or

Profes of Aparant Church 261

who we shold cownt for brethren or whom we shold count for heathen & publycanes by the determynations of the churches sensors. therfor these pishes ar not the churches of christe.

14 The psalme speaketh thus ; owt of Sione which is the pfection of bewtye the lord hath shined. but they y^t speaketh the best or favorablyest of these churches do confes y^t in the state of owtward govñment ther be many Imperfections, coruptions & deformities, which darken the face therof ; yea, such deformities they be as is fowll and ugllye, as is proved. therfor they have not syone which is the church.

<small>Salm 50.2.</small>

15 Also of the people of the church it is written lette the highe accts of god be in ther mouthes & a towe edged sword in ther hands, to execut vengance upon the heathen & corrections among the people ; such honour have all his saynts. but in ther church ther is no such autorytye ; nor any such honour unto the saynts y^t they shold execut vengence & corections upon the wicked, but contrarywise they them selves are smiten of the wicked & dispitfully abused for rightteusnes sack ; yea, the guides them selves lay downe ther neckes willyngly & slavishlye to antychristian offices, and to be displaced by those courts & such lyck senseurs : so far of ar they from bynding in chaynes & ffetters of Iron. therfor they have not the church of christ aparant amongst them.

<small>Salm 149.6.</small>

16 paull to the Romans speaketh thus : we have many members of on bodye, & all members have not on offyce ; so we being many ar on bodye in christ, & every on of us onanothers members. seing then we have gifftes that ar dyvers, according to the graces wch is geven unto us, whether we have provesey according to the pporsyon of faythe, or an offyce, lett hime wayt on his offyce, or he that exorteth on his exortations ; he that distributeth lett him do it with simplisite, and he that rulethe with diligence, he that sheweth mersye with chearfulnes Thus hathe the apostell sett downe the offyces & callings of the church & the menistry of them, namlye of the profyts, pastors, docctors, elders, relevers, & widowes ; thus declaring y^t in the house of god we be mad on anothers members by the Deversitye of those callynges, gyftes, graces, wherin we sarve on to anothers perfection & going forward unto godlynes. but in ther pshes they have not these offices, much les the exercision of them, nather any gyftes of graces tending therto ; for yf any such gifftes spring up in any by the gyfte of god, for want of styring up and not pracktysyng of it it is quenched. then, as the tallent head in the ground, So y^t the pishners ar not by these gyftes & callings Joined together as ffelowmembers of christ ar knite by these as by the synewes & bands of the church. thefor they have not the church of christ aparant amongst them.

<small>Rom 12.</small>

17 Yf they say they have som of these offyces, as passtors & doctors, we denye that a pson or a vicar plased by a patron or a lord byshop can be a pastor; but he must fyrst renownce that evell calling, & then to be lawfully called, both by God and bye the consent of godlye christians to be ruled and guided by hime so fare as the word of god doe lead them; & furder executyng of his dutye not in gathering of the good and bad together, but in sepatyng of the good from the bad. & as for the docter, in som fewe places wher he is he cometh to smale effecte; for most comonlye he is adioyned with some Idoll sheperd or some tym-server, and withdrawethe not the people from those abhomynactions afornamed, nor do not plant the church among them; So y^t the lyght of those churches is nothing but darknes. O how great is that darcknes! when the chefest ordars is full of confution, what then is the disordar offe them. thes things ar not in the churches of god.

18 Also thosse which psecut the church of christ ar not the church of christ; for christ is not devided wthin (?) hime self; & thei which hate sione ar not of sion but they psecut those which ar gethered to gether in the name of christ, hollding on law & govment under christ, & whom they ar not abell to charg of any abhomynaciones unremoved, nather in the outward worshipe of god nor in the maner of lyffe. Therfor they psecut the church of christ & ar not his churche.

19 And wheras they say we rend ourselves from the church, it is childyshe and slaundering of us: for although they wear the church, we myght leve on congregation as many occasions may fall out, so that we joyne with another which is the congregation of gods people. now if they can prove y^t we have joyned agaynest christ in any antychristian, then we will retorne & refforme our selves.

20 David speaketh thus: be favorable unto sione for Thie good
Salm 51.18.   pleasuer, byld the walls of Jerusaleme; then shalt thow exept the sacrifyes of ryghteusnes, the burnt oferings & oblations; then shall they ofer calves upon thiene alters. So that the exeptyng of our sacrifyses, even all our prayers & good deds & thancks geving in the true worship and service of god, dependeth upon gods ffavor toward syon and the building of Jerusaleme, & the place where his honour dweleth. & his honour dweleth where his ark resteth; & when his ark depteth his honor & glory depteth, as ffineas wyf speak saing the glorye is depted from Israell for the ark of god is taken. but in these churches They have not brought home the arke of god ffrom the philystians which is christ bearing his septer; therfor the glory of god is not among them; & they Refuse to bring it home, & that wylfullye: Therfor they Refuese the lords honor. the ark of god is the facce of god & the presence

Profes of Aparant Church 263

of his grace : therfor they not having it in his resting-place, nor going about to fetche it home, they canot behowld the lord as he is, nor the facces [sic] of his anoynted. & for the walls of Jerusaleme, and the lords house, they Refeuse to build ; not as the Isralytes did in the dayes of agge the pfytt, which pronised [sic] unto them from the mouthe of the lord, y^t all that they did was uncleane & not exepted because the lords house was not bylded ; for they being admonished speedylye obayed : nether do they as the Isralytes did in the dayes of nehemiahe and annan, which sayd it was a tyme of troubullacion & Reproche because the walls offe Jerusalyme was not builded ; for then thei aplyed them selves carfulye to the work untyll it was ffynished. but these mynisters do as the Isralyts Did in meribay, and as in the dayes of massay in the wyldernes, when they tempted and proved god, & seenne (?) his works, & wold not enter into his reste when they wer comanded ; to whom the lord swar in his wrath that they shold not enter into his rest. now these which have not the walls of Jerusalem bylded, nor his temple builded, & refuese obstinatlye to build being admonished therto, there sacrifyses is not excepted of the lord, & ther relygion but a burden to the lord, & he werye to bear them ; and therfor not his church.

<small>Esaie .1.13, 14, 15, f.</small>

The tabernacell was a figuer of the church of the lord ; & the lord gave strayght charg y^t it shold be mad according to the pattern showed to mosses in the mount. & so our savior christ was fortye dayes after his ressurrection conversant with his apostells, teaching them those things which conserneth the byldyng of his church & kyndom. & the apostels, according as they reseved instructions of hime, so they bylded & have left us a patroun. Now these churches are not framed affter this pattron ; yea, they fayll not only in a pine or a curtayn, which want myght not be suffered, but they fayll in the cheffe pillers & walles therof. therfor they be not the churches of christ.

Also David speakethe thus : Jerusalem is bwilded as a cittye y^t is compackte together in it self, wherunto the tribes goo upe, evene the tribs of the lord goe up, according to the testimonies to israell, to prays the name of the lord there : for ther ar trones sett for Judgment, even the trones of the house of David. Jerusalem is a figuer of the church ; the trones of David a figure of the holye eldership of the church : but in thes churches they have neyther cowrts nor consystory, counsyll nor synod, holden of our David, christ Jesus, nor in his name ; but only those unlawfull courtts, consistoryes and seann [sic] holden by the strength of the canone law, even the sharpest edge of antychrists sword, & that by the confesshion of them all. therfor they have not the church of christ aparent to be seene.

<small>Salm 122 8 fo.</small>

Thus being so manifestlye pved y̌ they be not the churches of christ ; they which be gathered to gether in his name as he hath apoynted to hear them, neyther cane they have his sacraments, which be seales only to the pmyses maed to the church. ffor there sacraments ar but dead synes, & pretended sacraments, because they cane prove no church ; and the true sacraments aplay unto the aparant church, & to be grafted into the church of god. nather have they the word of messag from the mouth of the lord preched among them, but Rezytall or historycall out of other historyes. for none can preach the [word] of messag but those that ar sent from the mouth of the lord onlye and alone. but they com not only & alone ffrom the mouth of the lord, but taketh ther warant by antychristian autoʳytye from the byshope. So they Ronne and ar not sent of god only and alone ; and so they speak gracious words, and so minister graces to the hearers, as anye child may doe, or any other man without callyng. Now lett this Reason teach you ; yf a man in a town com to the wicked and disobedient, & saye I com in the nam of a constable, & say I charg you in the princes name y̌ you leve your wickednes & flowe me, & is no constable nor have no lawfull autorytye nor callyng ; the wicked will not nor hath not to obay hime : but yf the lawfull offiser com that hath his autoritye from the prince, hime they will and must obay, and so do wee.

The callyng of those ministers, & autorytye that they have, cannot be waranted by the word of god ; therfor no autorytey

Now lett every on xamine hime self by the word of god, & show his obedienc ; for withowt his obedience ther is no promyse, and without a promise ther is no true fayth. now

That preaching and govñing ar joyned to gethere and can not be sepated the word of god is manifest : Mat. 24, Accts 20 : 28, I tim. 5 : 17, I petter 5 ; 2, Ezra 3 : 9, Zacha. and wheras they mak ther xscuse of doing of ther dutie, for tarieng for the miestrats begining, that is that the maiestrat must warant them by lawe, because they dar not do ther dutye for fear of lawe, yea, I say againe for fear of trobell by law in lossing of ther lyvings, as thowgh the maiestrats wear against the truth of god, & did lett the buildyng of the church of god, I saye in this they slander the maiestrat ; ffor the maiestrate is not against the bylding of the house of god & fudarying of his glory : for the maiestrat being a christian maiestrat hath bed them go fforthe & build the church of god ; or else lett them challeng the maiestrate in that poynt yf there dare.

Matt. 24, 45.

Profs for sepation upon just cause, being dulye examyned by the word of god.

1 Corenth 5 : 9, 10, 11, 12, 13 ; Rom. 16 : 17 ; 1 Cor. 7 : 23 ; 2 tessal 3 : 14 ; 2 cor. 6 : 13, 14, 15, 16, 17, 18 ; ephess 5 : 6, 7, 8,

9, 10, 11 ; Acts 19 : 8, 9. christ sayeth he y^t hearethe lett hime tack head what he hearethe ; bewar of the leaven of the pharises.

Yf they aleag the Kyngs of Juda & moses & Kings of Isreall for begining of reformation in the church——

we answer that y^t they did in ecklesiastical or spirtiuall matters they did it as they wear sygnes of christ ; & that y^t they did sivillye in fforsyng they did it bye the sevyll sword, for they had autoritye in bothe cases y^t our kings & princes want ; ffor the fyguratyve maner was ended ỉn Christe.

List of Members

Hon. Members marked *H*, Life Members marked *L*.

Anderton, W. E., Rev., M.A.
Andover (U.S.A.) Theological Seminary
Andrews, William, Esq.
Astbury, F. T., Rev.
Atkinson, S. B., Esq., M.A., M.B., F.S.S.
Avery, John, Esq.
Baptist Union, The
Barrett, Geo., Rev., A.T.S.
Bartlet, J. V., Rev. Prof., M.A., D.D.
Basden, D. F., Esq.
Bate, Frank, Esq., M.A.
Bax, A. Ridley, Esq.
Beaumont, E., Esq.
Bell, J. Barton, Rev.
Boag, G. W., Esq.
Bragg, A. W., Esq.
Brown, J., Rev. Dr., B.A.
H Brown, W. H., Esq.
Brownen, G., Esq.
Burrage, Champlin, Esq.
Carter, W. L., Rev., M.A.
Cater, F. Ives, Rev., A.T.S.
Chevalier, J., M.
Clapham, J. A., Esq.
Clark, J. H., Esq., J.P.
Clarkson, W. F., Rev., B.A.
Claydon, George S., Esq.
Cocks, J., Esq.
Congregational Library, Boston, Mass.
Crippen, T. G., Rev.
Dale, A. W. W., Esq., M.A.
Davies, J. Alden, Rev.
Davis, C. H., Rev.
Davis, J. E., Esq.
Davy, A. J., Esq.
Dawson, E. B., Esq.
Didcote, C. Page, Esq.
Dimelow, J. G., Esq.
Dixon, H. N., Esq., M.A., F.L.S.
Dixon, R. W., Esq.
H Dore, S. L., Esq., J.P.
L Ebbs, A. B., Esq.
Ebbs, W., Rev.
Ellis, C. W., Esq.
Evans, A. J., Esq., M.A.
Evans, G. Eyre, Rev.
Evans, Jon. L., Esq.
Evans, R. P., Esq.
Firth, C. H., Prof., M.A., LL.D.
Flower, J. E., Rev., M.A.
Forsyth, P. T., Rev., Dr.
Friends' Reference Library
Galloway, Sydney V., Esq.
Gasquoine, T., Rev., B.A.
Glasscock, J. L., Esq.
Gordon, A., Principal

Gosling, Howard, Esq.
Green, Joseph J., Esq.
Green, T., Esq.
Grice, T. E., Esq.
Grieve, A. J., Rev., M.A., B.D.
Groser, W. H., Esq., B.Sc.
Hall, C. W., Rev.
Hall, W. H., Esq.
Harris, W. J., Esq.
Harrison, G. W., Esq.
Harwood, W. Hardy, Rev.
Hawkins, F. H., Esq., LL.B.
Henderson, A. D., Esq.
Hepworth, Frank N., Esq.
Hepworth, J., Esq.
Hepworth, T. M., Esq.
Heslop, R. Oliver, Esq., M.A., F.S.A.
Hewgill, W., Rev., M.A.
Hitchcock, W. M., Esq.
Hodgett, C. M., Esq.
Holt, Edwyn, Esq
L Hounsom, W. A., Esq., J.P.
Huckle, Attwood, Esq.
Iliff, John S., Esq.
Jackson, S., Esq.
James, Norman G. B., Esq.
H Johnston, W., Esq.
Jones, A. G., Esq.
Keep, H. F., Esq.
Key, James, Rev.
King, Jos., Esq., M.A.
H Lancashire Independent College
(Goodyear, C., Esq.)
Lawrence, Eric A., Rev.
Lester, E. R., Esq.
Lewis, D. Morgan, Prof., M.A.
Lewis, Geo. G., Esq.
Lewis, H. Elvet, Rev., M.A.
Lewys-Lloyd, E., Esq.
Linell, W. H., Esq.
Lovatt, J., Esq.
Low, G. D., Rev., M.A.
Macfadyen, D., Rev., M.A.
Mackintosh, R., Rev. Prof., D.D.
Manchester College, Oxford
Massey, Stephen, Esq.
May, H. A., Esq.
H McClure, J. D., Dr.
Minshull, John, Esq.
Mottram, W., Rev.
Mumford, A. A., Esq., M.D.
Musgrave, B., Esq.
New College, Edinburgh
H New College, Hampstead, N.W.
(Staines, Howard, Rev.)
Nightingale, B., Rev.
H Palmer, C. Ray, Rev. Dr.

List of Members (*continued*)

Palmer, W. M., Esq.
Parnaby, H., Rev., M.A.
Pierce, W., Rev.
Pitt, Walter, Mrs.
Powicke, F. J., Rev., Ph.D.
Poynter, J. J., Rev.
Pugh, Mrs.
Rawcliffe, Edwin B., Rev.
Reed, E. P. S , Esq.
Rees, J. Machreth, Rev.
Richards, D. M., Esq.
Ritchie, D. L., Rev.
Robinson, W., Rev.
Rollason, Arthur A., Esq.
Rudge, C., Rev.
Rutherford, J., Esq.
H Rylands, Mrs., D.Litt.
Scamell, J., Esq.
Sell, W., Esq.
Serle, S., Esq.
Shaw, H., Rev.
Silcock, P. Howard, Esq., B.A.
Simon, D. W., Rev., D.D.
H Smith, W. J., Esq., M.A.
Smyrk, C. Watt, Rev.
Souter, Alex., Prof., M.A.
H Spicer, Albert, Sir, Bart., M.P.
H Spicer, George, Esq., M.A., J.P.
Standerwick, J. W., Esq.
Stanier, W. H., Esq.
Sutton, C. W., Esq.
Sykes, A. W., Esq.

H Thacker, Fred. S., Esq.
Thacker, Henry, Esq.
Thomas, D. Lleufer, Esq.
Thomas, John, Esq., J.P., C.C.
Thomas, Wm., Rev.
H Thompson, J., Esq.
Thorpe, F. H., Esq.
Titchmarsh, E. H., Rev., M.A.
H Toms, C. W., Esq.
Turner, G. Lyon, Rev., M.A.
Tyson, R. G., Esq.
U.S A. Congress Library.
Wallis, R. B., Esq., J.P.
Walmsby, L. S., Esq.
Watkinson, J., Esq.
H Webster, Isaac., Esq.
L Whitley, A. W., Esq.
Wicks, G. H., Esq.
H Wilkinson, W., Esq
Williams's Library.
Williams, Mrs.
Williamson, David, Esq., J.P.
Williamson, David, jr., Esq.
Wilson, T., Esq.
Windeatt, E., Esq.
Wing, Lewis, Esq.
Winterstoke, The Rt. Hon. Lord
Wontner, A. J., Esq.
Wood, Leonard B., Esq., M.A
Woodall, H. J., Esq.
Young, Hugh P., Rev.

OFFICERS OF THE SOCIETY.

President	Rev. Dr. John Brown, B.A., Hampstead, London, N.W.
Hon. Treasurer	Rev. G. Lyon Turner, M.A., Wheatham Hill, Hawkley, Liss, Hants.
Hon. Auditor	Mr. John Minshull, Memorial Hall, London, E.C.
Hon. Editor & Librarian	Rev. T. G. Crippen, ,, ,, ,,
Hon. Secretaries	Rev. T. G. Crippen, ,, ,, ,,
	Mr. Henry Thacker, ,, ,, ,,

CONDITIONS OF MEMBERSHIP.

(a) LIFE MEMBERS, paying twenty guineas in lieu of annual subscription.

(b) HONORARY MEMBERS, paying an annual subscription of one guinea or more.

(c) ORDINARY MEMBERS, paying an annual subscription of five shillings.

Subscriptions should be made payable and remitted to the Hon. Treasurer, as above; and are due *in advance* on January 1st in each year.

New members are entitled to all the publications issued by the Society in the year they join.

Transactions

Vol. III., No. 5] [MAY, 1908

Contents

Congregational Historical Society : Annual Meeting	269
Editorial	270
Early Nonconformist Academies	272
Penry's Last Journey to London	291
T. Gasquoine	
Seventy Years of Church Building in the West Riding	293
J. A. Clapham	
Early Conventicles in Cumberland and Westmorland	300
G. Lyon Turner, M.A.	
The Later Years of Robert Browne	303
F. Ives Cater	
The Ancient Meeting-House at Walpole, Suffolk	317
Unpublished Doddridge Correspondence	319
Surrey Congregational History	331
List of Members	335

Can be obtained direct from the Book Saloon, Congregational Union of England and Wales, Inc., Memorial Hall, London, E.C.

Printed for the Society by
Fred. S. Thacker; 3 Dyers' Buildings, Holborn, London

Congregational Historical Society

Annual Meeting

Our eighth Annual Meeting was held in Room 28 at the Memorial Hall, on Wednesday, 13th May, 1908, at 4 p.m., the Rev. J. Brown, D.D., in the chair.

After prayer by the Rev. J. Alden Davies the SECRETARY read the Report, which was for the most part a statement of what had been published during the year; notice being taken of work in progress by members of the Society—Mr. Boag, in Northumberland; Mr. Watkinson, in Kent; and Mr. May, in Staffordshire. Reference was also made to MSS. of the late Rev. B. Dale, which the Society had been requested to publish; and to the urgent need for research in counties where no history of Congregational Church life and work had yet been undertaken. The present number of members was stated to be 178.

The TREASURER presented a provisional statement, the accounts being not yet audited.

Resolved on the motion of the Rev. J. A. DAVIES, seconded by Mr. A. R. BAX, F.S.A., "that the accounts be henceforth made up to 31st December in each year."

The Officers and Committee were unanimously re-appointed.

Conversation ensued as to the best way of increasing our membership, without which it was felt that no satisfactory progress was possible. It was arranged that a circular should be prepared for distribution by members among their friends. Several suggestions as to publications were discussed, some of which were not entertained, and others remitted for fuller information.

Reference was made to the recently established Baptist Historical Society. A general feeling found expression that the movement deserved a hearty welcome, and that practical co-operation might be highly beneficial to both Societies.

The Rev. G. LYON TURNER, M.A., gave an account, with extracts, of a Report which he had discovered relating to Conventicles in 1665.

In view of the Autumnal Meeting to be held in Liverpool, the Secretary was directed to endeavour to obtain a paper on the history of Congregationalism in that city.

Editorial

We regret the delay of the present issue beyond the usual time of publication, which is due to the fact that our esteemed contributor, the Rev. F. J. Cater, was unable sooner to complete his examination of the Peterborough diocesan archives. We think members will prefer this delay to the postponement until autumn of Mr. Cater's illuminative paper.

Thanks to the laborious researches of Mr. Cater, and the fortunate discoveries of Mr. Burrage, we have now before us as much as is ever likely to be known about the career of Robert Browne. Some other of his writings which are known to have existed may perchance hereafter be discovered; but they are not likely to throw new light on his life or character. The statements of Fuller are now both justified and explained; the "poor old wife" is shewn scarcely to deserve the sympathy claimed for her by Baillie, even if her ill conduct did bring on her some such chastisement as he alleges; Browne's conformity is ascertained to have been very partial, and although the local tradition of his late reversion to separatism is not actually proved, it is shewn to be by no means unlikely. The obloquy which has been cast upon his memory by several prominent Nonconformist writers is now seen to be for the most part undeserved; and although it is impossible to assign him a place among the heroes beside Penry and Robinson, he will henceforth hold honourable rank among the pioneers of religious liberty.

May we therefore venture to express a hope that before very long some fitting memorial will be raised to the author of *Reformation without Tarying for Anie*? Probably the most suitable form it could take would be a brass in St. Giles's church, Northampton, near which his remains rest in an unmarked grave.

* *

Our Society has sustained serious loss in the death of Mrs. Rylands, of Manchester. We have endeavoured, without success, to obtain a brief biographical sketch suited to our pages. It may be that her characteristic modesty would have preferred that no such narrative should appear. It was noticeable that, amidst the unstinted eulogy of the newspapers at the time of her decease, very few facts were given, except such as related to her large benefactions—which were by no means limited to her own city.

Her name will live as long as men can appreciate a singularly energetic and unselfish life. The Rylands Library is her lasting monument; and for the rest, "let her own works praise her in the gates."

* *

In the paper on *The Ancient Meeting-house at Ravenstonedale* (iii. 94) we have detected a rather ludicrous blunder. At lines seven *et seqq.* is a quotation from Evans's MS. as follows: " Russendale . . . . 10 disc. James Malleson 1716 (rem) "; which is explained "that, after Mr. Mallison's removal, about ten of his adherents, calling themselves Presbyterians, continued to hold a separate meeting, etc." This is evidently due to a misinterpretation of the " 10 disc."; which really means—as is shewn by comparison with many similar entries in other parts of the MS.— that, in addition to the Independent church of which Mr. Magee was pastor, there was a Presbyterian church under the charge of Mr. Mallison, which received £10 from the Presbyterian fund; but Mr. Mallison had removed, and the grant was *discontinued*.

* *

We have great pleasure in calling attention to *The Colonial Missions of Congregationalism*, by our honoured President, the Rev. Dr. Brown. To one point, however, we must take exception—the title, which is by no means adequately comprehensive. The book should have been called *A History of Congregationalism in the British Colonies;* for it begins the story with 1597—two hundred and thirty years before our Colonial Missionary Society was dreamed of. It is crammed full of facts, narrated in a popular and instructive manner, and is by no means the least valuable of the venerable author's contributions to the history of the Church. We would urge all our members first to read it, and then circulate it among our young people.

Early Nonconformist Academies

A COMPLETE history of the Nonconformist academies and colleges is a desideratum not likely soon to be realized. There is abundance of scattered material, but its collection and arrangement would need much patient research. Of the character of this material a fair sample is afforded in the accounts of Frankland's academy, *Trans. II, 422*, and in the Rev. B. Dale's supplementary communication, *Trans. III, 21*. It would be desirable to put on record the time when and circumstances under which every such institution originated, migrated, was reconstructed, or came to an end; the succession of tutors, their academical qualifications, and literary, pastoral, or other work; the number of students in training from time to time, with particulars of those who gained especial distinction as preachers, authors, or otherwise; and any matters bearing on the relation of the institutions to each other, to the churches, to the national universities, and to educational and theological movements in general.

The academies and colleges may be conveniently arranged in three groups: 1. Those conducted or initiated by the ejected ministers; 2. Those of later origin which have entirely ceased to exist; 3. Those which still remain, or are represented by existing institutions.

In the present and following papers it is intended to give in a concise form such information as lies readily to hand about the academies of the first group—those founded by the ejected ministers.

The available sources are the *Nonconformists' Memorial*, Calamy's *Continuation*, Toulmin's and Bogue's *Histories of Dissenters*, W. Wilson's *Dissenting Churches*, various memoirs and funeral sermons, and MSS. collected by Mr. J. Wilson, in the library of New College. Any additional information, whether by way of correction or supplement, will be heartily welcomed.

LIST OF ACADEMIES FORMED BY EJECTED MINISTERS

1. In or near London

Newington Green. (1) By Theophilus Gale, 1665-78, continued till about 1706.

     ,,   ,, (2) By Charles Morton, 1667-85, continued till about 1696.

Islington. (1) By Ralph Button, 1672-80.

    ,, (2) ,, Thomas Doolittle, 1672-1700 [?]

Wapping. By Edward Veal, 1680-1708 [?]

2. In the English Counties

Coventry (Warwickshire) By Obadiah Grew and others, 1663-93 [?]

Sheriff Hales (Salop) By John Woodhouse, 1663-96 [?]

Broomsgrove (Worcestershire) By Henry Hickman, 1665-92.

Nettlebed (Oxon) By Thomas Cole, 1666-97.

Lincoln By Edward Rayner, 1668-80.

Whitchurch (Salop) By John Maulden, 1668-80.

Tubney (Berks) By Dr. H. Langley, 1668-79.

Dartmouth (Devon) By John Flavel, 1668 [?]-91.

Wickhambrook (Suffolk) By Samuel Cradock, 1670-1706.

Rathmell and elsewhere (Yorks) By Richard Frankland, 1672-98

Taunton (Somerset) By Matt. Warren and others, 1672-1750 [?]

Manchester (Lancs) By Henry Newcome, 1672-1716 [?]
Sulby (Northants) By J. Shuttlewood, 1680-88.

3. In Wales
Brynllwarch (Glamorgan) By Samuel Jones, 1668-97.

ACADEMIES IN OR NEAR LONDON

At NEWINGTON GREEN, now represented by a small square a furlong northward from Mildmay Park railway station, but then a pleasant rural village, there were two academies, both commenced soon after the Great Fire. One of them was conducted by Theophilus Gale, and the other by Charles Morton.

Theophilus Gale was born in 1628, at King's Teignton, Devon; where his father (of the same name) was vicar, holding likewise a prebend in Exeter cathedral. Young Gale received his early education under a private tutor and at a local grammar school, and in 1647 entered Magdalen College, Oxford. He graduated B.A. on 17th December, 1649; being permitted to do so after a shorter residence than the statutes demanded in recognition of his unusual proficiency. He was elected Fellow of his college in 1650, and proceeded M.A. on 18th June, 1652. He was a successful tutor at Oxford, one of his most distinguished pupils being Ezekiel Hopkins, afterwards bishop of Derry. He also gained distinction as a preacher; and in 1657 was chosen one of the stated preachers in Winchester cathedral. At the Restoration he lost both his preachership and his fellowship; and in September, 1662, accepted an engagement as travelling tutor to the two sons of Lord Wharton, who is still remembered for his sturdy Puritanism and his large-hearted beneficence. The elder of the two sons, though his personal character reflected no credit on his tutor, left his mark on English history as an energetic promoter of the Revolution; and especially as the author of the celebrated political song Lillaburlero, with which he boasted that "he had rhymed a foolish king out of three kingdoms." After spending a considerable time with his pupils at Caen, Gale appears to have sojourned for a while at Lord Wharton's house in Buckinghamshire; and, journeying to London, arrived during the progress of the Great Fire. Fortunately a desk full of papers, which he had left in charge of a friend, had been saved by what might be deemed a mere accident; the MS. thus rescued being that of the book with which, more than any other, his name is associated, *The Court of the Gentiles*. The main object of this once renowned treatise is to develop, for apologetic purposes, the opinion advanced by several early Christian writers, that the heathen philosophers borrowed their most rational sentiments, and all that is best in their theology and philosophy, from the Hebrew Scriptures.

Soon after his settlement in London he became colleague with John Rowe, M.A., in the pastorate of an Independent church which during the Commonwealth had met in Westminster Abbey, but which now worshipped in some obscure retreat in the parish of St. Andrew's, Holborn, and subsequently in Bartholomew's Close. He also established an academy at Newington Green; where his richly stored mind and proved tutorial aptitude enabled him in large measure to supply the educational needs of young men whom ecclesiastical and political intolerance excluded from the universities. Unfortunately we have no complete list of his pupils; the only names that have come down to us being those of Thomas Rowe, the son of his colleague and his own successor; Benoni

Rowe, brother of the former, and John Ashwood. Both of these were distinguished ministers in the next generation.

John Rowe died in October, 1677; and Mr. Gale had for a few months, as colleague, Samuel Lee, M.A., the ejected rector of St. Botolph's, and the author—amongst other works—of a curious folio on the structure and spiritual significance of Solomon's temple. It does not appear whether or not Lee co-operated in the work of the academy. Gale died in February or March, 1678. By his will he left to Harvard's College in New England the whole of his valuable library, except the philosophical books, which were to be reserved for young students at home. He also left the whole of his real and personal estate to be managed by some of his Nonconformist brethren for the benefit of poor young scholars. He was buried in the tomb of his friend Rowe, in Bunhill Fields.

The following is a list of his writings:

The Court of the Gentiles: *or a Discourse touching the Original of Human Literature.* 5 vols. 4to., 1669, '71, '77, '77, '78.
  (The 5th vol. is chiefly occupied with an endeavour to vindicate Calvinism from the charge of making God the Author of sin).
The True Idea of Jansenism. Preface by J. Owen, 12mo., 1669.
Theophilie; or the Saints' Amity with God. 8vo., 1671.
The Life and Death of Mr. Thomas Tregosse [an ejected minister in Cornwall] 16mo., 1671.
The Anatomie of Infidelitie. 8vo., 1672.
A Discourse of Christ's Coming. 8vo., 1673.
Idea Theologiae tam Contemplativae quam Activae, 1673.
Sermon on 1 John 2 : 15 in the Morning Exercise, 1674.
Philosophia Generalis, in duas partes disterminata. 8vo., 1676.
A Summary of The Two Covenants; prefixed to a discourse on that subject by William Strong, 1678.
Christ's Tears for Jerusalem's Unbelief and Ruin, posthumous, 8vo., 1679.

Shortly before his death he issued proposals for printing a folio *Lexicon of the Greek Testament* which was to be more complete than any then extant. This design was never realized.

Gale was succeeded both in his pastorate and in the conduct of the academy by his pupil, *Thomas Rowe*, who had only just completed his 21st year. Notwithstanding his youth he proved a successful pastor and an able tutor. As an author he was not conspicuous ; but there is evidence that he won, in an unusual degree, the personal affection of his students, several of whom attained to eminence in various departments of public life. Among these the foremost place is due, by common consent, to Dr. Isaac Watts, poet, theologian, and philosopher. Others were Dr. John Evans, whose historical collections have been of incalculable value ; Dr. Jeremiah Hunt, pastor at Pinners' Hall ; Daniel Neal, the historian of the Puritans ; Henry Grove, metaphysician, and tutor at Taunton ; Samuel Say of Westminster ; John Wilson, first pastor of a dissenting congregation at Warwick ; Josiah Hort, who conformed to the State Church and became archbishop of Tuam ; and John Hughes, poet and dramatist. During Mr. Rowe's time the church migrated to Girdlers' Hall ; and afterwards to Haberdashers' Hall, where it was finally disbanded about 1826. The academy was also somewhat migratory ; being in Little Britain about the time of the Revolution, again at Newington Green when Watts was a student, and at another time at Clapham. It came to an end with the life of Mr. Rowe, who died suddenly on 18th August, 1705. He was riding along a London street when he was taken with a fit, fell from his horse, and immediately expired.

Charles Morton, the originator of the other academy, was born at Pendavy in Cornwall, probably about 1617. He was descended from an ancient family in Nottinghamshire ; one of his ancestors having been Thomas Morton, secretary to King Edward III. Cardinal Morton, archbishop of

Canterbury in the fifteenth century, and Thomas Morton, bishop of Durham in the time of James I., were of the same family. His father, Nicholas Morton, was rector of Blisland, near Bodmin ; who, being driven thence for nonconformity in the time of Charles I., removed to London, became rector of Newington Butts, and died in 1652. Young Charles Morton entered Wadham College, Oxford, at a very early age. By his proficiency in mathematics he won the special regard of the warden, Dr. Wilkins —brother-in-law of Cromwell, and afterwards bishop of Chester. Having attained to the degree of M.A., and to a fellowship in his college, he was presented to the rectory of Blisland, formerly held by his father. He was at first a strict Conformist, and zealous for all the prescribed ceremonies ; but on the outbreak of the Civil War was much impressed by the fact that many of the worst characters flocked to the royalist standard, while the most sober and pious men of his acquaintance took the side of the Parliament. This led him to reflections which issued in his becoming a decided Puritan.

Being ejected by the Act of Uniformity, he preached for some time in a house of his own in the parish of St. Ives. But sustaining severe loss by the Great Fire he came to London to secure the remains of his property ; and was urged by several friends to undertake the instruction of youth in academical learning, for which he had ample qualifications. To this end he settled at Newington Green, where he is said to have trained "some scores of young ministers, as well as many other good scholars." This statement of Calamy may be a little exaggerated ; but unquestionably his pupils were numerous, as he "had a familiar way of making difficult subjects easily intelligible." For their use he drew up several brief systems of various arts and sciences, which the students copied out, and which he expounded in his lectures. These lectures, contrary to the prevailing fashion of the day, were not in Latin but in English.

After a time the tutors of dissenting academies, who were all graduates of Oxford or Cambridge, were assailed with an accusation that by privately " teaching university learning " they had violated the oath which had been administered to them on taking their degrees. To this charge Morton thought it necessary to make an elaborate reply, which is printed in Calamy's *Continuation of the Account of Ejected Minsters, 1727*; (see pp. 177-197). It is not worth reprinting as a whole, but a brief summary may be of some interest. He points out (1) that the terms of the oath were explained in one way by those who desired to claim for Oxford and Cambridge an educational monopoly and to stigmatize Nonconformists as perjurers, and in another way by persons of ordinary common sense : (2) that the oath was designed to obstruct the possible growth of a rival university, such as had once been attempted at Stamford ; and that, the occasion no longer existing, the former oath was nugatory : (3) that the Nonconformist teachers could claim good precedents, as several prelates and dignified persons had privately "read university learning" to young men of their own party during "the late times"—the archbishop of York having 16 or 17 such students : (4) that the accusers' contention would not only condemn Sion and Gresham Colleges, but would challenge the king's right to appoint English graduates to professorships, if it should please him to constitute another university : (5) finally he urges the necessity of private academies, unless Nonconformists are to be false to their own consciences ; and anticipates that these will benefit the ancient universities, by stirring them up to emulation and improvement, until at length "private students may come all to supplicate their public graces, when they can receive them without incumbrance."

Another small treatise of Morton's, also preserved by Calamy (*Continuation* pp. 198-210), is entitled *Advice to Candidates for the Ministry under the présent discouraging circumstances*. It well deserves to be reprinted in full; but the headings must here suffice:—

1. See that in all Study and Preaching you chiefly mind Jesus Christ. 2. Call to mind the End of Preaching; which is to teach *what men should*, not *what you can* do. 3. Use notes, not proudly and foolishly, but humbly and wisely. 4. Endeavour, by Prayer and Meditation, to have your hearts well affected with the matter you are to deliver. 5. Lay the stress of all your discourses on plain and pertinent texts of Scripture. 6. Be diligent in hearing the most pious and practical preachers, and such as you see do most prevail with the hearts of men. 7. Let your discourses be mostly Practical, both as to the Subjects and Manner of handling. 8. Be well disposed as to the present or future dispensations of Providence towards you. Under this last head he specially warns against plausible tempters to conformity; saying "Be sure, unless you be complete and thorough-paced renegades, you will be always suspected, and then trusted and favoured accordingly. My advice therefore is, that you tamper with them as little as may be."

There is no complete list of Morton's students; but the following attained to some measure of distinction:— Samuel Lawrence, pastor for 24 years at Nantwich; John Beaumont, pastor at Deptford; Thomas Reynolds, for above 30 years at the King's Weigh House; Joseph Hill, of Swallow Street, afterwards at Rotterdam, and finally at Haberdashers' Hall; William Hocker of Edmonton, afterwards at Gravel Lane; John Shower and Joseph Bennett, both of Old Jewry; Timothy Cruso of Poor Jewry Lane; Nathaniel Taylor of Salters' Hall; James Hannot of Yarmouth; Richard Lardner—father of the celebrated Dr. Lardner; Samuel Wesley, who conformed in 1684, and was afterwards the well known rector of Epworth ; while among the lay students were Kitt. Battersby, William Jenkyn, and one of the brothers Hewling, who laid down their lives "for Faith and Freedom" among the victims of Jeffreys' Bloody Assize in 1685 ; and, more distinguished than all the rest, Daniel Defoe, politician, pamphleteer and novelist. It is noteworthy that Reynolds, Hill and Bennett were ordained with four other young ministers in Dr. Annesley's meetinghouse, Little St. Helen's, on 22nd June, 1692, this being the first *public* Nonconformist ordination in London since the time of the Commonwealth.

In this, however, Morton had no part. Worn out with vexatious proceedings in the ecclesiastical courts, he retired in 1685 to New England; and there became pastor of a church at Charlestown. He was also chosen vice-president of Harvard College; and died in April, 1697, aged about 80 years. His publications were numerous, though mostly small ; for he was fond of quoting the proverb Μεγα βιβλιον μεγα κακον : so that it is somewhat strange to find him entirely unnoticed in Ant. Wood's history of Oxford writers. The ensuing list of his works is probably incomplete.

The Little Peacemaker, discovering Foolish Pride the Makebate, 1674.
The way of Good Men, for Wise Men to walk in, 1681.
Debts' Discharge (on Romans 13 : 8), 1684.
The Gaming Humour Considered and Improved, 1684.
Season's Birds; an enquiry into the sense of Jerem. 8 : 7.
Meditations on the History of the first 14 chapters of Exodus.
The Ark, its Loss and Recovery (on 1 Sam. 4-6 cs.)
The Spirit of Man—Meditations on 1 Thes. 5 : 23.
Of Common Places, or Memorial Books.
Ευταξια : (*a treatise on principles of public polity, agreeable to the English Constitution*).
A Compendium of Logic (Once used as a text-book at Harvard's).
Letters to a Friend, to prove Money not so necessary as is imagined.
Considerations on the New River.
A Discourse on Improving the County of Cornwall (In the Philosophical *Transactions.*)

At the removal of Mr. Morton some of the students went to pursue their studies on the continent, especially at Geneva. But the academy was not immediately dissolved. For a time, at least, three London ministers read lectures to the remaining students ; viz. Messrs. Wickins, Lobb, and Glasscock.

William Wickins was born in London in 1614, and educated at Emanuel College, Cambridge. After being chaplain to Sir E. Scott in Kent he occupied successively the two sequestered benefices of St. Andrew Hubbard and St. George's, Southwark. Vacating the latter at the Restoration he was chosen preacher at the Poultry Comptor, whence he was ejected by the Act of Uniformity. He subsequently became pastor of a small congregation at Newington Green, having for a colleague, first, Mr. Starkey, ejected minister of Grantham, and afterwards Joseph Bennett, mentioned above as one of Morton's students. He is said to have been a hard student, especially of Jewish antiquities and Oriental learning ; and to have usually read the Scriptures (in private) in the original languages. He took part in several private ordinations; one of the latest being that of Matthew Henry, 9th May, 1687. He died at the age of 85, and was buried in Bunhill Fields, 22nd September, 1699.

Those of his works of which we have found any trace are :

The Kingdom's Remembrancer, 1660.
The Warrant for Bowing at the Name of Jesus examined, 1660.
A Plea for the Ministry.
And something on *The Dates of Paul's Epistles*.

Of *Stephen Lobb's* early history we have but little information ; which is somewhat surprising, as he "made a very considerable figure in his day." He was a Cornish man, probably born during the Protectorate. His father, Richard Lobb, was high sheriff of Cornwall, and M.P. for St. Michael in 1659. It is believed that Stephen received his education partly in one of the early dissenting academies, and partly in Holland. His first pastorate is supposed to have been in the west of England ; as he married a daughter of the Rev. Theophilus Polwhele, Independent minister at Tiverton. In 1681 he became pastor of Fetter Lane, in succession to Dr. Thos. Goodwin ; and four years later commenced his tutorial work at Newington Green. On the issue, in April 1687, of King James's " Declaration for Liberty of Conscience " Lobb was one of the few Nonconformists who believed in his sincerity, and one of those who presented the Address of Thanks. James, believing that the good man's simplicity fitted him to be a useful tool, took him into conspicuous favour, and conversed with him frequently and familiarly. Lobb earnestly endeavoured to use the influence he seemed to possess in the interest of his dissenting brethren ; and is said both to have advised the king to set aside the Test Act, and to have expressed approval of the prosecution of the seven bishops. However he may thus have erred in judgement, it was in company with such men as the Presbyterian Vincent Alsop and the Quaker William Penn ; and he was sufficiently chastised by the reproaches of many of his brethren and the revilings of the High Churchmen. On the outbreak of the Neonomian controversy he took the High Calvinistic side, in common with most of the Independents, and in opposition to Alsop and most of the Presbyterians. He is described as a faithful and laborious pastor, a diligent student, a keen and yet charitable controversialist, and a man of large beneficence and deep spirituality. He died very suddenly on 3rd June, 1699.

His writings were numerous, and mostly controversial. They include:

A Modest and Peaceable Inquiry into . . . Mistakes . . . in Dr. Stillingfleet's Unreasonableness of Separation, 1681.
Reply to the Defence of Dr. Stillingfleet (written jointly with John Humphries) 1681.
The True Dissenter, or the Cause of those who are for Gathered Churches, 1685.
The Healing Attempt : being a Representation of the Government of the Church of England, 1689.
The Glory of Free Grace Displayed, 1690.
A Peaceable Inquiry into the Nature of the Controversy about Justification, 1693.
A Letter to Dr. Bates on the Doctrine of Satisfaction, 1695.
A Report of the present state of the Difference in Doctrinals between some Dissenting Ministers in London, 1697.
The Growth of Error ; or Rise and Progress of Arminianism and Socinianism, 1697.
A Defence of the Report ; and Further Defence, both 1698.
An Appeal to the Bishop of Worcester [Stillingfleet] *and Dr. Jonathan Edwards, about the Controversy between him and Mr. Williams*, 1698.
A Further Defence of his Appeal, 1698.

Of *Francis Glasscock* still less is known. He is understood to have studied at one of the Scottish universities, and to have been minister of a Presbyterian congregation that met near Drury Lane, and some time after 1695 in Hanover Street, Long Acre. Although a Presbyterian, he was one of the lecturers at Pinners' Hall. According to W. Tong, who preached his funeral sermon, he was an enthusiastic student of the prophetical Scriptures, especially Daniel and the Revelation. He died in 1706 ; and a treatise of his *On the Two Covenants* was published posthumously.

Matthew Henry narrates that while reading law at Gray's Inn, in 1685 or -6, he once attended "a divinity disputation kept up weekly by Mr. Morton's young men, six or eight of them, when scattered from him." Mr. Glasscock presided, and the question was : "Whether we are justified by

Faith alone?" The balance of opinion seems to have been on the Solifidian side.

How long the academy was carried on after the removal of Morton is a matter about which we have no certain information. That it did not collapse on the departure of the last of Morton's students is evident from the statement that Wickens, Lobb and Glasscock lectured not only to them but "to others who, through the severity of the times, were deprived of more public means of improvement." But as none of the students who, from 1696, were educated under the patronage of the Congregational Fund Board is mentioned as receiving instruction from either of these gentlemen, it may reasonably be supposed that the academy was discontinued very soon after the Revolution.

There were also two academies at ISLINGTON, one conducted by Ralph Button, and the other by Thomas Doolittle.

Ralph Button was the son of Robert Button of Bishopstown, Wilts. He commenced B.A. at Exeter College, Oxford; and in 1633 became Fellow and tutor of Merton. One of his pupils was the once famous Zachary Bogan. On the outbreak of the Civil War he removed to London, and was appointed professor of geometry in Gresham College. In 1647 he was delegated as assistant to the visitors of Oxford University, and in the following year was elected public orator, and appointed to a canonry in Christ Church, though he was not "in orders," and at that time was no preacher. In 1650 he exercised his influence on behalf of the eminent Hebrew and Arabic scholar, Edward Pococke, and thus enabled him to retain his post in the university. He welcomed the Restoration both in Latin and in Hebrew; but experienced the usual Royalist gratitude of being

B

deprived both of his oratorship and his canonry; of which the former was given to R. South and the latter to Dr. J. Fell. He thereupon removed to Brentford, where he commenced a school for the sons of gentlemen; his pupils boarding with his next door neighbour, the Rev. T. Pakenham, the ejected minister of Harrow. For doing this without taking the "Oxford oath" of non-resistance he was imprisoned for six months. After the Indulgence, in 1672, he removed to Islington, where he "trained up many young persons, both for the dissenting ministry and for secular employments." The most distinguished of his students was Sir Joseph Jekyll, the son of a clergyman in Nottinghamshire: he became an eminent lawyer, was one of the managers of the trial of Sacheverel, and in the reign of George I. was appointed Master of the Rolls. Other pupils of Button who attained distinction were Mr. King, minister of Wellingborough, and Samuel Pomfret, of Gravel Lane, Houndsditch. Mr. Button died in 1680.

Thomas Doolittle was born at Kidderminster in 1630 or -31. His spiritual awakening was due to some of those sermons of Richard Baxter which were afterwards embodied in the *Saints' Rest*. He entered an attorney's office, with a view to the legal profession; but withdrew owing to some conscientious scruples. Encouraged by Baxter he entered Pembroke Hall, Cambridge, where he graduated M.A. Coming to London in 1653 his lively and pungent preaching attracted attention, and he was elected by the parishioners as minister of St. Alphage, London Wall. Being ejected in 1662 he commenced a boarding-school in Moorfields; in which he was assisted by Thomas Vincent, the ejected minister of St. Mary Magdalen, Milk Street. On the outbreak of the plague in 1665 he removed with his pupils, nearly 30 in number, to Woodford Bridge in Essex. Returning after the abatement of the pestilence, he fitted up a meeting-house in Bunhill Fields, which gave place, after the Great Fire, to another in Monkwell Street. From this he was forcibly driven away by soldiers, and the chapel was seized : Doolittle escaped arrest through a friendly hint conveyed privately from the Lord Mayor.' On the issue of the Indulgence he resumed his ministry, and commenced an academy in Islington. Whether in this he had any co-operation from Vincent is uncertain. In 1680 he had 28 students in his charge. An outbreak of persecution in 1685 compelled the temporary closing of the academy ; and Doolittle removed successively to Wimbledon, Clapham and Battersea ; the students boarding in neighbouring villages, and attending the lectures by stealth. He was often in danger; and at Battersea his goods were seized and sold. After the Revolution he resumed his regular work as pastor and tutor; but the academy is believed to have been discontinued some time before his death. He died 24th May, 1707, in his 77th year ; being the last survivor of the ministers ejected from London churches. There is no complete list of his students ; but the following names are recorded :—

Walter Bedford ; Robert Bozier (a kinsman of Philip Henry), died while a student; Samuel Bury, pastor successively at Bury St. Edmund's and Bristol ; Edmund Calamy, D.D., biographer of the ejected ministers ; Ebenezer Chandler, second successor of Bunyan at Bedford ; Henry Chandler, of Malmesbury, Hungerford, and Bath ; Samuel Doolittle, son of of the tutor, minister at Reading ; Thomas Emlyn, Unitarian, who endured much persecution for his belief; Matthew Henry, the commentator ; **Dr. Kerr**, physician and tutor successively at Highgate and Clerkenwell ; John

Mottershead, assistant to the tutor, afterwards pastor at Ratcliff; Thomas Ridgley, D.D., tutor and theologian; Thomas Rowe, who had also received instruction from Theo. Gale, and succeeded him at Newington Green; and J. Waters of Reigate, afterwards of Uxbridge. We also find the following names, which we fail to identify: Benson, Clark, Saunders, and Wells.

Doolittle's published works are numerous, and several of them were frequently reprinted. The following list is believed to be complete:

Sermon "Concerning Assurance" in the *Morning Exercise*, 1661.
A Spiritual Antidote against Sinful Contagion, 1665.
A Treatise Concerning the Lord's Supper, 1665.
A Serious Enquiry for a Suitable Return, answered in xiii Directions, 1666.
Rebukes for Sin by God's Burning Anger, 1667.
The Young Man's Instructor and the Old Man's Remembrancer, 1673.
Captives bound in Chains made Free by Christ their Surety, 1674.
Sermon "Concerning Prayer," in the *Morning Exercise*, 1674.
Sermon on the Novelties of Popery, in the *Morning Exercise*, 1675.
The Lord's Last Sufferings shewed in the Lord's Supper, 1682.
A Call to Delaying Sinners, 1683.
Sermon "On Eyeing of Eternity," in the *Morning Exercise*, 1683.
A Scheme of the Principles of the Christian Religion, 1688.[a]
The Swearer Silenced, 1689.
Love to Christ Necessary to escape the Curse at His Coming, 1693.
Earthquakes explained and practically improved, 1693.
The Mourner's Directory, 1693.
A Plain Method of Catechizing, 1698.[b]
The Saint's Convoy to Heaven, 1698.
A Complete Body of Practical Divinity (posthumous), 1723

The last named is a huge folio of 20 + 644 pp. His *Solemn Form of Covenant with God*, dated 18th November, 1693, occupies 5 pages. The treatise is based on the Assembly's *Shorter Catechism*, on which Doolittle had already published two smaller expositions [a] and [b] above. The treatment is chiefly practical and devotional, a feature which characterizes most of the author's works. He generally ignores, indeed does not seem to perceive, the difficulties of the Calvinistic system. Toulmin justly says: " though a very worthy and diligent divine he was not very eminent for compass of knowledge or depth of thought."

As above stated it is uncertain whether *Thomas Vincent* is entitled to a place among the academical tutors; but his moral courage and spiritual greatness demand a brief recognition. He was born at Hertford in 1634; studied at Christ Church, Oxford, and graduated M.A.; was ejected from St. Mary Magdalen, Milk Street; and assisted Doolittle in his school at Bunhill Fields. On the outbreak of the Plague he refused to leave London; and remained throughout the whole time of the visitation, tending the sick, comforting the bereaved, and preaching—in defiance of law—to large congregations in parish churches from which the conforming ministers had fled. On Doolittle's return he assisted him in his ministry at Monkwell Street until the meeting-house was seized. Afterwards he ministered to a congregation which met first in Hoxton, later in Hand Alley, and finally in New Broad Street; and died at Hoxton in 1678. He published several small works, devotional and practical; of which the most important is *God's Terrible Voice in the City*, 1667.

The remaining London academy of this period is that conducted by *Edward Veal* in WAPPING. He was born about 1631 or -2, and studied at Christ Church, Oxford, where he graduated B.A., 13th February, 1651, and M.A., 21st February, 1653. He also studied at Trinity College, Dublin, of which he became senior Fellow. On 14th August, 1657, he received Presbyterian ordination at Winwick, Lancashire; being designated to a pastorate at Dunboyne, a village about 11 miles from Dublin. He was admitted B.D. at Dublin in July, 1661, but before the end of the year was deprived for Nonconformity. He came to London with a testimonial signed by seven Dublin ministers, and was for some time chaplain to Sir Wm. Waller. Afterwards—from 1680 till shortly before his death—he was pastor of a Congregational church in Old Gravel Lane, Wapping. We are told that "he had several pupils, to whom he read university learning," but only three names have been preserved—Nathaniel Taylor of Salters' Hall; John Shower, and Samuel Wesley; all of whom studied also with Chas. Morton. Thomas Simmons, his successor, says, in a funeral sermon: " God made him extremely useful in the educating of young persons for the sacred office of the ministry, at a time when the harvest was great and the labourers few. He has met with good success that way; some that were under his care approved themselves able ministers of the New Testament, have done their work betimes, and are gone to receive their crown. Others have —most of them—approved themselves faithful and useful; and are living witnesses of his soundness in the faith, and the care he had upon him that their judgements might be well informed in the great fundamental points of the Gospel."

Mr. Veal died 6th June, 1708. His only published writings of which we have any knowledge are four sermons in the *Morning Exercise*, and the annotations on the Ephesians in the continuation of Matthew Poole's monumental work.

Penry's Last Journey to London

November or September—Edwards or Penry?

(See p. 182 : Sept., 1907)

THERE is a singular discrepancy as to the date of Penry's last journey from Scotland in 1592 ; Edwards, apparently, saying definitely that it was in November, Penry that it was " about September " ; and it is not easy to account for the discrepancy or to reconcile it. I have recently made a special examination of the MSS. in regard to this point, and the following notes may be of interest.

It may be well at the outset to give the exact words involved :

> Examination of John Edwards :—" John Edwards came out of Scotland with Penry—His coming out of Scotland was in November last."
>
> Examination of Penry :—" Item he sayth that he came out of Scotland about September last, in the company of John Edwards."

It may then be noted : 1. As the Harleian MSS. are confessedly copies of still earlier MSS., it is possible, and not at all improbable, that in one case there has been a mistake in copying. The two words have the same termination, —ember.

2. It is not likely that in regard to events so comparatively recent—the examination of Penry being dated April 5, 1593, and Edwards's having taken place, apparently, a few days earlier—there was with either of them a mistake of memory.

3. The apparent vagueness of Penry : " about September," is not to be unduly pressed. It is clear from the construction of the sentences that all the items of Penry's examination are in answer to questions, which are not given. The vagueness was probably in the question ; " Did you leave Scotland with Edwards about September last ? " To which the answer would be in the affirmative.

4. If there has been miscopying of dates, this seems to be less likely with the evidence of Penry. (*a*) It is given in formally arranged items. The deposition of Edwards is given in the style of narrative ; and owing perhaps to some looseness

in the examination there is a certain confusion in the order of the recital of events. Edwards goes forward and backward; there are, too, evident gaps in the story, and a want of completeness. There are signs that only a part of his evidence appears. (*b*) At the close of Penry's evidence there is the note, "concordat cum originale." (*c*) September agrees better than November with all the other indications of the journey.

5. In Edwards's testimony, after mention of November, there are the words: "They came *first* to one Mr. Urèton's house besides Darby six miles." Here there must surely be a preceding gap, as from the southernmost point of Scotland to Derby must be some 150 miles, a distance further than any mode of locomotion known at the time would be likely to accomplish. If "November" be retained as, after all, Edwards's word, then the question is suggested whether he is not dating from a time and place somewhere in England in the course of the journey.

6. Waddington (*Penry*, p. 120) has a singular and somewhat irritating variation. Instead of any mention of Scotland, in giving the evidence of Edwards he has the words: "In November last he came with him *out of the country*." It would seem unwarrantable for an historian to alter words; and yet there is no note to say he is quoting from some earlier MS. In any case he shews his conviction that the journey Edwards describes as beginning in November is from a point south of Scotland.

7. One suggestion of the gaps in the preservation of Edwards's evidence arises from the statement, as if of habit, that he lay wherever Penry lay. Yet in the very next place named, Northampton —which however could hardly be reached from Derby in a day,—he does not lie with him, but stays alone at the Bull; and St. Alban's, also within a day's journey from Northampton, is the only place left for this habit.

Locate, however, a number of places between Edinburgh and Derby, and suppose a number of weeks spent between the two, and there is room for the habit, and some possible explanation of the naming of November.

T. GASQUOINE.

Seventy Years of Church Building in the West Riding

AT the accession of Queen Victoria, in 1837, the Congregational churches in the West Riding of Yorkshire numbered about 107. Ten of these, mostly in small towns and unprogressive villages, are to-day extinct; but the growth of our great cities, and the development of rural hamlets into thriving towns, have necessitated such additional provision for the spiritual needs of the population that there are at present within the West Riding above 200 Congregational churches, together with at least 35 preaching-stations—many of them substantial buildings—where churches have not yet been organized. In addition to these 42 of the older church buildings have been replaced since 1837; so that Congregationalism is responsible for about 175 ecclesiastical buildings, great and small, erected in the West Riding within the last seventy years.

Of the edifices existing in 1837 very few had much architectural character. Of the majority the style was domestic; in a few cases there was a more or less successful imitation of the Italian style; a small minority—like Salem church, Bradford—were really handsome buildings of their kind; but in too many instances the architecture was that of a factory. Yet some of the least attractive of these structures bore witness to much devotion and self denial; for example, the old sanctuary at Allerton, erected in 1814 and removed in 1872, was largely built by volunteer labour.

The internal arrangements were usually those of the Puritan meeting-house; the pulpit was often in the longest side of the building, with a large table pew in front, and deep galleries so constructed as to bring their occupants as near as possible to the preacher. Sometimes the pulpit had a sounding-board, over which at Mixenden hung a dove with expanded wings. Pews were usually high backed, sometimes square and sometimes narrow, but seldom shewing much regard for comfort. As the leading idea was that of an auditorium it was natural to mass the congregation as much as possible in front of the preacher; and therefore a central alley was unusual, except in the smallest churches. Organs were rarely found in "Dissenters' meetings"; but Yorkshire was then, as now, renowned for its church psalmody; and the table pew, or front gallery, furnished accommodation for "cornet, flute, harp, sackbut, psaltery, and dulcimer, and all kinds of music," as miscellaneous as Nebuchadnezzar's court band, and much more tuneful.

By far the finest Congregational church building of the early Victorian period in the county was that in East Parade, Leeds, erected in 1840. It was in Grecian style, with a stately Doric portico; and well deserved the admiration it commanded. Its removal sixty years later, owing to the shifting of population, deprived the city of a notable ornament; but was less to be regretted than some possible uses to which it might otherwise have been applied. Another noteworthy building is the church at Saltaire, erected in 1857 by Sir Titus Salt, entirely at his own cost. This is a Roman classical edifice, artistically faultless; and with its richly coloured marbles, arched roof with elaborate panelling, and fittings at once elegant and solid, was probably up to that date the most

beautiful church that had ever been dedicated for Free Church worship in England. Its belfry, moreover, was the first attached to a Congregational church in which there was more than a single bell. Unfortunately its acoustic properties were thoroughly bad; and the mischief was only overcome, after several costly experiments, by the introduction of heavy draperies.

A third church that demands notice is that in Horton Lane, Bradford, erected in 1862 to replace a huge factory-like meeting-house which had stood for about 80 years. The style of this is Elizabethan, with Italian details, from the designs of Messrs. Lockwood and Mawson. It is at once commodious, beautiful, and comfortable, and its acoustic properties are excellent. It seats about 1,300, and, with the adjacent schools, cost £12,000. A concise description appears in the Congregational Year Book of 1864.

But these churches, large, conspicuous, and beautiful as they are (or were), must yield in historic importance to a very modest village sanctuary which accommodates 300 worshippers. This was built in 1840, at Burley-in-Wharfedale, and is noteworthy as the earliest Congregational church in Yorkshire in the so-called "Gothic" style. It is a pretty little building, though no doubt architectural purists might find much in it to criticize; and its builders had to contend against not only ignorance but prejudice. In those days many excellent people seriously believed that a "churchy" style of building was somehow incongruous with the "principles of dissent"; and there is a story—perhaps apocryphal—that the architect had to conciliate ultra-Protestant susceptibilities by substituting another kind of finial for the floreated cross which he had proposed to place on the front gable. However, the success of the experiment was such as to warrant repetition; and it was soon practically demonstrated that, if anything better than the baldest and ugliest utilitarianism was desired, a better effect could be obtained at less cost by the adoption of some form of Gothic than by feeble imitations of the classical or the renaissance.

No doubt many blunders were made; that was inevitable. The ecclesiastical Gothic of the earlier years of the nineteenth century was of the most debased type. Churches were built, or rebuilt, in which were blended architectural features of every age from Henry II. to Henry VIII. Difference in style may be seen in most of the cathedrals; but the Episcopalian churches built with parliamentary grants, all in one style, were as debased Gothic as any in the country.

And the fact that the systematic study of mediaeval architecture was intimately associated with the religious movement popularly nicknamed "Puseyism" was disadvantageous to Free Church architects. Hence from time to time we had deep transepts, heavy stone or clustered iron pillars, open roofs, wide aisles — often filled in with galleries which cut right across tall narrow windows. And not infrequently there were timber or plaster imitations of features which must be ridiculous if not executed in stone—in short a cheap pretentiousness which gave point to the gibe about "Dissenters' Gothic."

But we learned by our failures. A fairly creditable church was built at Rawden in 1846; Greenfield, Bradford, followed in 1852, Stanningley and Lister Hills, Bradford, in 1854, and in the same year Wicker, Sheffield. In 1856 there arose the slender spire and richly decorated front of Regent Street, Barnsley; and every former success was surpassed in 1857, when the Square Church, Halifax, reared its stately head.

From this time forward the majority of our new churches in the district were designed in the style which most unmistakedly proclaims their religous purpose, and is associated with the most memorable incidents of our national history. Many of them bear witness not only to the zeal and liberality of the congregations, but to the fine taste and constructive skill of the architects. Externally at least, Harrogate (1861), Knaresborough and Hillhouse, Huddersfield (1865), Pudsey (1866), and Ilkley (1868), may safely challenge criticism. But it was long before our architects abandoned the attempt to enclose a conventional "meeting-house" within a mediaeval shell, or resisted the temptation to insert lofty side windows which were afterwards to be obstructed by the erection of deferred galleries. This constructive error was avoided at Halifax Park (1868), and Dewsbury Ebenezer (1884); but late examples indicate that it was abandoned with some reluctance. Of downright structural falsehoods—such as vestries simulating chancels, and of pretentious fronts on buildings otherwise mean and shabby, we have happily few instances in the West Riding. But somehow it has come about that often our most successful buildings, those most suited for Congregational worship, are found not in great cities, but in small towns and rural villages. Perhaps it may be that there is less temptation to provide the largest possible number of seats at the smallest possible cost. However, churches like those at Drighlington and Holywell Green (both 1868), Ripponden (1869), and Boston Spa (1877), are each in its own way admirable. While for the requirements of a great city church it would not be easy to imagine provision that should surpass that of Trinity, Leeds (1901), the majestic edifice which carries on the work of the once famous East Parade.

This is a review of architectural progress which would do honour to any Christian denomination. Some of the churches that have been mentioned are not perfect, for who has ever seen a perfect building? But they are a wonderful improvement upon the meeting-houses of the eighteenth or nineteenth century.

This slight sketch would be wanting indeed if it were to close without reference to the most valuable work which the English Congregational Church Building Society, under the able and painstaking leadership of the Rev. J. C. Gallaway, M.A., has effected in the improvement of our church buildings. The moneys granted and the loans made have been but a small portion of the good accomplished.

How many churches could be named that have cost over £10,000, which if their plans had been submitted to Mr. Gallaway or his successors before the works were let, would be much better to hear or preach in! Sometimes the transepts are too deep, the naves too lofty and the inner wagon headed roof been found wanting. Instances could be named where there are no transepts and there is an under drawn roof, and still by the faulty construction of the building the acoustics are wretched.

More than 50 years ago the society published a *Manual of Practical Hints*, embodying the views which the committee then held as to the buildings themselves and the methods by which such undertakings should be carried out.

Taking as their motto " Strength and beauty are in His Sanctuary " the committee have tried to combine such important requisites in the buildings they have aided, and have been of untold benefit to Congregationalists in the hundreds of churches they have aided throughout the land. The English Congregational Church Building Society started in 1853 on an experimental career of five years, with a guaranteed income of £2,500, proposing in that time to aid in the building of fifty places of worship. It is pleasant to be able to report that in 1905 the committee could say that nine hundred and eighty seven cases (874 churches and 113 manses) have been aided by the society in the fifty two years of its existence, with loans and grants, paid and promised, amounting to £205,444.

Besides the English Church Building Society there have been or are the Metropolitan, the London, the Yorkshire, the Lancashire, and other societies of a similar nature, which have by practical advice as well as by grants and loans been of great service in the erection of suitable buildings in advantageous and commanding situations.

The writer has had to do, more or less, with the erection of more than fifty Congregational churches and schools, and can speak from practical experience of the great improvement that has taken place in the adaptability of the structures for which they are designed. The purposes to which we apply our buildings are prayer, psalmody, preaching, teaching, conference and fellowship; and the more we make them suitable for our requirements the more serviceable they will be for the wants of the community and the efficiency of our work for the Master.

J. A. CLAPHAM.

Early Conventicles in Cumberland and Westmorland

IN the last issue of *Transactions* an attempt was made to illustrate and supplement Mr. Colligan's paper by a map of the two counties and lists of ejected ministers, licences under the Indulgence, early Friends' meetings, etc. But nothing was said about the conventicles that were reported in 1669. The Rev. Geo. Lyon Turner, M.A., who has made a special study both of the Sheldon returns and of the licences, enables us to complete the record.

*Conventicle Returns—*1669.

(1) The returns for *Cumberland* are given in three brief sections:

i.—*Copeland* deanery as follows :

DEANE.	Meetings of Quakers, sometimes to the number of 200.
DISTINGTON.	Quakers.
EMBLETON.	Some Quakers.
COCKERMOUTH.	Some Nonconformists and some Quakers.
EGREMOND.	Conventicle of Nonconformists.
BRIGHAM.	Quakers.
LOWESWATER.	Quakers.
LAMPLUGH.	Quakers about 20.

Then follows a list of 21 places, with the note : "Noe Conventicles in any of these places." They are :

Ardleiden	Whitehaven	Millam	Innerdale	Waverthwayt
Corney	Nether Wasdale	St. Bees'	Nuncaster	Ponsonby
Breg	Wicham	St. John's	Haill	Hornington
Bootill	Work	St. Bridgett's	Irton	Morasby
				Gofforth

ii.—*Lonsdale* deanery :

LORTON. Some few Quakers.

iii.—In the diocese of *Carlisle.*

This part of the return is given in five columns—as was intended —and as it is given in all the returns from the southern counties.

Parishes & Conventicles in them	Sects.	Numbers.	Qualitie.	Heads and Teachers
Bridekirke ...	Independents	50 or 60	Meane for the most part	One George Larkham some time minister att Cockermouth.
Brampton ...		30 or 35	Meane most of them, but some rich	One Nathaniel Burnand some time vicar there, but is now a Farmer or Drover.
Hesket	}			Simon Atkinson.
Lozenby	} Independents	60 or more		One Slee.
Kirk Oswald	}			One Nicholson.

There is likewise a meeting of Quakers, sometimes in one parish, sometimes in another, very tumultuous.

(2) The returns for *Westmorland* are very meagre—only three in number; all in the return for the *Kendal* deanery, and all for Quakers.

They are:
    1. GRIESMERE. A meeting of Quakers, about 80 or upwards.
    2. BOLTON. Meeting of Quakers, to the number of 40, sometimes more.
    3. BURTON. Quakers, 50, sometimes more.

Mr. Turner also furnishes corrections of several inaccuracies in the lists above referred to—*Transactions* 3., pp. *229-232.*

Some of these are trivial—as where the licences for the preacher and the house are separate documents, but are not so distinguished in the list; or where licences are not dated in the entry book, but the dates have been supplied by the compiler of the calendar. But the following are important :

LICENCES IN CUMBERLAND.

ALLONBY is an error for Allerby.
BRAMPTON. Nathaniel Burman should be Burnam. The person meant is the ejected vicar, whose name was Burnand.

BRIDEKIRK. The dates 2nd May and 26th July should be 8th May and 16th July.
BRIDEKIRK. House of Edward James was at Carlisle—not Bridekirk [printer's error]; the correct entry is
CARLISLE. "The House of Edw. James of Blackfryers in Carlisle in Cumberland, Pr."
GREYSTOCK is spelled Graistock in the entry book.
A more serious fault is the omission of
SCALEBY CASTLE. "The house of Rich. Gilpin at Scarby Castle in Northumberl. Pr." (The name is misspelled in the calendar, and the county is wrongly stated.)

LICENCES IN WESTMORLAND.

KENDAL. Whitehead was ejected from Dalton in Lancashire (which of the two Daltons is questioned); and Benson from Bridekirk. Garrett is an error for Garnett; he is the same as Gernet mentioned below. Cook is an error for Cork; he is described as " of Kendall Park in Westmorland."

ERRORS ON THE MAP.

ALLONBY is given by error instead of Allerby, which is about two miles to the south.
BRIDEKIRK should be underlined for a Presbyterian meeting.
HESKETH in the map is Hesketh Newmarket; it is doubtful if the licence was for that place or for Upper or Nether Hesketh, both of which are about nine miles to the NE.
KENDAL should be doubly underlined for several Presbyterian meetings.
WHINFELL and HEVERSHAM, both Presbyterian, are omitted; the former is about six miles NNE. and the latter six miles S. of Kendal.
SCALEBY CASTLE, Presbyterian, is also omitted; it is NE. of Carlisle, about halfway between Kirklinton and Crosby.

The Later Years of Robert Browne

IN the first paper of this series (*Transactions* Vol. II. No. 3, p. 151) I ventured to remark " It seems to be the fate of every writer about Robert Browne to fall into some misstatements." Unfortunately that fate befell the present writer in that very paper, but he is now in the happy position of being able to correct some, at least, of his own errors.

I.—Browne's Matrimonial Troubles

The last section of the above mentioned paper dealt with the question of Browne's second marriage, and set forth a theory as to the second wife which seemed to fit in admirably with ascertained facts. It is now my duty to say that that convenient theory has been shattered completely by further discoveries among the diocesan records at Peterborough. Browne did marry a second time (and therein another of Dexter's conclusions goes to the wind), but the woman was not, as I conjectured, Joane Story of Stamford. In the parish register of St. Martin's, Stamford, I had found this entry:

> 1612 Robert Brown, gent, & Eliz. Warrener, married Feb 14th

But that entry I rejected as not relating to our Browne, firstly because it was unlikely that a " clerk " would be termed a " gent," and Browne we know had been ordained ; and secondly because the Joane story seemed so pat. However, I soon had proof that the name of his second wife was Elizabeth, yet it was not until this month (April, 1908) that I found the entry to settle all further doubt. In the Special Licence book (vol 1.) it is recorded

> That on Feb 5th 1612/13. a licence was granted for the solemnization of the rites of holy matrimony between " Robert Browne Clerk, Rector of Achurch & Elizabeth Warrener of Stamford S^t. Martins, widow." And permission was given for the marriage to take place " either at Achurch or Stamford S^t. Martins "

The entry at St. Martin's was evidently made by a clerk who had not been informed that Browne was in orders, yet knew that he was a member of the influential Tolethorpe family.

Elizabeth Warrener, widow, seems to have brought to Browne but little domestic happiness and much parochial disturbance. The next entry relating to her is as follows:

> "Before Mr Wm Pritherghe LL.D. Commissary general, Surrogate & official of the Archdeacon of Northanton. In the Chapel of Blessed Mary the Virgin by the Cathedral church of Peterborough. Wednesday 12 October 1614. Present Tho. Amy : Not. Publ. etc.
> Thorpe cū Achurche
> Wm Lynhall : pñtat^r for speakeinge of unreverent speeches of Elizabeth Browne the wyfe of Mr Robt. Browne o^r minister.

The case was deferred until November 25th. Unfortunately the proceedings on that day were entered on a leaf which has been torn from the record, and the only thing which remains clear is that Wm. Lynhall was excommunicated or suspended. Therefore the charge was admitted to be true, although, as we shall see presently, apparently Wm. Lynhall had some grounds of justification for speaking "unreverently" of Mrs. Browne. This presentation, of course, was made by the churchwardens of the parish.

Some light is thrown upon this unhappy domestic story by the following and similar entries:

> Court of the Archdeacon of Northamton
> 17 Octobrio   Before Mr Richus Meredith, clerk, surrogate
> 1615   etc.
>   In the parish church of Oundle.
>   Tuesday 17 Oct 1615
>   In the presence of Tho. Amy, Notary Publ.
> Thorpe Achurche
> Magistr Robtm Browne } Presentatur our parsonage houses (sic)
> clerc. Rector : ibidem } to be in decay and 4 Tenants dwellinge
>   } in them.
> Mrm Browne p^{r}dictum : Presentatur for not being resident on his parsonage.

Again a year hence, on October 30th, 1616, in the same place and before the same official, Browne was presented "that the parsonage house is oute of repaire."

Yet again on December 9th, 1617, he was charged with the same offence "for sufferinge his parsonage house to go to decaye."

Upon these entries all that I have to remark at present is this : that Browne's handwriting disappears from the Achurch parish register in June, 1616, that the house at Thorpe Waterville which he lived in (and built ?) bore the date 1618 ; and that his successor to the living of Achurch, the Rev. Peter Asheton D.D., built the present rectory in 1633 upon the site of the old parsonage house allowed by Browne to go into decay.

To return to Browne's wife, we find the following records, parts only of which I give :
"Before Mr. Johanes Lambe LL.D. Vicar General of the Lord Bishop of Peterborough as well as Official of the Lord Archdeacon of Northamton.
In the parish Church of Oundle, 14 October 1618
In the presence of Tho. Amy, N.P.
Achurche
Elizabeth Browne: Presentatur M^{rs}. Eliz: Browne and Bartholomew Smithe of Wadenhoe, for keepinge Companie together in the parsonage house of Thorpe Achurche as the fame goeth, in the nighte . . . ."

On the same day and before the same court she was likewise presented with John Broughton of Pilton on a similar charge. Both the men appeared to answer the charge and were ordered to find four honest neighbours apiece as compurgators to swear to their innocence. The case came before the same official on October 30th, 1618, in the parish church of Uppingham; it was declared that the citation had been served upon Elizabeth Browne by an apparitor named Washinglie on the previous Wednesday, but again Mrs. Browne put in no appearance. As she did not appear again on November 20th, 1618, she was pronounced by the court sitting at Oundle to be contumacious, and condemned to the usual penalties. However, on December 10th, 1618, Mrs. Browne did appear before the court sitting in the parish church of Oundle, "et solvit 2^s. debet 16^d." for her contumacy. Bartholomew Smithe and John Broughton also appeared, and presented their compurgators, viz.: "Thomas Saunderson. Tho. Thirlby de Pilton, Millicent Hunt de Yaxley, Wm. Wolasson de Allwinckle." These were accepted for Broughton, and when he and they had sworn on oath that he had never misconducted himself with Elizabeth Browne the court declared itself satisfied, and formally stated that Broughton's reputation was cleared. Bartholomew Smith, however, apparently was not able to clear his character. The case came up again on March 14th, 1619, and May 16th, when Smith was declared contumacious for not paying all the court fees; and there the case disappears.

Our present entries relating to Browne's wife end with the following :
"Court held before Mr Anthony Wells, surrogate of Mr John Lambe Vicar-general of the Bp of Peterborough, in the parish church of Oundle 29. Oct 1623. present Thos. Amy. N.P.
"Elizabetha Browne de Achurche uxor Roberti Browne, cl, contra Robertum Browne predictum eius maritum } in causa restituonis obsequiorum conjugalium etc.

Evidence of the service of a citation on Robert Browne was given by the Officer of the Court, but Browne put in no appearance. The case was called on November 11th, November 25th, and December 9th in the same year but no progress was made with it.

Piecing together these bare records we conjecture that the story of Browne's second marriage was somewhat as follows : Early in 1612/13 he married this Mrs. Warrener who was probably many years his junior. Her conduct was such that within eighteen months she was the subject of gossip, and plain spoken Wm. Lynhall was moved to unreverent speech concerning her. Sometime during 1615 Browne leaves his old parsonage house to reside at the other end of his scattered parish, and possibly builds there the house with which his name has ever since been associated. Whether his wife Elizabeth went with him, or stayed on in the large old parsonage house, we cannot say. The plural "houses" in the entry of October 17th, 1615, probably refer to the outhouses and other buildings adjacent to, and connected with, the parsonage house proper.

His wife's conduct may have been the cause of his removal to Thorpe Waterville, and even the reason why he ceased to officiate at Achurch for a while. This much is clear that henceforth at least Browne refused to live with his wife. She sued him in 1623 for the restitution of conjugal rights, but he took no notice of the suit, and in all probability never lived with her again. She outlived him some years.

Fuller (*Church History* vol. 5, p. 68) therefore is proved to be quite correct when he stated that Browne "had in my time a wife with whom for many years he never lived, parted from her on some distaste, and a church wherein he never preached." But I doubt whether we can place much reliance upon the assertion of Robert Baillie ("a Dissvasive...." 1645) "I have heard it from reverend Ministers, that he was a common beater of his poor old wife, & would not stick to defend publikely this his wicked practice." Had Browne beaten his wife she could have presented him before the ecclesiastical court, but there is no evidence of such a procedure.

2.—Browne's Parochial Troubles, 1616 to 1631

I regret that I am still unable to give the complete story of Browne's life as rector of Achurch. The new evidence which follows is very disjointed and usually the records break off just where the interest is keenest. However, from the following items (taken chiefly from the archdeacon's Visitation and Court Book at Peterborough) some fresh light is thrown upon the tangled history of Browne. And here the present writer desires to make the fullest acknowledgement of the ever courteous assistance of the

The Later Years of Robert Browne

Rev. E. A. Irons, M.A., rector of North Luffenham, Stamford, whose knowledge of the records at Peterborough is equalled by no man. But for Mr. Irons's generous help probably many of the following facts would never have emerged to light.

It is of interest to note, first, his relation to the ecclesiastical authorities as indicated by his appearance or non-appearance at the archdeacon's visitation.

Achurch is in the rural deanery of Oundle, from which place it is distant about 4½ miles. Thither then Browne and every incumbent, curate, etc., in the deanery was expected to come, or send an adequate excuse.

The archdeacon's visitation books prior to 1607 have been lost. The following is Browne's record:

1607. No appearance.
1608, 1609, 1610 and 1611. Appeared. (1611 paid 2/6 procuration fee).
1612. No appearance, excused. Thurlbie (his curate) appeared.
1613. Appeared.
1615. No appearance; he was therefore suspended, but probably absolved on paying the usual fine.
1616 (April 10) Appeared, also Henson, his curate, who had been licensed as deacon on Sept. 24, 1615.
1617. No appearance. But Arthur Smith, his curate, appeared and he was "asked by his Lordship's judge if he have worn the surplice, admitted he hath not since he served the cure, he was suspended from the exercise of his office & absolved, & admonished to wear the surplice every Sabbath & to do other rites & solemnities according to the book of common prayer."
1618, 1619, 1620, 1621. Browne made no appearance, Smith appears each time. In 1621 occurs the note "Mr. Smith is gon from Achurche." (He was instituted vicar of Oundle that year).
1622, 1623, 1624, 1625, Browne—no appearance. John Barker, curate, A.M., appeared each time. In 1622 there is the note "There is a strange preacher."
1626 (Oct. 10) Browne appeared by proxy, paid 3/4. Barker also appeared.
1627 (2 courts) No appearance. Barker appears.
1628 (Oct. 23) Browne appears.
1628/9 (Mar. 31) Browne appears.
1629 (Oct.) No appearance, paid 2/4.
1630. No appearance, but excused.
1632. No appearance.
1633 (Nov. 2) Peter Asheton, D.D. (his successor) appears.

On the whole, therefore, Browne fulfilled this ecclesiastical duty up to April, 1616, and from October, 1626 to the end of his residence in Achurch, but not during that strange period of ten years. There is no evidence from this source of any breach with the ecclesiastical authorities. He simply made no appearance then, as on certain other occasions, but no special notice is taken of his absence.

Turning, however, to the records of the archdeacon's court we find there is mention of a suit "Officium dni g^a Robtum Browne R. of Achurche" begun on Wednesday 4th June 1617 in the Oundle parish church, but no particulars of any kind are given, probably because the proceedings never took form. But the entry, such as it is, is of great interest. First, because of its date. It synchronizes with the first appearance of Arthur Smith's handwriting in the Achurch parish register—June 17th, 1617. Secondly, it indicates that the suit—whatever may have been its character,—was promoted not by the churchwardens of the parish but by the ecclesiastical authorities—"his lordship's officer."

I have no trace of any action against Browne during the interval 1617 to 1626 except those mentioned above in the section dealing with his second wife. But on April 26th, 1626, there is an important record. It is of a suit brought by "his lordship's officer," not against Browne, but against the churchwardens of Achurch because they had not presented Browne.

It was tried before John Lambe, LL.D., vicar-general of the lord bishop of Peterborough and official of the archdeacon of Northampton, in the parish church of Oundle.

His Lordship's officer against Wm Deacon & Henry Wiles wardens of Achurche } Information is given to the court by John Barker, clerk, & Thomas Olyver of Achurche

"That the sd Mr Browne beinge suspended ab execucone officii sui clericalis did notwithstandinge upon Palme Sonday last reade dyvine service & preache on the same daye. And that upon the 15 of Aprill now instant beinge the Sabothe daye he did reede prayers & preache and Administer the Sacramente in the Churche there."

We are not told what happened to the unhappy wardens. This entry gives us the exact date of Browne's resumption of duties—"Palme Sonday," 1626 : his handwriting reappears April 9th, 1626, His suspension may have been of short duration ; as we saw above, suspension was sometimes only for a few hours—till a fine had been paid ; but I think, putting the 1617 and 1626 entries together, we may legitimately infer that he was suspended from his clerical duties for the whole of that period. The cool, independent way in which he returns to his duties, without waiting for the annulment of his suspension, is quite characteristic of the man. It is the Robert Browne of pre-clerical days reasserting himself, and this same independent spirit is indicated in the remaining records.

The "Old Chapel House," Thorp Waterville (Achurch Parish); built for R. Browne, 1618

The Later Years of Robert Browne 309

Had we a full knowledge of the forty years spent at Achurch, we might find that that spirit had never left him.

The next entry is dated Thursday, 8th November, 1627.

> Before Mr. Anthony Wells, S.T.B., Surr. etc. in the parish church of Oundle etc.
> M^{rm} Robtum Browne, R. etc is presented "for not using of the crosse in baptism, & for not wearinge of the surplice, & for omittinge of some parte of the booke of comon prayer."

This suit was brought, presumably, by the churchwardens. From the time of his return we have evidence that an active section of his parishioners, including apparently the churchwardens, were opposed to his lax conformity. It may well be, as I suggest above, that all through his incumbency he had exercised a certain freedom with reference to the rubric, but that his withdrawal in 1617 was a more emphatic declaration of nonconformity, and that on his return the conforming section were less complaisant. The rebuke his curate Smith received at the archdeacon's visitation in 1617 is evidence of an atmosphere of freedom in Achurch.

It is worthy of note also that whereas we have evidence that Browne employed curates from 1611 to 1626, from 1627 there is no mention of one. Browne *now* discharges the duties himself, with what result we see.

The growing hostility to Browne comes out clearly in the following and subsequent records.

On the same day (November 8th, 1627) and at the same court at which Browne was presented for his nonconformity, one of his parishioners Thomas Sanders was presented "upon a fame for givinge the Minister evill speeches in the Churche." Sanders put in an appearance to meet the charge and declared "that that wc^h Mr Browne sayd to him in the Churche was A lye." Sanders was deemed guilty, he was suspended from entering the church and ordered to perform a penance.

Then follows a list of parishioners of Achurch presented for "absenting of themselves" from the parish church: "Thomas Olyver & his wyfe & all his familye. Robt Dust, Wm Osberston, Edmund Quincey & Judith his wyfe. Robt Peake, Johana Peake widow, Johana Greene." (Note that the first named, Thomas Olyver, had together with Barker the curate been the prime mover against Browne on his return on "Palme Sonday," 1626.

On November 27th Thos. Sanders still remaining suspended was absolved; he was ordered to perform a penance of which the wardens were to certify the performance, and a fee of 2/6 was paid. The certificate had not been sent by December 6th.

There is a lull as far as the records are concerned for the next two years, then the final storm slowly gathers. In the Achurch parish register (*vide Transactions* Vol. III. No. 2, p. 135) occurs this entry :

> 1629 Christenings October 25, 1629 Allen Greenes child baptized in schisme at Lyllford named John.

In the archdeacon's book we find the following :

> Business transacted before Mr Anthony Wells S.T.B. Surr. etc. in the parish church of Oundle, Thursday 19 Nov. 1629. In presence of Tho: Amy, N.P. Dep. Reg.
> Thorp Achurch.
> " Magrum Browne Rcorem ibm—Presentatur for that he refused to baptize the child of Allen Greene & turned it from the church."
> Evidence was given that the citation had been served on Browne on the preceding Sunday, but he made no appearance. John Browne his son appeared and declared on oath " that his ffather is not able to come to this courte without danger of his healthe." The case was deferred to the next sitting of the court, when Browne was ordered to appear in person.

Then immediately following there are also these separate charges made, each being held over for the same reason.

> " Magrm Browne predictum : Presentatur for that he refused to bury the dead. Similiter.
> Magrm Browne predictum : Presentatur for that he doeth not read divine service according to the booke of Comon prayer. Similiter.
> Magrm Browne, antedictum : Presentatur for that he doeth not weare the surplice. Similitr.
> Magrm Browne, predictum : Presentatur for that he doeth not use the Crosse in baptisme. Similiter."

The case came up before the same official at the same place on Thursday, 10th December, 1629. All the charges are repeated in precisely the same form. Again Browne made no appearance, and this time his son Thomas took the oath and made the same declaration. Then his lordship's official ordered Browne to appear at the next court.

The case was called again on Thursday, 7th January, 1629/30, in the same place. On this occasion the entry simply states that Browne did not appear to answer the charge, and that he was to appear at the next court.

How often during the year 1630 Browne was ordered to appear and refused I cannot say ; there are no more entries relating to the case until December, 1630, when the case is taken to a higher quarter.

"Business transacted before the Reverend Father and Lord in Christ the lord William by divine permission bishop of St. Peter's Borough or Peterborough in a certain parlour within the bishop's palace at Peterborough on Sat. 4 Dec. 1630 between the hours of 9 and 12 a.m. in presence of Thos. Amy, N.P. Dep. Reg."

Officium domini promotum per Allenum Greene unum Gard. de Achurche et Robtum Dust unum. Inquisit, ibidem contra Robtum Browne, Cler, Rcorem de Achurche } Then follows the usual court jargon at great length.—I give only a summary: Roger Mason certified that he personally had served the citation upon Robert Browne, on last Wednesday at his rectory of Achurch. When Browne's name had been called three times, and no appearance been made, Greene and Dust accused Browne of contumacy in not appearing to answer the summons, and prayed that he should be considered and declared contumacious and that he should be excommunicated; but the Reverend Father from reasons specially known to him ("ex causis eum specialiter novendis") ordered Browne to appear at the next court to be held at Oundle viz. on the 16th of December, and he postponed and held over the case to the aforesaid time and place.

Accordingly the scene is transferred back to the parish church of Oundle, before Mr. Anthony Wells, S.T.B. Surr. etc., on Thursday, 16th December, 1630.

There is a similar entry:

"Officium domini promotum etc." This time Browne appears and immediately Allin (a proctor, practising in the archdeacon's court, and appearing here for Greene and Dust) took the oath and produced the articles which his lordship had admitted on his petition and ordered Browne to answer to the aforesaid articles at the next court.

The next court was held in the same place, before the same official, on 12th January, 1630/31. Browne appears and presents his answers to the articles. Allin accepts the answers; and on the prayer of Allin his lordship fixes a date for the proving of the articles, etc. All this, of course, is merely the complicated court procedure. The case comes up at the next court on January 26th, 1630/31. Browne is called three times, but does not appear. Allin forthwith accuses him of contumacy and petitions that he should be pronounced contumacious and condemned to the usual fines. This his lordship decreed upon Allin's petition. Then Allin produced the witnesses who should prove his articles, viz.: Thos. Sanders, James Holledge, Robert Woodruffe, Wm. Deacon and Geoffry Tuckerson, all of Achurch. These witnesses are admitted by his lordship, and they are warned that their questions (examen) shall be written by the time of the next court.

February 17th, 1630/31, is the date of the next (and for us final) court. The witnesses on behalf of Greene and Dust are produced, and examined. Browne is called, but does not appear; thereupon much more court formality and court jargon, of which nothing clear is the upshot; and the entry concludes with the statement that his lordship ordered the aforesaid testimony to be published.

There, so far as these records go, it all ends. Browne's handwriting disappears from the Achurch register on June 2nd, 1631, and the curtain falls.

3.—WAS BROWNE EVER EXCOMMUNICATED?

The present writer thinks he was not. In a former paper (*Transactions* Vol. II. No. 4., p. 239) he brought forward certain considerations to prove that the excommunication, if it ever happened, did not happen in 1586, as Dexter and some subsequent writers allege. Those considerations have been accepted by Mr. Champlin Burrage in his invaluable work *The True Story of Robert Browne*, (p. 43), and he there agrees that the excommunication did not take place in 1586. Mr. Burrage, however, is loath to dismiss the excommunication story altogether. He fixes upon 1617 as the date of the excommunication, and argues very ingeniously to prove that the disappearance of Browne 1617 to 1626 was due to sentence of excommunication (*ibid.*, pp. 68-71). Now, Mr. Burrage's knowledge of Browne's life and writings is unrivalled, and his judgement weighty. The present writer therefore considerably hesitates to differ from such an eminent authority. Yet he cannot accept Mr. Burrage's theory. To make his theory square with known facts Mr. Burrage is obliged to alter, in two important particulars, the earliest account of (and sole authority for) the excommunication, *i.e.*, that given by Dr. Thomas Bayley in the preface to *Bibliotheca Scriptorum Ecclesiae Anglicanae*, 1709. For Northampton he would write "Achurch near Northampton" (it is 26 miles distant), and for Bishop Lindsell, Bishop Dove. Even then one can hardly believe that when Dr. Bayley wrote "This [the sentence of excommunication] so struck the old gentleman, that he submitted himself to the bishop," he was referring to an excommunication, which according to Mr. Burrage must have lasted nine years. That would be rather a slow striking of the imagination of the old gentleman. An excommunicated person was practically an outlaw, certainly he was put in quarantine. None dare even associate with him. It is difficult to believe that Browne should live thus in his own parish for nine years! More-

BROWNE'S HOUSE, THORP WATERVILLE
Door of the room where he is said to have held Religious Meetings

over, the records at Peterborough contain not the slightest tissue of evidence of excommunication. Robert Browne's name never appears in the list of excommunicated persons; for persons were occasionally excommunicated, and their names recorded, but they usually soon gave in to the ecclesiastical authorities. Further, in the entry of December 9th, 1617 (*supra* p. 304) he is termed rector, as usual, and is held responsible for the upkeep of the parsonage.

Had he been excommunicated from 1617 to 1626 we should have had reference to it on April 26th, 1626, if nowhere else. The present writer thinks that for some time preceding 1626— possibly from 1617 to 1626, Robert Browne was, for some reason at present not known (possibly for nonconformity), simply suspended "from the discharge of his clerical duties"—a very different condition from that of excommunication.

Browne came nearest to excommunication on Saturday, 4th December, 1630, as we have seen above; and if ever that sentence fell upon him it was in the year 1631, at the close of his life, and as the result of the "contumacy" indicated above. But of that we have not the slightest trace, and the probability is against such a conclusion.

What then was the origin of Dr. Bayley's circumstantial story? Another confusion! Not Robert but Philip Browne was excommunicated. For on the same days, and before the same courts that Robert Browne was presented (viz. December 16th, 1630, January 12th, 1630/31, January 26th, 1630/31, and February 17th, 1630/31), a Philip Browne was presented. Who this Philip Browne was, we cannot say, probably he was that younger brother of Robert who had been deprived of the living of Little Carterton in 1604 (*cf. Transactions*, Vol. II., p. 154). Nor can we say what accusation had been brought against him. The first entry relating to him discovered at present is that of December 16th, 1630. It commences (as Robert's):

> "Officium domini promotum per Alanum Greene et Robtum Dust gᵃ Philippum Browne de Achurche."

Like Robert, he was to answer certain articles. Mason certified that personally he had served the citation upon the aforesaid Browne at Achurch. As Philip did not appear Allin took the oath and accused him of contumacy in not appearing etc., and petitioned that he be deemed contumacious and be declared excommunicated. The court granted the petition and Philip Browne was declared to be in danger of excommunication. When the case came up on January 12th, 1630, it is simply recorded that Philip Browne did not appear, and he is excommunicated.

On January 26th, 1630, the entry relating to Philip reads: "Browne remains excommunicated."

The last entry (February 17th, 1630) states that he had been denounced in church "in festo Natalis Domini 1630" and that he "remains excommunicated."

Here then is the origin of Dr. Bayley's story, for this did occur while he was chaplain to Bishop Lindsell, or more accurately one year before. It should be noted that in Dr. Bayley's account no Christian name is prefixed to Browne.

4.—THE "SCHISM" ENTRIES IN ACHURCH PARISH REGISTER.

The various records reproduced above throw light, I believe, upon the "schism" entries which occur in the Achurch parish register (see *Transactions*, Vol. III., p. 126, *et seq.*). In those records certain of Browne's parishioners are found to take action against him, either by presenting him, or witnessing to the truth of the accusations brought against him, or simply absenting themselves from church.

In the first column below I give the list of such persons, and in the second I give the names of the "schismatics."

PERSONS OPPOSED TO R. B.	SCHISMATICS.
Thomas Saunders	Thomas Saunders
Wm. Osberston	Wm. Osbaston
Edmund Quincey	Edmond Quincey
Allen Greene	Allen Greene
James Holledge	James Holdich
Thomas Olyver	Sylvester Greene
Robert Dust	Thos. Meakins
Robert Peake	Richard Denis
Robert Woodruffe	John Cranfield
Wm. Deacon	James Connington
Geoffrey Tuckerson	Robert Greene

Each list contains eleven names, 5 of which appear in both. Clearly, then, there was a party opposed to Browne from 1616 onwards, who refused his ministrations by going to neighbouring parishes for various rites, and who were guilty, therefore, in his opinion, of "schism."

Further consideration has led me to believe that all the "schism" entries are in Browne's handwriting; and that the "doubtful" entries of 1616 are in his hand.

5.—WAS THERE A PARTY IN FAVOUR OF BROWNE?

The parochial upheaval of 1616 is reflected in the disturbed condition of the parish register for that year, especially by the unique formal setting forth of all the parochial officers for that year—churchwardens, sidesmen, constables, are all named as if to record the passing of an old order and the bringing in of a new. (*cf.* plate No. 2 *Transactions* Vol. III., p. 130).

Now one of the churchwardens who testified to the accuracy of the register in the spring of 1616, and therefore belonged to the old *régime*, was William Dust. In the archdeacon's Court Book, under the date 30th October, 1616, we find that Mr. Henson, curate of Achurch (he was licensed as deacon on September 24th, 1615) was presented:

> "For that he contrary to lawe doth reade dyvine service when the excommunicate person Wm. Dust is in the church... Henson admits that he did read prayers when Dust was present in the Churche at Achurche, but did as he saeth not know that Dust was excommunicate, because the same was not denounced at Achurche." Then there follows a list of persons presented "for keepinge companie in the Churche & in other places with the said Dust (— Wiles & Mary his wife,— Harbord & Mary his wife,—Nicholsen" and others whose names have decayed from the margin where they were written).

Have we here the nucleus of Browne's party in the parish, his "most forward" ones who possibly worshipped with him afterwards at Thorpe Waterville?

6.—AFTERMATH.

Robert Browne's troubles with the ecclesiastical authorities are recalled to mind by the following entries of later years. They refer to his widow and his second son.

> "Business transacted before Mr. John Smith cler. A.M., Surrog. of Thomas Heath A.M., LL.B. Vicar-general of Ffrancis bp. of Peterborough & Official of the Archdeacon of Northampton in the parish church of Oundle Thursday 22 May 1634. In presence of Robt. Rowell N.P. Reg. deput. Thorpe Achurch.
> Mrs. Eliz. Browne. Presentatur for a non communicant at Easter last etc.
> Willm Browne. Similiter.—Browne appeared & was warned to receive the sacrament & to certify that he had received it before the next Sunday after the feast of S^t. John the Baptist, & to pay the fine at the next court.

Both cases came up on June 6th, 1634, when Wm. Browne paid the fine of 3/4.

The cases appear again on June 25th, and again on July 9th, 1634, when it is remarked "She was gone from thence before the presentment against her." Thus disappears Browne's second wife.

On July 24th, 1634, Wm. Browne had not produced the certificate.

The last entry relates to William Browne's wife. On October 27th, 1636, before Thomas Heath, LL.D., Vicar-general, in Oundle church, she was presented "for a comon scold and in particular for abusing our Minister Mr. Tuthill by unreverent speeches."

F. IVES CATER.

Oundle.

[We have pleasure in presenting photographs of "The Chapel House" at Thorpe Waterville, probably built by Browne in 1618, and in which—according to local tradition—he held services when he was "turned out" from his parish church.—See *Transactions* Vol. II. pp. 243-4.]

Walpole Meeting-House

The Ancient Meeting-House at Walpole, Suffolk

THE Congregational church at Walpole was organized in the year 1647. Its history, so far as it can be recovered, is given in Browne's *History of Congregationalism in Norfolk and Suffolk*, pp. 437-440, and therefore need not be repeated here in detail. The first pastor was the Rev. Samuel Habergham, who declined an invitation to become assistant to the Rev. W. Bridge at Yarmouth, but removed in 1652 to Syleham, from which he was ejected ten years later. He was succeeded at Walpole by the Rev. John Manning; who within two years removed to Peasenhall, and was ejected in 1662. His brother, the Rev. Samuel Manning, M.A., was appointed to succeed him at Walpole by the Parliamentary "Committee for Plundered Ministers"; and remained until he, too, was ejected by the Act of Uniformity.

All these were at the same time incumbents of the parochial benefice and pastors of the "gathered church" within the parish. It is therefore a pretty safe assumption that the parish church was the usual meeting-place of the Congregational society. S. Manning continued to reside in the village after 1662; and on the issue of the Indulgence he was licensed as a Congregational teacher in his own house, the licence being dated 18th May. Another licence was granted to one Thomas Folkerd, for "his house" on 1st July. "Own house" in these licences does not invariably stand for a dwelling-house; and there is every probability that either Mr. Manning's or Mr. Folkerd's "own house" was the venerable meeting-house of which we have pleasure in giving illustrations. It is possible, however, that the latter was built a little later, perhaps immediately after the Revolution. That the meeting-house was coeval with the "gathered church" is altogether unlikely ; before the Restoration there could be no reason for its erection.

Mr. Manning died in or before 1697. Eleven pastors followed him in regular succession, the last of whom, the Rev. R. A. Cliff, resigned in 1877. Since then the church has usually been associated under the same pastor either with Cratfield or Halesworth, each of which places is about two miles distant.

The people of Walpole, though few in number, are duly sensible of the historic interest that attaches to their venerable sanctuary ; which we may hope will long remain as a monument of the heroic days of East Anglian Nonconformity.

In the interior view notice will be taken of the sturdy mast by which the M shaped roof is supported, the curious pulley arrangement by which the hanging lamp is raised or lowered, the sounding-board over the pulpit, and the remarkable manner in which the window is set in the wall—the upper part inclining outwards.

WALPOLE MEETING-HOUSE : INTERIOR

Unpublished Doddridge Correspondence

OF the huge mass of Doddridge correspondence preserved in the library of New College, all that is of much historical or biographical value has already been printed, either in Dr. Stedman's volume, Shrewsbury 1790, or in the five volumes of *Doddridge's Correspondence and Diary*, edited by J. D. Humphreys, London, 1829. The six letters now for the first time printed seem all to be of considerable interest. Two of them, Nos. 2 and 3, are preserved by the Congregational church at Market Harborough, and were kindly lent for transcription by J. H. Clarke, Esq., J.P.; the others form a part of the valuable collection of autographs brought together by Sir John Bickerton Williams, and now in the Congregational Library.

(1)

DR. HENRY MILES to DR. DODDRIDGE.
TOOTING,
8th March 1738/9

REVD & DEAR SIR
I rec^d y^r kind L^r with pleasure on Saturday tho I confess it made me ashamd of myself to think that you might justly expected a line from me long ago, especially as I had obtained the promise of y^r endeav^{rs} to serve a poor Destitute Church in Glo^{r}shire. I did not neglect to acquaint them with y^r concern for y^m, but they were then (unknown to me) applying themselves to a young Gentleman lately settled in that County—and since Xtmas wrote me word they had prevailed on him to accept their call: at y^t time a report was Current in Town that you would be in London very shortly, wch I gave credit to, till I saw y^r last to Mr. Neal, which (glad as I shoud be to see you) I could not be dissatisfyd with, because of the difficulty of a journey under such circum-

stances of bad weather. I most thankfully acknowledge the encouragem.ts you have been pleased to give to that good design on foot for the relief of the distressed Wid : & orphans of the Min.rs of I. Xt. and y.r very kind offers to promote it further ; be pleased to make my acknowledge.mts to such friends as have been pleasd to send their contributions by y.r hands. I pray G. reward y.r & their work and labour of love with his best blessings—I paid the 12 Guineas to the Treasurer, Mr. Corbett, on Monday last, and desired it might be entered among other Benefactions as Money Coll: by you, among y.r ffriends in and ab.t Northamp.n. The sd Treasurer, and such of the Society as I have Communicated it to, acct themselves much obliged to you for the assistance you have been pleased to lend us, and will I doubt not be always ready to think of any case which shall be recommended by you—But the body of the Managers meet not till next month, being chose yesterday, after an affectionate sermon preached by M.r Wilson a Baptist Min.r the Coll: was 211.l, being 5.l more than last y.r : there have been above 50 New Subscribers last year amounting to abt 270.l there has been beside a benefaction of 300.l sent in by a private Gentleman. So that besides Distributing 400.l they were able to purchase 300.l more S. Sea Annuity Stock, of which if my memory fails me not they have as their Capital 3000 and fifty odd pounds—the round Sum I am sure I remember—thus G. has caused his grace to abound toward his serv.ts, that they might abound in this good work. Thanks be to him for this unexpected encouragem.t. It woud I am sure rejoyce you to see the chearfulness that sits on the Countenances of the Contributors and the Gentlemen who take the trouble of managing the affair upon 'em—nothing abates our pleasure, or gives any discouragem.t to this pious design, but the Conduct of Sev.ll of our leading min.rs in Town who have taken offence at some Circumstances of missmanage.mt. at the beginning, as they conceive, in M.r Chandler. I considerd the matter seriously with myself as far as I was acquainted with it before I preachd, and thôt myself warranted to give that short hint in my Sermon, which it seems has given offence too—I am very sorry to say it, and it concerns me much to think that any for whom I deservedly have the highest esteem, shoud think anything a sufficient reason to discourage a Work of this nature, confessed to be good in itself and very necessary in y.e Circumstances—however I have the Consolation to tell you that there are 6 min.rs new Subscribers.

I am very sensible the Cases you mention deserve regard, perhaps among the first—I will do my endeav.r y.t they shall (the first opportunity the Laws of the Society will admit of it) be considered. I perceive you are sensible they distribute not to any more than twice toge.r. I now add that no money is given to Children in any circumstance but with the View to place y.m out as apprentices—or to buy such Clothes who chuse to go into Service :

Any such you can recommend I may venture to promise you shall be immediately considered. the business of the day taking up much time yesterday, I coud not get you a Copy of the rules of the Society, but will speedily do it. I presume you already know that Subscribing one 5 Guineas qualifies a Person to be a member of the Society & to recommend an Object. I have got a few Sermons left if they woud be acceptable to any of your ffriends I woud convey you some by Mr Hett in y^r next parcel, or otherwise as you shall direct.

I am very sorry a mistake was committed this last year by some ffriend of Mrs King's of Oundle. I am not able to find out by what means it happend. I shoud have been informd who recommended her, and had I known where her ffriend [Mrs Wildboar (*in margin*)] lives in Town that gave her the missinformation, I woud have examind into it ; however I shall be obligd to inform Mr Goodrich with my affectionate service to him (when opportunity offers) that the Treasurer told me the money was given to her self —On casting my Eye on y^{rs} I woud add, lest what I have before sd. shoud not be explicit eno'—that Relief is given to Widows as such, whether heads of Families or not, and to Children male and ffemale for the intentions I mentioned before, only.

I have been under a necessity of making some alteration in my Study, and to take a Catal: of my Books, which and Sev^{ll} avocations have unavoidably restraind me from doing little more than casting my Eye here and there into the body of y^r Book, which has been no small uneasiness to me—I think y^r dedication to the Princess merits the thanks of every one that loves the Royal Family & the Protestant Interest, for the decent freedom you have taken in suggesting such good Counsel to her—which I hope she will not fail to read and Consider—it cannot offend, and I think it is admirably adapted to promote her usefulness and happiness.

The period beginning ab^t ye middle of the 6th page in y^r Preface I can never sufficiently admire—in those sentiments may I live and dye. I have more than once seen reason to make the same Remark you do of the great obscurity of Some modern Paraphrases on Some texts, and am ready to think that you particularly mean a passage or two in the Evangel. John—but permit me to mention for your encourage^{mt} that so far as I can learn the performance meets with very great and universal acceptance—With my thanks, and my hearty Prayers for your health and a large Measure of Divine light and influence to carry you thro' what remains. You have, I doubt not. those of many in Town and Country. Mention not Elsner or any other Book I am able to furnish you with, with any mañer of Concern, till you want 'em no longer I desire 'em not. Tho I could not tell how to think Philo had any such Passage as that you mention—I was willing to examine by the help of the Index, but was only confirmd in my Opinion, especially after I had lookd into Fabric. Bib. Graeca, who takes no notice of it—however, I wrote to Mr Lardner, but it unhappily fell out that he was then going to preach, which somew^t retarded his answer. I will give his own words. I believe there is no such thing in Philo. I reckon it to be a thing generally allowd that he has nowhere made any express mention of the Xtians. Some indeed suppose that what he relates of the Essenes or Therapeutae in Egypt belongs to ye Xtians of his time &c—But I cant at present recoll^t anything in this author like what you mention. Such a thing is mentioned by Just. Mart. Dial. cum Tryh. Jud. p. 234.235 Paris. 171. Thirlb. Is it possible that any one shoud have writ or read Phil. Jud. pr Tryph. Jud. ? So far he. I am not so happy as to have a Justin by me, and am sorry I did not receive the passage transcribed from Mr Lard: and I was afraid of delaying my Answer too long. He adds when you write to Dr Doddridge be pleased to present my service to him. I am obliged to him for the honb^{le} mention he has made of the Credibility &c in his notes upon his excellent Paraph: a good part of which I have read with a great deal of pleasure.

I had like to have forgot to tell you y^t Mr Neal has been in Bath ab^t a fortnight, is well, and ye waters agree well with him. I will not forget to procure for you a Philo the first opportunity, or to send you my own.—Mr Hett sent me your sermon at Wellingb^{ro}, for which I return you my very hearty thanks, tho he has not done me justice in the list of subscribers, as I subscribe for Seven Setts—it matters little, only I gave you my promise to do so. I shall very much rejoyce when the time comes you so kindly mention, of your spending a day with me at Tooting; nor do I speak my own sentim^t alone, but that of Mr Collyer & Family, who send you their Sincere Service and good wishes. If you shall have occasion to write to me ag^n relating to ye Passage or ab^t anything which may require a speedy reply I will endeav^r to write you (if possible) p ye 1st Post. I have great need to crave y^r Candor in excusing so tedious an Ep: which had been shorter and more to the purpose but that I have been frequently hindered since I began it—Be pleased dear Sir to number me among those who share in y^r earnest requests when before the throne of grace, and you will add to the many obligations with which I am

Y^r most affectionate tho' unworthy
bro^r & humble Servt
HENRY MILES.

[This letter is interesting as an early account of the "Society for Relief of the Widows and Orphans of Dissenting Ministers," founded 1733, and still continuing its beneficent operations under the name of "The Widows' Fund." Its grants at present average about £2,060 annually. Dr. Miles, F.R.S., was pastor at Tooting from 1731 until his death in 1763.]

(2)

DR. DODDRIDGE TO THE DEACONS AT MARKET HARBOROUGH.

To Mess⁽ʳˢ⁾ Bayes, Knee, Tayler, &c.

NORTHAMPTON,
Oct. 29th, 1740.

MY DEAR FRIENDS
  I have received your most affectionate & respectful Letter with that Regard which I owe to a Society of so great importance as Harborough, as well as to the particular personal Friendship which I do & ought to bear to the valuable persons by whom it was subscribed in the Name of the rest.

Your Invitation to Mr Orton was no Surprize to me; & I cannot but approve it as a very prudent Step; for I know no Man living more fit to repair the Loss you have sustained by the Removal of the great & good Mr. Some. And I am so sensible of the Importance of your Congregation that I do not & will not set my self directly to counteract & oppose you in your present Scheme, how contrary soever it may be to my own Inclination to part wth so excellent an assistant. I have just now told Mr Orton that I love [?, *paper torn*] him as a Brother, & perhaps more tenderly than Brethren by Nature commonly do; & that I most earnestly desire his Continuance wth me if he judge it consistent wth his Duty to Christ & to his Church; yet if on serious Deliberation & fervent Prayer for Divine assistance & Direction he judge it most subservient to his Comfort & usefulness in Life quickly to leave Northampton & undertake ye Stated Care of a People, there is no Situation in which I should so much desire to see him as that of your Minister.

Further than this I cannot go, because I really think and I am perswaded that you also know, it is not my personal Interest & Comfort alone, but the good of the Publick wh is concerned in the Supply of my Academy wth a person of Learning Prudence & Serious Piety, capable of presiding over it wth a becoming Influence in my Absence, & also furnished wth such popular Talents as might render him fit to Succeed me both as a Tutor & pastor if God should remove me. I cannot therefore think it justice to Mr Orton, to my Self, or to the Publick to urge Mr Orton to accept your Invitation, tho' I have weighed your Case with the Bowels of Compassion which present Circumstances require.

On the whole, Gentlemen, seeing the Weight and Difficulty of the Affair, I humbly refer it to Divine Providence, which I doubt not will shew a gracious Regard to your Concerns & mine, or to speak more properly to the Interests of Religion at Northampton & at Harbro'. I heartly pray that if the Glory of God & the good of the Church may be more effectually promoted by Mʳ Orton's Removal to you than by his Continuance wᵗʰ me, he may be so re[]oved, & I hope you will remember that it is yᵉ Counter part of your Duty to pray that if God see otherwise he may be continued.

More upon this tender Head I flatter my self you did not expect & will not desire from me. Be assured that if Mʳ Orton decline your Proposal you will have a part in my most affectionate Cares ; & I will never cease my Endeavours to serve you according to the best of my Capacity, till I shall, if God permit, see you comfortably settled, for I can truly say there is no Congregation now vacant in yᵉ whole Kingdom for which I feel so sensible a Concern.

As for your Request of giving you a Sermon next Thursday Sevnight, tho considering how near it is to the fifth of November there may be some Difficulty attending it, I purpose to comply with it if I can ; yet I must beg you would endeavour to secure a conditional Supply if bad Weather, Indisposition, or any unforeseen Accident should prevent me. In the mean time I commend you & your Interest to the tender Care of the Great Shepherd of Israel, with a Regard becoming

Gentlemen
Your very affectionate Friend
& obliged humble Servant
P. DODDRIDGE.

(*Address*) To Mʳ Bayes
in Market Harborough,
Leicestershire.

NOTE —Mr. Some, referred to above, had been pastor at Harborough since 1709, and died 27 May, 1737. He had been succeeded by a Mr. Toaker, of whom little is known. On 9th May, 1740, Mr. Isaac Wilkinson, one of Doddridge's students, was to have been ordained at Harborough; but this may have been for Kibworth, five miles distant, where we find him located. Mr. Orton did not accept the invitation of the church; which was still vacant in 1741, when an invitation was also declined by the Rev. S. Wood of Rendham, Suffolk.

(3)

REV. SAMUEL WOOD TO DR. DODDRIDGE.

PENDHAM,
Oct. 27 1741

MY DEAR DOCT. AND MUCH HONᴰ FFRIEND

I recᵈ yʳˢ and have diligently considered the Contents, and, upon the most earnest Seeking to God & impartial Enquiry into Circumstances, am obliged to think it my Duty not to remove, at present, from Sweffling ; I own, dr Sʳ sincerely, it has cost me no small Uneasiness to come to this Determinatⁿ ; for tho' I'm conscious of my Unfitness for any such publick Service as Harborough, my ffears on this Head were greatly overbalanced by the

Thots of being placed so near that d.r Gentleman, whose Company & Convérst.n J value beyond any Ones in the World ; A Situat.n so near Northampton, S.r, I assure you, gave the Affair so pleasant an Aspect, that it was w.th much struggle and Difficulty my Judgm.t prevailed over Inclinat.n, and indeed to say the Truth its with sensible Reluctance, at last, that I sacrifice this sweet Circumstance, tho' my Duty now seems plain and pointing ; this unwillingness to w.t app.rs my Duty, I know, S.r, w.d be my ffault in any other Case, but where there was so fair a Prospect for my Improv.t and Pleasure, as, I'm sure there is, in the Society of my dr. D.r Doddridge, I can't but be much affected w.th the Loss, and must be very stupid to find it otherwise. However, d.r S.r upon the most mature & serious Attention that I've been capable of giving this important Affair, it app.rs that I ought not yet to leave my People, and for these I think material and governing Reasons ; I have Peace here, and the hearty affect.n of my People ; the Situat.n is made as pleasant as my Wife's Relat.ns, my surrounding Acquaintance, & the love of my Hearers can render it ; but w.t is more than all (and w.t has been the chief Motive w.th me to form my present Resolution) is, that tho' our Number is very small, the Ministry has been very remarkably succeeded since my being here, and, by the Blessing of God, the Work is still going on, so that tho' we have been much fewer in Number, we are confessed to have had much more apparent Success, than any of our Neighbouring Congrega.tns ; besides, such is the present Posture of our Affairs, that my Removing just now w.d cause several ffamilies to desert and attend in another Place, w.ch w.d certainly very much injure, if not ruin, the Interest here, to all w.ch I might add that (insignificant as I am) my ffriends w.d be willing I sh.d think that my Continuance here is necessary not only for the sake of Religion among my own People but for the Service of some others in the Neighbourhood, for it was only last Satturday Evening that I rec.d two very pressing Letters from diff.t Congreg.tns, signed by several of the leading people, solliciting my Stay at Sweffling, and indeed w.th such argm.ts, w.ch, tho' I care not to mention, yet if true ought to determine my Conduct in this Case. on Lords Day I had others y.t personally importuned me w.th argum.ts of the like kind, tho' I tho't y.e Affair had hardly been at all known (?) abroad, for I had communicated it only to 3 or else 4 of my own People. These Th.gs I mention d.r S.r, to give you to understand that I took the Case into very close Considera.tn and sh.d not have been perswaded to have withstood y.r kind Sollicitat.ns & my own Inclinat.ns but upon the ffullest Evidence & Convict.n of Duty. The Motives abovementioned (w.ch I believe y.or Self will not condemn or think impotent) were, if I know my Heart, the very Reasons that overul'd in this Affair and dictated Sufficiently w.t I ought to do.

I thank you, dr Doct.ʳ, for yo.ʳ too kind Tho'ts & Care for me ; how glad, sincerely glad, sh.ᵈ I be to see you ; the Tho'ts of You in this Affair have given me more Pain than I can express ; Please, S.ʳ, to render my affectionate Wishes for Harborough acceptab[le to] my good ffriends there ; I'm satisfied they'l be much better supplied than by me, while D.ʳ Dodd.ʳ is so so kind as to negotiate for them ; it gives me a singular Satisfact.ⁿ to think they have so able a ffriend. [*a whole line obliterated.*] I'm in no great Pain for their future Welfare.

We often speak of you, d.ʳ S.ʳ, and pray for you. I hope it was a singular good Providence to all these parts that directed yo.ʳ last Circuit, for as I'm sure many, both Ministers & people, were much affected w.ᵗʰ y.ʳ Lab.ʳˢ at Denton Publick & private, and speak often of them w.ᵗʰ y.ᵉ utmost Marks of Esteem & Thankfulness, so I have the Pleasure to assure you y.ᵗ w.ᵗ you offer'd at that Time has been a happy means to revive religion & produce a laudable zeal in Several Congregat.ⁿˢ w.ᶜʰ I c.ᵈ name ; I'm sure this will be highly pleasing to you if you have not heard it before ; I tho't to have wrote to you very shortly to have informed you of it, if I had not rec.ᵈ y.ʳ Letter. This I hope, d.ʳ S.ʳ will be an Encouragem.ᵗ to y.ʳ Triennial Visitat.ⁿ, w.ᶜʰ you have been so good as to encourage us to hope for, & w.ᶜʰ we think & speak of w.ᵗʰ great Satisfact.ⁿ. Yo.ʳ kind Wishes, d.ʳ S.ʳ for my Welfare I retalliate w.ᵗʰ prayers equally fervent for y.ʳˢ. You, d.ʳ S.ʳ, are in my warmest wishes every day ; I'm sure I love you, I value you and hon.ʳ you. I think of you w.ᵗʰ Pleasure, and think I can't better improve my Interest at the Throne of Grace than by a daily Sollicit.ˢ for the Continuance of a Life so reputable, so singularly useful, and on w.ᶜʰ the Hopes of the dissenting Interest so much depend. I wish you, d.ʳ S.ʳ, all possible pleasure & Success from yo.ʳ Young Gentlemen, and in every Branch of yo.ʳ great work. My wife (yo.ʳ particular ffriend) and I join in hearty Respects to Self & Lady and all yo.ʳ dear little ones ; we often speak of M.ʳ Parminter as a very desireable & excellent Young Gentleman, & send our kind Service. My little girl has often lisp'd y.ᵗ dear name & sends her duty ; we have had two meet.ᵍˢ since y.ᵗ at Denton, one at Yarmouth where M.ʳ Scott sen.ʳ preach.ᵈ, y.ᵉ other at Beccles where my Uncle preach'ᵈ ; Miss Scott has been so kind as to write me out her ffather's Sermon ; at Each place we had a good number of Ministers. I've not seen Mr. Badley since I rec.ᵈ y.ʳˢ, but am sure he loves you and w.ᵈ be glad I sh.ᵈ send his Service. I'll take Care ab.ᵗ all the other particulars of yo.ʳ Letter. Might I be so happy at any Time to be favour'd with One Line w.ⁿ d.ʳ Dodd.ʳ has a vacant Moment. Let me hope for y.ʳ Remembrance, & be asured, d.ʳ S.ʳ, that tho' among y.ʳ correspondents you have none less worthy, Ile venture to say there is no one that loves and hon.ʳˢ you more truly than yo.ʳ most obe.ᵈᵗ [*illegible*] SAMUEL WOOD.

I suppose you have heard of the death of that Pious and excellent

Lady Mrs Burward of Bury. Captn Kell, Miss Kell's ffather, at whose House Mr Parminter was at Woodbridge, dyed at London last week.

<small>The Rev. S. Wood, son of a minister of the same name at Lavenham, was pastor at Sweffling from June 1733 to 1747. (Sweffling and Rendham are adjacent villages, divided only by a stream). He removed to Norwich, as successor to the Rev. T. Scott at the Old Meeting, received a diploma of D.D. from one of the Scottish universities, and died 2nd November, 1767. (See Brown's *History of Congregationalism in Norfolk and Suffolk*).</small>

(4)

REV. JOHN BARKER TO DR DODDRIDGE.

DEAR AND REV^D SIR,

I had y^r Letter att Mr Jacksons, and what I have to say to it is this : You, Good and Good natured Man, are very apt to thinke well of every body ; what You believe of Me I know I do not deserve, I am sure is not true, & it is a Great Reason ag'st my consenting to y^r Request that you really think too well of me & will be apt to speake too much in my praise : otherwise I am not only Content, but should be pleas'd the world should know I am y^r Freind & that I love & assisted Mr Steffe.

Mr Clark I know & honour ; He is a judicious Man, & a Good Scholar, & were he a lively preacher he would be as acceptable as he is valuable. There is a vacancy in London by the death of Mr Wood, but I imagine it will be filled up by Mr Langford.

Your Meetings of Ministers are very entertaining as well as instructive, but I am not able to attend with you on those occasions, but only please myselfe with thinking & talking of doing so. I rejoice in all your prosperity usefullness and comfort, & heartily recommend you to Gods Blessing.

Mrs Doddridge being better increases my joy. I have had the opportunity of assisting Mr. Hunt 3 Lord's Days successively—I suppose He returns this Weeke.

My hearty love attend all my Brethren, & I send the most particular Respects to you

being yrs faithfully & affectionately

May 24, 1742.   J. BARKER.

(*Superscription*)   "To The Revd Dr Doddridge
att
Northampton."

(5)

JOSEPH WILLIAMS TO DR DODDRIDGE.

KIDDER^M

10th Octo^r 1743

REV^D & GREATLY HON^D SIR

Mr Crane related to me ye Conversation he had wth you, & I doubt not you are willing to know what we have been doing.

Mr Crane, at his return, set himself, somewhat unfairly, to oppose & beat down Mr Halford's Interest among us, wch was very strong, just as strong as Mr Adams's had been, & earnestly to recommend Dr Steward; upon whose Character, & ye expected Good Fruits of his settling wth us, he flourished wth an unbounded Profusion of what Rhetorick he is master of. And this he did, as I apprehend, not so much from a Dislike to ye former, as from a fond attachment to ye latter above all other min^{rs} in Engl^d, joined wth a prevailing Fear of a Division in case ye former sh^d settle wth us. Four Days he laboured earnestly, & in vain, to shake our attachment to Mr Halford; but on Friday ye 23^d past, thro' ye Advice & Persuasion of a very Good Friend, Mr. Simon Reader of Bedworth, finding y^t Mr Crane had Gained ye Adverse Party, & apprehending yt they would not fail to take Occasion from our Refusal to unite wth them in inviting a man so unquestionably Orthodox, to load us wth Reproaches, & charge to our account all ye bad Consequences of a Separation, Mr Symonds first inclined, & thro' his Persuasion added to all ye former I was prevailed on to try ye Expedient, & this we the rather complied wth, in hopes y^t on ye one Hand ye Drs. settling wth us would probably preserve ye Union, & promote ye Prosperity of our Church, so on ye other hand if ye Providence of God should any way prevent his Coming, this our Compliance might be of use to facilitate Mr Halford's access to us: for Mr Crane promises, in that Case, to join his own Edeavours with ours to procure for him a fair and candid Hearing: & Mr Reader advises us to stick at no Difficulty, nor regard any Opposition, w^h may then be laid in his way. And we ye rather acceded to it from an uncertainty whether Mr Halford did incline to us or not, wch seemed dubious, nor had he given us so much Ground to expect him as we hoped he would have done.

Accordingly on ye 24th I wrote to Mr Halford, & having assured him y^t he had not lost one Friend in Kidderm^r, & largely explained to him ye Reasons of our Conduct both toward him & toward ye D^r., I beg'd of him to defer his Answer to our repeated Invitation till he should hear further from us. On ye 26th we kept a Day of publick Prayer for Direction, & on ye 28th an Invitation to the Pastorship was sent to ye D^r signed by our whole Church, scarce one refusing, tho' indeed it was wth great Reluctance y^t many came into it from ye Great Regard they have for Mr Halford: and now we are waiting ye Determination of Providence.

[What follows is a lengthy narrative of an accident, and reflections thereon. About 14 months previously the writer had sustained a fractured skull, through the collapse of an old building; but had at length been restored to health.]

Your Goodness and Friendliness will excuse this long Detail of ye Circumstances of an Accident so long past, & rejoice wth me in ye joy wch far more than compensated for all ye Grief it occasioned:

a Joy built on a Foundation wch will never fail. I thank you for recommending to me Mr Clark's Nature and Causes of Irresolution in Religion. Be pleased to commend me wth Great Respect to Mrs Doddridge, & to all my Young Friends. I beg ye Continuance of your Prayers for our yet unsettled & destitute Church, & in particular for

Dr Sir, Y^r much obliged and
Most obed. Servant for Jesus Sake
Jos. Williams.

(*Superscription*)   To
The Rev. Dr Doddridge
in
Northampton.

Note —The pulpit of the Old Meeting at Kidderminster was vacant from the death of Matt. Bradshaw, November, 1742, till the coming of Benj. Fawcett, one of Doddridge's students, in August, 1744. Meanwhile there was much dissension "Mr. Halford" was presumably the minister in Back Lane, Horsleydown; of Dr. Steward we have no information.

(6)

The Countess of Huntingdon to DR Doddridge.

My most excellent Friend

    Since my last to you I have received a letter from my beloved Dutchess of Somerset, who thus writes in speaking of you —" I should be very glad to see any Sermon of Doctor Doddridges, and should look upon a letter from him as an honour provided he will write to me as a person who wants both Instruction & reproof, but not as one who has attained any share of that Christian piety & Self Denial without which all pretentions to the name of a Disciple is vain."—I could not satisfie myself till I had sent it, as it will not only Incourage you to write to her but show you in a degree to how amiable and Humble a disposition You have to address. I pray God improve this Friendship to you both, & I shall think myself of <u>some use</u>, since I have only now to lament my Great unprofitableness. My kindest respects to Mrs Doddridge and the Young Gentlemen who were with You hear, & to Mr Jones who I shall be—well extreme Glad to see whenever he has an opertunity of Comeing my way. You have, you ever will have, my prayers, poor and bad as they are, alass! You do not want them, your lively & active heart is ever soaring toward heaven from whence you look with transport for the Lord Jesus. O may he for ever rejoice in You that you you (*sic*) may delight Yourself eternally in him ; & may the last trumpet sound 'Arise, my Love, my fair one, Come away': this may we hear, & till then, love, watch, pray to (?) endure till every Cloud vanishes before us. We are now Confessing him, he will then Confess us, & all sorrows will be lost in endless day : bright Morn, O hail thou bless'd thou transporting thought, thou [*illegible*]   Glorious & Celestial world fraught with all Joy God has to bestow on Creatures so redeemed. Farewell, I am running beyond time, too fast, my friend ; forgive, and live assured of a most unworthy but best meaning affection of your sincere friend

S. HUNTINGDON.

(*Superscription*)   To
The Revd Docter
Doddridge at his
House In
Northampton.
The Care of the Postmaster
at Northampton.

[Undated · endorsed in Doddridge's hand "Countess of Huntingdon," with a note in shorthand. Probably written not long before 15th September, 1750, which is the date of the earliest known letter of the Duchess of Somerset to Doddridge. The Duchess is the "Hartford" complimented at the beginning of Thomson's *Seasons*.]

Surrey Congregational History

FORTY-TWO years ago the late Rev. John Waddington, D.D., published an interesting and instructive volume with the above title. There were then about seventy Congregational churches and preaching-places in the county, nine or ten of which have since disappeared; but, notwithstanding this loss, the present number stands at one hundred and forty. Three or four years ago the executive of the Surrey Congregational Union thought it desirable that Dr. Waddington's book, which had long been out of print, should be re-edited and brought up to date. The task was undertaken by the Rev. E. Cleal of Mortlake; but he soon found that a mere *rifaccimento* of Waddington's history would not meet the necessities of the case. Not only had the number of churches in the county doubled; the Congregational ideal had enlarged, and the isolated independency of former times was seen to be no longer a thing to be gloried in. Besides this, many facts had come to light relating to early nonconformity in the Metropolitan area, and Dr. Waddington was found to have been seriously mistaken on several points. Mr. Cleal therefore found it necessary to undertake an entirely new work; and the result is before the public in a handsome illustrated volume entitled *The Story of Congregationalism in Surrey*. Of the literary character of the book it would be unbecoming to say anything; because the failure of Mr. Cleal's health necessitated editorial assistance, which was afforded by the Secretary of the Congregational Historical Society. But to Mr. Cleal is due the credit of a diligent and laborious collection of facts from a great variety of sources, and the bringing together for the first time of a fairly complete record of Congregational church life and work in the county. Indeed, so far as our knowledge extends nothing of importance has been omitted except the story of a few isolated congregations, mostly extinct, in which hyper-Calvinistic or Huntingtonian teaching prevailed, and which have left no permanent mark on the religious life of the community.

There are given by way of appendix lists of the ejected ministers of the county, the conventicles reported by Sheldon's emissaries in 1669, the licences issued under the Indulgence in 1672, the Nonconformist meetings enumerated in Evans's MS. of 1718-28, and the registers of Surrey Congregational churches in the custody of the Registrar General. It is convenient to have these together at hand, though most of the lists were separately accessible without much difficulty. But a *full list* of the Surrey licences under the Indulgence had not, we believe, been formerly printed. We have therefore obtained permission from the executive of the Surrey Union to reproduce this list; and also the map which exhibits all the most important Nonconformist sites in the county—from which however it was necessary to omit the licensed meetings in Southwark to avoid overcrowding.

LICENCES GRANTED IN SURREY UNDER THE INDULGENCE, 1672

(O.H.—Own House)

BATTERSEA. Thomas "Harrockes," M.A.,*Presb.*, O.H. 20 April.
  „   Thomas Pace, *Presb.*, O.H. and General 22 April.
BLETCHINGLEY James Parkins, *Presb.*, Genl. 22 May.
  „   House of John Buttery, *Presb.* 22 May.

William Burnett, *Presb.*, H. of William Longhurst	9 May.
Arthur Squibb, *Bapt.*, O.H.	28 Oct.
Thomas Lye, *Presb.*, O.H. [this licence was applied for 5 times]	30 April.
Dr. Henry Wilkinson, *Presb.*, O.H. or Schoolhouse	25 May.
William Hughes, *Presb.*, O.H.	30 Sept.
House of James Towers, *Presb.*	29 May.
Francis Smith, *Bapt.*, "a room formerly a Malthouse"	20 April.
Edward Baker, *Congl.*, H. of Nathaniel Read	25 July.
House of John Worrell, *Presb.*	28 Oct.
John Wood, O.H.	11 April.
James Fisher, *Congl.*, O.H.	1 May.
Thomas Strickland, *Bapt.*, H. of Wm. Wilkinson	28 Oct.
J. Wheeler, *Bapt.*, H. of Edward Billinghurst	18 Nov.
James Prince, *Presb.*, H. of Richard Whithall	15 June.
John Faroll, *Presb.*, H. of Richard Collier	15 June.
House of William Bicknoll, *Presb.*	(30 Sept / 11 Nov)
Richard Bures, *Presb.*, O.H. and General	(30 April / 18 Nov)
Noah Webb, *Presb.*, O.H. and General	(30 April / 11 Nov)
John Bernard, *Bapt.*, H. of Richard Humphrey	9 May.
House of George Bridges, *Presb.*	29 May.
John Manship, *Presb.*, O.H.	25 May.
House of Thomas Bradford, *Presb.*	29 May.
William Simons, *Presb.*, General	2 April.
House of Mr. Piccard, *Presb.*	2 April.
Richard Mayo, *Presb.*, H. of John Pigot	13 April.
(Kennington) Charles Morton, *Presb.*, O.H.	11 April.
,, Christopher Fowler, *Presb.*, O.H. and General	25 May.
David Clarkson, B.D., *Presb. and Congl.*, H. of John Beamish	30 April.
Robert Fisher, O.H. in Stone Street	
House of Richard Margesson in Stone Street, *Presb.*	1 May.
House of Thos. Stone, *Presb.*	3 Feb. /73
Samuel Wickham, *Presb.*, General	30 April.

some cases, seems to indicate a second licence issued because of some rst. One date has been inadvertently overlooked.

SOUTHWARK*	William Whitaker, *Presb.*, H. in Court Yard, Bermondsey	2 April.
	Andrew Parsons, *Presb.*, O.H. in Deadman's Place and General	2 April.
	Nathaniel Vincent, *Presb.*, O.H. in Farthing Alley, St. Olave	2 April.
	William Carslake, *Presb.*, General	11 April.
	Thomas Kentish, *Presb.*, General	11 April.
	James Janeway, *Presb.*, O.H. in Salisbury Street, Rotherhithe	11 April.
	John Chester, *Presb.*, O.H. in Maid Lane	13 April.
	House of Richard Hill in Winchester Street, *Congl.*	1 May.
	Jeremiah Baines, Horsley Down, *Presb.*, General	2 May.
	Stephen More, *Indept.*, H. of Barnabas Bloxom, Winchester Yard	4 May.
	House of Humphrey Aldersley, St. Olave's, *Presb.*	13 May.
	John Luffe, of St. Mary's Parish, Bermondsey, *Presb.*, General	16 May.
,,	House of George Ewers, *Presb.*	22 May.
,,	John Peachye, *Presb.*, General	22 May.
,,	James Jones, *Bapt.*, O.H.	30 Sept.
,,	House of James Walker, *Congl.*	30 Sept.
WALTON-ON-THAMES	House of John Daberon, *Presb.*	16 May.

---

*See note on the map.

SOUTHWARK*	William Whitaker, *Presb.*, H. in Court Yard, Bermondsey	2 April.
	Andrew Parsons, *Presb.*, O.H. in Deadman's Place and General	2 April.
	Nathaniel Vincent, *Presb.*, O.H. in Farthing Alley, St. Olave	2 April.
	William Carslake, *Presb.*, General	11 April.
	Thomas Kentish, *Presb.*, General	11 April.
	James Janeway, *Presb.*, O.H. in Salisbury Street, Rotherhithe	11 April.
	John Chester, *Presb.*, O.H. in Maid Lane	13 April.
	House of Richard Hill in Winchester Street, *Congl.*	1 May.
	Jeremiah Baines, Horsley Down, *Presb.*, General	2 May.
	Stephen More, *Indept.*, H. of Barnabas Bloxom, Winchester Yard	4 May.
	House of Humphrey Aldersley, St. Olave's, *Presb.*	13 May.
	John Luffe, of St. Mary's Parish, Bermondsey, *Presb.*, General	16 May.
	House of George Ewers, *Presb.*	22 May.
,,	John Peachye, *Presb.*, General	22 May.
,,	James Jones, *Bapt.*, O.H.	30 Sept.
,,	House of James Walker, *Congl.*	30 Sept.
WALTON-ON-THAMES	House of John Daberon, *Presb.*	16 May.

*See note on the map.

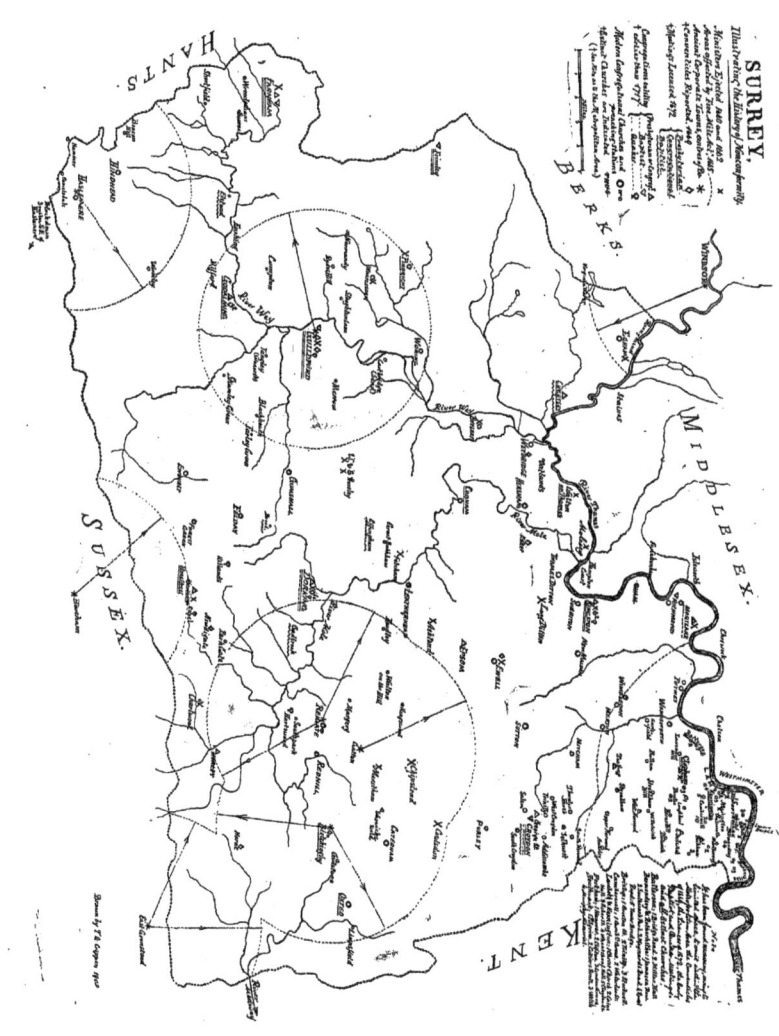

334

List of Members

Hon. Members marked *H*, Life Members marked *L*.

Adeney, W. F., Rev. Prof., M.A., D.D.
Andover (U.S.A.) Theological Seminary
Andrews, William, Esq.
Ashworth, W., Esq.
Astbury, F. T., Rev.
Atkinson, S. B., Esq., M.A., M.B.
Avery, John, Esq., F.S.S.
Baptist Union, The
Barrett, Geo., Rev., A.T.S.
Bartlet, J. V., Rev. Prof., M.A., D.D.
Basden, D. F., Esq.
Bate, Frank, Rev., M.A.
Bax, A. Ridley, Esq.
Beaumont, E., Esq.
Bell, J. Barton, Rev.
Boag, G. W., Esq.
Bragg, A. W., Esq.
Brown, J., Rev. Dr., B.A.
Brown, W. H., Esq.
Brownen, G., Esq.
Burrage, Champlin, Esq.
Carter, W. L., Rev., M.A.
Cater, F. Ives, Rev., A.T.S.
Chevalier, J., M.
Clapham, J. A., Esq.
Clark, J. H., Esq., J.P.
Clarkson, W. F., Rev., B.A.
Claydon, George S., Esq.
Cocks, J., Esq.
Congregational Library, Boston, Mass.
Crippen, T. G., Rev.
Dale, A. W. W., Esq., M.A.
Davies, J. Alden, Rev.
Davis, C. H., Rev.
Davis, J. E., Esq.
Davy, A. J., Esq.
Dawson, E. B., Esq.
Didcote, C. Page, Esq.
Dimelow, J. G., Esq.
Dixon, H. N., Esq., M.A., F.L.S.
Dixon, R. W., Esq.
Dore, S. L., Esq., J.P.
Ebbs, A. B., Esq.

Gordon, A., Principal
Gosling, Howard, Esq.
Green, Joseph J., Esq.
Green, T., Esq.
Grice, T. E., Esq.
Grieve, A. J., Rev., M.A., B.D.
Groser, W. H., Esq., B.Sc.
Hall, C. W., Rev.
Hall, W. H., Esq.
Harris, W. J., Esq.
Harrison, G. W., Esq.
Harwood, W. Hardy, Rev.
Hawkins, F. H., Esq., LL.B.
Henderson, A. D., Esq.
Hepworth, Frank N., Esq.
Hepworth, J., Esq.
Hepworth, T. M., Esq.
Heslop, R. Oliver, Esq., M.A., F.S.A.
Hewgill, W., Rev., M.A.
Hitchcock, W. M., Esq.
Hodgett, C. M., Esq.
Holt, Edwyn, Esq.
L Hounsom, W. A., Esq., J.P.
Huckle, Attwood, Esq.
Iliff, John S., Esq.
Jackson, S., Esq.
James, Norman G. B., Esq.
H Johnston, W., Esq.
Jones, A. G., Esq.
Keep, H. F., Esq.
Key, James, Rev.
King, Jos., Esq., M.A.
H Lancashire Independent College (Goodyear, C., Esq)
Lawrence, Eric A., Rev.
Lester, E. R., Esq.
Lewis, D. Morgan, Prof., M.A.
Lewis, Geo. G., Esq.
Lewis, H. Elvet, Rev., M.A.
Lewys-Lloyd, E., Esq.
Linell, W. H., Esq.
Lovatt, J., Esq.
Low, G. D., Rev., M.A.
Macfadyen, D., Rev., M.A.

List of Members (continued)

Nightingale, B., Rev.
H Palmer, C. Ray, Rev. Dr.
Palmer, W. M., Esq.
Parnaby, H., Rev., M.A.
Phillips, Maberley, Esq., F.S.A.
Pierce, W., Rev.
Pitt, Walter, Mrs.
Powicke, F. J., Rev., Ph.D.
Poynter, J. J., Rev.
Pugh, Mrs.
Rawcliffe, Edwin B., Rev.
Reed, E. P. S., Esq.
Rees, J. Machreth, Rev.
Richards, D. M., Esq.
Ritchie, D. L., Rev.
Robinson, W., Rev.
Rollason, Arthur A., Esq.
Rudge, C., Rev.
H Rylands, Mrs., D.Litt.
Scamell, J., Esq.
Sell, W., Esq.
Serle, S., Esq.
Shaw, H., Rev.
Silcock, P. Howard, Esq., B.A.
Simon, D. W., Rev., D.D.
Smith, Norman H., Rev.
H Smith, W. J., Esq., M.A.
Smyrk, C. Watt, Rev.
H Spicer, Albert, Sir, Bart., M P.
H Spicer, George, Esq., M.A., J.P.
Standerwick, J. W., Esq.
Stanier, W. H., Esq.
Sutton, C. W., Esq.

Sykes, A. W., Esq.
H Thacker, Fred. S., Esq.
Thacker, Henry, Esq.
Thomas, D. Lleufer, Esq.
Thomas, Sir John
Thomas, Wm., Rev.
H Thompson, J., Esq.
Thorpe, F. H., Esq.
Titchmarsh, E. H., Rev., M.A.
H Toms, C. W., Esq.
Turner, G. Lyon, Rev., M.A.
Tyson, R. G., Esq.
U.S.A. Congress Library.
Wallis, R. B., Esq., J.P.
Walmsby, L. S., Esq.
Watkinson, J., Esq.
H Webster, Isaac., Esq.
L Whitley, A. W., Esq.
Whitley, W. T., Rev., LL.D.
Wicks, G. H., Esq.
H Wilkinson, W., Esq
Williams's Library.
Williams, Mrs.
Williamson, David, Esq., J P.
Williamson, David, jr., Esq.
Wilson, T., Esq.
Windeatt, E., Esq.
Wing, Lewis, Esq.
Winterstoke, The Rt. Hon. Lord
Wontner, A. J., Esq.
Wood, Leonard B., Esq., M.A
Woodall, H. J., Esq.
Young, Hugh P., Rev.

Congregational Historical Society

Transactions

Vol. III., No. 6] [OCTOBER, 1908

Contents

Editorial - - - - - - -	334
The Episcopal Returns of 1665-6 - - -	339
G. Lyon Turner, M.A.	
The Oldest Chapel in Wales - - - -	354
Broadway Meeting, Somerset - - - -	357
J. W. Standerwick	
London Conventicles in 1683 - - - -	364
The Pastoral Letters of Thomas Maidwell - -	367
John Penry in Scotland - - - - -	379
William Pierce	
Early Nonconformist Academies, II ; Sheriff Hales	387
List of Members - - - - - -	399

Can be obtained direct from the Book Saloon, Congregational Union of England and Wales, Inc., Memorial Hall, London, E.C.

Printed for the Society by
Fred. S. Thacker: 3 Dyers' Buildings, Holborn, London, E.C.

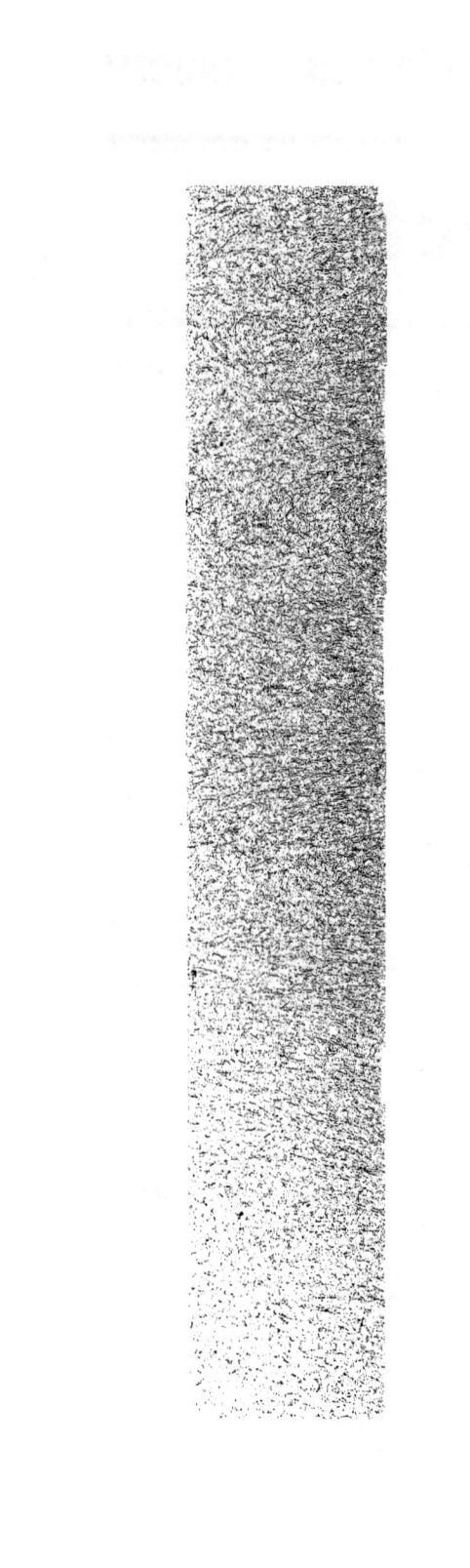

THE usual Autumnal Meeting of the Congregational Historical Society will be held in connection with the meetings of the Congregational Union at Liverpool, on Wednesday 21st October, at 4.30 p.m., in the Common Hall, Hackins Hey. A paper will be contributed by G. W. Boag, Esq., of Gateshead, on *Early Congregationalism in Northumberland and Durham.*

* *

We have unusual pleasure in announcing the speedy issue by Messrs. Constable of a work of national importance, which our esteemed contributor the Rev. W. Pierce has had for several years in preparation. It is entitled *An Historical Introduction to the Marprelate Tracts; a chapter in the Evolution of English Liberty, Civil and Religious.* It will be a demy 8vo. volume of about 400 pp.; and is expected to be ready before the end of October. Mr. Pierce has aimed at setting in order the chaos of information which is available about these celebrated satires, and defending their authors against the persistent vilification which has been customary among writers of all sects and parties. His position is that the Marprelate controversy was the summation of all the ecclesiastical conflicts from the accession of Elizabeth onward. There was practically no controversy of a doctrinal or ecclesiastical character between the Roman and Anglican churches at that time; no one, Conformist or Nonconformist, dreamed of a possible eirenicon with Rome; to every Protestant, whether Puritan or prelatist, the pope was merely Antichrist. The crucial question was: How far was the doctrine, in which all Protestants agreed, imperilled by the retention of traditional forms and usages?

Mr. Pierce has elucidated many doubtful points, and brought to light some important evidence that is now printed for the first time. We earnestly hope that the book will attain such a circulation as its historical importance deserves; and as will encourage the author to follow it with an annotated edition of the much talked of but little known tracts, and thus supply a literary need which has long been clamant.

* *

In *Transactions*, vol. iii, pp. 151-2, mention was made of certain Doddridge relics the whereabouts of which was then unknown. We are informed that the German Bible with remarkable historical associations is the property of Elliot Reed, Esq., of Hampstead, and the old trunk is, or was a few weeks ago, in the hands of Messrs. W. Williamson & Sons, Guildford.

* *

We are not accustomed to occupy our pages with a chronicle of current events; but the death of the venerable Thomas Lord in the hundred and first year of his age and seventy fifth of his ministry is, we believe, a thing unique in the annals of Congregationalism. Mr. Lord was born amidst humble surroundings at Olney, Bucks, on 22nd April, 1808. In his youth he worked as a shoemaker, and was almost entirely self educated. In early manhood he became an ardent advocate of temperance, and was enrolled among the then despised teetotallers. In 1834 he was called to the pastorate of a small church at Wollaston, Northants, which he served efficiently for eleven years. He afterwards ministered for 17 years at Brigstock, 4 years at Horncastle, 6 years at Deddington, and 5 years at West Bromwich (Great Bridge), whence he retired at the age of 70. He was three times married, celebrating a golden wedding with his second wife; but was a widower at the time of his death. During his later years he lived with his daughter at Horncastle; and notwithstanding the failure of his sight he constantly served churches of various denominations, often at a considerable distance from home, until within a few days of his death. On his hundredth birthday he received a sheaf of congratulatory telegrams, including one from the King and one from the Congregational Union. His last sermons were preached in the Congregational church at Horncastle on Sunday, 9th August; the following Sunday he was taken ill, and died on Friday the 21st. His preaching was always of a practical character, strongly evangelical in tone, and latterly tinged with regret that "the good old word repentance seemed to have gone out of fashion."

* *

We would earnestly request our friends to use what personal influence they possess to increase our number of members. There is much research work needed, numerous records that ought to be printed, and several important treatises of the sixteenth and early seventeenth centuries that urgently need reprinting; but it is impossible for us even to think of such undertakings with our present limited resources. Browne's *Book that Sheweth &c.*, Penry's *Korah, Dathan and Abiram*, Peters's *Good Work for a Good Magistrate*, and several of the early Cavalier lampoons against the Independents, may be taken as specimens of the work that might be put in hand if our membership were doubled.

* *

We respectfully remind members of the Society that subscriptions are due at the beginning of the year. In future no current year subscriptions can be cancelled after the first issue of *Transactions* has been forwarded.

The Episcopal Returns of 1665-6

IT has long been known that the Conventicle Returns of 1669 are preserved at Lambeth, being contained in vol. 639 of the MSS. department—one of the 250 vols. of the Tenison collection. They have been frequently consulted, and numerous extracts of local interest have been printed; but they have never been published as a whole. Having understood from the highest authorities that they had never even been completely transcribed, and believing that a complete transcript would be an invaluable aid to students of Nonconformist history, I undertook the task. But in executing it I found that the volume contained two other sets of documents of great value, which I also transcribed; one being the Returns given herewith, and the other some interesting schedules of statistics as to the relative formists: while for some unknown reason the Bishop of St. Asaph's gives as his first item "Ordinations" instead of "Hospitals and Almshouses." It would be interesting to know why he departed in this particular from the archbishop's directions: to the historian of the Episcopal Church in Wales, Asaph's list of ordinations must be of great interest. Whether these returns only were sent to Lambeth, or whether the rest were lost or destroyed through neglect, we cannot tell. But such as they are their historic interest is very great, giving as they do a first hand report of the whereabouts and circumstances of the nonconforming clergy only three years after their ejectment in 1662, and furnishing authentic information as to their attitude towards the ecclesiastical and political authorities of the day. They thus enable us to confirm, supplement, or correct the account given by Calamy of the earlier part of their career as Nonconformists. On this topic I propose to treat at some length in the next issue of the *Transactions*.

I have transcribed the whole of the documents contained in the Lambeth MS. 639, so far as they relate to Nonconformity; as well as the Licence Documents of 1672, and the State Papers relating to Nonconformity during the first decade or so of its existence. All these I hope some day to publish.

G. LYON TURNER.

I. In Diocese of ST. ASAPH.
pp. of MS.
    Return in 1665—of Ordinations, Pluralists, Lecturers,
300-303b Schoolmasters, Physicians, & Nonconformists.
 303b 6. Nonconformists and Ejected Min^{rs}
    None such in this Diocese.
    Per R^{dum} Prēm ac D^{num} Georgīum Asapheñ. Epūm. sub Chirographo proprio. Cum lris missivis 1665

EXETER Diocese

Schoolmasters.

on]
:PFORD[1]. John Drake teaches Schoole unlicensed
MPTON MORRICE[2]. A Private Schoole taught by John W^{ms} who also preacheth there not-conformable and unlicensed.
:TMOUTH. Edwd Manning, Wm Ball, teach English schooles But neither Licensed nor well-affected.
RY POMEROY. Dan Upton teaches youth Not licensed & Excommunicate.
:UM[3]. Margaret Underdon & Wm Coule, unlicensed.
ISTOCK. Mary Mollins and Lauercomb, both un-licensed.
NBRIDGE. Wm Lea, not licensed.
STLEIGH. Eliz. Loueman, not licensed & excommunicate.
rnwall].
NERY OF WEST. There are also severall women teachers in St. Martin's, Eastlow, Pelicit, and Likeyard—disaffected psons.
JEY. Mr. Hugh Warren. Gram. Schole, not Licensed.
). Mr. Mich. Prestwood; English, Writing, Arithm : not licensed.
YN. Nicholas Hodge teaches a Schoole
KEVERNE. Mr. Thomas Cocken. } all unlicensed.
:Y. Mr. Rob. Coode.

Practisers of Physick.
n].
ERY ST. MARY. Mr. John Staple—no graduate, Unlicensed, Disaffected.
RINGDON. John Symonds, Anabaptist, Ignorant, Unlicensed.
'DON. Rich. Bethog A.B. Disaffected. Expelled All Souls, Oxon.
Tho. Spencer, Chirurgion & Practiser of Physic, notoriously disaffected.
ST ALLINGTON. Wm. Hingston. Notorious Quaker.

ourtney, *cf.* R. 403b.
. Maurice.

307b 6. Non-Conformist ejected Minist^rs.
[1 Devon]

EXETER. 1. M^r. Thomas Ford. 2. M^r. John Bartlet. 3. M^r. Rob. Snow. 4. M^r. Thos. Trescott. 5. M^r. Downe. 6. M^r. Atkins. 7. M^r. Tickle. 8. M^r. Caryll. 9. M^r. Tapper. 10. M^r. Hill. 11. M^r. Hollett. 12. M^r. Jordayne. The whole Doz. Presbyterians. But not keepers of Conventicles, wch these 3 following Independents doe, viz: 13. M^r. Lewis Stukeley. 14. M^r. Powell. 15. M^r. Mall.

TRUSHAM. 16. Wm Stooke. A.B. now husbandman & peaceable.

KENNE. 17. Rich. Herring. A.M. husbandry & peaceable.

ST. THOMAS PARISH. 18. Edw. Hunt, sayd to live peaceably.

OTTERY ST. MARY. 19. Rob. Collins. Conventicle hold^r. 20. M^r. Mawditt. 21. M^r. Ambrose Clare, peaceable. 22. M^r. Groves, a wanderer.

TIVERTON. 23. Theoph. Polewheele, of Tiverton formerly, & there keepes seditious Conventicles. 24. Richard Sanders, a lurking wanderer & seditious convent:

HALBERTON. 25. James Haddridge, thence ejected, there remains Seditious still. 26. Steph: Coven. A wandering Seditious Seminary.

THORNECOMBE. 27. John Hodder. 28. M^r. Branker. 29. M^r. Wakerly & 30. M^r. Trottle.

HONYTON. 31. M^r. Fran. Sourton, thence ejected.

AXMINSTER. 32. M^r. Barth Ashwood, thence ejected.

MUSBURY. 33. M^r. Rich. Farrand, thence ejected.

UPLYME. 34. M^r. Josias Wyat.

SAMPFORD COURTNEY. 35. Tho. Maynard, inoffensive.

EXBORNE & BARNSTAB. 36. Thomas Triney, ejected from Exborne.

JACOBSTON. 37. Tho. Bridgman, inoffensive & poore.

ASBERRY. 38. Dan: Moreton, thence ejected, lives still in ye Pars. house, but not inoffensively.

308 CLAWTON. 39. M^r. Hump. Sanders: temporall estate, quiet.

HOLSWORTHY. 40. Nich. Taylor, quietly.

TAVISTOCK. 41. Tho. Larkeham, thence ejected, stands Excommunicate.

The Episcopal Returns of 1665-6   343

PLIMMOUTH. 42. Geo. Hughes, B.D. & Mʳ. Thomas Martin. Private perverters.
    43. Sam. Austen. 44. Nich. Sherwill. Notoriously disaffected.
WEST ALLINGTON. 45. Leonard Hyne. A temporall estate.
    46. Tooker, a Conventicler.
TOTNES.   47. Mʳ. Fran. Whiddon.
    48. Mʳ. Bickley   } Peaceable
    49. Mʳ. Mortimer.   livers.
STOKE FLEMMING. 50. Mʳ. Wᵐ. Bayley.
DARTMOUTH. 51. Mʳ. Kempster.
DARTMOUTH. 52. Mʳ. Jam. Burdwood. 53. Mʳ. Joh. Flavell. Conventiclers.
BARNSTAPLE. 54. Jonathan Hanmer, A.M. Privately & peaceably.
ILFARNCOMBE. 54. Mʳ. Bifeild, privately.
COMB-MARTIN. 55. Mʳ. Stokes. Preacheth abroad sometimes.
GR. TORRINGTON. 56. John How, A.M. peaceably.
[2. Cornwall].
LANCESTON. 57. Mʳ. Oliver, he is residᵗ, someᵗⁱᵐᵉˢ at Plimmouth.
SALTASH. 58. Mʳ. Tomes. 59. Tyash. 60. Mʳ. Hicks. 61. Mʳ. Wyne. 62. Mʳ. Leadstone. 63. Mʳ. Tavers. All notoriously disaffected to K. & Ch.
ST. MABYN. 64. Jonathan Wills. Keepes frequent Conventicles.
NEWLYN. 65. Mʳ. Wᵐ. White, lives peaceably.
FOWEY. 66. Nathan. Tincomb, peaceably.
HELSTON. 67. Joseph Halsey, thence ejected. But peaceable.
FOWEY. 68. Joh.: Tutchin.
HELSTON. 69. Mʳ. Rob. Jagoe
GUENDRON. 70. Mʳ. Rog. Flamock.   } peaceable
CONSTANTINE. 71. Mʳ. Joh. Langford.
PERANARWORTH-ALL. 72. Mʳ. Joseph Allen.
BUDOCK. 73. Mʳ. Tho. Tregose. a Great Conventicle keeper.
Per Dⁿᵘᵐ Sethum Exoñ Epū͡m 1665.

310   III. Diocese of BRISTOL.

315   6. Concerning Non Conformist Ministers.
There are many Non Conformist ministers in the County of Dorset within my dioces, who neither hath nor wil

take the oath enjoyned them by the late Act of Parliament, but have gotten them private habitations 5 miles from any Corporate towne, where they often meet together (about what, noe man knowes) And holds Conventicles frequently in divers places, vizt:

Mr Benn, late Rector of Alsaints in the towne of Dorchester, is now Resident at Maiden Newton.

M^r. Thorne, late Rector of Radipole, is now Resident at Compton Valence[4].

M^r. Churchill late Vicar of Fordington is now Resident at Compton Valence aforesaid.

M^r. Lawrence, late Rector of Winterborne Came, is now Resident at Frampton.

One M^r. Swessell, late of the dioces of Sarum is now Resident at Frome Vawchurch.

M^r. Fuoward[5], late of Bubbourne[6] is now Resident at Woolcomb in the same pish.

M^r. Secheverell, late Rector of Tarrant Hinton is now Resident at Winterborn Zelston.

M^r. Moore, late Rector of Hammoone, is now Resident at Milton Abbas.

M^r. Hallett, late Rector of St. Peters in Shaston, is now Resident at Helton.

Mr Lambe, late Rector of Beer Rs., is now Resident at Alton.

M^r. Rowe, late Rector of Litchet Matravers, is now Resident at Hampleston[7].

M^r. White, late Curate of Beer Rs., is now Resident (at) Helt nere Wimborne.

M^r. Martyn, late Rector of Tarrant Munckton is now Resident at Wimborne.

M^r. Dummer late of......hath taken the oath required by the late Act of Parliament, and is Resident at Dorchester.

M^r. Hammond, late Rector of the holy Trinitie in Dorchester, hath taken the oath required by the said Act of Parliament, And is Resident at Dorchester aforesaid.

M^r. Way, late Rector of West Staffor hath alsoe taken the said oath, and is now Resident at Dorchester aforesaid.

---

[4] *i.q.* East Compton.
[5] *i.e.* Forward.
[6] *i.q.* Melbury Bubb.
[7] *i.q.* Hampreston.

Mr. Hodder, late of Hawchurch, in the County of Dorset & Dioces of Bristoll. Resided there till of late, but is now removed, as I am informed into the County of Devon.

317 Endorsed :—Nonconformists at Bristoll. T. C. 1666. A list of the names of such Nonconformist Ministers whoe are now Inhabiting wthin the Cittie of Bristoll, contrary to the late Act of Parliament, vizt. :

Mr. Chroughton	Mr. Hibbert
Mr. Ewins	Mr. Jennett
Mr. Hazard	Mr. Brock
Mr. Taylor	Mr. Griffin
Mr. Voyle	Mr. Paule
Mr. Blindman	

IV. Diocese of St. David's.

321 Diocess Menevensis
extracted from the archives 1668.

336b To the 6 Article Concerning Non Conformist Ministers. Daniel Higgs, Clerke, was ejected out of the Rectory of Portynon in the Deanry of Gowre & County of Glamorgan and Diocess of St. Davids for non-subscripcōn, hee is removed from my diocesse.

John Griffith, Clerke was ejected out of the Rectory of Oxwich in the Deanry of Gowre in the County of Glamorgan & Diocesse of St. Davids for non-subscripcōn, and for all I heare, hee lives very peaceably in the Countrey in Relation to both Church & State.

Thomas Freeman clerke was ejected out of his benefices in the County of Pembroke for non-Subscripcōn, but since, hee conform^d and enjoyes one Benefice againe & lives peaceably in the Countrey in Relation to both Church & State.

Adam Hawkins clerke was Ejected out of the Vicaradge of St. Ismaels in the County of Pembroke for non Subscripcōn, and now lives quietly and peaceably in the Countrey in relacōn to both Church & State.

337 Rice Powell clerke was Eiected out of the Vicaradge of Llampeder pont Stephen in the County of Cardigan for non Subscripcōn, but since

hath subscribed and does conforme and live very peaceably and quietly in the Countrey in relacon to both Church & State.

John Harries clerke was a Non Conformist, but since he did subscribe and conforme and preached a Recantation Sermon, and my Ld Chancello^r gave him a Benefice in Cardiganshire, and now hee lives very quietly and peaceably in relacon to the Church and State.

Richard Swaine clerke was Ejected out of the Vicaradge of Clirowe in the County of Radnor, for non-Subscripcon and has now left the Diœcesse.

John Dennis, clerke, was Ejected out of the Vicaradge of the Hay in the Countie of Brecon for non Subscripcon and hath now left the Diœcesse.

Thomas Vaughan, clerke, M.A. was Ejected out of the Rectory of Llansanffread in the County of Brecon for non Subscripcon and left the Diœcesse.

Thomas Edwards clerke Master of Arts was Ejected out of the Rectory of Llandevayllogge in the Countie of Brecon for non-Subscripcon, hee lives in Hereford diocœsse.

M^r. Littleton clerke was Ejected out of the prebend of Llandugroie in the Collegiate Church of Brecon for non Subscripcon, hee lives out of this Diœcesse.

Thomas Evans, clerke, was Ejected out of the Vicaradge of Llanbister in the Countie of Radnor for non Conformity, but since Conformed and now lives very quietly and peaceably in the Countrey in relacon to both Church and State.

Concordat : cum Archivis Reverendi in xpo pris ac dnē diñ Gulielmi Meneven Epī.

308 [Another handwriting].
6. Nonconformists.
1. Dan Higgs. 2. John Griffith. 3. Tho. Freeman.
4. Adam Hawkins. 5. Rice Powell. 6. John Harries.
7. Richard Swayne. 8. John Dennis. 9. Thomas Vaughan. 10. Tho: Edwards. 11. M^r. Littleton.
12. Thomas Evans.

Per D^num Epūm Meneveñ sub sigillo Epāli suo. 1665.

354 BP OF NORWICH—HIS CERTIFICATE 1665 1666.
Nothing Concerning Non Conformists.

III. Diocese of EXETER.

Anno D. 1665
An Account of
Hospitals & Almeshouses
Clergymen holding pluralities
Scholemasters } in the Diœcesse
Lecturers } of Exeter.
Physicians
Ejected Non-Conformist Ministers
Bp of Exōns Certificate of the things above written.

Archdeaconry of EXON.
Decanatus CHRISTIAN^{TS} EXON./
Concerning Non Conformists.
Item I present
That there are inhabiting wthin the Citty and Suburbs of the Cittie of Exeter 12 Presbyterian Ministers who above 3 years since have laid down the publique exercise of their ministry & functions, and 3 Independents. But I think never were in Orders.

They are M^r. Thomas Ford, M^r. John Bartlett, M^r. Robert Snowe, M^r. Thomas Trescott, M^r. Downe, M^r. Atkins, M^r. Tickle, M^r. Caryll, M^r. Tapper, M^r. Hill, M^r. Hollett, and Mr Jordayne, besides M^r. Robinson who is come out of the County of Somerset. I do not know that any of these have kept any Conventicles, but only these Independants M^r. Lewis Stukeley, M^r. Powell, and M^r. Mall.

Decanatus KENNE.
Non-Conformists
There are 3 Non-Conformist Minist^{rs} in the Deanery. one in Trusham named Wm Stooke Bach^r of Arts, he liveth upon a Tenem^t of his owne as a husbandman, and cometh sometymes to that Churche and heareth divine service as well as preaching & behaveth himself Quietly and peaceably as to the Church as Comonwealth.

Another in Kenn, is named Richard Hering M^r of Arts who liveth upon a Tenem^t of his owne. He cometh sometime to ye neighbour Church Eu and behaveth himself Quietly and peaceably.

A 3rd in St. Thomas Parish, named Edward Hunt, but whether he hath taken any Degree he cannot learne. But is informed that he liveth peacably.

WESTBEARE Deanery

a person of no note or Learning, an Anabaptist, and one that keeps Conventicles, he is neither Licenced nor Conformable.

Non-Conformist Ministers.

M^r. Robert Collins, sometymes Rector of Tallaton & eiected for inconformity lives now in Ottery St. Mary in his owne house neare the Church where he keepes Conventicles frequently, but especially upon Sundayes in tyme of divine Service to the Scandall of many; but, for want of a Justice of Peace, the Churchwardens, or Constables, dare not enter the house to take them, and their privacy is such that they cannot yet proove enough agst them to convict them by Lawe. I am told he was never at Church in ye tyme of Comon prayer since the Act of Conformity, and is a very pertinacious Nonconformist.

One M^r. Mawditt of Exeter a Minister & Nonconformist is lately come thither, where as yet he carryes himself peaceably.

M^r. Ambrose Clare sometymes Rector of Poltimore lives in the same Parish still upon his owne meanes and carryes himself peaceably as farre as I can learn.

M^r. Groves sometyme an Intruder into Pinhooe & ejected thence for his Nonconformity wanders up and downe, sometymes in one place and one while in another. I knowe not where to find him nor how he lives.

400b   The Deanery of PLIMTREE.
Nonconformists.
No Non Conformist Minister in ye Deanery.

401   Decanat CHIVERTON.
Non Conformists.

M^r. Theophilus Polewheele, sometyme a minister in Tiverton, but eiected for non Subscripcōn, yet still remayneing in that Towne, & (as I am informed) drawes seditious persons in Conventicles to him; so doth

M^r. Richard Saunders, sometyme Rcor of Loxbeare ejected for inconformity, sometymes lurking in Tiverton, sometymes in Loxbeare, & other places for like ends.

There is also one M^r. James Haddridge eiected out of Halberton, remaynes still in y^t parish & acts in like manner. And also one Stephen

The Episcopal Returns of 1665-6

Coven sometyme of Sampford-peverell, who goes about from place to place teaching sedition, but where his Constant abode is we cannot learne.

402b   HONYTON Deanery.
Non-Conformists.

M^r. John Hodder, sometymes minister of Hawkchurch in Dorsett, now living in Thornecomb on his owne demeasne.

M^r. Branker, sometymes minister of Sturminster Newton in Dorsett, teaching Schoole in Thornecomb.

M^r. Wakeley, sometymes minister of Lawrence Lydiat in Somersett, now liveing in Thornecomb on his owne demeasnes.

M^r. Trottle, sometymes minister in Dorsett, now liveing in Thornecombe.

M^r. Francis Sourton sometymes minister of Honyton, now liveing in Honyton.

M^r. Bartholomew Ashwood sometymes minister of Axminster, now liveing in Axminster.

M^r. Richard Farrand, sometymes min^r of Musbury, now liveing in Musbury.

M^r. Josias Wiat, sometymes minister of Podimore in Somersett, now liveing in Uplime.

403   TOTNES Arch^{ry}.

OKEHAMPTON Deanery.

403b   Schoolmasters.

In Sampford Courtney one Drake teacheth Schoole without Licence.

Non-Conformist Ministers.

Thomas Maynard who left Northtawton for Non-Conformity, now liveth inoffensively in Sampford Courtney on a tenem^t he holdeth in right of his Children.

Thomas Finney who left Exborne for ye like liveth sometymes at Exborne & sometymes at Barnstable.

Thomas Bridgman who left Inwardley for want of Tytle, liveth in Jacobstow inoffensively and poorely.

Daniel Moreton who left Asberry for Nonconformity lives still in ye Parsonage house, but not altogether inoffensively.

404   HOLSWORTHY Deanery.

Conc^s Non Conformist Minist^{rs}.

M^r. Humfry Sanders was eiected out of ye Parish of

Holsworthy for Non Conformity who liveth now in yᵉ parish of Clawton upon his Temporall Estate, and behaveth himself peaceably and Quiet to yᵉ Church & State.

Mʳ. Michael Taylor was eiected out of Pyworthy for Nonconformity who liveth now in Holsworthy Peaceably and Quietly.

TAVISTOCK Deanery.

Concerning Non Conformists.

At Tavistock liveth Mʳ. Thomas Larkeham sometyme minister of Tavestock and stands at psent excōmunicated for Contempt of Ecclicall Lawes.

TAMERTON Deanery.

One Non-Conformist minister liveth in this Deanery, viz: Theophilus Wines Mʳ of Arts, eiected of Tamerton Foliot for inconformity.

PLIMPTON Deanery.

Schooles.

Mʳ. John Williams Resident in Plimpton Morris keepeth a private schoole and preacheth there, a person disaffected to yᵉ Governmᵗ & Discipline of yᵉ Church of England & unlicenced.

Phisitians.

Mʳ. Richard Bithog B.A. practiseth Phisick, he was, as I am informed turned out of All Souls Oxford for inconformity, he is a person wholly disaffected to yᵉ Government of yᵉ Church of England & unlicenced.

Mʳ. Thomas Spencer a Chirurgion sometymes practiseth Phisick, a person notoriously disaffected to the Governmᵗ of his Maᵗⁱᵉ & yᵉ Discipline of the Church of England.

Non Conformists.

There are Resident in yᵉ Towne of Plimouth

Mʳ. George Hughes B.D. and Mʳ. Thomas Martyn sometymes Publique now private perverters in this Towne.

Mʳ. Samuel Austin turned out of Minkinnett yᵉ Right of Dʳ. Hall yᵉ Bishop of Chester.

Mʳ. Nicholas Sherwill Episcopally Ordayned as he saith But notoriously disaffected to yᵉ Church of England in her discipline, and two yeares since endited at yᵉ Towne Hall for a disturbance made by him at a funerall whiles the Comon Prayer was read.

WOODLEY Deanery.
Phisitians.
M^r. William Hingston liveing in West Allington, an open and knowne Quaker, and hath frequently (as I am informed) unlawfull meetings and Conventicles in his house.
Nonconformists.
There are two in this Deanery liveing in the parish of West Allington, viz :
M^r. Leonard Hyne liveing in a Temporall Estate of his owne.
And one Tooker who hath as I am certainly informed frequent and unlawfull meetings.

TOTNESS Deanery.
Schoolmast^{rs}.
Edward Manning and William Ball teach an English Schoole at Dartmouth, but not licenced nor well affected.
Non Conformists.
In TOTTNESS. M^r. Francis Whiddon, M^r. Bickley, & M^r. Mortimore,
in STOKE FLEMMING. M^r. William Bayley ;
in DARTMOUTH. M^r. Kempster,
all of them liveing upon their owne & behaving themselves peaceably & Quietly.
In DARTMOUTH, there are also M^r. James Burdwood and M^r. John Flavell ; who are reported to have private meetings.

IPPLEPEN Deanery.
Practition^{rs} of Phisick.
M^r. Smith practiseth Phisick at Woolborough, not Licensed sometymes of Wadham Colledge & afterwards of Hart Hall B.A.
One Gabriel Pridham professeth phisick at Little hempston, who is not licenced, but is conformable in frequenting prayers.

MORETON Deanery.
Non Conformists.
John Nosworthy a Non Conformist liveing in Manaton, formerly Rector of that place.
Jonathan Bowden a Non Conformist liveing in Moreton, formerly Rector of Littleham.

no way disturbing ye Peace of Church or State.

SHERWELL Deanery.
408b Non-Conformists.
One M^r. Bifield lives privately at Ilfardcombe, but from whence came, or whether he were eiected, I knowe not.
Also one M^r. Stokes y^t lives at Comb-Martin & preacheth sometymes abroad, but whether he is in orders or hath any Lycence is not knowne.

TORRINGTON Deanery.
409 Non Conformists.
M^r. John Howe, A.M. inhabiting in great Torrington who behaves himselfe peaceably.

HARTLAND Deanery.
Non-Conformists.
M^r. Wm Bartlett } Liveing in Bideford.
M^r. Jo: Bartlett   }
M^r. Anthony Downe in Northam.

409b Archītus Cornub.

Deanery of **TRIGG MAJOR**.
Non-Conformists.
There is one M^r. Oliver sometymes a Preacher of Lanceston, was eiected for non-Subscription, and that he sometymes resides in Plimouth, as he hath heard.

Deanery of **EAST**.
Non-Conformists.
There are residing in ye Towne of Saltash. Six Non-Conformist Ministers, viz :
M^r. Tomes, M^r. Tiack, M^r. Hickes, M^r. Wine, M^r. Leadstone and M^r. Travers, who are reported to be notoriously disaffected to ye Government of ye Church established in ye Kingdome of England.

Deanery of **TRIGG MINOR**.
Non-Conformists.
411 There is one Jonathan Wills who never tooke any degree in the Schooles yet in ye tyme of sequestracōn intruded himself into ye Rectory of Mabyn, and from thence removed to ye Rectory of Lanteglos nere Camelford, from whence being eiected he returnes to the house of Anne Silly in St. Mabyn where he still shelters himselfe where as is strongly

The Episcopal Returns of 1665-6

reported, he keepes great & frequent Conventicles.

Deanery of POWDER.
Non-Conformists.

M^r. Nath. Tincomb eiected out of Laselles liveth upon his Temporall Estate in Fowey peaceably.

M^r. Joseph Halsey eiected of Michael Penkevell liveth now in ye parsonage-house there which he renteth of ye present Incumbent and is peaceable and Quiet.

Deanery of PENWITH.
Non Conformists.

M^r. Joseph Sheawood eiected out of St. Hillary for Non-Conformity lives usually in ye parish of St. Earth in ye Quality of a Husbandman he was lately imprisoned for presuming to preach publiquely in ye Church there Contrary to ye Act of Uniformity.

Deanery of KERRIAR.
Concern^g Non-Conformists.

In HELSTON. M^r. Robert Jago A.M. and M^r. Tobias Butcher.

In CONSTANTINE. M^r. John Langton.

In PERANARWORTHAL. M^r. Joseph Allen.

All these have been eiected for in Conformity, but as farre as I can learne do behave themselves Quietly in Referrence to ye Church & State.

In BUDOCK. M^r. Thomas Tregosse lately imprisoned for holding a Conventicle.

The Oldest Chapel in Wales

THIS honourable distinction is assigned by common consent to the ancient chapel at Maesyronen—the name may be translated "Field of Ash Trees." Its location is near the southern corner of Radnor county, about two miles from Glasbury-on-Wye, and at a considerable distance from any village. The church undoubtedly represents the religious movement initiated by the itinerant labours of Walter Cradock (1606-59) and Vavasor Powell (1616-70); and its origin is usually dated 1640, that being the year in which Powell's itinerancy commenced. The church in its earlier years was a large and widely scattered community, having its headquarters at Llanigon, near Hay; but dispersed over the country from Hay, on the borders of Herefordshire, to Cefn Arthen in Carmarthenshire, and from Troedrhiwdalar in Brecon to Merthyr Tydfil in Glamorgan. Its first pastor was Richard Powell, whose ministry extended from the early days of the Long Parliament to 1668. He was assisted by lay preachers; the most conspicuous being Lewis Prytherch, and Henry Williams of Merthyr. These local men kept up the interest until 1672, when Henry Maurice was called to the pastorate, who laboured till his death in 1682.

The meetings were necessarily held in private houses. One of these, near Maesyronen, was called "The Bendy"; and there is a firmly established tradition that in it, on one occasion, at least, Oliver Cromwell attended divine service. Soon after the

MAESYRONEN CHAPEL, 1696

MAESYRONEN CHAPEL, INTERIOR
From photographs by the Rev. D. M. Lewis, M.A.

passing of the Toleration Act (1689) the scattered church divided into several local societies; nine are named altogether in the four counties of Brecon, Carmarthen, Glamorgan, and Radnor, which branched off from the Llanigon fellowship.

All these, Maesyronen, Tredwstan, Brecon, Llanwrtyd, Troedrhiwdalar, Beilihalog, Gwenddwr, Cefn Arthen, and Merthyr (Congregational), and Maesyberllan near Brecon (Baptist), still subsist. The site of Maesyronen chapel was given by Lewis Lloyd, Esq., Maesllwch, who was probably a member of the church. About the date there is a little uncertainty; a local tradition says 1689, and Beriah G. Evans names it as one of the chapels built between 1689 and 1735; but Dr. Rees, a very careful inquirer who made investigations on the spot, fixes the date as 1696. (This is not really inconsistent with B. G. Evans, but only with a traditional story).

When the present minister endeavoured to set in order the history of this venerable sanctuary, he found " MSS. and church records in a deplorable state." He has been able, however, to furnish an approximately complete list of the pastors from the beginning of the eighteenth century:

> David Price, 1700-1742; Lewis Rees, 1745-1748; James Davies, 1749-1759; Walter Bevan, -1762; William Llewellyn, -1775; Thomas Bowen 1781-1796; David Jones, 1797-1846. (A memorial tablet within the chapel says of Mr. Jones: " He began early, continued late, met with enemies of a most malignant type, but he overcame them all, and in the end did cry Hallelujah !")
>
> Thomas Havard, a student of Cheshunt college, was at this time pastor of Tredwstan, a few miles distant in Brecon county. On the death of Mr. Jones Maesyronen was united with Tredwstan under his single pastorate until 1861. In 1863 M. A. Harvey became pastor of Maesyronen only; and three years later a new and commodious chapel was erected in the neighbouring village of Glasbury, where

there is a more numerous population. The two cc
gations have ever since constituted a single past
Mr. Harvey retired in 1867, and was followed in 18
J. R. Lewis from Brecon college, who remov
Dorrington, Salop, in 1871, and still ministers there.
was succeeded by H. B. Shankland, 1872 ; who in
removed to Domgay, Salop. Then came J. Thomas
Brecon college in 1878, who removed to Trecastle in
After him came D. Watkins from Carmarthen colle
1882, and left in 1884. The church met with conside
trouble during these two pastorates, through the
conduct of some of the members. In 1885 cam
Fairhurst from Ystalfera, he removed to Barrow in
and was succeeded by the present minister, D. C. L
who came from Shipley, Yorkshire, in the same year

The statistics of the ancient church, last y
shewed 32 church members, and 25 Sun
scholars, with 4 teachers. But with these ot
in all fairness to be reckoned the 49 church m
bers and 30 scholars with 4 teachers at Glasbu
who, though now separately organized, are hist
cally a branch of the ancient church.

Most of the above particulars have been furni
by the Rev. D. C. Lloyd.

Broadway Meeting, Somerset.

BROADWAY Meeting owes its existence to a split between the Trinitarian and Socinian sections of the old chapel at Ilminster, about 1739. The former section, living in localities of which Broadway was a convenient centre, and recognizing the need of further spiritual provision for it and the district round about, took steps for the erection of a chapel. A suitable piece of land was purchased there by the Rev. John Lavington, of Exeter, and the Rev. John Walrond, formerly of Ottery St. Mary, who conveyed it to a regularly constituted trust; whereupon the chapel was built. The original trustees consisted among others of the principal members of the Standerwick, Hayes, and Horsey families; and the foundation stone was laid by Isaac Standerwick the younger, then a child, whose grandson in later years exercised the pastoral office. The first pastor was the Rev. John Lavington, junior. It is not known how long his ministry lasted; but in July, 1763, the Rev. John Samuel was, and apparently had been for some time, the minister. At that time George Betty, a labourer, of Hatch Beauchamp (a place some four miles off), charged his property with an annuity of ten shillings, payable to Mr. Samuel and his successors; which is paid unto this day. By March, 1765, Mr. Samuel had been succeeded by the Rev. John Peacock, whose sermon on the death of Mr. William Johnson, preached in Paul's meeting, Taunton, in 1768, reached a second edition. In

1776 he published a collection of hymns designed to supersede those of Dr. Watts, which however they have not yet done, either at Broadway or elsewhere. Many of them are however of considerable merit, fully up to the average of those in use nowadays, and might well take a place in the present service of the sanctuary. About 1777, the Rev. T. Lewis became the pastor, and added to this duty the conduct of a superior school for young gentlemen in the house which, until it was burnt down, was practically, though not formally, the parsonage. From April, 1792 (and perhaps earlier), to Lady Day, 1793, a Mr. Allen received £40 salary as minister. On June 30th, 1793, Mr. Crook commenced his ministry, which terminated about the close of the last century ; this pastorate was notable for the establishment of the Sunday school, which was founded in 1797. It was followed by an interregnum, during which Mr. Thorn, of Grilston, near Crediton, and others supplied the church, though without pastoral charge. In 1803 the Rev. Thomas Pyke was called to the pastorate. He was by birth and behaviour a gentleman of the old school, and his ingenuity was witnessed by (among other things) his invention of a machine for calculating the mileage of coaches ; which, however, was never formally adopted. Towards the close of his life his mental powers failed, and although he retained his position he was practically laid aside, the death of his only child (a daughter) having largely contributed to this result. It may, perhaps, be mentioned without offence after this lapse of time, that on dark nights he used to place a lantern in his shrubbery, in order that his daughter if she came down to visit him might not break her wings among the laurels. In consequence of Mr. Pyke's incapacity, the Rev. William

Standerwick became co-pastor in 1837. He had been minister at Dulverton, and built the chapel there, the cost of which was mainly paid out of his own pocket and that of Mr. Heudebourck, of Taunton. During his ministry Mr. Pyke had been largely assisted by his gifted sister, Sarah Leigh Pyke, who under the pseudonym of "Serena" had published *Israel, a Poem*, *The Triumph of Messiah*, and *Eighty Village Hymns*, all of which enjoyed an extensive popularity. The last of these works was written in the very plainest style; but was by just so much the better suited for the rural community among which her lot was cast, and much good may be traced to its publication. The year 1843 was a noteworthy one in the annals of Broadway; it witnessed, with other significant events, the deaths of Mrs. Standerwick, mother of the junior pastor and the last surviving subscriber to the clock, "the young people's gift," which still forms a striking feature of the meeting; Mr. Robert Collins, of Horton, an important and invaluable supporter of the cause; and of Mr. Pyke himself; also the destruction by fire of a large part of the village, including the parsonage house. During Mr. Standerwick's ministry the church attained its highest measure of success, the gallery and pulpit stairs being habitually occupied by persons who could not find seats elsewhere; and in the end the chapel was considerably enlarged, although the work was not completed until after Mr. Standerwick had been compelled by ill health to resign his charge. He emigrated to America, but subsequently returned to England and died in 1876, within a stone's throw of the building with which he had been connected from his birth. After his retirement the church was supplied by the Rev. Richard Penman, the Rev. J. S. Underwood, Mr.

Victor Herschell (uncle of the late Lord Chancellor), who as a clergyman of the Church of England lost his life in the Jamaica disturbances; and by students of the Western college, notably Mr. Chapman, subsequently of Montreal and Plymouth, and Mr. Bryan Dale, since of Halifax. In 1855 the Rev. Stephen Ross was called to the pastorate, during his tenure of which the present parsonage was built. Failing health, however, necessitated his retirement in 1865; and he was succeeded by the Rev. William Lang, during whose ministry the church fabric underwent extensive restoration. Mr. Lang was succeeded in 1872 by the Rev. George Osborne, also previously of Dulverton, who died in 1906.

The principal features of interest in the history of Broadway Meeting are, first, that its foundation was the direct outcome of the Trinitarian Controversy of 1719, and second, that it has never received a penny of assistance from outside sources. It has had from time to time a complete church organization, mission stations at Donyatt, Windmill Hill, and Buckland St. Mary (near "the Hare and Hounds"), a Bible Society auxiliary, Dorcas, maternity, and tract distributing societies, and a flourishing Sabbath school. This was founded in March, 1797, with a stipendiary teacher, retained to conduct school three times on a Sunday and attend two services with the children at a remuneration of 1s. a week. Many of that teacher's pupils remained to their dying day earnest members of the church, and adorned during the course of long lives the Christian profession. The original rules are appended, and will doubtless be of interest, if only by way of contrast with modern Sunday school methods.

Broadway Meeting, Somerset

Articles and Rules for the Establishment of a Sunday School, in the parish of Broadway, March, 1797.

1. That this school shall be supported by voluntary subscriptions.

2. That a Treasurer shall be appointed by a majority of the Subscribers, who shall receive the subscriptions, and therewith pay the Salary of the Master, and defray all other Expenses attending this Institution.

3. That Mr. Bennet be, and he is hereby, appointed Treasurer of the said School, for the year ensuing.

4. That a Master shall be appointed for this school by a Majority of the Subscribers, who shall instruct the Scholars in Spelling and Reading, at his own House, and shall regularly attend them to and from the Place of Worship, on every Lord's Day, agreeably to the rules of this Institution: and the said Master shall receive for his care and Trouble the sum of Two Pounds and twelve shillings a year, to be paid Quarterly.

5. That Thomas Whitfield be, and he is hereby, appointed Master of the said School.

6. That no Child shall be admitted into this School, who is less than seven years of age, or more than Fourteen.

7. That no Child shall be admitted into this School, without the Recommendation of a Subscriber; and any Parent who is desirous to have a child admitted into it may apply to the Master, who will give the necessary information as to the Names of the Subscribers.

8. That the Name of every Child admitted into this School shall be entered in a Book to be kept for that purpose by the Treasurer; in which Entry, the Age of the Child shall be specified, and the Name of the Subscriber, at whose Recommendation the Child was admitted.

9. That the Subscribers be requested to visit the said school, in Turn, as often as they can make it convenient, for the Purpose of observing the manner in which the Children are instructed, and the Progress they make, as well as to inquire into their general Conduct and Behaviour.

10. That from Lady Day to Michaelmas, in every year, the children of this school shall attend at the House of the Master precisely at eight o'clock, in the morning of every Lord's Day, and from Michaelmas to Lady Day, precisely at nine o'clock in the morning, to be instructed in Spelling and Reading, till the time of Divine Service, when they shall go in decent order to the Place of Worship, conducted by their Master.—And on every Lord's Day throughout the year, they shall attend at the Master's House, precisely at one o'clock, to be further instructed till the Time of

Divine Service in the Afternoon when they shall again go in decent order to the Place of Worship, conducted by their Master. And from Lady Day to Michaelmas, in every year, when Divine Service in the Afternoon is ended, they shall return, in the same decent order, to the House of their Master, to be further instructed till Six o'clock.

11. That if any Child shall fail to attend at the Place and Time before appointed, without sufficient reason (of which sufficiency the Master shall judge), such child shall, for the first default, be admonished and reprimanded by the Master, and for the Second Default, shall be confined in a dark and solitary place, for the space of one Hour, after the other Scholars are dismissed; and for every other the like Default shall suffer such further Punishment as the Treasurer, or any Visitor of the School shall order the Master to inflict.

12. That the Parents of the Children shall send them to School, as neat and decent as their circumstances will permit, with their Hands and Faces washed clean, and their Hair combed.

13. That if any Child shall come to the School, whose Hands and Face are not washed clean, and whose Hair is not combed, such Child shall, for the first, second, and every other Default of the like Kind, be punished in the manner directed by the Eleventh Rule for the punishment of those who fail to attend at the Place and Times before appointed.

14. That if any Child belonging to this school shall be guilty of cursing, Swearing, or Lying, or of talking in an indecent manner, or of Pilfering and Stealing, or of any other Misbehaviour, the Master shall, on the first offence, point out the Evil of such Conduct; and if, after his reproof and admonition, the Child shall be guilty of either of the said offences a second Time, every Child, so offending, shall be confined in a dark and solitary Place, for the Space of One Hour, after the other Scholars are dismissed; and if the said Child shall offend a third Time, then the Master shall make a particular Report of such Offender to the Treasurer, who shall order such Punishment to be inflicted, as he, in his Discretion, shall think proper.

15. That a Book shall be provided for the Master, which shall be called the Black Book, and the Master shall enter therein a regular Account of the Misbehaviour of any of the children of this School, mentioning the particular Nature of every offence; which Book shall, from Time to Time, be laid before the Visitors of the School, that they may have an opportunity of publickly reproving those children who shall in any respect misbehave themselves, and of encouraging those who behave well.

16. That proper Books for the Instruction of the Children shall be provided by the Treasurer; and the said Books shall be carefully kept in a Box by the Master of the School.

17. That at the end of every year, The Black Book shall be opened and examined by the Treasurer, and other Visitors of the School, in the Presence of the Master and Scholars ; and those children whose Names shall seldom or never appear in the said Book, and who shall be found to have made a good Progress in Spelling and Reading, shall receive some mark of Approbation and Encouragement.

18. That a copy of these Articles and Rules shall be delivered to the Master of this School, to be by him read over to the scholars, on the first Lord's Day, in every Month.

The above narrative has been furnished by J. W. Standerwick, Esq., son of the Rev. William Standerwick, and one of an old Nonconformist family, some of whose members fought "for faith and freedom" under the blue flag in 1685. Mr. Standerwick served the nation for many years in a public office; and also served the Church and the world as secretary to the society which has printed the Latin works of John Wiclif, previously existing only in MS. On retiring from the public service he settled at Broadway; where he now ministers to the congregation with which his ancestors have been associated from its commencement.

[ED.]

London Conventicles in 1683

THE following list is of interest, as an enumeration of Nonconformist meetings at the time when the Rye House plot furnished a pretext for renewed persecution. The pamphlet seems to have been printed as a guide to constables and informers. Its press mark in the British Museum is 491, K4. No. 12.

> A List of the Conventicles or Unlawful Meetings within the City of London and Bills of Mortality Humbly presented to the Lord Mayor, Recorder and Aldermen, the Justices of the Peace of Westminster, Middlesex and Surrey; and all Constables, Church wardens, Overseers, and all other Officers and Ministers of the Peace.

Lond. Printed by Nat. Thompson, 1683.

Conventicle.	Faction	Preacher (if given)
In City and Liberties.		
Leadenhall St., near Creech	Independ.	Dr. Owen
Bishopsgate Street within, Crosby House	Presbyt.	
Bishopsgate Street without, Devonshire Buildings	Independ.	
A Quakers' Meeting at the same House		
Meeting-House Alley, near Bishopsgate Church..	Anabap.	Griffis
A Meeting-house in Petit. France	Independ.	
Pin-makers' Hall, near Broad Street	Presbyt.	
Near All-hallows the Wall	Independ.	
Whites Alley in Little Moor-fields	Presbyt.	
Another in the same alley	Independ.	
Ropemakers' Alley near Whites Alley	Presbyt.	
Lorimers Hall near the Postern, between Moor-gate & Cripple-gate	Presbyt.	

Between White Cross Street & Red Cross Street, near the Peacock Brew-House	Independ.	Cockin
Paul's Alley in Red Cross Street at the Old Play-house	Anabap.	Plant
Beech Lane at Glovers Hall	Presbyt.	
Another in the same lane, near it	Independ.	
Jewin Street	Presbyt.	Jenkins
Westmoreland House in Aldersgate Street	Independ.	
Bartholomew-close	Presbyt.	
St. Martin's le Grand, Bull & Mouth	Quakers	
Embroiderers' Hall in Gutter Lane near Cheapside	Presbyt.	S. Smith
Near Cripplegate	Presbyt.	Doelittle
Staining Lane, near Haberdasher's Hall	Presbyt.	Jacomb
High Hall, near S. Sepulchre's	Presbyt.	
Cow-lane, in a School-house	Independ.	
Stonecutter Street near Fleet Ditch	Presbyt.	
Wine Office Court in Fleet Street	Independ.	
Goldsmith's Court in Fetter Lane	Presbyt.	Turner
Blackfriars, near the King's Printing House	Scotch Presbyt.	
Another near Scotch Hall		
Broken Wharf, George Yard	Anabap.	Knowles
Three Cranes, in Thames Street, near Dowgate, over Stables	Presbyt.	
Joiners' Hall near Dowgate	Independ.	
Chequer Yard on Dowgate Hill	Anabap.	
Bell Inn in Walbrook	Presbyt.	Leigh
Exchange Alley, at a Coffee House	Independ.	
Bartholomew Lane, by the Exchange	Presbyt.	
Freemans Yard, near the Exchange	Presbyt.	Cruyo
Grace-Church Street, near Lombard St.	Quakers	
Grace-Church Street, Talbot Court	Independ.	
40] S. Martins Hill, near Crooked Lane	Anabap.	

For the out-parts of Middlesex and Westminster within the Bill of Mortality.

Lower end of Limehouse, next the fields	Presbyt.	
Near Stepney Church	Independ.	Mead
School-House Lane, near Ratcliff Cross	Presbyt.	
A Quakers' in the same place		
Near Shadwell Church	Anabap.	Collings
Meeting House Alley between Shadwel and Wapping	Presbyt.	

In a Carpenter's Yard near the Hermitage	Anabap.	
At a Ship-Chandler's, near it	Presbyt.	
Looking glass Alley in Westsmithfield	Anabap.	
In Bell Lane, near Spittle-fields	Presbyt.	
Quaker's Street in Spittle-fields	Quakers	
Windford Street	Anabap.	
Near the Spittle	Presbyt.	Dr. Ansloe
At Hackney, near 3 or 4 but at present are all suppressed.		
Near Hog Lane in Shoreditch	Presbyt.	
Old Street	Presbyt.	Partrige
S. John's Lane near Hicks's Hall the Peel	Quakers	
Greys Inn Lane, in Red Lyon Yard	Presbyt.	
Near Montague House in Bloomsbury	Presbyt.	Read
In Swallow Street, St. Martin's in the Fields	Presbyt.	Lobbs
Near Tothill Street, Westminster	Presbyt.	Alsop
In the same place	Quakers	
Savoy, near the Church	Quakers	
23] Clare-Market at the Old Playhouse	Presbyt.	Farindon

In Southwark & County of Surrey, within the Bill of Mortality.

Farthing Alley	Presbyt.	Vincent
Little Maze Pond	Anabap.	
Horse-ly-down, Fare Street	Quakers	
Horse-ly-down, Free School Street	Anabap.	
Horse-ly-down	Millinar	Wheeler
New Shad Thames	Anabap.	Clayton
Near Horse-ly-down, New Street	Presbyt.	Flavel
Unicorn Yard near Stony Lane	Presbyt.	Castle
Globe-Alley, near the Bear Garden	Presb. Ind	
In Street in Winchester Park	Quakers	
11] Winchester Park, near Lownands Pond	Anabap.	

The Pastoral Letters of Thomas Maidwell

THE Congregational church at Kettering is widely known on account of the ministry of the Tollers, father and son, who together held the pastorate nearly a hundred years. But apart from its association with these honoured worthies, the church has a history of which it is justly proud, and which is given with much interesting detail in Coleman's *Memorials of the Independent Churches in Northamptonshire* and in Stephens's *Album of the Northamptonshire Churches*. Its first pastor was the Rev. Thomas Maidwell; who was ejected from the parish church by the Act of Uniformity, and continued his ministry (with some interruptions) till his death on 9th January, 1692, at the age of 83.

Amongst the most cherished possessions of the church are three letters written by Mr. Maidwell in 1683, when, by reason of the renewed persecution, for which a pretext was found in the Rye House plot, he was compelled to remove to a distance. They are supposed to have been written from the house of H. Barwell, Esq., of Marston Trussell, about 12 miles N.W. of Kettering. The first of these letters was printed, with some inaccuracies, in Palmer's *Nonconformists' Memorial;* but by the courtesy of the deacons we are enabled to place before our readers the entire series.

By the kindness of Mr. C. A. Percival, of Gold Street, Kettering, we are also able to give two prints of Hazlewood House, otherwise called the Conventicle House, where Mr. Maidwell and his flock were accustomed to meet for worship in times of persecution. Under the Indulgence of 1672 he was licensed to preach "at Widow Cooper's"; but at other times he preached "in his own and other people's houses," as might best afford safety or secrecy. One of the most frequently used meeting-places was the house here represented, situated in an alley called Hazlewood Lane, and then the property of Mr. Maidwell's granddaughter, Mrs. Hazlewood. At the back of the house was a small window, of which only the framework now remains; and the tradition is that several times when the congregation were assembled for worship, and constables or informers —local tradition says soldiers—were forcing an entrance, the minister and his followers escaped by this window to the adjoining roof, and so over the fields towards Rothwell.

The historic house being for the time untenanted, an interesting memorial service was held within its walls on Wednesday evening, 11th March, of this year. The room was lighted with candles in ancient candelabra and brackets, and adorned with engravings illustrating incidents of Puritan history. Mr. C. A. Percival first conducted a short service for the children; and afterwards the Rev. D. Stephens, pastor of Toller church (and so the lineal successor of Mr. Maidwell) read the eleventh chapter of Hebrews from a Bible dated 1612; which was followed by the reading of one of Mr. Maidwell's pastoral letters. A devotional service was held in the same place on the following Sunday evening.

I.

My dear friends,' July 31st 1683.

Grace and peace be multiplied.

Since I heard of the great distress you are in on several accounts, it cannot but affect and afflict me; and the rather because my present danger and sufferings add to yours, which makes the

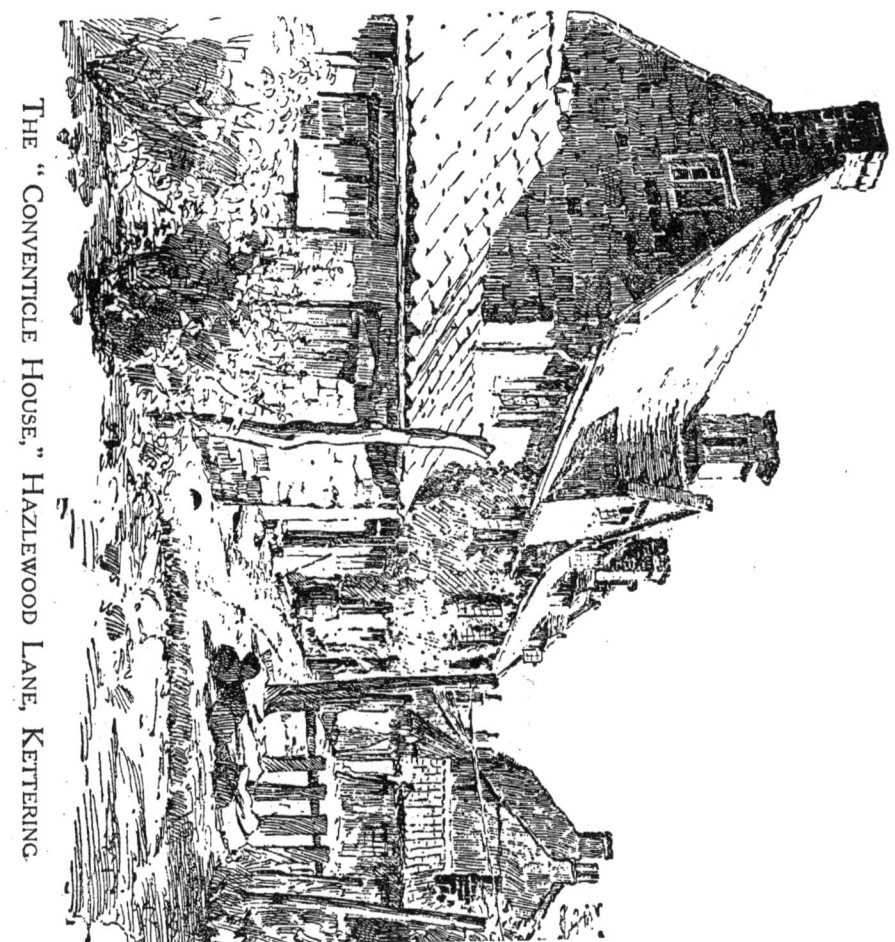

The "Conventicle House," Hazlewood Lane, Kettering.

burden heavier to us both : but if our God who directs, helps us to "cast our burden on him," he will sustain it and us under it ; as at present he doth, blessed be his name : for though we are troubled on every side, yet we are not distressed ; tho' perplexed, yet not in despair ; tho' persecuted, yet not forsaken ; tho' cast down, yet not destroyed. Tho' we bear in our outward man the dying of the Lord Jesus ; yet if the life, spirit, and vigour of Christ be exercised in our inward man, we shall (live) to him eternally hereafter as spiritually here : but the want of that divine vigour and true christian magnanimity fill most souls with despondency, bowels with sighs, and tongues with complaints. Yet we have no reason to murmur against, or complain of our God, who doth all things justly, wisely, and well ; but of ourselves, who neither know, do, nor suffer as we ought ; but "in many things we offend all" and therefore all suffer justly. It's true, you will say, What is to be done under present sufferings? what ?

(1) Let every one search and try his and her ways, and say seriously ; what have I done to kindle so great a fire of God's indignation against myself, and the church of God ? The sin of any one of His may provoke him against every one ; as of Jonah, David, and Hezekiah. God is calling the sin of his people to remembrance and shall not they do it, as he to afflict them so they to repent them ?

(2) Let not self examination be common, (superficial) inaffectionate ; but special, thorough, affectionate, heart-melting, soul-afflicting, extraordinary ; becoming so dark a day. Judgment is more than begun at the house of God ; and therefore it becomes God's house to be a house of mourning indeed, for their own and others sins, like that of Hadadrimmon in the valley of Megiddo.

(3) Let us not now take up with a formal search, confession, and humiliation as heretofore, but press after a personal, relative, and thorough reformation of what is amiss in Heart, Tongue, and Life. Let us forsake sin confessed, that we may obtain mercy ; and let us indeed so turn from all our sins of life actually, of heart affectionately : and so turn to the Lord our God, that he may turn to us in mercy to heal our hearts, lives, church, and land.

(4) Let us indeed have a daily, vigorous recourse, by a lively faith unto Christ and his blood of sprinkling, that by virtue thereof all the blessings of the new covenant may more powerfully, effectually, and experimentally be conveyed into our hearts and lives, more to assimilate both to the heart and life of our dearest Lord Jesus, in grace here, and glory hereafter.

(5) Let that faith, in the reality and eminence of it, be daily more and more manifested in our new obedience, especially in our united affections of love to and delight in our God thro' Christ, and thro' him in each other ! Oh ! where is that fervent love to God and each other with purity of heart ! Is not the love of many

waxen cold in this day wherein iniquity abounds ? Where is that union of hearts and ways Gods covenant promises and calls for ? Enemies are one to destroy us, studying all artifices imaginable to do it, and shall not we be one for mutual edification, confirmation, and consolation ? By what strength of arguments, what holy and fervent passion is this often argued by the apostle, 1 Cor : 13 Ephes : 4 Phil : 2^d. He saw the excellency and necessity of it in the church of Christ in his day, and is it not so at this day ? O God let us be found in the spirit of it !

(6) Whatever you do in the worship and service of God, carefully see that your chief motives therein, and thereto, be not the examples of others, slavish fear of men, and persecution by men ; this will not bear you out before God : but let them be obedience to a divine precept, general or particular ; a persuasion of God's spirit with yours, that the way of worship you walk in is agreeable to God's revealed will, (for what ever is not of faith is sin) and that love to God in Christ engages you so to worship and walk.

(7) Wherein you differ in your opinion and practice from others, take heed of contemning or reproaching each other ; of animosity and bitterness of spirit against one another ; but rather pity each other, and in love, counsel, instruct and pray one for another, waiting patiently for God's blessing on these counsels and prayers : in the meantime 'forbearing one another in love' until God by his spirit shall reveal his mind to them that differ from you. If any be overtaken in a fault, you that are spiritual, restore such a one with the spirit of meekness, considering thyself, lest thou also be tempted.

(8) Take heed of all sinful compliances and mixtures of human inventions with divine institutions in the worship of God. Will worship will prove vain worship. We must not be men's servants, but Christ's ; not seek to please them but him. We must not lift our tool on God's altar, lest we defile it, nor set our post by His, our Dagon by his ark, lest we be broke in pieces.

(9) Take heed of a spirit of estrangement from each other but maintain a holy christian communion as you can. God promises his presence to the meeting of two or three. When you meet, let it be for the better ; for mutual edification, (Mal. III. 16). Strengthen one another's hands in God as Jonathan did David's when he was in the wood.

(10) Sit loose to the creatures, and all creature-enjoyments. Sit near and cleave close to your dear Lord Jesus. Seek not great things here for yourselves, but seek the things above, where Christ sits at the right hand of God ; Let your affections and conversation be in heaven, and lay up your treasures there where thieves cannot break through nor steal. Many Demas's there are who do and will forsake Christ's interest, to embrace the present world. What is written aforetime is written for our learning.

(11) Really and frequently in your thoughts resign up yourselves with all that you are and have to the sole and sovereign disposal of the only wise God, and Almighty Creator and Governor of all ; and seeing our times, our all, are in his hand, a hand so good, so powerful, so tender, so safe, let us humbly, quietly, and contentedly leave all there with all patience and long-suffering; verily believing that he will order all for His glory and for the good of His.

(12) Give all diligence to make your calling and election sure ; to get assurance of God's love and favour in Christ to your souls in particular. All we have is now going ; there is no assurance of liberty, estate, relations, or life to any. O that this might awaken us to assure God in Christ to us ! that while evil men are devising and endeavouring to take all from us, we may on good grounds say, The Lord is our portion, and he being ours, in him we inherit all things.

(13) Get and maintain in your souls an inward spiritual joy and peace in believing. In every thing give thanks. Rejoice in the Lord always. Again I say rejoice. This will be your strength, to mortify corruptions, resist temptations, perform all duties absolute and relative, and with courage to undergo the worst of sufferings you can meet with ; to persevere to the end in doing and suffering God's will, that therein being faithful unto death, you may obtain a crown of life ; That you may embrace the counsel given O pray, pray, watch and pray ; pray for your selves, for me, and for all that love Christ in sincerity, that I, you, they, may be accounted worthy either to escape those dismal things that are coming upon us, or if not, yet may stand before the Son of Man, when he comes to judge the world in righteousness, with courage, confidence and comfort.

Thus my dear hearts, I have answered your desires in your last I received, heartily letting you know, that though I am absent in body from you to my great grief, yet I am present with you in Spirit, daily praying for you, longing to see you, which I should have done once and again, had not Satan hindered ; which he will do till Christ comes and binds him in chains and removes him, out of the way and gives his people a quiet and full enjoyment of himself in each other. Which that he may is the earnest prayer of your unworthy pastor, solicitous for your soul's good.

T.M. Senr.

Communicate this to ours.

II.

October 19, 1683.

Mercy unto you and peace and love be multiplied.

My dearly beloved and longed for in the bowels of Jesus Christ, in whom I bless God for you that you yet stand fast in the faith, and in the Bible where with Christ hath made you free and are not yet entangled in that Yoke of Bondage again in which you formerly were ; and that my last contributed to that freedom as your last I thankfully received testified to my no little refreshing in my banished wandering state which is such that unfits me for converse with you either personally or literally. However I cannot but sometimes overcome myself to express my mindfulness of you in my inforced absence from you, which separation is, as soul from body, a Death to me being a forerunner of my Final Departure which cannot be long, having more than filled up the days of my years and being disabled to serve you those few that yet remain, I conceive it advisable to choose some other who may not be under my circumstances, may be resident with you, and be more capacitated for your edification than I possibly at present can. I propose this not to grieve or discourage any, or to give you the least room to think that I am about to desert you in your present sufferings. No, no for God strengthening me, its in my heart to live and die with you, but I understanding to my great grief what sad breaches there are among you, some going off one way, some another, is it not the best expedient to preserve the remainder in their present station, to have one among you in whom you may cordially unite. However know and consider that you who yet stand, stand by faith and dependence on Christ. If he withdraws you fall, therefore be not high minded but fear ; humble yourselves to walk with God for he will give more grace unto, and will save the humble person. Hath the way ye have walked in been God's way or no? Have ye had any comfortable meeting with God thro' Christ in that way? If so, what reason have ye to leave it? Are not ordinances divine appointments in which He communicates Himself graciously to His people far beyond what the things of themselves can do, and have you experienced this and will you desert this and try some other you are doubtful of wither God be in it or no? If you judge it the right way, its the counsell of Jehovah to his people (Ezekiel 46: 9) relating to gospel times that when they went to worship before the Lord, if they went in at the North gate, they must go out at the South ; they must go forward and not back again. Job. 17: 9 tells us that the righteous shall hold on his way and they that have clean hands shall be stronger and stronger. Those that are gone off, is it their strength or weakness? If this, follow not others in their infirmities. Did you not promise to endeavour a reformation according to God's word and have you not in some measure done it accordingly? And is not God's word the same it was and will not you be the same likewise? Will you begin in the spirit and end in the flesh, will you build again that you have destroyed? In so doing will not you make yourselves transgressors? Deal plainly and truly with me and your selves. Who do you verily think have most freedom and boldness with God at the throne of grace, have most sweet communion with the Father and Christ, have most comfort in holy

Pastoral Letters of Thomas Maidwell

es, have most interest in the heart's prayers
 the most strict and powerful Godly; wither those
om reformation begun, or those who resolutely pe
these then see you be found in their number.
consider, whither a compliance at present with
nterest in the worship of God in all the parts of it, c
ll the impositions and human inventions in God's v
those who willingly submit to them, as if they v
ations, and whither such compliances doth not harden
ossly ignorant atheistical profane persons who be
n baptism, confirmed therein in the Lord's Supper,
m of rising to life at the last day and that they are
of God and their way of serving God is the only
cause those that had left it are turned again to it u
ght as the best. [*Sic. Sense rather obscure.*]
sider whither this practice doth not grieve the he
ly pious ones, laying a stumbling block in their wa
eir ruin, and whither it doth not condemn themse
 so long from them to whom they are returned.
 worship was good, why did they leave it? If evil, v
rn to it again.
consider how they will avoid that reproachful branc
d levity, pretending conscience in following God's w
 yet now desert that out of slavish fear of men, or
ve of the world. Lastly consider what sad wou
made upon their spirits by so doing, to the loss of tl
he endangering of the loss of their reason, their li
rieving God's spirit, dishonouring his name, reproach
which things are not easily repaired. These conside
eighed may prove effectual, if not to reduce those 1
lers, yet to preserve those who stand from fall
 further Are you indeed willing to be one bread
ith the most ignorant and profane, as those are saic
ake with them in that one bread of the Lords Sup
: 16-17, and would you have your souls gathe
h them in the great day of the Lord? If not then
vicked ones from your communion now.
: "But its not in our power to do it."
Do you do your utmost in order to it? If not,
lt. Or doth the church you join with own a powe
o put from them such wicked persons upon complai
 is a great defect in discipline. If there be and
ere is a great neglect to Christ's dishonour
ent to them that join with them, seeing little probabi
mation.
: "The matters we differ in are but little and
ontest."

Answer: That we call little God may call great. Adam's eating the forbidden fruit. Uzziah's touching the Ark with a good intention. The Bethshemites looking into the Ark. Nadab's and Abihu's offering of strange fire. Annanias and Saphira's telling a lie, seemed small things in man's eyes, but how great and offensive in God's the dreadful punishment thereof demonstrated. His command is thou shalt not add to or diminish from his word. Deu. 12.32, Rev. 22, 18.19, especially in his worship for he is a jealous God. He will not bear an Idol set up in the heart. He is a Great God and there is not properly any little sin against a Great God.

Objection: "If we comply not we are undone."

Answer: Had that been a good argument there never had been a martyr. Christ says: "He that will save his life shall lose it, but he that shall lose it for my sake and the Gospel's, shall find it and shall have a hundred fold here with persecution, and hereafter life eternal." If that believed, will not satisfy you, I know not what will.

Objection: "But many professors do or will comply."

Answer: God's word, not the example of others is our rule. God's flock is a little one and that of slaughter. You hear [Paul] himself complain all men forsake him and prays God it may not be laid to their charge. However things be my counsel is that you choose suffering rather than sin. Suffer not when you can avoid it without sin and sin not to avoid suffering.

(2) Whoever reproaches you let not your hearts reproach you. Maintain Job's resolution, Job 27 : 6. Do nothing doubtingly, especially in religious worship lest you contract guilt. Let every one be fully persuaded in his and her own mind, Rom. 14 : 8, 21, 23, and wisely consider though any of you can freely hear a gifted person declare the truths of the gospel to you, yet whither you can with a clear and good conscience join in a complete and constant communion with that church in all her appointments, whose constitution, matter, officers, practices, order and government is disagreeing with the word of God, and that wants power in itself or willingness to reform according thereto.

(3) As for those who differ from you, follow the apostle's counsel, 2nd Thess. 3, 14, 15 ; Gal. 6, 1, 2 ; Rom. 14 and 15, 1 to 7 ; 1 Thess. 5, 11 to 15 ; James 3, 3, 14, 15 and 5, 19, 20 ; Gal. 5, 13, 14 ; Heb. 11, 14, 15. I know sorrow will fill your hearts for the departure of your brethren, yet count them not as enemies, but admonish mildly as brethren. Make the breach no wider than needs must ; Satan and his agents, the sowers of discord among brethren, will do that. As what you see evil in them you disallow and shun, so what you see of good in them commend and cherish. Outstrip them in acts of kindness and condescension, which you will find the nearest and best way to win them to Christ and you in a nearer conjunction. Use candid words void of passion, manifesting bowels

towards them when you use the strongest arguments. If nothing will do, cry to God on their behalf, and in the meantime say to your souls "wait on the Lord and keep his way, be of good courage and he shall strengthen thine heart, wait I say on the Lord" and if you cannot this present day have and enjoy what you would, in everything give thanks to God for what you have.

(4) Grow in grace daily and in the knowledge of and acquaintance with Christ. The more you trust and love him, the more you shall enjoy his love shed abroad in your hearts, which will render your joy in him more unspeakable and glorious. A little strength will hardly enable us to keep his word as not to deny his name. Therefore press after greater measures, after Christ, stature and fulness, that through him you may be more than conquerors. Methinks when Christ is on the throne in the heart, all the evils and glories of self and the world vanish at his appearance, and fall before him as those wicked ones did that came to take him.

(5) Look to your relative duties; slumber not over secret prayer; mind the matter more than the manner; its not length, but strength; mind what God says to you as well as what you say to God.

(6) Disquiet not yourselves with imaginary evils which oft times are more distressing than real. Inure yourselves to do God's precepts and will daily, then you will more easily suffer his afflicting will.

Lastly: Live what lies in you in the believing view of heavenly glory, so as to be transformed from glory to glory, which I find by experience a great help to sweeten present sufferings. Christ for the joy that was set before him, endured the cross, despised the shame and is set down gloriously on the right hand of the majesty on high. Was it the best for Christ? Is it not the best for us? Let's overcome with him, and we shall sit in the throne with him. Now to Him that is able to keep you from falling and present you faultless before the presence of his glory with exceeding joy, to the only wise God, our Saviour be glory, majesty, dominion and power, now and ever Amen.

Yours unfeignedly,

III.

January 24:

My Dearly Beloved in our dearest Lord,

    I had visited you long ere this, either personally or literally, or both, had not the severity of the season and my own illness prevented so that I could not comfortably either hold my pen to write or my bridle to ride, and truly its no little affliction of soul to me that our sins should be such and so provoking our God as to separate us so much from our God and each other. Oh the many miseries and calamities that the sins of God's people have brought on themselves and others this day, for their sins being acted against most light, strength and love are most God-provoking, therefore his controvercy is chiefly with them everywhere and with us amongst others which cries aloud to us for our awaking from our carnal security more strictly and severely than ever, so to search our hearts and ways. Wherefore our God contends with us as to reform whatever is discerned amis that God may turn to us with ordering and healing mercy. And may we not fear that there are some sins lurking in us and amongst us which are little notified by us and make least noise in the world, as sinful self love, inordinate love of the world, spiritual pride in gifts and graces, crying sins, insensibleness of God's severe hand stretched out amongst us, of the departing of gospel glory from us and of too many from it. What secret distrust of God's care for us and ours ; what unthankfulness for mercies ; what unfruitfulness under means ; what formality in God's worship and quiet resting in outward forms in the want of life, spirit, and power, and that in such a day as this is hath much provocation in it ; these and the like evils I see myself too much guilty of and is matter of great rebuke to me. I believe its so to you, but this I hope we can all say, its our daily burden and grief and that we have frequent recourse to Christ in a covenant of grace for pardon of it and power over it, and that we are returning to our first love, our first works, our first husband, for then it was better with us than now. For all that love Christ in sincerity shall by experience find that suitable to their drawing nigh to God in religious worship and walking, He will draw nigh to them as He hath said James 4.8, And the Lord is with you while you are with him but if you forsake him he will forsake you. 2 Chron. 15.2. When He is less sought, slightly and formally, He is less found and the soul hath less communion with Him, is under much darkness, distress, and unquietness ; but when He is vigorously sought and the heart makes near approaches to Him by the lively actings of faith and love then usually God makes his near approaches to that soul in tastes of his goodness and manifestations of his love to the soul as he promised John 14,21. Now I am jealous over you as over myself with a Godly jealousy lest you are fallen under some spiritual decay. Some under more who thro' slavish fear of men, or loss of creature comforts are gone out of the inward court to the outward, to the condemning reproach of their own hearts and grief of others. Some under less who tho' they kept their standing in the work of reformation engaged in, yet through unwatchfulness, and embracing the present world slightings of spirit in holy performances, and many discouragements from themselves and others, may grow remiss and lukewarm and thereby lose their sweet communion with God. Oh my friends how bent are our hearts to backsliding, tho' the backslider in heart shall be

The "Conventicle House," Kettering
shewing at X the window by which the preacher escaped

filled with his own ways, therefore let's all take up the resolution and practice of the church Jeremiah 3, 22. Behold we come unto Thee for Thou art the Lord our God. And Hosea 2, 7. When the church cannot find contentment and quiet in seeking other lovers, saith, I will go and return to my first husband for then it was better with me than now ; which words have of late left some impressions upon my heart and I wish they may upon yours in which you may observe :

(1) Seeking after other lovers rather than after God in Christ who is love, we shall meet with great disappointments. They shall seek them but shall not find them.

(2) That we may weary ourselves in byways and find no rest until we return to God. I will return to my first husband. Return to thy rest O my soul.

(3) A heart effectually touched by God resolves to return unto God, as before verse 5, She said I will go after my lovers, now resolves, I will return to God.

(4) There's nothing got by departing from Christ. The church confesses it was best with her when she was nearest Christ Job. 27.8. A man that backslideth from Christ may think to gain riches, credit, freedom from troubles, but what will he gain saith Job when God takes away his soul. Demas.

(5) There must be a conviction of sin and shame for it before the sinner will return from it to God. The Prodigal.

(6) Sometimes its better, sometimes its worse with God's people. Better when they are nearer in union and communion with God in Christ their husband. Worse when they thro' their backsliding are distance from Christ and Christ from them.

(7) The main thing as one observes in those words is that a clear sight,—how much better it was when the heart did cleave to Christ over it was now since its departure from Christ—is an effectual means to cause the heart to return to him. This Christ advises Rev. 2.5, and this we may understand by experience wither our present departure be it more as in some or less as in others, may not Gods people now under spiritual decay say as one observes :—

(1) Heretofore when I did cleave to God in Christ and walked close with him, I could thro' God's mercy behold the face of God with joy thro Christ, shining on me, but now there is a cloud over that face, the light of his countenance is darkness to me to my great grief. Oh then it was better with me than now !

(2) Then I had free access to the throne of God's grace and could pour out my heart to him with a holy and humble boldness and confidence. Oh but now I am filled with slavish fear. I have sad apprehensions of God as an enemy and its rather dictates of conscience than earnest desire of communion with God that puts me upon duty. Oh then it was better with me than now !

(3) Then I could look on the precious promises, lay claim to them, take hold of them, rejoice in them as my own, my own legacies and inheritance ; but now I question my interest in them and good title to them. They are not precious to me as heretofore. Oh then it was better with me than now !

(4) Then Christ and His spirit made frequent and gracious visits to my soul which had then sweet communion with him. The glimpses of God's face and seals of His loving kindness was sweeter than life to me, but now its far otherwise. He scarce looks thro' the lattice to me. He stands behind the wall. My beloved hath withdrawn himself and is gone. Oh then it was better with me than now !

(5) Then the ordinances of God was indeed divine ordinances unto me. I met with God in them. I heard God speaking to me in the word. I had sweet intercourse with him in prayer. The sacrament was a seal of God's pardoning love in Christ to me, but now its far otherwise. Having changed my pastor, I want the green pastures which formerly my soul fed in and tho' the pasture of itself be good, yet I find not the sweet incense of Christ refreshing my soul thereby. Oh then it was better with me than now !

(6) Then all grace was vigorously acted as Faith, Patience, Humility and God in the creatures comfortably enjoyed. The company of saints was dear to me and mine to them. I sat under the shadow of God's care and protection with great delight. The thoughts of death and suffering for Christ was rather desirable than terrible to me. Then I had much joy and peace of conscience in believing and doing God's will, but now its far otherwise with me. Grace if any is at a very low ebb. Many mercies are enjoyed but I want the God of those mercies. I have sometimes the company of God's people but methinks they look shy on me. Its not so delightful as heretofore. God is not such a sun and shield to me as he hath been. The thoughts of death and suffering for Christ are rather terrible than desirable and that inward peace and tranquility I had is turned to dissatisfaction, unquietness and trouble so that I may truly say that it was better with me then than now. If so let this be a forcible argument to me and you all to turn to our first husband Christ from whom we have in the least revolted and let it be considerate, rational, speedy, unfeigned, effectual, and persevering, and then it will be better with us in poverty than in abundance, in a prison than at liberty, under the wrath and rage of a wicked world and devils than under all their smiles and commendations, in sickness than in health, in adversity than in prosperity, in the worst of deaths for Christ's sake than in the best of lives without Christ. Which that it may be to me and you all is and shall be fervent and daily prayer of your souls friend and servant in Christ.

T.M. Sen.

John Penry in Scotland

AFTER the printing of the last of the Marprelate tracts, the *Protestatyon*, we learn from Matt. Sutcliffe that Penry "lurked here and there" in the Midlands; but always in touch in Job Throkmorton; by whose directions Jenkin Jones was able to find him in a certain odd ale house eighteen miles from Fawsley (*Ans. to Job Throk.* 73). Sutcliffe goes on to say that Throkmorton still kept in touch with Penry "when the sun began to shine so hot in England that Penry could not abide it, but must seek for a colder region." One definite trace of this journey to Scotland occurs in the statement of John Udall before the Privy Council on January 13th, 1590. For the previous twelve months Udall had been labouring at Newcastle-on-Tyne.[1] "A quarter of a yeere" earlier, that is, in the beginning of October, Penry called at his door. It was a hurried visit. The fugitive did not pass the threshold nor even receive any refreshment. (Wall's *New Discovery*, 93). Early in 1590 we begin to find evidence of Penry's residence in Scotland.

Robert Waldegrave, the well known Puritan printer, after printing *Hay any Worke* at Coventry relinquished his dangerous post as Marprelate's printer and escaped to Rochelle. He and Penry were present at the Haseley conference, which we assign to the interval between the printing of

---

[1] Udall preached before the king and court on the occasion of his visit to the General Assembly at Edinburgh in June, 1589.—*Reg. of the Priv. Council Scot.* IV, 518. Dr. Masson's note.

Marprelate's *Protestatyon* and Penry's appearance at Udall's door at Newcastle. Waldegrave brought with him to Haseley the editions he had printed, presumably at Rochelle, of *M. Some in his coulers* and Penry's *Appellation*, desiring Throkmorton's instructions as to their disposal. (*Answere to Job Throk.* 72 rect. 73 rect.) These dangerous commodities were not allowed to stay at Haseley. The stock of both tracts and almost the entire edition of the *Protestatyon* were taken to the house of Henry Godley of Northampton; and the natural conclusion is that they were carried thither by Penry and Waldegrave. Then the two men would continue their journey north. That Waldegrave did not call at Udall's door (Udall does not say that he did not) need not surprise us. Waldegrave was as circumspect and as cautious as Penry was risky in his movements. In any case Waldegrave was in Edinburgh early in 1590, established as a printer. *The Confession of Faith* printed by him at Edinburgh has the authorization of the Lords of the Council dated March 13th, 1590. In the following month, as seems probable, he printed Penry's *Reformation no Enemie*, and on the 16th May Robert Bowes, the English ambassador, formally complains to king James that Penry is in his realm publishing books against the government of England (*S. P. Scot* [Eliz.] 45.44). Bowes points out to the king that Penry had " falne wth in the case of treason," and asks that he should be banished from Scotland. The king appears favourable to the request and promises to enquire into the matter and to give orders accordingly.

We hear nothing further of Penry until Bowes' letter to Burghley on August 1st (*Ibid.* 46.22) which reports that " The k. at this convencōn hathe giuen order for the banishm[t] of Penrie, and directed the Chancelo[r] to see the same executed at his returne hither from Dunfermling on Mondaie next." The chancellor appears to have lost no time in taking up the case. On the following Thursday, August 6th, the writ of banishment was issued by "The Kingis Majestie with advice of the Lordis of his Secreit Counsall" (*Reg. of Priv. Council of Scot.* IV. 517*f*). Officers of arms and sheriffs are to proclaim "John Pennerie, Inglisman," at the "mercat croces of the head barrowis [burroughs]" charging him to depart from the realm "within ten dayis nixt eftir he be chargeit thairto," under severe penalties. The king's lieges are also warned under similar penalties not to have intercourse with him "or furneis him meit, drink, hous or herbery." The proclamation was doubtless made in due form at the market crosses, but as the months went on the information which reached the ears of Elizabeth's government was to the effect that Penry was still in Scotland and that Waldegrave was openly working at his craft. Morever there was evidently a suspicion that Robert Bowes, who belonged to Berwick-on-Tweed, was not as zealous as he might be in seeing that the decree of banishment was actually carried out. It is certain that neither at Berwick nor at Edinburgh was there any excess of zeal in pursuing a man whose treason consisted in opposing Elizabeth's episcopal system and in appealing for the evangelization of Wales. Robert Bowes, however, is at great pains as her Majesty's representative to clear himself of any such suspicions; writing to that effect on November 20th, 1590 (*S. P. Scot.* [Eliz.] 46.64). He had duly informed his Majesty that "it was merveiled in Ingland" that Penry should still be suffered to remain in Scotland, or that "Walgrave the printer" should be "permitted freelie to print seditiouse bookes against his natiue countrie"; his Majesty was urged to carry out the

order of banishment. The king and the chancellor
both disavow any knowledge that Penry is still in
Scotland, having been "credibly informed that he
was departed"; but they promise that a search
shall be made. With regard to Waldegrave the
case is different. The reason is that Scotland
"standeth nede of a printer"—there had been no
king's printer appointed since the departure of
Vautrollier. Besides, "Walgrave with submission
had acknowledged his fault in printing ... a
booke set forth by Penry," and had entered into a
"great bonde" only to print in the future by permission and allowance of the king. As for Bowes
himself he had truly thought that Penry had departed. He was so informed by "some of good
creditt," and "sondry godlie ministers in the
Towne" still held that opinion. As for his zeal
in the matter, and his statement on this point is
important, he says that:—

> "Sundry ministers here haue m^{r}ueiled to behold
> the earnestness of my course herein, and left my
> company for the same. Whereupon I have not
> thought it profitable for her Ma^{tis} seruice in my
> charge (wch I respect more than my life) so sharpelie
> to prick the rest, as I should chaise them also from me,
> together with the losses of the best affected in the
> nobilitie. All wch haue no litle regard to the course of
> the ministery, as in all services I haue had good
> experience."

Over against these lines there is a note in the
margin in Burleigh's hand: "I wrote Sōe what
rōdly to Mr bowes not to be ledd away w^t the
unruly ministers." At the close of the year,
December 18th, Bowes again refers to Penry and
Waldegrave. Concerning the latter the news is
that he has been appointed king's printer. But
the king has been informed "by persons very
honest" that Penry had departed. And we are
given the interesting information that "his wife

John Penry in Scotland 383

)weth in this Towne supported by benevo-
f his friends here. Whereof some of them
;sured me that he departed indede from her
 while past, and hath no repair to her,
is it knowne where he is." This concludes
erences to Penry in this collection of MSS.
y now draw out the significance of one or
 the statements.
, we have plain proof how the ministers
ly regarded the decree of banishment
against Penry and the zeal manifested by
in seeking to get it executed. They boy-
 the ambassador. He had to deal very
 with those with whom he had had hitherto
ercourse about Penry, lest the whole of the
y should hold aloof from him. The
y, barons and burgesses had such regard
 ministry that they also would in all like-
 follow their example. The ministers
iot stay the promulgation of the order of
ment against Penry, but they regarded with
ient the too careful enquiries of Bowes into
rying out of the order. The information
y spies in Scotland to Burleigh, and the
ige of the Penry-Throkmorton correspon-
by Bancroft's minions (Sutcliffe's *Answere*,
;., and Baker MSS. [Camb.] Mm. 1-47[28])
tve convinced Burleigh and Whitgift that
 was in Scotland. It was clear, however,
e ministers meant to shield him against the
on of decree of expulsion from Scottish soil.
t was the autumn of 1592 before Penry
 left his harbourage among the Presby-
; but apparently until the last they shielded
[n proof of this let us turn to the deposition
n Edwards concerning his journey from
d in company with Penry. (Mr. Gasquoine
ently drawn particular attention to the

discrepancy between the date given for this journey by Edwards and that given by Penry in his companion deposition). The document is itself a rudely penned record of Edwards's examination, and Edwards himself was only imperfectly acquainted with the inwardness of the facts about which he is led to speak. His words on the point of the decree of banishment are:—

> "Penry was not banished out of Scotland, but there was Banishment decreed against him and the mynisters ever stay the proclaiming thereof."

The testimony though incorrect in form is amply sufficient for our purpose. This is the information which Edwards brought out of Scotland at the close of Penry's sojourn in that country. It explains why, after the issuing of the decree of banishment on the 6th of August, 1590, Penry remained in Scotland until September (or November), 1592. This is not to say that Penry never paid a furtive visit across the border during this period. It would be unlike this daring spirit to be confined to Scotland by a sense of danger, if his chivalrous heart believed that a journey into England were required in the interests of the cause of Christ. What is sufficiently plain from the letters of Robert Bowes, the complaints of Burleigh, the testimony of John Edwards, as well as the facts concerning the intercepted correspondence passing between Haseley and Edinburgh, is, that Scotland was the general residence of Penry from October, 1590, to the autumn of 1592.

But there is a second point in the Scottish letters which demands a further brief notice. It is that concerning Mrs. Penry. On December, 18th, 1590, Bowes reports that she "contineweth in this Towne supported by benevolence of [Penry's] friends." The assumption was that Penry was gone and ha left his wife destitute to depend upon the generosity of his Presbyterian friends. We know there was a little child born before this date. Penry was married in September, 1588, and was hanged in May, 1593. Four daughters were born to him, and before his death he wrote them a final message, to be read to them when they should attain to years of discretion. He charges them to be kind to "all strangers, and unto the people of Scotland, where I, your mother, and a couple of you, lived as strangers and yet were welcome and found great kindness in the name of our God." Thinking pathetically of their helpless infancy he says "the eldest of you is not yet four years old and the youngest not yet four months." We have to arrive at some reasonable theory why Penry should mention only two of his children as having received kindness from the people of Scotland.

The youngest child was clearly born in London. When Edwards and Penry reached Stratford-by-Bow they found Mrs. Penry already there. She had a chamber at " ye sign of the Cross Keys." The imminence of the birth of her child may have dictated her earlier departure from Scotland. The eldest child was the Deliverance Penry whose marriage with Thomas Whitaker the bombazine worker, on May 14th, 1611, is happily recorded in the Amsterdam register (see *Transactions*, vol. ii, p. 165). She was then 21 years old and stated to be native of Hamptonshire (that is, Northamptonshire). To make the round figure 21 years quite exact we should have to add or to deduct a certain number of months. Let us suppose she were born in July, 1589. She would then be 3 years 9 months old when her father described her as "not yet four years," and 21 years all but two months at her marriage. This we may regard as satisfying the chronological data. The little Deliverance would be a year and five months old when Bowes reported that Mrs. Penry continued to reside in Edinburgh. But the ambassador mentions no child. Indeed by all reckoning a second child was soon to be born. And from the particularities of Bowes' reports we cannot help the conviction that if he knew there was a child he would undoubtedly have mentioned it in his report to Burleigh. Nor is it any easier to believe that in so small a community as Edinburgh was in 1590, there was a child as well as the wife of Penry, without Bowes knowing the fact. No hypothesis therefore meets so well the requirements of the case, as to suppose that the Northamptonshire child should have remained in the house where it was born, in the charge of its grandparents, when the mother felt it her duty to undertake the journey to Scotland to join her husband. She was at the time in delicate health, and the care of a baby on that journey would have added enormously to her burden. This leaves us free to believe that the two children to whom the people of Scotland shewed such kindness were the second and third daughters. The fourth we know was born in (or near) London early in December, 1592. Since we have such strong reasons for believing in Penry's continuous residence in Scotland between October, 1590, and the autumn of 1592, and since it is necessary to exclude one of the three oldest children from the kind ministrations of the Scottish people, the remaining of the eldest child with its grandparents, when Helen Penry went on her hazardous journey to dwell with her fugitive husband among strangers, is the most natural hypothesis that suggests itself to us.

WILLIAM PIERCE.

Early Nonconformist Academies: Sheriff Hales

II

ONE of the most important of the provincial academies was that at Sheriff Hales, near Newport in Shropshire, conducted by the Rev. John Woodhouse. Unfortunately our information respecting him is very incomplete; we know neither the place nor the date of his birth, nor his college, nor the time of his entering or leaving the University. He must, however, have been at Cambridge during the period of Puritan ascendancy; having previously, it would seem, experienced a spiritual awakening in very early life. Dr. D. Williams, who preached his funeral sermon, says that "he was so remarkably serious as to be admitted into the intimate society of some of the gravest divines of that place." But he removed thence while still young, and became private chaplain to one Lady Grantham in Nottinghamshire. He held this post for several years, devoting much time to study, but also, as occasion offered, preaching and visiting the sick. Calamy says "God was pleased to give a signal blessing to his ministry. About the Vale of Belvoir he diffused saving light, and was an instrument in the conversion of great numbers." Not holding any ecclesiastical benefice he cannot be strictly counted among the ejected ministers; but the Act of Uniformity effectually prevented him from taking office in the Established Church. Conformity, says Dr. Williams, "he disallowed upon maturest thoughts, and few were so well qualified to manage that controversy as he was."

He seems to have resided in Nottinghamshire or Leicestershire till 1667, when he married Mary, daughter of William Hubbard of Rearsby who had been a major in the army under Monk. She is described as "a lady of singular piety, as well as handsome fortune." It is probable that soon after his marriage he became tenant of the manor house at Sheriff Hales, which was vacated in 1667 by the death of Francis Fowler, the adopted son and heir of the last of the Levesons—the old family to whom it formerly belonged. It is not, however, certain when Mr. Woodhouse took up his residence there. There are indications that he was at Saxleby, Leicestershire, in 1669, and at Wartnaby in the same county in 1670, 1672, and 1675; but these may have been temporary visits. On the other hand the first *certain* evidence of his presence at Sheriff Hales is in 1676.

It was presumably about this time, or a little earlier, that he commenced his academy. "He piously managed his house as a nursery for heaven, as well as a school for promoting learning; and the many excellent ministers in the church, and eminent gentlemen both qualified and disposed to serve their country, who were educated by him, were sufficient proofs of his ability for his office and fidelity in it. Many of his pupils owned him as their spiritual father. Possessed of an ample fortune, he educated several students entirely at his own expense, and was liberal to his brethren who stood in need of relief." We are told of threatenings, losses, fines and imprisonments which he endured, but which failed to divert him from the course which he had adopted only after ample consideration; of these persecutions, however, no details have come down to us.

In Toulmin's *History of the Protestant Dissenters*

may be found a full account of the course of study pursued at Sheriff Hales, with the names of the authors read in each department. This was derived from papers furnished to Dr. Toulmin by a descendant of Mr. Woodhouse. It may suffice to say that, in addition to Latin, Greek, Hebrew and mathematics, instruction was given in history, geography, and natural science, logic, rhetoric, ethics and metaphysics, as well as in anatomy, law and divinity. All the students were required to read Grotius *De Veritate Religionis Christianae*, Wilkins's *Principles of Natural Religion*, Baxter's *Reasons of the Christian Religion*, Bates *On the Existence of God, Immortality of the Soul*, &c., Fleming's *Confirming Work*, Stillingfleet's *Origines Sacrae*, with parts of Bochart. The divinity students also read the *Westminster Confession of Faith* and *Larger Catechism*, Corbet's *Humble Endeavour*, Ruffonius's *Compendium of Turretin*, Calvin's *Institutes*, Pareus on Ursinus, Baxter's *End of Controversy* and *Methodus Theologiae*, Williams's *Gospel Truth*, Le Blanc's *Theses*, and Dixon's *Therapeutica Sacra*. Once a week the tutor was accustomed to read to the senior class a didactic or polemical lecture either on Wollebius's *Compendium Theologiae*, or on Ames's *Medulla Theologiae;* and on Sunday mornings, at the time of family prayer, the junior class were expected to give an account of some part of Vincent's *Exposition of the Shorter Catechism*. The students were accustomed to hold "disputations after a logical form"; and were practised in English composition in the form of letters and speeches. The divinity students were also exercised "in analysing some verses of a psalm or chapter, drawing up skeletons or heads of sermons, and short schemes of prayer and devotional specimens according to Bishop Wilkins's method; and were called on to pray in the family in the evening of the Lord's day, and to set psalms to two or three tunes."

It may be worth while to enumerate the authors chiefly studied in the arts course at Sheriff Hales:

In Mathematics. Galtruchius, Gassendi, Gunter, Leybourn, Moxon, "and Euclid's Elements, which were read late."
In Natural Science. De Carte's *Principia*, De Stair, Heereboord, Magirus, Rhegius, Rohault.
In Logic. Burgedicius, with Heereboord's commentary; Sanderson, Wallis, Ramus, and his commentator Downam, for private perusal.
In Rhetoric. Quinctilian, Radeau, Vossius.
In Metaphysics. Baronius, Facchaeus, Frommenius; also Blank's *Theses* and Ward's *Determinationes*.
In Ethics. Eustachius, Heereboord, More, Whitby.
In Geography. Eachard.
In History. Puffendorf.
In Anatomy. Gibson, Bartholine, and Blancardi *Anatomia Reformata*.

The law students read *Doctor and Student*, Littleton's *Tenures*, and Coke upon Littleton.

The Hebrew text books used were Bythner's grammar, and his *Lyra Prophetica*.

A leading characteristic of Mr. Woodhouse's tuition seems to have been thoroughness. Each day an account of the preceding day's lecture was required before a new lecture was read; most authors were read over twice; and on Saturdays the business of the past five days was reviewed. To the lay students various practical exercises were occasionally assigned, such as land surveying, constructing dials, or dissections. To the divinity students "a plain and familiar way of preaching" was constantly recommended, as best suiting "a faithful diligent aim at usefulness in saving immortal souls."

The last appearance of Mr. Woodhouse's name on the parish register of Sheriff Hales is in 1691, when his daughter Mary was married to a Mr. Oliver Cromwell. The identity of this gentleman

for an alleged share in the "Yorksh
was afterwards the guest of Bishop R
Norwich; and died at his birthplace in

Oliver the son of John Cromwell had
Mary a son John, born at Basford, 2nd
and voted in a Nottinghamshire electi
Whether these Cromwells were at all
the family of the Protector is uncertair
connection was remote.

It is *supposed* that Mr. Woodhouse w
in the work of tuition by the Re
Beresford. He was a native of Shrews
student at King's College, Cambridge,
graduated B.A. in 1651, and M.A. in
was ordained at Wirksworth 21st July,
ministered at St. Werbergh's, Derby,
1657, to the ejectment in 1662. On the
the Five Mile Act he removed to Sh
where he commenced a school, but fa
to his lack of disciplinary power. He
up his abode at Weston, near Shiffnal,
patronage of Lady Wilbraham; and
16th October, 1697.

Not long before this Mr. Woodhous
strained by "some unhappy circums
break up the academy. The facts are
stated; but indications point to 1
feeblement by some painful distem
compulsory retirement occasioned
distress. "Now," said he, "every field is 1

for I fear I shall live to no purpose." The break-up of the academy was presumably late in 1696; for on the 15th February, 1697, a lease of the manor was granted to the Rev. Edward Aston, rector of Kemberton.

The fear of uselessness which distressed Mr. Woodhouse was of no long continuance. In a short time he was invited to succeed Dr. Annesley as pastor of a congregation in Little St. Helen's, Bishopsgate, of which he took charge before the end of 1697. His ministry there, though of short continuance, was abundantly fruitful, and ended only with his life. A few days before his death he "took a kind of solemn farewell of his people in a sermon which he preached with his usual warmth." The date of his death is not recorded; but it was toward the end of 1700.

As a theologian he appears to have been sound without narrowness. Dr. Williams says: "In disputed articles of faith ... he was ... skilful as well as orthodox; though disallowing extremes, particularly as to the Extent of the death of Christ, and Conditionality of the Covenant, with several things depending thereupon." His only published works are *A Sermon on the death of Mrs. Jane Papillon*, 1698; *A Sermon before the Society for Reformation of Manners*, 1697; and *A Catalogue of Sins, highly useful for Self-Examination*, &c. 1699.

The following list of ministers trained by Woodhouse at Sheriff Hales is chiefly derived from the Wilson MSS. at New College; but is supplemented from other sources. As there is no evidence on which to found a chronological arrangement, it seems best to place the names alphabetically.

Benjamin Bennett, Newcastle-on-Tyne : author of *The Christian Oratory, &c.*, died 21st September, 1726, aged 52.

Chewning Blackmore : son of W. Blackmore, M.A., ejected from St. Peter's, Cornhill; minister at Worcester ; died 1742.

SHERIFF HALES MANOR HOUSE.
Photo kindly lent by the Rev. A. T. Michell, M.A., F.S.A.

Sheriff Hales

Richard Carver : minister at Stretton-under-Fosse ; still living in 1745.
Matthew Clark : son of Matthew Clark ejected from Narborough ; minister at Miles Lane ; died 27th March, 1726.
Mr Doughty (name added in another hand at the foot of the list among the Wilson MSS.)
George Flower : domestic chaplain to Mr. Foley, afterwards first dissenting minister at Stourbridge ; ordained 14th April, 1698 ; died 1st June, 1733, aged 60.
Daniel Greenwood : minister at West Bromwich, afterwards at Birmingham and Oldbury ; died about 1730.
Jonathan Hand : assistant to Chewning Blackmore at Worcester ; ordained 30th May, 1699 ; died December, 1719.
——Hayley : minister at Leominster ; died 1719.
John Newman : minister at Salter's Hall ; ordained 20th October, 1697 ; died 25th July, 1741.
John Norris : minister at Welford, Northants ; died 8th February, 1738, aged 63.
Edward Oasland : son of Henry Oasland ejected from Bewdley, minister in the same town ; died 1750.
Samuel Philips : minister at Bromyard ; died 1721.
John Ratcliff : minister at Jamaica Road, Rotherhithe ; ordained 1705 ; died 16th February, 1728.
Benjamin Robinson: ordained at Findern, October, 1688; opened a grammar school there ; removed to Hungerford 1693, and trained a few students there for the ministry ; removed to London 1701, succeeding Mr. Woodhouse at Little St. Helen's ; died 30th April, 1724.
Paul Russel : itinerant in Staffordshire and Worcestershire ; associated with work at Coseley, but usually lived at Gnossall.
Ferdinando Shaw : son of S. Shaw, ejected from Long Whatton, Leicestershire ; minister at Derby from 1697 ; died 1743, aged 72.
John Southwell : nephew of Richard Southwell ejected from Baswick, Staffordshire, successively chaplain to Ph. Foley, Esq., assistant to Mr. Woodhouse, schoolmaster at Kidderminster, and minister at Dudley and Newbury, where he died about 1694. [See below.]
John Spilsbury : son of J. Spilsbury, M.A., ejected from Bromsgrove ; minister at Kidderminster. He was nephew and executor of Dr. John Hall, bishop of Bristol ; died 31st January, 1727, aged 60.
Joseph Stokes : minister at Dudley, 1701-43.
James Thompson : minister at Bromsgrove from 1699 ; died 1729.
William Tong : (also studied under Frankland at Natland), ordained 1687, minister at Knutsford, Chester, Coventry, and London ; died 21st March, 1727, aged 65.

Robert Travers: native of "Laniboy" (? Llanboidy), Carmarthenshire; studied also under James Owen at Oswestry; minister at Longdon and Lichfield; ordained 27th September, 1692, still living in 1747.

James Warner: minister at Tewkesbury to 1737, afterwards at Walsall; died 1741.

John Warren: chaplain to Ph. Foley, Esq., near Kidderminster; then for nearly fifty years at Coventry, as assistant, co-pastor, and sole pastor; died 1742, aged 70.

Edward Warren: his brother; minister at Birdbush, Wilts.; living in 1736.

Wm. Willets: minister at Dudley from 1694; died Mar. 2, 1700.

William Woodhouse: son of John Woodhouse, is not mentioned in the list, but most likely received tuition from his father. He was ordained for Rearsby, Leicestershire, 21st August, 1702.

The lay students were very numerous, the total number in residence being at one time above forty; but only the following names have been preserved:

Robert Harley, afterwards Earl of Oxford; political celebrity, and collector of the *Harleian MSS.*; died 1724, aged 63.

Edward Harley, his brother.

Henry St. John, afterwards Viscount Bolingbroke, political adventurer; died 1751, aged 79.

Thomas Foley, afterwards Lord Foley.

Thomas Hunt of Boreaton; friend of Philip and Matthew Henry.

T. Winnington.

—— Leechmere.

—— Yates of Deanford; living in 1764, the last survivor of the Sheriff Hales academy.

NOTE.—Toulmin gives a tradition that the academy was carried on for some time by Mr. Southwell, and mentions Dr. Wm. Harris of Poor Jewry Lane (died 1740) and Thomas Leavesly of Little Baddow, afterwards of Old Jewry (died 1737), as among his students. But Southwell died before the removal of Mr. Woodhouse, having left the neighbourhood at least ten years earlier. If he "carried on" the academy it must have been as *locum tenens* during the absence—perhaps imprisonment—of Mr. Woodhouse; at which time Dr. Harris would be a boy of ten years old or less. He and Mr. Leavesly *may* perhaps have been pupils of Southwell at Kidderminster or Dudley; but the statement is most likely to be a mistake.

[For several of the facts above related we are indebted to the Rev. A. T. Michell, M.A., F.S.A., vicar of Sheriff Hales.]

[With reference to the London academies, the Rev. G. Lyon Turner furnishes the following additional information :

Charles Morton (p. 278) obtained licences for himself as a Presbyterian teacher, and for "a room in his dwelling-house at Kennington, in Lambeth" as a Presbyterian meeting-place, on 11th April, 1672 ; and for his house at St. Ives on 22nd July. In each case the application was made three times before the licence was issued. [These dates make it probable that the academy at Newington Green was not commenced before 1673].

William Wickens (p. 282) was licensed on 16th May, 1672, "to be a Pr. teacher in the house of John Forth in Hackney in Middlesex" ; the house was also licensed as a Presbyterian meeting-place.

Thomas Doolittle (p. 286). In Sheldon's *Return of Conventicles*, 1669, he is reported as having a congregation of 300 every Sunday, in Mugwell Street, in a house built on purpose. On the issue of the Indulgence he was one of the first to obtain a licence. It is dated 2nd April, 1672 ; and is recorded in the Entry Book as "allowing a certain Room adjoining the dwelling house of Thomas Doelittle in Mugwell Street to be a place for a Presbyterian teacher. Desired by Mr. Ja. Innes, & sent to him 4 Apr. 72." This Mr. Innes was the ejected minister of St. Breok, Cornwall ; he now lived in London, had some interest with Lauderdale, and enjoyed the personal favour of the king.

Thomas Vincent (p. 289) is represented in the Conventicle returns of 1669 as having a congregation of 500 "in Hand Alley, in Bpsgate Street, in a spacious Roome new built with galleries." He seems also to have occasionally visited Wiltshire ; where he figures as one of several preachers "at St. Lawrence Chapel, & at Mr. Buckley's house" at Warminster, to a promiscuous congregation of 200 or 300 Presbyterians, Independents, and Anabaptists ; also to a meeting of 400 or 500 in a barn at Hornington.

Edward Veal (p. 289) is mentioned both in the Conventicle returns of 1669, and in the licence documents, in such a way as to suggest that there was something unusual about him. In the former we have, written across the page, disregarding the columns, "Also one Mr. Veale an Independent hath lately set up a meeting in this parish, and first solicited for subscriptions before he would come." By 1672 he had evidently made himself a name in Wapping ; for the notice in the Entry book reads :

Wapping Congr.	The howse of .... near the hermitage by Wapping licensed to be a Congr. Meeting-place. 13 Apr. 1672.
Veale Pr Wapping	Licence to Edmund Veale to be a Pr. Tr. in the howse known by all in Globe Alley in Wapping 13 Apr. 1672.

It will be seen that there is a little discrepancy between these entries; but Globe Alley was "near the Hermitage," and no place was licensed as Presbyterian.

Some additional facts of interest are furnished by the controversial pamphlets of Samuel Wesley against the Nonconformist academies, and those of Samuel Palmer in their defence.

Wesley, then aged about 16, came to London in March, 1678, intending to study under Gale; but finding him "newly deceased" was placed under the tuition of Veal. With him he was for two years "reading logic and ethics." After which, "being prosecuted by the neighbouring justices, he broke up his house, and quitted that employ." This fixes the commencement of Veal's academy some years earlier than is commonly stated; and its termination in 1680 or -81.

Wesley then removed to Morton's academy at Newington Green, where he remained nearly two years longer; proceeding to Oxford in August, 1683. Of Morton's house he says it had a fine garden, with bowling green and fishpond; and within a laboratory and all kinds of mathematical instruments and scientific apparatus. "We had a list of all who had been entered of our society—some hundreds it amounted to, but I cannot be precise in the number—with a distinction of the faculties and employments of everyone, whether law, divinity, physick, or what else." "Our tutors, having no power, could use but little discipline; we having besides, for what order we had, a sort of democratical government amongst us; every one having power to propose a law, and all laws carried by the ballot as the greater number determined, and pains and pecuniary mulcts accordingly inflicted, as it seemed best to our own discretion. We had two houses at Newington, our number 40 or 50, over or under." It is not quite clear whether this means that Morton's students occupied two houses, or that they and Gale's together numbered 40 or 50.

It is to be regretted that Wesley gives no intelligible account of the curriculum or of the text books employed. He says indeed that among the books recommended were Ames's *Medulla, Altare Damascenum, Bellarminus Enervatus, Charnock,* and Baxter's books of controversy and devotion; adding that most of the students had Milton's *Defence* and *Eikonoclastes,* which the tutors did not direct them to, and other books "which the tutors knew not of." When pressed for further details, he strung together in doggerel Latin verse the names of several obscure writers, adding that he could give more if necessary.

If Wesley's statements are at all reliable we may gather that two or three students out of the 40 or 50 were men of loose morals: also that many of them cherished advanced liberal if not republican sentiments. In this, he acknowledges, they were not encouraged by the tutors. Mr. Morton always rebuked language implying disaffection to the government, and taught that " it was none of their business to censure such as God had placed over them."

Mr. Morton was much harassed in the renewed persecution which broke out in 1682. He was formally excommunicated, " and a *capias* issued out against him, on which he was taken; but while he was in custody of an officer, before he was actually committed to prison, the officer in whose house he lay accidentally died during his stay there; on which, there being none to detain him, he returned home."

Being in danger of a second *capias* he concealed himself some time in the house of a friend, "leaving the senior pupils to instruct the juniors"—a course which Mr. Wesley evidently thought highly improper, for he speedily disassociated himself from the academy and from Nonconformity; and did not feel any obligation to refund the exhibitions he had received from Gale's trustees.

The property which Gale had put in trust was to furnish exhibitions of £10 each for young students designed for the Nonconformist ministry. So strong was his confidence "that times would speedily alter," and that learning acquired at a private academy would, ere long, be allowed to qualify for degrees in the national universities, that he wished the exhibitioners to enter their names at some Oxford or Cambridge college, but not actually to matriculate or take the prescribed oaths. This statement rests on the authority of S. Wesley; who says that an exhibition was offered to him by "Dr. O." (? Owen) on such conditions.

Concerning Rowe's academy S. Wesley writes, "Mr. R. lived, when I first knew his people, at Hackney. After that he removed with his pupils to London and lodged in Rowse's house, who was executed in West's plot for high treason; whither his pupils used to come daily, and he read to them, as well as afterwards in other parts of the town. Since . . . I hear that he lived in Jewin Street; and now or very lately (1703) in Ropemaker's Alley, in Moorfields."

It should be observed that Wesley's three pamphlets are characterized by intense bitterness against the party which he had deserted.]

List of Members

Hon. Members marked *H*, Life Members marked *L*.

Adeney, W. F., Rev. Prof., M.A., D.D.
Andover (U.S.A.) Theological Seminary
Andrews, William, Esq.
Ashworth, W., Esq.
Astbury, F. T., Rev.
Atkinson, S. B., Esq., M.A., M.B., J.P.
Avery, John, Esq., F.S.S.
Baptist Union, The
Barrett, Geo., Rev., A.T.S.
Bartlet, J. V., Rev. Prof., M.A., D.D.
Basden, D. F., Esq.
Bate, Frank, Rev., M.A.
Bax, A. Ridley, Esq.
Beaumont, E., Esq.
Bell, J. Barton, Rev.
Boag, G. W., Esq.
Bragg, A. W., Esq.
Brown, J., Rev. Dr., B.A.
H Brown, W. H., Esq.
Brownen, G., Esq.
Burrage, Champlin, Esq.
Cater, F. Ives, Rev., A.T.S.
Chevalier, J., M.
Clapham, J. A., Esq.
Clark, J. H., Esq., J.P.
Clarkson, W. F., Rev., B.A.
Claydon, George S., Esq.
Cocks, J., Esq.
Congregational Library, Boston, Mass
Crippen, T. G., Rev.
Dale, A. W. W., Esq., M.A.
Davies, J. Alden, Rev.
Davis, C. H., Rev.
Davis, J. E., Esq.
Davy, A. J., Esq.
Dawson, E. B., Esq.
Didcote, C. Page, Esq.
Dimelow, J. G., Esq.
Dixon, H. N., Esq., M.A., F.L.S.
Dixon, R. W., Esq.
L Dore, S. L., Esq., J.P.
Durant, W. F., Rev.
H Ebbs, A. B., Esq.
Ebbs, W., Rev.
Ellis, C. W., Esq.
Evans, A. J., Esq., M.A.
Evans, G. Eyre, Rev.
Evans, Jon. L., Esq.
Evans, R. P., Esq.
Firth, C. H., Prof., M.A., LL.D.
Flower, J. E., Rev., M.A.
Forsyth, P. T., Rev., Dr.
Friends' Reference Library
Galloway, Sydney V., Esq.
Gasquoine, T., Rev., B.A.
Glasscock, J. L., Esq.

Gordon, A., Principal
Gosling, Howard, Esq.
Green, Joseph J., Esq.
Green, T., Esq.
Grice, T. E., Esq.
Grieve, A. J., Rev., M.A., B.D.
Groser, W. H., Esq., B.Sc.
Hall, C. W., Rev.
Hall, W. H., Esq.
Harris, W. J., Esq.
Harrison, G. W., Esq.
Harwood, W. Hardy, Rev.
Hawkins, F. H., Esq., LL.B.
Henderson, A. D., Esq.
Hepworth, Frank N., Esq.
Hepworth, J., Esq.
Hepworth, T. M., Esq.
Heslop, R. Oliver, Esq., M.A., F.S.A.
Hewgill, W., Rev., M.A.
Hitchcock, W. M., Esq.
Hodgett, C. M., Esq.
Holt, Edwyn, Esq.
Hooper, A. E., Rev.
L Hounsom, W. A., Esq., J.P.
Huckle, Attwood, Esq.
Iliff, John S., Esq.
Jackson, S., Esq.
James, Norman G. B., Esq.
H Johnston, W., Esq.
Jones, A. G., Esq.
Keep, H. F., Esq.
Key, James, Rev.
King, Jos., Esq., M.A.
H Lancashire Independent College (Goodyear, C., Esq.)
Lawrence, Eric A., Rev.
Lester, E. R., Esq.
Lewis, D. Morgan, Prof., M.A.
Lewis, Geo. G., Esq.
Lewis, H. Elvet, Rev., M.A.
Lewys-Lloyd, E., Esq.
Linell, W. H., Esq.
Lovatt, J., Esq.
Low, G. D., Rev., M.A.
Macfadyen, D., Rev., M.A.
Mackintosh, R., Rev. Prof., D.D.
Manchester College, Oxford
Manchester Free Libraries
Massey, Stephen, Esq.
May, H. A., Esq.
H McClure, J. D., Dr.
Minshull, John, Esq.
Mottram, W., Rev.
Mumford, A. A., Esq., M.D.
Musgrave, B., Esq.
H New College, Hampstead, N.W. (Staines, Howard, Rev.)

List of Members (continued)

New College, Edinburgh
Nightingale, B., Rev.
H Palmer, C. Ray, Rev. Dr.
Palmer, W. M., Esq.
Parnaby, H., Rev., M.A.
Phillips, Maberley, Esq., F.S.A.
Pierce, W., Rev.
Pitt, Walter, Mrs.
Powicke, F. J., Rev., Ph.D.
Poynter, J. J., Rev.
Pugh, Mrs.
Rawcliffe, Edwin B., Rev.
Reed, E. P. S., Esq.
Rees, J. Machreth, Rev.
Richards, D. M., Esq.
Ritchie, D. L., Rev.
Robinson, W., Rev.
Rollason, Arthur A., Esq.
Rudge, C., Rev.
H Rylands, Mrs., D.Litt.
Scamell, J., Esq.
Sell, H., Esq.
Serle, S., Esq.
Shaw, H., Rev.
Silcock, P. Howard, Esq., B.A.
Simon, D. W., Rev., D.D.
Smith, Norman H., Rev.
H Smith, W. J., Esq., M.A.
Smyrk, C. Watt, Rev.
H Spicer, Albert, Sir, Bart., M.P.
H Spicer, George, Esq., M.A, J.P.
Standerwick, J. W., Esq.
Stanier, W. H., Esq.
Sutton, C. W., Esq.

Sykes, A. W., Esq.
H Thacker, Fred. S., Esq.
Thacker, Henry, Esq.
Thomas, D. Lleufer, Esq.
Thomas, John, Sir.
Thomas, Wm., Rev.
H Thompson, J., Esq.
Thorpe, F. H., Esq.
Titchmarsh, E. H., Rev., M.A.
H Toms, C. W., Esq.
Turner, G. Lyon, Rev., M.A.
Tyson, R. G., Esq.
U.S.A. Congress Library.
Wallis, R. B., Esq., J.P.
Walmsby, L. S., Esq.
Watkinson, J., Esq.
H Webster, Isaac, Esq.
Whitebrook, J. L., Esq.
L Whitley, A. W., Esq.
Whitley, W. T., Rev., LL.D.
Wicks, G. H., Esq.
H Wilkinson, W., Esq.
Williams's Library.
Williams, Mrs.
Williamson, David, Esq., J.P.
Williamson, David, jr., Esq.
Wilson, T., Esq.
Windeatt, E., Esq.
Wing, Lewis, Esq.
Winterstoke, The Rt. Hon. Lord
Wontner, A. J., Esq.
Wood, Leonard B., Esq., M.A.
Woodall, H. J., Esq.
Young, Hugh P., Rev.

Lightning Source UK Ltd.
Milton Keynes UK
UKHW010306220119
335963UK00013B/970/P